OVERKILL

A volume in the series

Culture and Society after Socialism

edited by Bruce Grant and Nancy Ries

For a full list of titles in the series, see www.cornellpress.cornell.edu

OVERKILL

SEX AND VIOLENCE IN CONTEMPORARY RUSSIAN POPULAR CULTURE

ELIOT BORENSTEIN

Cornell University Press
Ithaca and London

First published 2008 by Cornell University Press
First printing, Cornell Paperbacks, 2008

Printed in the United States of America

Library of Congress Cataloging-in-Publication Data

Borenstein, Eliot, 1966–
    Overkill : sex and violence in contemporary Russian popular cul-
ture / Eliot Borenstein.
        p. cm. — (Culture and society after socialism)
    Includes bibliographical references and index.
    ISBN 978-0-8014-4583-5 (cloth : alk. paper) —
    ISBN 978-0-8014-7403-3 (pbk. : alk. paper)
    1. Popular culture—Russia (Federation)   2. Culture—Social as-
pects—Russia (Federation)   3. Sex in popular culture—Russia
(Federation)   4. Violence in popular culture—Russia (Federation)
5. Sex in mass media—Russia (Federation)   6. Violence in mass
media—Russia (Federation)   7. Popular literature—Russia (Federation)—History and criticism.   8. Post-communism—Social aspects—Russia (Federation) I. Title.   II. Title: Sex and violence
in contemporary Russian popular culture.   III. Series.

HM621.B67 2007
306.70947'090511—dc22

2007028831

Cornell University Press strives to use environmentally responsible
suppliers and materials to the fullest extent possible in the publishing of its books. Such materials include vegetable-based, low-VOC
inks and acid-free papers that are recycled, totally chlorine-free, or
partly composed of nonwood fibers. For further information, visit
our website at www.cornellpress.cornell.edu.

Cloth printing   10 9 8 7 6 5 4 3 2 1
Paperback printing   10 9 8 7 6 5 4 3 2 1

For Stanley Russell Borenstein
(1925–2006)

Отец мой был доверчивый к люлям, он обижал их восторгами
—Isaac Babel.

CONTENTS

PREFACE

The average human body contains between five and six liters of blood. The average Russian novel and film contain far more. Nor is blood the only bodily fluid that threatens to spill out onto the page and the screen: contemporary Russian books, films, and televisions shows abound with beautiful women who are sexually available by definition—indeed, that would often appear to be their primary narrative function. Yet just twenty years ago, this was not at all the case. Late- and post-Soviet culture, in opening itself up to sex and violence, adopted an aesthetic of boundlessness. This most recent Russian popular culture has had many virtues, though restraint has not been among them. The culture's focus on sex and violence did not arise in a vacuum, and it reflects the very real changes that have happened in recent years; yet these preoccupations suggest something more than a simple response to changing realities. Both the unrelenting excess of recent Russian popular culture and the periodic decrying of perceived lapses in morality and taste are part of a process that has defined the field of mass culture and entertainment in the post-Soviet period, particularly in the 1990s. This process simultaneously thematizes and evokes anxiety about the fate of the nation, identifying both entertainment and truth with the pessimistic and the extreme. Contemporary Russian slang suggests a number of terms to characterize this cultural moment; for the convenience of the English-language reader, I have chosen to call it *overkill.*

In the last decade of the twentieth century, the people of the Russian Federation had to cope with the multiple and interdependent shocks and traumas of their new social order. In addition to the economic and political hardships of postsocialist life (unemployment, poverty, social stratification, and widespread corruption), the collapse of the seventy-four-year-old Soviet system opened up the possibility that both public and private life could be radically transformed. Russia had lived through such a decade of transformation immediately after the 1917 Revolution, but if both the 1920s and the 1990s were periods of chaos and vast social dislocation, the first post-Soviet decade did not seem quite prepared to present a grand narrative of optimism and progress. After the initial euphoria of the early Yeltsin years subsided, there was little sense that the country's hardships heralded the advent of a "new post-Soviet man." The misery of the 1990s was undeniable: ethnic violence, terrorism, sexual slavery, increased morbidity, and organized crime could not be ignored. It would be naive to expect that the media and culture industry would not incorporate these themes, but Russian popular culture of the 1990s went beyond the mere representation of previously taboo subject matter. Explicit sex and violence had an obvious novelty in the late- and post-Soviet years, but their pervasiveness as the 1990s drew to a close suggests that novelty alone could not explain the prevailing content and tone of post-Soviet popular culture. Rather, Russian popular culture was heavily invested in portraying a dangerous, violent, and cynical postsocialist world.

The logic of cultural pessimism demanded a constant intensification of post-Soviet decline, resulting in a popular culture that indulged in the depiction of increasingly ingenious debauchery and crime. In 1995, Daniil Korestkii published a best-selling novel called *Antikiller*, which served as the basis for Egor Mikhalkov-Konchalovskii's blockbuster movie seven years later. The novel contains a memorable set piece, only partly (but graphically) reproduced in the film. Watching a man's severed hand spurt blood on a chopping block in a meatpacking plant, a mob boss decides that human dismemberment is probably a first even for this particular butchery, a longtime site of scandal and crime. His thoughts drift back to an orgy that took place there a few years before, when the plant's director "demonstrated his male strength" to his guests by penetrating a drunken woman with the help of a bull's penis, "specially stocked" for that purpose:

> But that wasn't the end of it: the girls were placed on the counters with their legs spread, like chicken carcasses, while the guys moved along, trying each one in turn. . . .
> It was crude entertainment, but fun. (Koretskii, *Antikiller* 79–80)

Though Koretskii's fascination with bestiality made him virtually unique among writers, filmmakers, and television producers in 1990s Russia, his penchant for scenes of violence and sexual coercion was far from exceptional. Koretskii's works represent the dominant post-Soviet aesthetic of overkill thanks to their utter lack of restraint. It is not enough to show criminals severing a rival's hand with an ax, nor is it enough to recall the assault with a (dead) bull's penis; only after describing a particularly baroque group sexual encounter with commodified female bodies can the narrator return to the events of the present. This last grotesque detail is crucial, since it moves from isolated acts to endlessly repeatable, mechanical violations of individual dignity. Koretskii stops only when there is no more stopping.

America and Western Europe have a long tradition of viewing Russia as a site of delectable atrocity, as Vladislav Todorov observes in *Red Square, Black Square*: "The East aestheticizes its monstrosity for the West," while the West "has been investing in the thrills of the ruins from the very beginning" (Todorov 183). Yet I contend that we lose a great deal if, out of a desire not to become complicit in the sensational, we leave the world of overkill unexamined. This book takes up overkill as its central theme, not by interrogating axiologically whether the crime statistics were right, whether morals were collapsing, or whether the coverage of these themes in popular culture was "too much." Rather, the "excess" in overkill provides this book's central operating principle, as the very dramas of excess become zones for contending with questions about the nation's role and fate that mattered a great deal to Russians in the 1990s. Overkill provides the arena for the public negotiation of these questions.

ACKNOWLEDGMENTS

This project has been with me for over a decade and has benefited from the insight and support of so many people that I am afraid I cannot possibly remember them all. David Bethea, Clare Cavanagh, Arlene Forman, and Judith Kornblatt, my teachers before this work began, continue to inspire me with their example and their observations. Adele Barker and Natalie Kononenko encouraged me to work on popular culture long before I ever thought to write a book on the subject. Over the years, numerous friends and colleagues provided their support along the way: Amy Singleton Adams, Ulrich Baer, Elena Baraban, Angela Brintlinger, Boris Groys, David Herman, Galina Khutorskaya, Laurie Iudin-Nelson, Martha Kuhlman, Jessie Labov, Andrea Lanoux, Judith Lobel, Birgit Menzel, Yuliya Minkova, Inga Pagava, Eric Naiman, Cathy Nepomnyashchy, Jenifer Presto, Elena Prokhorova, Dianne Sattinger, Lisa Siegel, and Ilya Vinitsky.

Preliminary versions of parts of this book were presented at Colorado College, the CUNY Graduate Center, the Harriman Institute, Miami University, Notre Dame, the University of California at Berkeley, the University of Colorado, the University of Virginia, and the University of Wisconsin. My research was facilitated by the generous support of the Council for the International Exchange of Scholars (Fulbright), IREX, New York University, and the Social Science Research Council. I would also like to express my gratitude to the Harriman Institute for paying for compiling the book's index.

Most of the work was completed after I joined the Department of Russian and Slavic Studies at NYU, where I have had the rare good fortune of finding excellent colleagues who have also become my friends. Genya Altman, our departmental administrator, not only provided excellent logistical support but also served as a pop cultural guinea pig; she is perhaps the only person in my daily life who has watched more contemporary Russian movies than I have. Irina Belodedova could usually be counted on to hash out the finer points of the latest Dashkova novel, while Anne Lounsbery's good humor and intellectual generosity always gave me the opportunity to brainstorm about my latest idea. Slavic librarian Diana Greene's bibliographic wizardry has yet to fail her, or me. Jane Burbank, Steve Cohen, Charlotte Douglas, Anneta Greenlee, Milan Fryscak, Diana Greene, Misha Iampolski, Nancy Ruttenburg, and Yanni Kotsonis have been wonderful colleagues and fine interlocutors.

Olga Bichko, Sasha Gelerman, Daniil Leiderman, Alex Morim, Elena Rosenberg, Irina Ryabaya, and Christine Wilson provided invaluable research assistance over the years. Mike Summers helped me greatly with his document scanner and his reliable good cheer. Special thanks goes to Jennifer Smith, who provided the child care that made any kind of work possible.

The people at Cornell University Press have been a sheer delight. My editors, Bruce Grant and Nancy Ries, are among the most careful and thoughtful readers I have ever encountered, and my book has benefited greatly from their advice. Peter Wissoker shepherded the book through the editorial process with sensitivity and grace. During copy editing, Jamie Fuller caught more errors than I would care to admit, saving me from my own sloppiness. Karen Laun was a superb, and, above all, patient manuscript editor, putting up with all my delays while gently reminding me of the latest missed deadline. I would also like to express my gratitude to Judith Kip for indexing the book.

Two friends deserve particular mention: Mark Lipovetsky, whose wide-ranging intellect and sheer enthusiasm helped me see this project through to the completion, and Helena Goscilo, who has shown us all that scholarship isn't worth it if you're not having any fun. Helena also read more versions of this manuscript than anyone should ever have to.

Though writing this book was a largely solitary endeavor, I could not have even begun it without the love and support of my family. I am grateful to my parents, Deborah and Stanley Borenstein, for giving me a solid education while allowing me to watch far too much television, and for providing a model of unabashed enjoyment of the popular. I dedicate this book to

their memory and also to my sons, Lev and Louis Bernstein, avid consumers of the best and the worst that the culture has to offer. May they
never feel the need to apologize for their taste.

Finally, my greatest debt of gratitude goes to Fran Bernstein, who saved
me, and continues to save me each and every day.

NOTE ON TRANSLITERATION
AND TRANSLATIONS

The Library of Congress transliteration system is used in this book whenever unfamiliar Russian words are introduced. For the sake of easier reading, however, when well-known Russian authors, politicians, and places are named in the body of the text, I have chosen the most familiar English spelling (e.g., "Dostoevsky" rather than "Dostoevskii"). The "Works Cited" section and internal citations use the Library of Congress system for ease of bibliographic reference; as a result, the writer who publishes in English under the name "Victor Erofeyev" is listed in Russian-language references as "Viktor Erofeev."

All translations are my own unless otherwise noted.

OVERKILL

INTRODUCTION

Why are people so attracted to all sorts of filth?

—Polina Dashkova, *Air Time* (*Efirnoe vremia*)

Less than half a year before Russia's relations with the United States were soured by the 1999 NATO bombing of Yugoslavia, the Russian State Duma began a war of words about an issue of no apparent significance, although its subject was literally earth-shattering: the Hollywood blockbuster *Armageddon*, whose depiction of a Russian cosmonaut wearing a fur hat as he frantically repaired the decrepit Mir space station was perceived as an unforgivable insult to Russian national pride. The fact that the movie was a runaway success in theaters throughout the Russian Federation only made matters worse, especially considering the sorry state of the domestic film industry. The legislators demanded that the chairman of the State Cinema Committee provide an explanation for his failure to ban the film entirely (Graff).

One need not follow the news from Russia all that closely to suspect that the nation's legislature had more serious problems to discuss than the latest Bruce Willis star vehicle, whose jerry-rigged plot about an impending meteor impact was cobbled together from at least as many spare parts as its cinematic depiction of the Mir. In a convenient parallel to the Russian media's own preoccupation with a nation on the verge of collapse, American newspapers and television present the latest events from the largest Soviet successor state only when they fit the familiar rubric of "Russia in Crisis," with the result that Russia's woes in the 1990s were familiar to anyone who turned on the TV: unemployment, the near-total impoverishment of the population, the resurgence of tuberculosis, and the growing threat of AIDS; prostitution and sexual slavery; the increasing "brain drain" and threat of nuclear proliferation; and, of course, terrorism and the war in Chechnya. Moreover, when the Duma was debating the merits of a forgettable Hollywood confection, barely a month and a half had passed since a nationwide banking crisis sent the country's economy into a tailspin. One suspects the Duma of engaging in the time-honored legislative tradition of diverting attention from problems that have escaped their control.

Yet even if the legislators' discussion of *Armageddon* may have been of little use to senior citizens waiting for their overdue pensions, it does highlight the ambient anxieties that characterized Russian public discourse in the 1990s. The country's material plight was inevitably framed within a larger context of moral blight, cultural degradation, and lack of national purpose, all connected with humiliation at the hands of the West. Hence another governmental initiative of dubious real-world pertinence, this time from the executive branch: President Boris Yeltsin's establishment of a commission in 1996 to develop a new "Russian idea" (Smith 158). Borrowed from the philosopher Nikolai Berdiaev's famous study of Russian intellectual history and national character, the term "Russian idea" need not be evaluated here in its long-term historical context, precisely because Yeltsin's charge to the commission suggests that previous Russian ideas no longer apply. The attempt to develop a national idea through a government committee may sound like the stuff of satire (Dostoevsky by way of *Dilbert*), but it was also a recognition of a growing sentiment, represented and generated by the media and culture industry, that postsocialist Russia was somehow morally adrift. A country that had grown accustomed to having an official national ideology for the better part of the century (and arguably longer, if one includes the discourse of Russia's historic mission as it developed before the October Revolution) was descending into chaos, at least in part because it lacked a sense of its own purpose and identity. Such an argument was simple for any Russian politician to make, for the evidence could be drawn from a realm that was easy to scorn but impossible to ignore: the emerging world of popular culture.

In the 1990s, it was popular culture, as produced and disseminated by the Russian media and culture industry (television, film, radio, the press, book publishing, and, to a lesser extent, the Internet) that most effectively defined and presented Russia and "Russianness" for domestic consumption, usually framed within the discourse of total collapse and cultural degradation.[1] Thanks to market reforms, the influx of Western cultural products, and the decline in the intelligentsia's traditional moral and aesthetic authority, the 1990s represent a turning point in the very notion of the popular. For the first time in the country's history, the culture industry was simultaneously free from the censor's watchful eye while beholden to the dictates of a cutthroat market. If this did not guarantee that the purveyors of culture were really "giving the people what they want," it did represent the first significant wide-scale attempt to appeal to all the instincts of Russian consumers, from the sublime to the most basic.

This is not a book about "real life" or everyday experience in the early years of the Russian Federation. Instead, I am operating under the assumption that, in a media-saturated world, we understand our lives and surroundings not only through empirical, lived experience but through simulated and mediated experience constructed on paper or on screen. Such a truism is almost obvious enough to go unspoken; it has been the stuff of media criticism for decades (witness Baudrillard's often-caricatured assertion that the 1990 Gulf War was created on TV) (29–30). Yet for Russia, and for the scholars who have spent decades studying the (former) Soviet Union, the relationship between mass culture and the consumer changed radically in the last fifteen years of the twentieth century.[2] Western scholars had a functionalist vision of the Soviet media that was far too focused on propaganda, attributing too much unanimity and cohesiveness to the centralized Soviet media.[3] Nonetheless, in the old days, *Pravda* could be carefully analyzed for signs of subtle shifts in Soviet policy or dissent in the ranks. But if the Kremlinologists, in their assumption that the Soviet media were crucial to understanding the mechanisms of the state, operated under an essentially *conspiratorial* model—the idea that texts have hidden meanings encoded by

[1] Though the Internet has taken off at an astonishing rate in the past several years, economic considerations and limited computer access still prevented the Russian Internet from being as much a "mass" phenomenon as its English-language counterpart in the 1990s or as domestic competitors in the traditional media. For the most part, the Internet in Russia functioned as a support system for the larger culture industry and as a cheap and efficient means for communication and "propaganda" among more marginalized groups (such as "Tolkienists," who have turned *The Lord of the Rings into* the basis of their subculture) and fans. It was only in the following decade that the Internet took on a greater role in the development of popular culture, as exemplified by the popularity of the Web cartoon "Masiania," which eventually made the leap from the Web to network television (Strukov 438–61).

[2] For a thorough and insightful overview of the challenges post-Soviet popular culture poses to Western models of cultural studies, see Barker, "The Culture Factory."

[3] Recent scholars have argued quite persuasively that the mass culture of the post-Stalin era was neither monolithic in form nor monosemic in reception (Roth-Ey, "Introduction"; Yurchak, *Everything* 36–77).

a guiding hand—my point of departure is that whatever can be learned about today's Russia comes from analyzing an ever-changing set of texts, representations, and myths that emerge from an essentially chaotic system. That is, Russian cultural consumers, like cultural consumers around the globe, come to conclusions about the world around them by processing messages that are by no means anchored to the messengers' intentions.

For the purposes of this project, I define "popular culture" as those forms of entertainment that aim for a wider audience than educated elites, reflecting their creators' understanding of their target audience. My material consists largely of (best-selling) fiction, film, television, mass-market periodicals, and pornography. On the surface, soap operas, mystery novels, and sword-and-sorcery sagas appear to be an unlikely source of insight into the experience or worldview of everyday Russians. I would argue that these forms of entertainment are a window onto the Russian imaginary: the conglomeration of set images, notions, and stereotypes that mediate the world through a kind of mental shorthand. They are the models with which we compare our own lived experience.

Even a cursory glance at Russian popular culture of the 1990s reveals a decidedly bleak picture. Indeed, this grimness characterizes both the predominant subject matter (joyless sex, violent crime, poverty, disease, and unhappy families) and contemporary critics' assessments of the state of culture itself. Without a doubt there was no shortage of things to lament. In addition to the earlier litany of the social and economic problems that beset Russian society, the industries that produced the mass media and popular entertainment started the decade in a sorry state. Vanishing state subsidies brought a once-vibrant film industry to a virtual standstill (Beumers 2–3); the airwaves were dominated by a seemingly endless supply of foreign-produced comedies, dramas, and soap operas whose quality varied sharply, at least in part as a function of the networks' ability to pay; and, as the heady days of civic debate under glasnost faded to a distant memory, both print and television journalism were taking on a decidedly yellow tint.

The only real success story was in book publishing, but here, too, the definition of success was shared by media critics only when framed in narrow economic terms. As the novelty of long-suppressed Soviet-era classics by the likes of Solzhenitsyn, Zamiatin, and Platonov wore off, and as the experimental prose of such contemporary authors as Valeriia Narbikova and Victor Erofeyev captured the attention of a dwindling intellectual elite, publishing houses reaped huge financial rewards by following the less refined tastes of the broader, but still highly literate, public. After a half-century of limited public access to novels written solely for the purpose of entertainment, the perestroika years had already seen a boom in editions of foreign writers who catered to a taste for mystery and crime: the British writers Agatha Christie and James Hadley Chase were best sellers in bookstores and among street vendors, printed and reprinted in high-end collected editions, separate hardback volumes, and, eventually, in paperback (a rarity in Soviet times). In the 1990s, the publishing industry responded with popular novels by Russian authors, who quickly toppled their dead British rivals from their book-market thrones.[4]

The reasons for the book market's early recovery are easy to deduce. Unlike film and television, books can be produced cheaply by individual creators rather than large, expensive teams, and the investment in equipment and technology is minimal. In the 1990s, the book market was far less vulnerable to the weak economy, for the switch to cheaply produced pocket paperbacks (many of which fell apart almost as soon as they were opened) made them accessible to all but the most desperately poor. Throughout the decade, the price of a cheap paperback was roughly equivalent to a loaf or two of inexpensive bread, making reading a relatively affordable pastime. If in Soviet times, books were as much an aesthetic object as they were a medium for conveying text (the varied colors of hardback editions were an integral part of the intellectual's home decor), now they were an interchangeable commodity. From an elite point of view, such a success was a double-edged sword: Russians were still reading, but the books themselves, whose sensationalist covers hardly helped matters, were a source of dismay.[5]

Though there were certainly many bright spots in the cultural landscape—the occasional successful film comedy, such as Aleksandr Rogozhkin's 1995 *Peculiarities of the Russian Hunt* (*Osobennosti natsional'noi okhoty*), the hit television series *Menty* (*Cops*), combining action with irony—public discourse and mass entertainment in the 1990s were marked by a logic of cultural pessimism, an ongoing fixation on cultural collapse, and an expectation of apocalyptic disaster mixing eschatology with the everyday. Popular culture was both a cause and a subject of extended anxiety in that it disseminated the idea of general collapse at the same time that its very existence, and its focus on the subject matter that facilitated the discourse of collapse, was seen as a sign of that collapse.

---

[4] Before perestroika, there were only about a hundred publishing houses in the entire Soviet Union, but by 2000, the Russian Federation alone had five thousand. By 2000, approximately fifty thousand titles were printed in the Russian Federation, roughly the same number as in the mid-eighties (Menzel, "Writing" 42).

[5] For more on the evolution of the post-Soviet publishing industry, see Lovell (*The Russian Reading Revolution* 129–42), Menzel ("Writing"), and Gudkov and Dubin (259–87).

From perestroika through the 1990s, Russian culture was caught in a state of almost permanent crisis: a free-floating but repeatedly expressed anxiety about the state of the country, its fate, its relationship with the West, the morality of its youth, and the hopeless chaos of a corrupt, criminalized society lacking a unifying idea. This generalized anxiety coalesced around certain general topics, such as sex, violence, and the drain of Russia's literal and metaphorical national resources. I approach this preoccupation with national collapse as a discursive phenomenon, constructed and reflected in the constituent genres and media of Russian popular culture. National collapse is simply too large-scale a problem to be apprehended or constructed as unmediated experience, even by someone individually suffering under miserable conditions. The scale of late- and post-Soviet collapse is beyond individual or local experience. The full sense of collapse requires a panoptic view that only the media and culture industry were eager to provide, amalgamating national collapse into one master narrative that would then be readily available to most individuals as a framework for understanding their own suffering and fears.

The scale of national collapse presents a peculiar set of aesthetic challenges. How can something so vast be represented through the particular? Russian popular culture's response is to try to do everything at once, creating local and particular examples that, through their frantic proliferation, reproduce a sense of global despair. This is the phenomenon that I call overkill: an insistence on patently excessive details of collapse, rooted in doubts about any example's capacity to be truly *exemplary*. Only through the endless accumulation of appalling details can an adequate picture emerge.

The narratives examined in this study oscillate wildly between condensation (focus on the particular) and expansion (generalization from the particular). On the one hand, the amalgamation of data on collapse immediately lends itself to reduction and simplification through the vehicle of narrative melodrama. Many of the films and novels discussed in this book create an individual whose experience functions as a distillation of anxiety, a synecdoche for total collapse. The protagonists of *Vultures on the Roads* (*Sterviatniki na dorogakh*), *Everything We Dreamed about for So Long* (*Vse to, o chem my tak dolgo mechtali*), and *You're Just a Slut, My Dear!* (*Ty prosto shliukha, dorogaia!*) are subject to so many varieties of baroque suffering that, in the hands of more ironic writers and directors, their stories could be the stuff of dark comedy (along the lines of John Waters or the early Pedro Almodóvar). Yet the trials they endure (kidnapping, organ harvesting, rape, attempted murder, forced drug addiction, servitude as gladiators to entertain the rich) are the stuff of the daily scandal sheet, already familiar to readers and viewers. Such an excess of misery is reminiscent of the long tradition of ten-dentious novels, as in Upton Sinclair's *The Jungle*: in the first chapters, the narrator informs us of all the disaster to which desperate immigrants in Chicago's meatpacking district are prey and then proceeds to subject poor Jurgis and his family to every one of them. Sinclair's earnest muckraking and the blithe horrors of Waters and Almodóvar are similar in content yet worlds apart in tone, suggesting that the line between moral outrage and camp is thin indeed. When combined with irony, the accumulation of hor-rific details ceases to be mere repetition, transforming atrocity into absurd-ity. When presented seriously as signs of unabated moral and social blight, such excess does not turn quantity into quality. Rather, the portrait being painted is so bleak that no examples can ever be enough.

Unhappily Ever After: Glasnost' and Chernukha

Such a surfeit of misery had become the standard fare in the last years of the Soviet Union, representing a sharp break with the immediate past. The Brezhnev era had been a retreat from previous waves of truth seeking and revelations of "hidden crimes" that had begun with Khrushchev's "Secret Speech" at the 1956 Party Congress, in which he denounced the brutal ex-cesses of Stalin's "cult of personality." The next several years, commonly called the "Thaw," saw the efforts for cultural liberalization stop and start several times before the mercurial Khrushchev was ousted and replaced by the widely perceived blandness of Brezhnev in 1964. To say that the two decades between Brezhnev's installation and Gorbachev's ascension were nothing but "stagnation" (the term subsequently adopted for the Brezhnev years) is certainly a caricature. The proliferation of countercultures and sub-cultures, as well as alternative artistic organizations, was never completely crushed by the state's repressive apparatus, to which it resorted with far less frequency and severity than in the Stalin era; the flowering of dissent and ex-perimentation that characterized perestroika did not come from nowhere.[6]

Nor could it be said that the Soviet Union lacked a popular culture be-fore perestroika. Quite the contrary: a great deal of recent scholarship argues convincingly that the official culture of the Soviet Union, socialist realism, was far more than simple propaganda forced on an unwilling and

---

[6] Indeed, Yurchak makes a persuasive argument that the ritualized forms of official culture in the Brezhnev years actually opened up a great deal of space for individual Soviets to create mean-ing (1–35).

uninterested populace. As an explanatory system, the propaganda model had already begun to lose its luster long before the Gorbachev era. Starting in the 1960s, Western scholars had already distanced themselves from the postwar paradigm of Theodor Adorno, who condemned mass culture as a means of inducing "human dependence and servitude" in both "totalitarian" and "democratic" societies (37). Poststructuralist critics in the West began to explore popular culture as a realm that, rather than rendering its audiences passive and complacent, left room for cultural consumers to express their own subjectivity. This more nuanced approach to the phenomenon of popular culture proved to be applicable to the Soviet experience as well. Though film, television, theater, radio, and fiction were officially supposed to reinforce the reigning ideology, in the post-Stalin era, simply steering clear of certain taboo subjects and political stances was often enough to facilitate publication or broadcast. More to the point, the ease with which Western scholars dismissed socialist realist culture during the cold war was largely the product of an inability to conceive of the pleasures to be found in narratives and images that outsiders saw as mere propaganda. Soviet readers and viewers created their own meanings as they consumed official culture, while writers, directors, and artists often paid serious attention to the reactions and criticisms of their audiences.[7]

Yet despite the complexities of the production and reception of Soviet popular culture, there can be no doubt that the cultural productions of the perestroika and post-Soviet eras differed significantly from their Soviet predecessors. The key questions here concern scale and content. In Soviet times, popular cultural production was subject to the same problem that plagued all other sectors of the consumer economy: scarcity. The Soviet economic system put a premium on heavy industry and the military, resulting in pent-up consumer demands that it was structurally incapable of satisfying. In the realm of culture, scarcity was only exacerbated by a profound pedagogical impulse. Ideally, entertainment should be more than innocuous: it should be useful. While the Soviet cultural industry was not deaf to the needs and desires of cultural consumers, it was neither willing nor able to produce and distribute enough products to meet demands, in terms of either variety or quantity.[8]

---

[7] The study of socialist realism in the West is indebted first and foremost to the work of Katerina Clark (*The Soviet Novel*). More recent works by Evgeny Dobrenko (*The Making of the State Reader*), Thomas Lahusen (*How Life Writes the Book*), and Stephen Lovell (*The Russian Reading Revolution*) have demonstrated the depth of engagement with socialist realism on the part of the country's readership. See also Richard Stites (*Russian Popular Culture*).

[8] Lovell notes the Soviet-era phenomenon known as "book hunger": the scarce supply of the books that most consumers really wanted to read (*The Russian Reading Revolution* 57–60).

While steering clear of the central tenets of Soviet ideology, film comedies such as El'dar R'iazanov's *Ironiia sud'by* (*Irony of Fate*, 1975) and *Sluzhebnyi roman* (*Office Romance*, 1978), the stand-up monologues of popular satirists such as Arkadii Raikin, and the urban fiction of Yuri Trifonov, particularly his 1969 novella "The Exchange" (*Obmen*), drew attention to many of the numerous flaws that characterized Soviet daily life: the limited supply of consumer goods and the concomitant long lines, the moral compromises brought on by the housing shortage, and the excessive privileges of the well connected. Perhaps the biggest cultural safety valve was the flourishing oral genre of the joke (*anekdot*), whose subject matter ranged from politics to sex to ethnic humor.[9] Yet it is indicative that the best jokes, while certainly an important part of Soviet popular culture, were excluded from the mass media entirely. The most subversive elements of Soviet popular culture thrived precisely through their opposition to the blandness and uniformity of official state discourse. Indeed, the sheer dullness of Soviet mass culture increased in direct proportion to the amount of political content or "news." The newspapers and television broadcasts featured interminable speeches by party leaders (and, in Brezhnev's case, their growing incomprehensibility added an unintended element of subversive entertainment), while the news from around the Soviet Union showed a seemingly endless progression of successful harvests, hyperefficient factories, and warm welcomes to the country's leaders by smiling delegations of workers and peasants. What bad news could be found tended to happen elsewhere; even natural disasters were more likely to befall capitalist countries, as if the bourgeoisie were being punished by a nonexistent God.

All of this changed with the advent of perestroika. Mikhail Gorbachev's policy of *glasnost'* (openness), with its emphasis on telling hidden, buried truths, opened up the Soviet Union's anodyne mass culture to an astonishing onslaught of sheer negativity. In his 1987 international best seller *Perestroika: New Thinking for Our Country and the World*, Gorbachev provides an upbeat characterization: "Today, glasnost is a vivid example of a normal and favorable spiritual and moral atmosphere in society, which makes it possible for people to understand better what happened to us in the past, what is taking place now, what we are striving for and what our plans are, and, on the basis of this understanding, to participate in the restructuring effort consciously" (75). As an expression of Gorbachev's hopes for his policy of cultural democratization, this passage is probably accurate, but what is

---

[9] On the history and function of Soviet jokes, see Draitser, Graham ("A Cultural Analysis"), and Krylova.

painfully clear decades later is the extent to which these words, like the entire book, reflect a much older Soviet ethos of optimism and engagement. While it is true that perestroika launched an unprecedented frenzy of civic activity, with politically and socially oriented independent organizations popping up all over the USSR, the public discourse produced by glasnost in the media and mass entertainment made Gorbachev's assertion of a "favorable spiritual and moral atmosphere" look like so much wishful thinking.

It is emblematic that the defining moments of glasnost in the media revolved around catastrophes: the 1988 earthquake in Armenia—which, in addition to demonstrating the shoddiness of Soviet architecture and the incapacity of the bureaucratic infrastructure, also revealed the importance and extent of ethnic as well as tectonic fault lines—and the 1986 Chernobyl disaster.[10] When reactor 4 exploded in the Chernobyl nuclear power plant on April 26, 1986, the government's response was near-total silence; sixteen days passed before Gorbachev appeared on television to discuss Chernobyl, after Western news reports and the rumor mill made such an admission unavoidable.[11] Everything about Chernobyl was exacerbated by the deep-rooted habits of secrecy, with the result that the Soviet coverage of and polemics about the disaster took on a decidedly self-reflexive character: talking about Chernobyl meant also talking about how one talked about Chernobyl. Chernobyl provides a metaphor for late-Soviet culture that is too compelling to ignore: a dangerous explosion whose invisible fallout would have repercussions for decades to come.[12] The metaphor contains an implicit value judgment that needs to be suspended, but the fact that the disaster loosed a literal toxic cloud over a swath of Soviet territory (and endangered the West as well) renders it exemplary of the tendency that truly characterized the changes in the Soviet media and mass culture: the phenomenon Russians call *chernukha*.

[10] The months preceding the Armenian earthquake saw the intensification of the crisis over Nagorno-Karabakh, a predominantly Armenian region seeking to break away from the Soviet Republic of Azerbaidzhan. By the time Gorbachev arrived to assess the earthquake damage, relief efforts had already been spearheaded by the Karabakh Committee, whose leaders were subsequently arrested by the Soviet government (Miller and Miller 34).

[11] Even when he finally addressed the Chernobyl question, Gorbachev spent much of his time denouncing the Western press for its "distortions" (Remnick 246), a theme he touches on again in *Perestroika* (236)("I won't recall all the lies concocted about Chernobyl").

[12] Months after the accident, the author Yuri Nagibin wrote: "The entire country is falling out, Chernobyl-like. Matter is disintegrating uncontrollably, and spiritual substance is dissipating" (Gessen, *Dead Again* 24). See also the assessment of doctor and journalist Yuri Shcherbak: "Chernobyl was not *like* the Communist system. They were one and the same. . . . The system ate into our bones the same way radiation did, and the powers that be—or powers that were—did everything they could to cover it all up, to wish it all away" (Remnick 245, italics in the original). For more on the social and personal meanings that have accrued to the Chernobyl disaster, see Petryna (*Life Exposed* and "Sarcophagus") and Phillips ("Chernobyl's Sixth Sense").

Chernukha, initially a slang term with its roots in the argot of the Soviet prison system, is derived from the adjective *chernyi* ("black"), bearing most of the negative connotations the word carries in the Russian language (darkness, filth, pessimism, and misery).[13] Broadly speaking, chernukha is the pessimistic, naturalistic depiction of and obsession with bodily functions, sexuality (usually separate from love), and often sadistic violence, all against a backdrop of poverty, broken families, and unrelenting cynicism. Chernukha has garnered the greatest attention in the study of late Soviet film, where it was so prominent as to constitute something close to a full-fledged genre.[14] Film scholars Andrew Horton and Michael Brashinksy provide a useful elaboration of the "chernukha formula," whose ingredients include the following:

1) The family, agonizing or already collapsed.
2) Average Soviet citizens unmasking their animal natures, ultimate immorality, and unmotivated cruelty. . . .
3) The death of all former ideals, leaving no hope for the future after the closing credits.
4) Packed everyday conditions in "communal apartments." . . .
5) Senseless hysterics and fights arising from nowhere and dying down in the middle of a scream.
6) Usually, a few "adult" scenes. (163–64)

More generally, Naum Leiderman and Mark Lipovetsky argue that late Soviet chernukha showed the "world as a concentration of social horror taken as the everyday norm" (81). Seth Graham emphasizes chernukha's "radical, indiscriminate, and ostentatious rejection of all ideals, especially those that are culturally marked, which signifies visually the trend's essential philosophical fatalism" ("Chernukha" 14). All these formulations are correct, but they do not tell the entire story. The sheer negativity of perestroika-era chernukha—the deliberate *épatage* and the dogged depiction of a world full of cynics—distract from the fact that chernukha functioned within a profoundly *moral* context, one that was all the more powerful for not being readily apparent.

[13] Graham cites several dictionaries and encyclopedias, noting that in prison camps, the term referred to "lying, cheating or slander," as well as "deceit," "crime," and even "radio" ("Chernukha" 23n2). When the term broke out of its criminal context, all that was left of its original meaning was the emphasis on negative phenomena.
[14] Horton and Brashinksy call chernukha a "new semigenre, or even antigenre" but argue that it "is not a valuable genre . . . since its artistic language is still neglected" (163).

Chernukha in the 1980s was a form of muckraking, much like that in Sinclair's aforementioned *Jungle*, and muckraking always situates itself within a higher moral or social purpose. The Russian antecedents of chernukha have also been noted by many critics: the nineteenth-century physiological sketch, the dramas and stories of Maxim Gorky, and even the gulag writings of that avowed Russian moralist Alexander Solzhenitsyn (Lipovetskii, "Rasstratnye" 194–95; Genis 91). Thus chernukha in the news media was part of an implicitly reformist agenda, zeroing in on precisely the sorts of problems that the Soviet media had ignored for decades, since pretending that they did not exist had presumably only allowed them to get worse.[15] Emblematic of this approach was Aleksandr Nevzorov's fast-paced, semi-sensationalist news program on Leningrad Television, *600 sekund* (*600 Seconds*), whose on-screen, second-by-second countdown until the end of each ten-minute episode lent each horrific story an added sense of urgency. In his early shows Nevzorov focused on mismanagement and corruption; in the best traditions of Sinclair, Nevzorov even did an investigative report on a factory that used spoiled meat to make sausages sold to an unsuspecting populace (Mickiewicz 100). In Nevzorov's reporting, at least before he took a turn toward the extreme nationalist right, the public interest in revealing such details was obvious: no one wanted to eat rotten meat.[16]

In film, fiction, and drama, the moral context was at times made clear through the speeches of a *raisonneur*, but more often, the audience was simply presented with a bleak picture and left to draw its own conclusions. While many a pundit decried the rise of chernukha (particularly in "high" art), the phenomenon nevertheless took on a certain epistemological significance: chernukha became implicitly identified with the "truth" (*pravda*), or at the very least with the absence of systematic lying (*vran'e*).[17] When one factors in the deeply rooted power of the Russian rumor mill, which fosters credulity in anything negative, horrifying, and contrary to official views, the

---

[15] This is not to say that the Soviet media had no experience portraying the negative. Quite to the contrary, one of the remarkable things about early perestroika exposés was how much they resembled the traditional Soviet portrayal of human suffering in countries such as the United States. Now it was the Soviet Union that was depicted as a land full of prostitutes, drug addicts, and homeless people.

[16] Nevzorov shocked his longtime liberal supporters in January of 1991, when his sixteen-minute documentary *Nashi* (*Ours*) portrayed Lithuanian separatists as bloodthirsty fanatics and justified the deaths of protesters at the hands of Soviet troops (Mickiewicz 100–101).

[17] Andrei Zorin makes a similar point in his excellent 1992 article about chernukha, one of the first attempts to look at the problem somewhat retrospectively. "At issue was not the responsibility of particular leaders for specific decisions, and not even the responsibility of the party or the regime for the character of the system or the general course, but the universal, total sin of lies and silence" ("Kruche" 201).

fascination with chernukha can be explained at least partially by its identification with reality. Despite the obvious "anti-Soviet" character of chernukha, it actually partook in a tried-and-true Soviet tradition: *razoblachenie* (exposure, unmasking).[18] Chernukha showed the seamy underside of Soviet life and ideology, revealing what we might already know but do not wish to accept. Though hard-line critics and many readers/viewers charged that chernukha was "immoral," its very role in the ideological debates gave it a distinct moral character. It functioned like satire without necessarily being satirical—that is, it exposed flaws and inspired outrage among readers/viewers who presumably would want to live in a different world. Hence violence and horror become tantamount to truth telling.

Chernukha could not have been what the architects of perestroika had in mind when they launched the campaign for glasnost, and yet, two decades later, each is inconceivable without the other. Unintended consequence or not, chernukha was the apotheosis of glasnost: the rejection of enforced optimism based on lies and an insistence on uncovering long-suppressed truths. By the very nature of the system (and its unsystematic dismantling), such truths could only be unpleasant. Politicians and leaders are not generally noted for false modesty; why would any regime forbid the publication of national success stories? Though the stories told in the chernukha vein were often near-dystopian nightmares of moral relativism, they unfolded against a backdrop of a rather naive and binary rhetoric of the "Truth" (often with a capital T). After years of deception, the Truth would literally set the country free.

When Nevzorov was asked to explain exactly what *600 Seconds* was, he replied, "The genre of the program is the truth" (Mickiewicz 100). After an open letter in defense of Stalinism sowed panic in the ranks of reformers, who feared it was a sign of the government's shift toward reactionary policies, an editorial in the April 5, 1988, edition of *Pravda* defined the goals of perestroika in no uncertain terms:

> We are rehabilitating Truth, cleansing it of phony and cunning truths that
> lead us into the dead end of social apathy; we are learning the lesson of truth

---

[18] In fact, chernukha's focus on character types and presumably common situations linked it to the discredited aesthetics of official Soviet socialist realism. Sergei Dobrotvorskii argued in 1992 that chernukha was a "pointless statement of the pointlessness of life. . . . Prison yards, hideouts, drunk tanks, barracks, and communal kitchens aspire to comprise the sorrowful symbolism of Soviet reality. Thus they allow a director to stay afloat without having to relinquish socialist realist slogans about 'typical character in typical circumstances'" (28–29, qtd. in and trans. by Graham, "Chernukha" 13).

offered by the 27th Congress of the CPSU. But Truth has turned out to be in many ways bitter. And so already an attempt is undertaken using references only to the extreme situation to whitewash the past, to justify political deformations and crimes before socialism. (Melville and Lapidus 65)

If the Truth did not automatically set the country free, at the very least it was essential for "rebuilding" a broken society—one of the central metaphors implied by the term *perestroika* (literally, "reconstruction"). As Andrei Zorin notes, the editorial writers and documentary filmmakers who exposed the country's hidden suffering "took on the function of healers" ("Kruche" 202).[19]

Yet the healing was more in the promise than in the execution. Or rather, in the tradition of socialist realism, which saw art as a means to spur the audience into action, chernukha narratives contained no solutions for the misery they depicted. Instead, viewers and readers, their eyes opened to the suffering that surrounded them, were supposed to take a renewed interest in social action. Consider the title of one of the documentary films that was most closely identified with chernukha, Stanislav Govorukhin's 1990 *Tak zhit' nel'zia* (*This Is No Way to Live*). In the original Russian, the title is a complete sentence, a declaration, and perhaps even a verdict: we cannot go on living like this. Equally evocative was the rock melodrama *Assa* (1987), which ended with the anthem by the quasi-underground band Kino: "Our hearts demand change/We want change."

Some of the more heavy-handed examples of chernukha narrative shared this tendency to drive their message home, even as they depicted acts of "immorality" that scandalized conservative viewers. In 1988, one of the sensations in perestroika theater, *Dorogaia Elena Sergeevna* (*Dear Elena Sergeevna*), became an equally sensational film in the hands of director El'dar R'iazanov, telling the story of a group of high school students who pay an unexpected visit to their teacher (the eponymous Elena Sergeevna) on her birthday, with the hopes of convincing (or eventually forcing) her to change their grades. Along the way, the students get out of control, in scenes complete with drunken brawls, threats of violence, and even the gang rape

---

[19] A rhetorical emphasis on truth was in itself nothing new to Soviet literature, both because socialist realism itself was supposed to lead the audience to higher, ideological truth and because the Thaw had already reestablished independent truth as a virtue, if even temporarily. As Genis notes, "[t]he overall subject matter of Soviet literature was always reducible to a revelation, that is, to a proclamation of Truth: about leaders, about the government, about the rural economy or heavy industry" (88). Perestroika, however, represented a moment of sustained common understanding between the party and the intelligentsia about the centrality of the "truth," even if the *content* of the truth was still a bone of contention.

of one of the girls, all of which cause Elena Sergeevna to hang herself in despair at the end of the film. At various times, when Elena Sergeevna expresses her outrage at her students' cynicism, they respond with a claim that served as the unofficial mantra of chernukha films: it was your generation that made us like this.

It stands to reason that youth would be at the center of so many chernukha narratives of the perestroika era. Even setting aside decades of slogans about "youth as the future" and "youth as builders of communism," young people could be expected to embrace the new options available to them in more liberal times and would be most cynical about anything their elders had to say. Indeed, one of the full-fledged, classic moral panics to arise under perestroika involved the moral failings of wayward youth (Pilkington 118–60). Chernukha indulged its audiences' fears of sexually depraved, drug-taking, irreverent young people devoid of guiding moral principles. To a large extent, chernukha was about a crisis that was at least as much pedagogical as it was moral: how can good young people be raised in such treacherous times?

Perestroika cinema (and, to a lesser extent, fiction) was populated with bad boys and bad girls who embodied their parents' worst nightmares: the hard-currency prostitute of Viktor Kunin's 1988 novel and Petr Todorovskii's 1989 film *Interdevochka* (*Intergirl*), whose lifestyle causes her mother to commit suicide (itself a hugely popular perestroika motif); the out-of-control daughter in *Malen'kaia Vera* (*Little Vera*) whose cynicism is highlighted by the movie's title, a pun on her name (Little Vera = Little Faith). *Intergirl* follows the rules of melodrama closely, meting out punishment to most of the transgressors along the way, the title character included, while *Little Vera* is more unsettling through its total lack of sympathetic characters or even a resolution to the plot. But there is no question that the very act of depicting such misery is supposed to be instructive. Though stories of juvenile delinquency throughout the world tend to have a strong element of smug moralism, the chernukha tales of the perestroika era elevate the problems of youth to a higher level. Thus Chingiz Aitmatov in his 1986 novel *Plakha* (*The Place of the Skull*) features a plot line with a young former seminarian who takes to the streets in order to fight the spread of marijuana and hashish.[20] His struggle is more philosophical than social, in that the

---

[20] Aitmatov's novel, one of the early breakthroughs of perestroika fiction, is not usually assimilated to the category of chernukha. Not only did the book appear before the concept became prevalent, but Aitmatov's own well-established reputation and the book's relatively restrained language also would seem to make it a poor fit. Nevertheless, the first section of the novel hits many of the notes associated with chernukha, and the novel's violation of taboos (particularly about drugs) justifies the connection.

ill-defined threat of "drugs" is presented as a metaphysical evil. The resulting novel is painfully high-minded, a leaden *21 Jump Street* with Russian Orthodox overtones.

The fact that chernukha was prominent in such disparate realms as film, news media, and fiction shows that the barriers glasnost broke down were ones of genre and cultural hierarchy as well as simply content: all three areas were able to combine the seriousness of purpose and the moral weightiness of high art with the all-but-unmentionable grotesque details of contemporary misery. Feature films and television documentaries tended to be the most overtly preachy; Aitmatov's *Place of the Skull* is an exception in this regard. The short stories and novels that had the "chernukha" label attached to them were, if anything, more vulnerable to charges of cynicism because their authors refused to provide a crystal clear message. Nonetheless, it took a remarkably obtuse critical eye to view their works as value neutral.

Political allegory or satire was never far from the surface of texts by Viktor Astaf'ev, Victor Erofeyev, or Vladimir Sorokin. The short stories of Ludmila Petrushevskaia were a bit more challenging in this regard: her depictions of pure, unedifying human misery (as in her apocalyptic plague tale "Hygiene") and family breakdown (*The Time: Night*) defy a socially engaged reading. If anything, Petrushevskaia transposes the generalized perestroika angst about Soviet youth in order to highlight the moral failings of the preceding (1960s) generation. Her most famous story, "Our Crowd," is narrated by a spiteful, unpleasant woman modeled after Dostoevsky's underground man, who, through her vicious wit and her calculated, public neglect of her own son, manipulates her circle of friends to make sure that the boy will be taken care of after she succumbs to the disease that is slowly killing her. Here Petrushevskaia is continuing the process begun decades earlier by Iulii Daniel, whose story "This Is Moscow Speaking" showed the murderous potential in a similar group of friends (as well as in society at large), unleashed by the government's declaration of an upcoming "Open Murder Day." In each case, one of the 1960s intelligentsia's most cherished myths about itself, its cult of friendship, is coldly dismantled, undermining the "humanism" that was the motto of an entire generation of the intellectual opposition. This was perhaps one of the most disturbing philosophical implications of chernukha, since, in its zeal to expose, it quickly subverted even the humanist impulse that helped spawn it.

The chernukha of the perestroika era, while appearing to be asocial or antisocial in its portrayal of everyday misery, unmotivated violence, rampant drug use, broken families, and loveless sex, replicated existing cultural norms, if only to invert them or tear them down. With its unapologetic pessimism as a counterpoint to earlier official Soviet optimism, chernukha skewered the old Soviet myths of cultural achievement and radiant future not through the pointed political satire of earlier critics of the regime, such as Vladimir Voinovich, but through a preponderance of counterevidence. Here, too, the traditional binary cultural patterns identified by Lotman and Uspensky are upheld: if, as we are told in "Ever Higher," the anthem of the Soviet Air Force under Stalin, Soviet citizens are "born to make fairy tales come true" (Lotman and Uspenskii 31–32; German and Khait 257), chernukha narratives functioned according to the logic of the inverted fairy tale: a miserable person encounters a set of often unlikely situations that, taken together, leave him or her even more miserable than when the story began.[21] In chernukha, everyone lives unhappily ever after.

Chernukha: The Next Generation

Given the bleak picture I have painted of chernukha in the perestroika years, readers might well wonder how such a dismal phenomenon could possible intersect with *popular* culture, or how it could last very long. Chernukha was exciting and novel, but it offered little in terms of sheer fun. Indeed, by the nineties, "classical" chernukha had begun to run its course in highbrow fiction, one of the media that spawned it, to be largely replaced by what Mark Lipovetsky calls "neo-sentimentalism ("Rasstratnye" 205). But in popular entertainment, chernukha was just beginning (the films of Quentin Tarantino would only add fuel to the fire). Post-Soviet chernukha in pop entertainment bears a superficial resemblance to its perestroika predecessor, but this similarity is only skin deep. Both describe torture, sex, humiliation, and "cynicism," but there is no longer the same impulse to "expose." After all, what remains to be uncovered? Taboos have long been broken; the old system is dead. Yes, these works often are critiques of the misery of post-Soviet life, but they are telling people what they already know (people barely have enough food to eat), what they already think they know but cannot prove (the government is stealing from the people), and what they are convinced is true but can neither prove nor rebut (that Russia is the victim of a conspiracy led by the scapegoat du jour). But chernukha is no longer the implicitly moral crusade to expose. Instead, in a world in which the private has been made public for the first time, and in which the publicly owned has

---

[21] Though the song was written in 1920, it came to prominence only a decade later (von Geldern and Stites 257).

been privatized, the rhetoric of neo-chernukha is, if anything, that of *overexposure*: let us see once again what horrifies us every day. This is the logic of *Dorozhnyi patrul'* (*Highway Patrol*), one of several nightly infotainment broadcasts featuring corpses, car crashes, and bloodied criminals and victims. The abundance of more or less identical material based on shock value suggests an almost obsessive relation to the entertainment concerned. Chernukha transforms post-Soviet moral anxieties into a discourse of anxiety, a symbolic language for both the expression and shaping of fears about crime, sexuality, and national status.

The centrality of chernukha is particularly revealing when it comes to the development of popular genres. Though action, mysteries, and fantasy/science fiction started out as "imports," they are now being supplemented (if not supplanted) by homegrown knockoffs. Yet in the 1990s, this was still not the case for an extremely popular genre, the romance novel. Romance novels were available everywhere, but virtually all of them were translations.[22] By 1999, I managed to find only a handful of domestically produced, truly Russian romance novels. As Helena Goscilo argues, Western-style romances "were thoroughly alien to Soviet readers," since Russia "lacks a love-story tradition as a solid foundation to build on" ("Big-Buck Books" 18, 20).[23] The optimism and the happy end of the romance novel do not fit in with the worldview that spawns the rest of Russian popular entertainment. And, of course, the romance novel relies on certain types of characters that are truly difficult to imagine in contemporary Russia (the rich "prince," for instance).[24] Thus the novels found had generic titles indicative of the dearth of viable domestic competition: *The Rich Husband*, *The New Russian's Wife*. The closest thing to a Russian romance, at least in terms of marketing and packaging, was the rubric "women's fiction" (*zhenskaia proza*). Publishing powerhouses such as Vagrius took books by long-established "serious" women authors such as Viktoriia Tokareva and gave them covers featuring flowers, pastel colors, and the general trappings of romance. Many of these books

---

[22] For a discussion of Harlequin Romance's wildly successful implantation in Russia, see Goscilo ("Big-Buck Books" 18–19).

[23] Indeed, Goscilo finds that the "remoteness and hyperbole of the romantic universe" render the romance analogous to science fiction and fantasy ("Big-Buck Books" 20). Mariia Cherniak notes that even though domestically produced romances became more common by the end of the decade, they still took second place behind translated works (158).

[24] Il'ia Fal'kovskii notes that the closest analogy to such a prince in Russia would be either ethnically unsuitable (a rich man from the Caucasus, for example) or ethically problematic (the "New Russian") (5, qtd. in Goscilo, "Big-Buck Books" 20). One Russian writer asserted that Russian romance novels have no future because the genre can only be American: "To make a Russian romantic novel is the same as making Lego out of breadcrumbs. Lego is Lego" (Sotnikova 171, qtd. in Cherniak 157).

were about family life and love, but they did not follow the pattern of mass-market romances à la Harlequin.

Even before the August 1991 coup attempt, the term *chernukha* was undergoing considerable semantic drift. Chernukha simultaneously signified the overall aesthetic of socially oriented unmasking discussed above and the simple presence of the themes and images that made chernukha so shocking. When critics, viewers, and readers complain that there is too much chernukha in popular entertainment, they are referring first and foremost to content. By the 1990s, chernukha had become an umbrella term for sex and violence. "Classical" chernukha was something of a Trojan horse, bringing sex and violence back to popular entertainment in the guise of high-minded social purpose. I do not mean to endorse a moralistic "slippery slope" argument here; rather, arguments for the freedom to use a particular kind of imagery or content inevitably invoke art's need to transgress, but since consensus on the distinctions between art and non-art is impossible, the principle of free artistic expression facilitates the violation of taboos for the sake of pure entertainment (and, of course, profit). The relaxation of censorship meant that violent, explicitly sexual films and publications produced in the United States, Western Europe, and Asia became readily available, and had a clear influence on domestic production.

Chernukha functioned discursively as an unhealthy habit widely enjoyed even as it was derided. As popular genres developed in the 1990s, creators and critics would talk of "good" crime fiction and films that avoided tasteless excesses: the hope was that one could choose to have one's entertainment with or without chernukha, like coffee with or without caffeine. In reality, however, chernukha-free entertainment was almost as hard to find in Russia as decaf: it existed, but one had to know where to look.[25] Otherwise, post-Soviet popular culture was dominated by sex and violence.

This dominance should not come as a great surprise. Where would consumer culture be without sex and violence? These twin pillars support not only the lowest common denominator of mass taste, but, equally important, the fierce ideological opposition to the perceived excesses of modern and postmodern culture. While it would be a mistake to reduce chernukha and its legacy only to this pair of cardinal sins, sex and violence form the

---

[25] One obvious place to find it was in popular music, which falls outside the purview of the present study. Though production values and musical styles changed greatly during the 1990s, the lyrics of popular songs were still dominated by the conventions of Soviet-era *estrada*, favoring a vague, romantic vocabulary that invoked the natural world, love, and fate.

basis of chernukha in that they condition the experience and subjectivity of the characters who live in this particular mode. In its focus on physicality, chernukha defines the human body in terms of sex and violence: the body is an object to be fucked, beaten, or killed.

The centrality of sex and violence to the chernukha phenomenon is indisputable, if for no other reason than their virtual simultaneity: chernukha was identified with the sudden upsurge in the representation of sex and violence in a country that had previously kept tight controls on both. Thus, whether or not a text is marked by the bleakness and cynicism that characterized chernukha at its height, it gets easily assimilated to this category owing to the mere presence of graphic sex and/or violence. Sex and violence are the fundamental features that distinguish late- and post-Soviet popular entertainment from the mass culture that preceded it, and their effect on the hyperreal construction of post-Soviet Russia in the mass media and culture industry can hardly be overstated. Yet despite the tendency to lump the two together (particularly in the United States, where "sex and violence" often functions as a single semantic unit), their deployment in the culture at large does not have identical effects on cultural forms and cannot be treated as an indivisible phenomenon.

The emerging discourse of sex and violence in post-Soviet Russia made the creation of any kind of female subjectivity particularly challenging. Though women's perspectives could be encountered on talk shows and in magazines designed for a female audience, the conjunction of sexuality with the discourse of national identity generally presupposed a male subject position. Cultural productions about violent crime quickly divided themselves along gender lines: some of the most successful crime narratives were produced by and for women, but the genres geared toward men tended to reduce female characters to the familiar functions of lovers, martyrs, betrayers, and victims.

The first part of this book explores the discourse of sexuality as it emerged during and after perestroika. The very fact that sex was being discussed (and simulated) openly caused enormous anxieties in the culture at large. At issue was sexual expression itself, rather than any particular kind of sexual expression or taboo activity. In its reflexive preoccupation with Russia's lost prestige and its perceived humiliation by a self-satisfied West, post-Soviet sexual discourse imagines itself on an international scale. Metaphors of sex easily lend themselves to political or metaphysical dramas, since all (nonsolitary) sex involves the encounter between self and other. The Russian discourse of sexuality in the 1990s combined great power anxieties with dramas of beset masculinity, allegorical rapes of the once-virginal mother-land, and outright whoredom.[26]

If the removal of taboos on sex has been integral to reconfiguring the discourse surrounding Russia's place in the world by using allegories of desire, conquest, and submission, the thematic and aesthetic predomi-nance of violence (and, in particular, violent crime and murder) has been crucial to the forms of storytelling that have become popular in the post-perestroika era. As I investigate the role of violence and violent crime in 1990s Russian entertainment, the goal is not merely to catalog the myriad representations of violence. Rather, the focus is on the worldviews created and supported by various modes of violence, worldviews that cannot be entirely separated from the forms and genres that produce them.

The growing emphasis on violence in Russian popular culture coin-cides with a renewed love affair with serial narrative. It is violent crime, rather than sexual subject matter, that has provided the thematic and philosophical basis for Russia's return to the serial form. Without a doubt, the aesthetics of violence and sex share a number of key characteristics. Their representation can easily be seen as pandering to prurient interest, appealing to an essentially voyeuristic impulse. Indeed, at least one partic-ular strain of Russian violent entertainment has clear and obvious paral-lels to pornography. Yet violence and sex differ in their relation to, and effect on, *narrative*. Certainly, sexuality can be expressed as action, as seen in the ubiquitous sex scenes in film and fiction. But the pervasiveness of sexuality is underscored at least as much by its static representation: much of the material I analyze in the first part of the book is images that are deployed in contexts inviting semiotic analysis (e.g., on billboards, plastic bags, magazine covers) but that do not necessarily tell a story. Violence, like sex, can be represented statically, but with a difference. What is shown is either the result (usually a corpse) or the threat (a man holding a gun or a knife). Of course, to the extent that it can ever be satis-fied, the pornographic imagination is indulged most fully though the representation of the act over time; however, the static image functions as a stimulus to fantasy to a much greater extent than any corresponding vi-olent picture. Violence does not have anything that serves quite the same function as the simple portrayal of nudity does for sexuality. The image of

---

[26] Katherine Verdery advises students of postsocialist cultures to pay close attention to the the-ories of procreation that underlie the images of nationalism taking hold in the wake of the Soviet collapse: "Theories that privilege men as genitors of the nation's eternal spirit while women pro-vide merely its vessel" (232–33).

the mutilated corpse is not the same as the pinup, even though both can be said to have a pornographic appeal. If nothing else, the naked body represents the beginning of the erotic story, an invitation to act, for sex is what happens next. In sexual terms, the dead body is, if not anticlimactic, then *post*climatic. Except in rare cases of necrophilia, the action is already over.

Of course, such schematic distinctions are difficult to maintain because they presume that sex and violence have entirely separate spheres, whereas the sexualized violence that characterizes so much popular entertainment suggests a much more complicated situation. Still, Russian novels and films do feature numerous works where either sexuality or violence presents the dominant mode of action, with clear consequences for their storytelling. The violence in Russian entertainment more often than not results in murder.[27] While the parallels between sex and death are well known (one need only recall the French phrase "little death" used to signify orgasm), they shape narration and storytelling along different lines. To borrow Umberto Eco's term, sex does not "consume" character; except in cases of an extremely moralized context (such as the American slasher movie, in which the indirect but inevitable punishment for teenage sex is death), the mere fact of engaging in sex poses no danger to the character's continued existence.[28] By contrast, violent entertainments are predicated on the threat of a fatal outcome, whether for the hero, the villain, or secondary characters. As the driving forces behind a narrative, sexuality and violence diverge in their relation to both temporality (the flow of action) and iterability (the possibility of repetition). On the face of things, sex would allow for an endless, episodic, or agglutinative kind of storytelling, while violence would lend itself to discrete plots that lead to an inevitable (and almost inevitably lethal) conclusion. However, closer examination of popular entertainment

---

[27] While this notion might seem too obvious to warrant mention, it should be recalled that there is an entire realm of violence that has not been adopted in Russia. Until recently, most violence in superhero comics did not result in death, or at least not permanent death—in the world of fantasy, death is not necessarily final; hence the notion of "cartoon violence," or violence that lacks the lethal consequences it would have in real life. Specific political and historical circumstances led to the rise of cartoon violence in the American context, in particular the public outcry and moral panic surrounding comics in the late 1940s and early 1950s, prompted by Frederic Wertham's *Seduction of the Innocent*. The result was the Comics Code of 1954, which set strict limits on both sexual and violent content (Pustz 35–43).

[28] In "The Myth of Superman," Eco argues that certain popular forms, particularly superhero comics, depend on a semimythic time frame, in which virtually no irreversible events happen in the protagonists' lives. This lack of development, combined with the illusion of the passage of time, allows the story to appear as though it were contemporary to the reader without "consuming" the characters (changing them, aging them, and bringing them that much closer to death) (333–35).

(particularly, but by no means exclusively, in Russia) shows that the narrative situation is exactly the opposite of what one might expect: it is violence, not sex, that lends itself to episodic storytelling.

Serials are predominant in the two most prominent and distinctly gendered genres of violent popular entertainment of the first post-Soviet decade: the *detektiv*, roughly equivalent to the murder mystery, and the *boevik*, action story. Each genre combines the temporality of the post-Soviet serial with a preoccupation with death and destruction, facilitating a compromise between crippling pessimism and naive optimism that allows both story and the consumer to go on. The serial frame proves incompatible with the mode of violent crime that is equally incompatible with hope: the random, meaningless destruction called *bespredel*. Bespredel takes chernukha to its logical extreme, presenting violence, crime, and collapse as phenomena that defy all logic, perpetrated by criminals whose amorality is so shocking that they are often rendered as inhuman.

In the post-Soviet context, pessimism is not surprising, and yet it was far from a foregone conclusion that the cultural production of the 1990s would be so overwhelmingly bleak. It would not have been inconceivable for the media and cultural industry to win over consumers through happy-go-lucky escapism. The patterns of muckraking and misery mongering established during the perestroika era could have faded with the regime. Instead, popular culture in the 1990s both condensed and magnified the anxieties that gripped the nation. The thematics of violent crime colonized virtually every narrative genre, ensuring that even comedy owed its success to liberal helpings of blood, gore, and guns. Nor did the commodification of sexuality fade along with the novelty of graphic sex (whether in prose, photos, or film). Together, sex and violence provided post-Soviet popular culture with a symbolic vocabulary for the expression of fundamental anxieties about national pride, cultural collapse, and the frightening new moral landscape of Yeltsin's Russia. Throughout the decade, the stories Russians told about themselves allowed cultural consumers to indulge in despair over the ills that beset their country and the threats they faced every day while at the same time building a notion of heroism that could be entertained even under the most miserable of social conditions. In all but the most extreme manifestations of chernukha, the logic of cultural pessimism contained intimations of a way out.

Chapter One

ABOUT THAT

Sex and Its Metaphors

"We'll never understand it," Anyuta tried to explain. "That was
the morality of the era when this country had no sex."

—Viktoriia Rostokina, *The Rich Husband* (*Bogatyi muzh*)

Walk into any sex shop in Moscow, and with enough cash or the right
credit card, you can buy a perfect plastic replica of international porn star Jeff
Stryker's erect penis. Clearly, the penetration of the Russian market has been
a success. To make an analogy unlikely to grace the pages of a college entrance
exam, Stryker's member is to the Russian sex industry as Snickers is to snack
foods: while both guarantee "satisfaction," the organ is a naked demonstration of the barely hidden erotic connotations of post-Soviet Russia's humiliating status as a weakened, passive importer of prepackaged cultural and
physical commodities. Though I have no statistics on sales (let alone consumption) in the Russian Federation, given the price ($59.95, as of June 2004,
on www.jeff-stryker.com/ for an autographed edition), it is safe to assume
that the vast majority of the country's impoverished citizens are not saving up
their rubles to buy imported sex toys. But here, as throughout this book, I am
dealing more with the symbolic and the imaginary than the real and the
everyday, and on that level, Stryker's commodified erection is a perfect fit.

The Stryker artifact is a powerful, if artificial, embodiment of so many of
the anxieties that surround the discourse of sexuality after the Soviet collapse,
starting with the fact that it is so unambiguously sexual: unlike the om-
nipresent representations of naked women in post-Soviet Russia, this partic-

ular prosthesis cannot pretend to be merely aesthetic. Moreover, it is erect, and erections are sexual desire at their most visible: according to the unwritten laws of international erotica, only the flaccid penis can be displayed without signaling the transgression from the erotic to the pornographic. Finally, the importation of an American man's mass-produced phallus conjures up an important set of Russian cultural anxieties surrounding masculinity, sexual humiliation, and globalization. Always erect, the plastic substitute can embody the phallus in a way that the biological penis cannot—in a bizarre echo of the Soviet cult of labor, it never stops working because it only *simulates* working. Stryker's dildo recalls the tropes of male decline and sexual anxiety that pervaded the discourse in the nineties: impotent and pathetic, the once-proud Fatherland even has to import a phallus.[1] The potential for humiliation is only increased by the gender ambiguity involved in selling dildos: who exactly is supposed to be buying them? Is it Russian women, who despair of finding a good man, or is it Russian men, who have thoroughly assumed a "feminine" position? The packaging on Stryker's package is deliberately ambiguous.[2]

The Stryker dildo is hardly the only sign of the intersection between globalization and sexual anxiety in post-Soviet Russia. More than a decade after "adult material" began to slip through the state censor's tight grip, sex in Russia still wore a distinctly foreign face. In November 1997, 30 percent of the sizable portion of the Russian television audience still awake after midnight was tuned in to a program on the NTV (Independent Television) network called *Pro Eto* (*About That*), Russia's first talk show devoted entirely to sex (Carpenter). The program, which featured frank discussions of such formerly taboo subjects as masturbation, sadomasochism, and homosexuality, was hosted by one Elena Khanga, a young journalist whose Moscow accent and blonde wig were a striking contrast to her black skin. Born and raised in Russia, Khanga was the grandchild of an American communist and the daughter of a Tanzanian nationalist, the indirect product of the Soviet Union's troubled love affair with the American civil rights movement and postcolonial Africa.[3] The fact that Khanga sounded Russian but looked foreign made her a fitting

[1] Cf. Victor Pelevin's ironic comment in *Generation P* (*Homo Zapiens*): "[W]as it worth trading an evil empire for an evil banana republic that imports bananas from Finland?" (18).

[2] In fact, Stryker is unusual among male porn stars not only for his celebrity (usually reserved for women) but for his unabashed bisexuality. While many men appear in both straight and gay porn films, Stryker flaunts rather than hides his sexual omnivorousness. His website reduces sexual ambiguity to a question of menu options: "Please make a choice below. Gay Entrance. Straight Entrance." (www.jeff-stryker.com/).

[3] Khanga is the author of a memoir about her life as a "black Russian" called *Soul to Soul*. For more on Soviet attitudes toward Africa and African Americans, see Blakely (chaps. 7–9).

icon for post-Soviet sex; like her subject matter, Khanga, who divided her time between Moscow and New York, was both an export and an import, a native daughter whom Russians seemed to have difficulty acknowledging as their own. The wig, added at her producers' insistence in order to bridge the potential gap between Khanga and her viewing audience, only heightened her exoticism: she was foreign sex in Russian drag.[4]

If *About That* was meant to acquaint Russians with "deviant" sexuality, the phenomenon of Khanga's show can provide foreign observers with a rather tidy illustration of the pleasures and anxieties of contemporary Russian sexual discourse. *About That* embodies all the problems of sex in 1990s Russian culture that are the subject of these first three chapters: the sexualized relationship between Russia and the West; the sexualization of politics (as opposed to the politicization of sex); the rigid but unspoken code governing the deployment of sex in "high" and "low" culture; and, fundamentally, the development of a sexual discourse that defies circumlocution and repression while simultaneously relying on them. Whether or not changes in mores and practices since the gray days of Brezhnev constitute a "sexual revolution," a phrase rendered virtually meaningless through overuse, the sexual scene in Russia changed radically in the course of a decade. Prostitution, a relatively small-scale phenomenon in Soviet times, was viewed by many young girls in the 1990s as a viable career choice, and male homosexuality was decriminalized for the first time in over fifty years; sex shops were scattered throughout the Russian Federation; and pornography was so prevalent in the streets and stores that it rarely merited a second glance.[5] Such facts form the backdrop of any study of sexuality in 1990s Russia, but they are not the primary focus of this section. Rather, in turning to the question of sex in Russia, my intent is to examine the way in which Russian culture addressed these empirical phenomena, the way in which Russia interpreted this so-called revolution. Positing Soviet sexuality in terms of absence or lack justifies an ethos of revelation and overexposure in the name of liberation and self-expression. Post-Soviet sexual discourse is an exercise in excess, a

---

[4] NTV executive producer Leonid Parfenov was quoted in the *New York Times* as saying, "A Russian black girl has never been seen on television. I believe in cosmopolitanism—showing that not all Russians are blue-eyed and blond." But when the show was in rehearsals, a stylist fitted her for a blonde wig and blue contact lenses; Khanga agreed to the wig but balked at the lenses. Parfenov's response: "We didn't want to go with an Angela Davis, Afro-American style. We had to make a step toward the viewers" (Stanley, "On Russian TV").

[5] Lesbianism in Russia has long had the dubious distinction of being legally and socially invisible; there have never been any laws in Russia forbidding female same-sex activity. Article 121.1 of the criminal code, which made male homosexual relations an offense punishable by imprisonment, was repealed on May 29, 1993. For an overview of the status of gays and lesbians in contemporary Russia, see Essig (5–24); Gessen, *Rights of Lesbians*; Kon (239–64); and Tuller.

pointed and self-conscious indulgence in overkill as remediation. Khanga's face and Stryker's dildo highlight the two key features of Russian sexual discourse on which the following two chapters rest: the paradoxes involved in expressing the repressed and the rhetoric of the "crisis of manhood" that haunts most of post-Soviet Russia's representations of sex and gender.

From the Ineffable to the Unmentionable

Just as the black Russian Khanga is a study in contrasts, the show itself exploited its own obvious disjuncture between form and content. One of the most explicit programs on Russian television hid behind the coy euphemism "about that." The producers were clearly winking at their audience, albeit in two different directions. In the traditions of "higher-class" Russian pornography, which constantly makes parodic references to the Russian literary and artistic classics in order to cover itself in the fig leaf of erudition, *About That* took its name from a Russian modernist masterpiece.[6] The educated Russian's first association with the phrase "about that" is in Vladimir Mayakovsky's famous 1923 poem of the same title, in which the speaker of the poem agonizes over his passion for a particular woman while meditating on the role of love in the new world. In the poem's prologue, the speaker proclaims the importance of his theme in typically hyperbolic terms and yet avoids writing out the word "love," as though it were a dirty word.[7] Mayakovsky's circumlocution flies in the face of the Russian literary

---

[6] Helena Goscilo explores the unlikely juxtapositions of "high" and "low" cultures in the first wave of contemporary Russian pornography, in which "the Venus de Milo is likely to rub elbows (*only* metaphorically speaking) with a *Playboy* centerfold, their sole common denominator being their gendered nudity" (Goscilo, *Dehexing* 146, emphasis in the original).

[7] The prologue ends with a rhymed couplet, the last line of which is "The name / of this theme / is . . ." (*Imia / etoi / teme / . . .*); the missing word (*liubov'*) is made all the more obvious in that it is meant to rhyme with the Russian *lbov* ("foreheads") (Maiakovskii 176). The forbidden character of the speaker's love is reinforced by the title of the section immediately following it, "The Ballad of Reading Gaol"; though Mayakovsky's passion in the poem is explicitly heterosexual, the reference to Oscar Wilde's poem written during the author's years in prison for sodomy suggests that homosexuality is not the only love that "dare not speak its name."

In the early years of Soviet power, particularly during the Russian civil war, love was seen by many revolutionary romantics as a theme that was too "bourgeois" for the "new world" they envisioned. In particular, the poets associated with the Proletarian Culture movement tended to relegate women, femininity, and love to the dustbin of history (See Naiman, *Sex in Public* chap. 1, and Borenstein, *Men Without Women* chap. 1. Even writers as distant from revolutionary ideologists as the formalist Viktor Shklovsky, for reasons of their own, would treat love as a matter for coy circumlocution. Shklovsky's 1923 novel *Zoo, or Letters Not about Love*, composed of personal letters between a man and a woman, is structured on the woman's prohibition on writing about love ("Don't write to me about love. Don't. I'm very tired") (177).

tradition, in which the paucity of sexual details is more than compensated for by dogged attention to emotion. Nineteenth-century Russia may not have had a publicly acceptable vocabulary for sex, but it certainly had a language of love. Khanga's show turned Mayakovsky's discomfort back to its more "appropriate" target, and just as the poet spends pages describing the love his title refuses to name, *About That* never flinched in its exploration of the seamier side of sex. In both cases, circumlocution facilitated discourse rather than hampering it.

Perhaps more important, however, is the very fact that the most popular television show about sex avoided the word entirely. Indeed, the word "that" ("eto") was a remarkably apt choice, reflecting a traditional reticence about discussing sexual matters. Though the Russian language is rich in obscene verbs and nouns related to sexual activity, the only polite way to refer to sex in mixed company is not to refer to it explicitly at all. The euphemism of Khanga's title recalls a crucial moment in late Soviet sexual discourse, a 1987 Soviet-American "space bridge" hosted by Phil Donahue and Vladimir Pozner. When asked about sexual practices in the Soviet Union, one of the Russian audience members-*cum*-citizen-diplomats responded "We have no sex!" (*U nas seksa net!*), an apparently paradoxical declaration when one considers that Soviet women managed to give birth to children without recourse to test tubes and pipettes. Obviously, physical sexual activity was not the issue here. As opposed to the native Russian *pol*, the word *seks* is a relatively recent import into the Russian lexicon; even the word's standard pronunciation (with an unpalatalized *s*) draws attention to its foreign origins.[8] Here I would translate *seks* as either "sexuality" or "sexual discourse," that is, sex as subject matter rather than activity. One usually imagines that frank discussions of sexuality are meant to titillate, resulting in arousal and even action; yet the issue here is what Michel Foucault calls the "incitement to discourse": the drive to produce more and more discourse about sex rather than sex itself (29–30). When examined in this light, a sexual (rather than verbal) response to sexual discourse constitutes a short circuit of desire; sexual discourse exists so that we can talk about sex without necessarily engaging in it. The two activities can (and do) exist quite independently of each other.

Thus despite the apparent absurdity of her claims, the woman who declared that the Soviet Union "had no *sex*" was actually correct: there was no

---

[8] See, for example, the title of M. Rezin's article about the lack of shame among contemporary Russian students: "In Latin, it's sex, but what is it in Russian?" (*Po latyni—seks, a po-russki?*). As the subject of seks grows less foreign, so too does the pronunciation of the word itself; one hears a palatalized *s* more and more frequently.

sexual discourse, no "sexual question," insofar as a question that has not been raised does not exist. But this comic phrase became fodder for jokes on both sides of the Atlantic, a mantra to be repeated and mocked whenever the occasion arose. Over the next ten years, when Russian or Western scholars and journalists would write about the sexual revolution in Russia, they would inevitably return to this phrase as the point of departure.[9] One might argue that the public denial of seks effectively called it into being; the word, once uttered, became infectious. Indeed, the comparison between sexual discourse and sexually transmitted disease is not made lightly, since the very scene of the introduction of seks would prefigure the dynamics of Russian sexual discourse for years to come. The sexual question was, after all, raised by an American; seks, like AIDS, penetrated the Soviet borders once vigilance became lax. Sexual discourse in Russia is therefore dependent on the West to a much greater extent than Western sexual discourse depends on Russia;[10] not only is there a great deal of borrowing on all levels, from medical literature to pornographic imagery, but we shall see that the relationship between Russia and the West takes on undeniably sexual overtones. Finally, one must not forget the particular genre that brought seks to Russia: the talk show. In America, the talk show has defined the limits of acceptability by testing and stretching them, inciting its participants to turn their own sexual experiences into narratives for mass consumption. Just ten years after Donahue and Pozner got their audiences talking, Elena Khanga's talk show continued the process begun during the space bridge, returning to the scene of the crime. If Russians still required a "foreigner" to pose the question of sex, they now had one who spoke their language, the language accustomed to euphemism and denial. Black and blonde, Khanga is both "about that" and "all that."

For the average Russian, frank discussion of sexual issues in the media must have felt entirely new, since few citizens of the Russian Federation would have been old enough to remember the last time sexuality had played such a prominent role in public discourse. The "sexual question" was already a pressing issue in the last decades of tsarist rule, with strong links to the growing political/revolutionary counterculture and the realm of Russian religious philosophy and mysticism. Nikolai Chernyshevsky's

---

[9] See, for example, Lynn Attwood, "Sex" (66); Gessen, "We Have No Sex"; and Kon (1).

[10] This is not to say that Russia plays no role in the Western sexual imaginary; quite to the contrary, Russia has often functioned as the source of "passion" in various Western narratives and fantasies, from Freud's metaphorical connections between Russia and the unconscious (Rice; Etkind, *Eros* 132) to Sacher-Masoch's use of Russian material in his most famous works (Etkind, *Sodom* 12–30). Elsewhere I argue that Western scholars' and journalists' interest in Russian sexuality is also erotic in character (Borenstein, "Slavophilia" 146–47).

Chto delat'? (*What Is to Be Done?* 1863), a tendentious novel aimed at raising revolutionary consciousness, showed its young readers the lives of the
"new people" who refused to be shackled by an outdated moral code.[11] On
the other end of the spectrum, Lev Tolstoy's 1889 *Kreitserova sonata* (*The
Kreutzer Sonata*) depicts marriage as nothing more than legalized prostitution, a debasement of both man and woman and a denial of their higher,
Christian calling. Sexual passion is purely animalistic and fundamentally
repulsive; rather than allowing any outlet for it at all, people would be far
better off living lives of total chastity. Tolstoy's novel caused a sensation,
both at home and abroad, and his polemic against sex did not fall on deaf
ears.[12] His views had much in common with the posthumously published
writings of Nikolai Fedorov, whose *Filosofiia obshchego dela* (*Philosophy of
the Common Cause* 1906) argued that sex and reproduction are intrinsically
evil, since they make us turn away from our parents and look to the next
generation. Such distractions help us make our peace with the seemingly
irremediable loss of our parents when actually we should be devoting all
our efforts toward the scientific resurrection of our dead ancestors.

Though both Tolstoy and Fedorov were hugely influential, other religious philosophers and mystics during Russia's Silver Age (1890–1917)
came to different conclusions about sexuality. Vladimir Solov'ev's *Smysl
liubvi* (*The Meaning of Love* 1892), while hardly a celebration of sexual passion for its own sake, posited a sexual relationship in which "the task of
true love consists not in merely doing homage to this supreme object [the
divine feminine principle], but in realizing and incarnating it in another
lower being of the same feminine form" (93). Vasilii Rozanov went further,
finding that sexual love is itself a transcendent force for good. Many of the
poets connected with Symbolism, the dominant artistic movement of the
Silver Age, were inspired in particular by Solov'ev, imbuing their works
with an eroticized spirituality that was unprecedented in Russian letters.[13]

Sexual expression during the Silver Age was by no means the exclusive
purview of poets and philosophers. The relaxation of censorship and increased urbanization that followed the failed 1905 revolution led to the rise
of "boulevard" culture: the newly literate workers and lower middle class

[11] For more on the role of Chernyshevsky's novel in the history of Russian sexuality, see Borenstein (*Men Without Women* 7–10); Matich ("Dialectics of Cultural Return" 60–66); Paperno
(29–36); and Stites (*Women's Liberation* chap. 3).

[12] A thorough study of Tolstoy's role in the development of public sexual discourse in Russia can
be found in Moller. See also David Herman's "Stricken by Infection."

[13] A more thorough discussion of sexuality in the Russian Silver Age can be found in Matich
("The Symbolist Meaning of Love") and Naiman ("Historectomies").

could choose from a wide range of racy entertainments, from bawdy vaudeville acts to endless serialized penny dreadfuls, whose heroines enjoyed erotic adventures and travails that could not have seen print only a few years before. Russian feminist movements, which trace their roots back to the 1860s, brought the "woman question" to increasing prominence, and even homosexuality, long criminalized and stigmatized, was discussed in pamphlets, books, and on the floor of the new legislature. Within just two years, Mikhail Kuz'min published Kryl'ia (*Wings* 1906), a short novel about a young homosexual man; Lidiia Zinovieva-Annibal came out with *Tridtsat'-tri* uroda (*Thirty-Three Freaks* 1907), a tale of lesbian love; Fedor Sologub published *Melkii bes* (*The Petty Demon* 1907), a "decadent" novel featuring voyeurism, transvestism, and homoeroticism; and Mikhail Artsybashev gained notoriety for his scandalous novel *Sanin* (1907), whose heroes' sexual cynicism and hedonism prompted an outpouring of anxiety over the morals of "today's youth" on a level not seen again until the age of perestroika. From 1908 to 1915, Aleksandr Kuprin, in *Iama* (*The Pit*), penned a frank and captivating chronicle about the lives of women who worked in a provincial brothel. Anastasiia Verbitskaia's *Kliuchi schast'ia* (*The Keys to Happiness* 1913), a saga about a sexually emancipated young woman, was a runaway best seller. In politics, the Marxists in Russia had long been advocating the complete abolition of the family and the establishment of total equality of the sexes; by the October Revolution of 1917, the sexual status quo had already been shaken.

Almost as soon as they came to power, the Bolsheviks passed legislation that entirely reconceived family and private life in Russia. The October 1918 Code on Marriage, the Family and Guardianship was the most radical document of its kind, not just for Russia, but for the entire world. It replaced religious marriage with civil marriage, making divorce available at the request of either spouse (no grounds were necessary). Alimony was to be granted to women and men, and the very category of legitimacy for new offspring was made irrelevant. Legal persecution of male homosexuality had ceased (lesbianism had not been technically illegal in tsarist times), and abortion was legalized in 1920 (Goldman 48–58). The transformation of Russian sexual life and legislation was staggering, equaled only by the proliferation of a burgeoning new discourse surrounding sex. The new Soviet men and women could choose from a wide range of sexual advice literature, whose quality and accuracy varied widely (Bernstein, *Dictatorship*; Kelly 266–70). Soviet medical doctors, particularly venereologists, tried to assert their professional authority over the sex question in order to create a sexually and eugenically healthy populace, but with mixed results (Bernstein,

Dictatorship). At the same time, the debate over proper sexual conduct grew increasingly heated, in part thanks to the writings of Bolshevik feminist Aleksandra Kollontai, whose call for "comradely love" in her 1923 article "Make Way for Winged Eros" was widely (and mistakenly) condemned for advocating hedonism. On the other side of the sexual barricades, Aron Zalkind argued that a truly revolutionary society can be based only on sublimation, since the task of building communism cannot afford the distractions of sex. His 1924 "twelve commandments" for sexual behavior called for abstinence before marriage, infrequent sexual relations within marriage, and as little sexual variety as possible (Kon 55–58).

The tensions between proponents of sexual freedom and advocates for revolutionary chastity were not based on ideology alone. The chaos stemming from nearly a decade of war and revolution (from World War I through the Russian civil war, ending in 1920) inevitably took its toll, while the relaxation of marriage laws was seen by many men as an opportunity to avoid family responsibilities altogether. Divorce, female poverty, and child abandonment rates soared, with homeless children rapidly becoming a serious problem on urban streets. The social benefits promised by Bolshevik dreamers in replacing the patriarchal family, such as communal kitchens and laundries and high-quality socialized child care, were slow in materializing, with the result that women, who were supposed to reap so many of the benefits of the new world, were bearing the brunt of the social upheaval.

Stalin's consolidation of power by the 1930s put an abrupt end to nearly all public discussions of sexual matters, and a more rigid family code quickly followed: male homosexuality was recriminalized in 1934 and abortion banned in 1936 (to be legalized once more in 1955). It would be an oversimplification to attribute this new sexual conservatism entirely to Stalin and his government, since the backlash against perceived sexual excesses had already begun, concurrently with the excesses themselves. Nonetheless, the sex question was now closed. Though women joined the workforce in even greater numbers in the 1930s than they had in the previous decade, the traditional family had been reinstated, now as a basic cell of Stalinist society. Even after Stalin's death in 1953, the Soviet media and culture industry remained decidedly reticent when it came to sex until perestroika began.[14]

---

[14] This is not to say that sexual silence remained absolute. The occasional foreign film did give audiences a glimpse at more risqué art, while the occasional (and prim) handbook on marital relations did get translated, starting in the 1960s. The 1960s also saw the birth of Soviet sexopathology, the return of the study of sexuality as a part of the medical disciplines (Kon 85–95).

The Expressive Hypothesis

Though the majority of participants in the new sexual discourse in the 1990s preferred the language of circumlocution, even the most reticent among them, including those who polemicized against the proliferation of sexual expression, only facilitated the transformation of sex into discourse. On a scale surpassing both the libertinism of the fin de siècle boulevard and the eroticized battlefield of the Russian civil war and New Economic Policy, Russian culture in all its manifestations would appear to have become thoroughly and overtly sexualized. Certainly, sexual expression was most evident in the lowbrow media: in the popular or "gutter" press, represented most notably by *SPID-Info* (*AIDS-Info*) Russia's best-selling newspaper, and by the controversial publication *Eshche* (*More*), whose editions and publisher were subject to detentions by Russian authorities; in the proliferation of pornography; and in the erotic imagery of television, radio, and newspaper advertising, where scantily clad women moaned the names of the latest indispensable consumer gadget. Far from being a mere verbal or audiovisual representation of glandular realities, sexuality also became an object of study for the professional writers, scholars, and artists who, in the wake of the Soviet government's failed attempts at a monopoly on expression, now shaped Russian public discourse. Sex manuals, both imported and homemade, were sold on every street corner; newspaper pundits either decried the collapse of morals or praised the end of sexual hypocrisy, and writers such as Valeria Narbikova and Victor Erofeyev put overt sexual situations in works printed by highbrow literary journals and publishing houses.

One could dismiss the simultaneous rise in both scholarly and nonscholarly discourse as mere coincidence, a happy accident of Western critical fashion and Eastern postsocialist experimentation. But the juxtaposition of scholarly and popular examples of Russian sexual discourse reveals a shared belief in the capacity of sex to signify, a belief that sex can speak of more than just itself. Both the Russian media and the scholarly literature took for granted that sexual discourse was politically significant, co-opting what might arguably have been considered the one sphere of Soviet life that was, thanks to the prudishness of the guardians of Soviet culture, beyond the limits of the official and the public. Now the state of affairs in Russia most closely resembled the situation that Foucault considered one of the defining characteristics of the modern era: "What is peculiar to modern societies, in fact, is not that they consigned sex to a shadow existence, but that they dedicated themselves to speaking of it *ad infinitum*, while exploiting it as the secret" (35).

Figure 1: Cover of *SPID-Info*, a popular lifestyle publication about sexuality.

Only recently had sexologists, sociologists, psychologists, and journalists begun to enjoin the populace to enter into a dialogue on sexuality. It was the public acknowledgment of sex as a medical problem that facilitated the spread of sex as discourse. A revealing case (in every sense of the word) was the newspaper *SPID-Info*, which had the highest subscription rate of all periodicals for 1994. Founded in 1989, *SPID-Info* was initially purported to have essentially "prophylactic" goals: to enlighten the public about sexual issues and to prevent the spread of venereal diseases in general and AIDS in particular. Homilies on sexual hygiene and protracted discussions of fatal diseases, however, do not sell newspapers; from the very beginning, *SPID-Info* carried numerous stories about porn stars, prostitutes, and the sex lives of historical figures.[15] If one charitably assumes that the newspaper's more sensational aspects were included in order to gain a wider audience for the paper's public health message, one is forced to admit that the situation rapidly reversed itself. The newspaper still contained detailed information for those with sexual questions, but such concerns were clearly secondary to the paper's popular appeal.

Indeed, the very meaning of the word "SPID" in the newspaper's title underwent a transformation that would startle even Susan Sontag. Since the newspaper now contained far less information about AIDS than it did about nymphomania and tantric sex, the word "SPID" had become little more than an advertisement of sexual subject matter.[16] In 1994 the editorial board decided to make the newspaper's name doubly exotic: in a rather dubious rhetorical sleight of hand, they explained that the newspaper's goal was to provide information as rapidly as possible; now the masthead uses Latin letters, spelling not "SPID" but "SPEED." Where "SPID" is a contagion best avoided by abstinence, "SPEED" insists on the necessity of its own transmission: " 'SPEED-INFO' is a whole world for a couple!" (*SPID-Info* February 1994)

Having freed itself from the less appetizing connotations of immunodeficiency, *SPID-Info* was not only a veritable encyclopedia of sexual life; it was a monthly advertisement for sex *as* life.[17] If the newspaper had been mere pornography, it would not have been at all memorable, for its scope would have been limited to stimulating and satisfying physical sexual desire. Instead, *SPID-Info* combined the typical photos of gravity-defying, airbrushed nudes with a relentless torrent of articles about sex and beauty,

---

[15] As Masha Gessen writes, "Though [*SPID-Info*] contained less AIDS information than Tema [an early gay newspaper], which ran safer-sex guidelines in every issue, and its provocative covers featured such topics as fetishes and prostitution, *SPID-Info* carried the morally upstanding cachet of being an AIDS information publication. No one had to be embarrassed about reading it. So everyone read it" (Gessen, "Sex" 220–21).

[16] Gessen notes that after its first few issues, *SPID-Info* "ceased providing AIDS-related information" altogether (Gessen, "Sex" 222).

[17] The newspaper does still contain detailed information for those with sexual questions. Indeed, if Russian men and women have taken some of the paper's more questionable contraceptive advice to heart, who knows how many blessed events may have occurred by now.

sex and the workplace, sex and humor, sex and money, sex and crime. This editorial strategy was different from that of Western magazines such as *Playboy*, which purports to rise above pornography by including articles and fiction on nonsexual topics. Rather, *SPID-Info* was a promotional brochure for a brave new, polymorphously perverse world in which sexuality always insisted on its place in any given aspect of culture or everyday life. The best of *SPID-Info*'s headlines and rubrics playfully suggested that life could be defined only in terms of sex. For years the newspaper printed articles under the heading "Coito ergo sum" ("I copulate, therefore I am").

The all-embracing grip of *SPID-Info*'s sexualized world was comically evoked in the paper's 1993 television advertising campaign. An average-looking man sits on his couch reading *SPID-Info*, oblivious to his surroundings. Meanwhile, his two-year-old son has discovered a neon green crayon, with which he proceeds to draw on the carpet, the walls, the furniture, and finally, even on his father's balding head. Only at this point does the man speak: he looks up from his newspaper, stares straight into the camera, and says, "A *very* interesting newspaper!" ("*Ochen'* interesnaia gazeta!"). After the name *SPID-Info* appears on the screen, the commercial is over. No mention is made of sex, nor do any of the paper's ubiquitous nubile young women make an appearance. One can, of course, analyze this commercial in any number of ways: in the absence of the wife/mother, the husband/father turns his thoughts to sexual fantasy, while his son (embodying sex's inevitable "hazards") runs rampant. But for the purposes of my argument, two things are important. First, that the newspaper, which is famous enough that it need not advertise its sexual content, is placed in a domestic, comforting context; that is, *SPID-Info* isn't just for sex shops any more. Second, the newspaper is so captivating that its sexual embrace completely replaces the everyday world.

Where some of the sex manuals created the appearance of reader participation through a question-and-answer format resembling a catechism, newspapers such as *SPID-Info* were truly interactive. People wrote in from all over the country with questions about impotence, menstruation, menopause, etc., and the newspaper printed the letters along with professional replies. *SPID-Info* featured a marvelously entertaining rubric entitled "Family Consultation," in which fictional patients confessed their most personal problems to Professor Konstantin Tumanovskii. In the early issues, the column was accompanied by a picture, in which "Tumanovskii" is seen talking to "real" people, whose eyes are blacked out to protect their identities, while the photo's perspective suggests that the reader is sitting with them in the office, watching unnoticed from the side. As in Russian newspaper interviews, all extraneous conversation was edited out of these sessions, resulting in a telescoping of the sexual plot to the point of absurdity. Dispensing with any therapeutic foreplay, Tumanovskii often pronounced a complex Freudian diagnosis after a mere two or three questions. Tumanovskii's "consultations" epitomized both the professionalization of sexual discourse and the paradoxical conflation of the public and the private. His fictional patients, whose problems were general enough to be relevant to the largest number of readers, were reassured about confidentiality, while millions of Russians eagerly awaited his next word. Time after time we saw a concerned wife drag her reluctant husband into the sexologist's office, finally convincing him to let the doctor (and the readership) into their sex life. Here, perhaps, was the true post-Soviet "primal scene": the Russian bedroom exposes its secrets to the concerned professional.

SPID-Info served not to provoke sexual desire but to provoke the verbalization of desire. The readers of *SPID-Info* learned their lesson well. Even more indicative than the practical-minded consultation was the letters section of *SPID-Info*; here people (mostly women) sent in letters about their own sexual experiences, more often than not unhappy ones. They could expect no reply and no advice; instead, they simply felt the urge to talk. Newspapers like *SPID-Info*, by their very existence, suggested to the reader the possibility of turning one's own sexuality into discourse, of joining the mass readership in a well-regulated, professionalized form of textual intercourse.

Publications such as *SPID-Info* trumpeted the virtues of the "private" (*chastnoe*) and the "intimate" (*intimnoe*), yet the constant exploration of this once-taboo realm constituted an all-out assault on privacy by bringing the private realm into public discourse.[18] The title of one of the more popular newspapers of 1990s Russia, *Chastnaia zhizn'* (*Private Life*), is emblematic of this problem. One section of *SPID-Info* was called "Intimacy Club" ("Intim-Klub"). Intim-Klub is, of course, an oxymoron, but a particularly revealing one: how can a club be intimate? This may well be the fundamental paradox of sexual discourse in 1990s Russia: we are enjoined to make sex a legitimate object of discourse, to read and write about sexual problems and sexual pleasures, all in the name of the private and the intimate. Yet one can argue that sexuality was far more intimate, if not more satisfying, when it could not be exposed in print.

---

[18] It has been argued that in Russian culture, the value placed on something is in indirect proportion to the amount one talks about it: the most truly valuable, intimate matters are protected from being tarnished by a presumably corrupt or profane public sphere through silence. See Pesmen (223–25).

Reactions to the sexual saturation of Russian popular culture ranged from approval to panic to parody. In Boris Akunin's literary mystery novel *F.M.* (2006), the search for a lost Dostoevsky manuscript is jeopardized because Filipp Borisovich Morozov, the literary scholar who found it, suffers from a postconcussive syndrome that has transformed him into his exact psychological opposite. No longer the least bit interested in Dostoevsky, Morozov will provide a clue to the manuscript's location only if the other characters tell him the most embarrassing sexual stories from their past: "I need the truth. Go ahead: tell me the most obscene story. Only it has to have a little sex in it (*Tol'ko obiazatel'no s seksikom*)" (F.M. I: 164–65). Fifteen years after the Soviet collapse, Akunin plays the scene for laughs, but the sex-obsessed Dostoevsky scholar quite handily represents the paradoxes and anxieties resulting from the broadening of post-Soviet sexual discourse. On the one hand, a brain-damaged intellectual's rejection of high culture in favor of filth could be a clear metaphor for the Russian intelligentsia's decline, but on the other hand, he also embodies the return of the repressed. Morozov's fascination with shame, sin, and scandal are not just contemporary; they are also quintessentially Dostoevskian.

Akunin's approach is light-hearted, but others took the "problem" of sexual expression more seriously. One man's utopia is another's apocalypse, and the numerous critiques of sexual excess seem to suggest that it is only a small step from scatology to eschatology. In one of the many prolonged attacks on utopian "liberation sexology" featured in *Nezavisimaia gazeta* (*The Independent Newspaper*), Valentin Aleksandrov complains that "plaster casts of reproductive organs are displayed for sale on Novyi Arbat and the central squares right under the nose of the Moscow mayor's office" (the Gogolian implications of this sentence are staggering). He then proposes that the vanguard of sexual revolution will need its own new titles, such as *Vashe Erotichestvo* ("Your Erotic Highness") and *Vashe Seksual'noe Erotichestvo* ("Your Sexual Erotic Highness") (Aleksandrov 8).

Aleksandrov's moral outrage is necessarily limited to invective and misinformation (he blames lesbians for the spread of AIDS), but governmental organs, on occasion, have resorted to the familiar harsher methods. Though dozens of graphic, hard-core publications circulate throughout the Russian Federation without resistance, the publisher of a peculiar newspaper called *Eshche* was imprisoned in 1993 for spreading pornography. If *SPID-Info* presented an erotic utopia that was left largely unexamined, *Eshche*—which its defenders, such as Zugar Gareev, call a "postmodern phenomenon" (Erotika 13)—comically proclaimed that the former USSR was a "Common Erotic Space" ("Edinoe Eroticheskoe Prostranstvo," a parody on then-current phrases such as a "Common Cultural Space" or a "Common Ruble Space"). Where *SPID-Info* took a decidedly international perspective, *Eshche* presented a sexual vision as seen through an entirely post-Soviet lens. Its erotic adventurers were truck drivers and collective farm workers, and its stories about sexual experimentation in other countries were told from the point of view of the bemused ex-Soviet sex tourist. Dmitrii Stakhov sees the newspaper as the catalogue of a "dying breed": "the Soviet people." He writes: "*Eshche* is a mirror for Soviet man. "Both you and your intimate manifestations are open to the gaze of another. Look at yourself!" *Eshche* seems to be calling. "You are still Soviet in a no-longer-Soviet world" ("Erotika" 14).

Whether or not Stakhov's assessment is accurate, it is worth noting that, even as he defends the newspaper from political persecution, he insists on defining the agenda of *Eshche* in political as well as cultural terms. Stakhov's interpretation of the newspaper has an added appeal, one that Stakhov himself does not make explicit: the very title of *Eshche* (which could mean both "still" and "more") would then combine Stakhov's idea of the Soviet who is "still Soviet" with the more obvious sexual connotation of "more" (that is, one can never get enough). Why this newspaper in particular had been targeted is still largely a mystery; Igor Iarkevich claims it is because *Eshche* refuses to restrict erotica to the "acceptable" realm of nightclubs and bars ("Erotika" 12). For Stakhov, the state repression only reinforces the newspaper's "Soviet" essence: it was even shut down in tried-and-true Soviet fashion ("Erotika" 14).

The Erotic Body Politic

If sexuality had entered the public sphere for the first time in over fifty years, one would expect to find it in that most public of all realms: politics. And, indeed, sexual questions continued to be debated in the Russian parliament and press: the means and advisability of fighting prostitution, the status of women, the pros and cons of the legalization of male homosexuality, the advisability of sex education, and the spread of venereal disease are repeated flash points in sexual politics.[19] But despite the widespread attention to such matters in the past decade, there is still some continuity with the early Soviet disdain for devoting too much time and energy to the sexual question; Lenin's dismissal of sex reform as "navel gazing" is a sentiment that might well be shared by political leaders today (Zetkin 61). Feminism is

[19] See, for example, Kon and Riordan (1–7, 129–273).

still largely a dirty word, and gender roles, which are assumed to be innate, are to be reinforced rather than questioned.[20] In a country where political and economic crises make the headlines on a daily basis, issues of sexual politics are almost always relegated to the features section of the more respectable papers and broadcasts (where they nonetheless do their part in maintaining circulation). It is politics (in the traditional sense) and economics that were the stuff of hard news in 1990s Russia, rather than sex per se. But the discourse of politics and economics itself became sexualized to an unprecedented extent: sex had begun to provide their metaphors.

Hence the relatively minor role played by sex scandals in the Russian popular imagination. Russia, like much of Europe, followed American coverage of the Bill Clinton/Monica Lewinsky story with a combination of bemusement and disgust. Though Lewinsky's semen-stained dress was described in lavish detail by the daily *Moskovskii komsomolets* (Bershidsky), the consensus in Russia seemed to be that this private affair should never have been made public (Bershidsky; Reeves; Shargodska; "Russia Would Prefer Sex Scandal"). Valentin Zorin of the USA and Canada Institute sees the Lewinsky story as evidence that "an element of sanctimoniousness . . . characterizes Americans" (Ustiuzhanin). The American media were particularly quick to note that, when polled, Russians see Clinton's alleged affairs as a sign that he is a "real man," unlike the old and ailing Yeltsin (Reeves; Shargodska; Howard and Gajilan).

On the rare occasions that Russian journalists attempted to stir up a sex scandal, they failed to hit the mark. In June 1997, the popular muckraking weekly *Sovershenno Sekretno* (*Top Secret*) published photos of Russia's justice minister, Valentin Kovalev, in the company of three naked women in a Moscow bathhouse reputed to be a mob hangout. Voices from across the political spectrum condemned the violation of Kovalev's privacy, including

---

[20] Susan Larsen argues that two ideas lie behind the conception of gender put forth in the Russian mass media: "first of all, normative axioms about the biological, and therefore 'natural' basis of the predetermination and life's purpose of women, and second, the conviction that 70 years of Soviet power have thoroughly deformed the 'natural' essence of women in all aspects of life—be they sexual, family, economic, or political" ("Zhenshchina" 178). Larsen echoes Lynn Attwood's 1990 study *The New Soviet Man and Woman: Sex-Role Socialization in the USSR*, which observes the growing concern over the perceived blurring of "natural" gender roles, the "feminization" of men and the "masculinization" of women (also noted by Goscilo, Dehexing 10–11). At the time of their research, Larsen and Attwood noted a great deal of concern over these issues, but in the past few years, this concern has taken a specific form. Headlines such as "Bureaucrats have taken everything away from men" (Proshina) continue the line of complaint noted by Larsen, but we now also see more and more calls to action and bold assertions of "natural" truths. See the article by sexologist Sergei Golod in the St. Petersburg paper *Chas-Pik* (*Rush Hour*) entitled "Despite everything, male sexuality is still different from female sexuality. And that's good."

Yeltsin's spokesman Sergei Yastrzhembsky, the popular reformer Boris Nemtsov, and Vladimir Zhirinovsky (Franchetti; Stanley, "The Sauna Scandal"). *Top Secret*'s editor, Artem Borovik, took pride in breaking new ground, as though coverage of sex scandals were a sign of political maturity: "We are absolutely delighted. This is the first scandal of its kind" (Franchetti). For *Top Secret*, the Kovalev story seemed to mark a subtle change of course. The very title of the paper embodies the informational paradox that characterizes the post-Soviet media. The words "Top Secret" customarily cover government documents not meant for publication, but the stories that appear in the newspaper of the same name have achieved the widest possible distribution. Since the paper was founded, the editors of *Top Secret* have devoted themselves to violating a long-standing taboo. The paper was predicated on a political, rather than sexual, fetishizing of information. The Kovalev story was an attempt to redirect this subject to a new object.

Thus the intersection of sex and politics in post-Soviet Russia lies elsewhere. The sexualization of politics and economics is predicated on a particular, and surprisingly consistent, gender-based metaphorical construction: Russia and the body politic are female, while those who lead (or exploit) the country are male.[21] To a large extent, this dynamic is culturally and linguistically overdetermined; Russia's very name (*Rossiia*) is grammatically feminine, and the metaphor of "Mother Russia" remains powerful to this day. It was "Mother Russia" and "the motherland" (*Rodina-mat'*) who rallied her sons to fight off the German invaders in World War II, not the masculine "Soviet Union." The Russian language does, in fact, provide a male counterpart to Mother Russia, the Fatherland (*otechestvo*), a grammatically neutral word that connotes civic responsibility (Zaitseva 32; Goscilo and Lanoux 14, 23–24). "Fatherland" is deployed in connection with the country's economic and industrial strengths (domestically produced goods are called *otechestvennye*—made in the fatherland) or in reference to the successful defense of the country from attack (the former Soviet Army Day is now called the "Day of the Defenders of the Fatherland"—*Den' zashchitnikov otechestva*). The operative word, however, is "successful": the country that is still in danger, the country that must be defended, is mother rather than father. In times of crisis, Russians seem to turn to a feminized sense of Russia almost automatically. Thus in the years immediately prior to and following the

---

[21] Aleksei Levinson has applied this particular gender regime to his analysis of the post-Soviet intelligentsia's initially hostile reaction to Western-style television advertising. The intelligentsia, which has long occupied a "feminine" position in relation to the "masculine" state structure, sees itself as the helpless victim of centralized manipulation by broadcasters.

revolution of 1917, the image of Mother Russia as either the helpless victim of rape or the wanton whore selling herself to the highest bidder could be found across the political spectrum. Such imagery recurs in contemporary Russia, where the country is frequently embodied as an alluring female misused at the hands of either the *gosudarstvennye muzhi* (an archaic phrase for leaders that in modern Russian sounds literally like "state husbands"), the country's perceived internal enemies (usually Jews, Chechens, and businessmen), or the depraved West.

It is Russia's most frankly sexual (and uninhibited) political figure, Vladimir Zhirinovsky, who most explicitly and playfully appeals to the sexual metaphor of the Russian feminine body politic. Zhirinovsky is unique among Russian politicians for both his frequent use of sexual imagery and his radical stance on a number of sexual issues. As with most of his political views, Zhirinovsky's statements on sex can hardly be considered a coherent political program. In March 1998, he attended a St. Petersburg gay club and expressed his support of "sexual minorities" ("Zhirinovsky Courts"). When the Monica Lewinsky scandal broke in January 1998, Zhirinovsky suggested that if Clinton were impeached, "Bill will have more freedom and I will be able to meet him more often. We will together recall our sexual experiences" ("Zhirinovsky to Clinton"). One of his more notorious moments occurred during an interview with Jennifer Gould for the American edition of *Playboy* (March 1995), when he proposed that Gould, her interpreter, and one of his bodyguards engage in group sex (Gould 248–49). In the same interview, Zhirinovsky boasts that he's "had more than two hundred women, and with every woman I've had it several times. And if you add masturbation, I've climaxed probably ten thousand times." (Gould 249).

Zhirinovsky, who once offered to personally impregnate all the lonely and childless women in Russia, turned his silver wedding anniversary into a political carnival. On February 11, 1996, Zhirinovsky and his wife, Galina, had a Russian Orthodox wedding for the benefit of the television cameras, dispensing free vodka to hundreds of pensioners waiting outside the church ("Zhirinovsky Throws Wedding"). Particularly significant was the fact that this ceremony was a renewal of vows, a nostalgic remarriage rather than a new union. Zhirinovsky was explicitly appealing to a longing for lost purity: "Against the background of general political prostitution, the LDPR [Zhirinovsky's party] is a long-haired, meek-eyed virgin in white," he said during a press conference. "Forty million men will desert all those prostitutes and rush after the virgin LDPR. Let's have group sex on June 16 [the day of the upcoming presidential election]" ("Zhirinovsky 'Like a

Virgin' ").[22] By conflating his personal wedding ceremony with the more public ritual of the election, Zhirinovsky underscored the election's role as a "life-cycle" rite for the body politic, at the same time mocking the solemnity of the event through his typically outlandish declarations.[23] The wedding ceremony, like all carnivals, inverted standard binary oppositions: now the men who lead the country are the blushing brides. But Zhirinovsky made it clear that this was only a temporary state of affairs, a necessary ritual for the renewal of the "great power": after the election, he declared, the wives of Gorbachev, Yeltsin, and Zhirinovsky himself would have to be sent "to a convent so they don't bother with their husbands running the country" ("Zhirinovsky Throws Wedding").

It would be all too easy simply to dismiss Zhirinovsky as an irrelevant sideshow—or to go to the opposite extreme that dominated American coverage of the LDPR leader in the early nineties, portraying him as a budding Hitler who could start World War III—and indeed, there is something decidedly clownish about Zhirinovsky's role in the public arena. One gets the sense that his reelections are almost akin to good Nielsen ratings: his constituents may or may not support what passes for his policies, but voting him out would be tantamount to canceling the most consistently entertaining show in contemporary politics. Yet when Zhirinovsky insisted on casting Russia's political fate in sexual terms, he was tapping into strong ambient anxieties about the fate of feminized Russia in the hands of her impotent male leaders. With his sexualized rhetoric of invasion, conquest, and great power/potency, Zhirinovsky provides the discursive counterpoint to the threat represented above by the Jeff Stryker dildo: Zhirinovsky's ideology is the politics of compensatory masculinity, trying to fight the West by speaking loudly and carrying a bigger stick.

Compensatory Masculinity

"The Russian man does not exist. That is to say, the concept has been preserved in the language by inertia, out of mental laziness, but essentially, it's a phantom, a chimera, a specter, a myth" (Erofeev, "Polet" 46). So writes

---

[22] The desire for such political purity was also parodically embodied by the short-lived All-Russian Virgin Party, an organization whose twelve members held their first public meeting in a Moscow nightclub in August 1997 (Beeston).

[23] This was not the first time that Zhirinovsky portrayed voting in sexual terms. Before the 1993 election, he declared," Political impotence is finished! Today is the beginning of orgasm. The whole nation, I promise you, will have an orgasm next year!" (from the *Washington Post*, December 17, 1993, qtd. in Tuller 197).

Figure 2: Illustration accompanying Victor Erofeyev's essay "The Flight of the Cloud in Trousers" when it first appeared in *Andrei*.

author and essayist Victor Erofeyev, who happens, of course, to be a Russian man. But as readers of Marx know, specters, despite their intangibility, can have a decisive impact, whether they are haunting Europe, Russia, or the post-Soviet national consciousness. Though Erofeyev is writing a veritable masculinist manifesto, a call for men to rise up and reclaim their "natural" prerogatives as leaders in both the public and private spheres, he is perhaps unwittingly continuing the decade-old Russian tradition of broaching issues of sex and gender in the negative: in the space of one short decade, we go from having "no sex" to having "no men." Years after dialectical materialism was dropped from the Russian school curricula, the concept of the "negation of the negation" seems to hold a special, if unexpected, relevance for questions of sexuality and gender.

Erofeyev's typically hyperbolic assertion that the Russian man is extinct must certainly be taken for the rhetorical flourish that it is. And yet, like the denial of sex, the negation of the Russian man is rich in implications even as it is divorced from biological reality. In a series of columns published originally in soft-core porn magazines and collected in 1998 in a slim volume of essays called *Muzhchiny* (*Men*), with a print run of five thousand copies, Erofeyev develops an argument that resonates throughout post-Soviet popular culture, whether or not it has any connection to everyday life: the crisis of Russian manhood. Certainly, the data on the life of the average Russian man give cause for alarm: poverty, military service, poor diet, inadequate health care, and, of course, alcoholism all contributed to a precipitous drop in the life expectancy of the average Russian male. But the data on Russian women are hardly encouraging either; though women live longer, they face the same day-to-day stressors as do Russian men, plus the added burdens of child rearing and domestic labor, not to mention—in extreme but by no means unusual cases—rape and sexual slavery. Even Erofeyev is careful not to indulge in comparative victimology with Russian women, since he tacitly acknowledges that the women would win this dubious honor hands down. His argument, as we shall see, is different.

If compensatory masculinity is a post-Soviet phenomenon, it has distinctly Soviet roots. Gender anxiety permeated Soviet culture from the early revolutionary days, when Bolshevik dreamers and utopian feminists argued for the emancipation of women from domestic labor and the virtual abolition of the family, at the same time that the traumas of war and revolution combined with the most liberal family code on the face of the earth to create domestic chaos: skyrocketing divorce rates, growing numbers of orphaned street children, and single-parent (i.e., single-mother) households. Women's entry into the industrialized labor force, a much-touted goal of the 1920s that became a truly widespread phenomenon in the thirties, would inevitably threaten traditional notions of gender and home life, and the virtual feminization of nearly all aspects of labor and daily life in World War II while the men were in the army would add to the sense of instability. But though women had every reason to complain that they were bearing a double burden, at work and at home, the frequent complaint was one of male inadequacy: as the Russian sexologist Igor Kon puts it, the "male character" had been "deformed": Soviet man was deprived of his traditional leadership role in the family and unable to express any social initiative when "in public life, absolutely everything came under the control of the powerful, maternal Communist Party, which knew better than anyone what was good for its members and which stood ever-prepared to correct mistakes by force" (150–51). It is worth noting, though, that Kon was one of the most liberal voices in public sexual discourse in 1990s Russia. Despite the fact that his *Sexual Revolution in Russia* is anything but an antifeminist rant, his choice of words still reflects a belief in the very idea of a "male character," partaking in the age-old Russian habit of identifying the feminine with the negative. Kon writes that "opposition to the idea of gender equality has been mounting and widening since the 1970s. . . . [A] mighty wave of conservative backlash has arisen, with thousands dreaming of turning back the clock not only to pre-Soviet times but to pre-industrial and even pre-Petrine times—literally to those ancient days when the *Domostroi* [medieval patriarchal] rules for family living were introduced" (153). Indeed, V. Pilipov's 1991 pamphlet "Was Domostroi Really so Bad?," with a print run of 210,000 copies, agitates for just such a return to the "radiant past."

Kon puts the start of the debate over the "feminization of men" and "masculinization of women" in 1970, with the appearance of articles on the subject in the weekly *Literaturnaia gazeta* (149). The argument can be found in numerous newspaper articles from the seventies and especially the eighties and is also featured quite prominently in a number of sex manuals and advice books dating from the last years of Soviet power to the present day. Indeed, there is a burgeoning literature devoted solely to the pathetic state of Russian manhood: Lina Tarkhova's 1992 *Vospitat' muzhchinu* (*Raising a Man*), V. Z. Vladislavskii's 1991 *Esli ty muzhchina* (*If You're a Man*), and A. Nuikin's 1990 *Muzhskoi razgovor* (*A Conversation for Men*) all share the basic premise elaborated by Erofeyev in *Men* in 1998: that Russian men are an endangered species, and that the Soviet regime in particular and modern society in general are to blame.[24] It is tempting to lump such works together with a similar phenomenon in Western countries that began in the 1960s: the antifeminist wing of the "men's movement," from Lionel Tiger's *Men in Groups*, which argued for men's basic need to form social structures that exclude women, to Robert Bly's mythopoetic *Iron John* and his laments over the lot of the "soft man," who, thanks to women's encroachment on traditional male prerogatives, does not know how to be a real man. But the Western men's movement (and again, I have in mind only the antifeminist branch) and the Russian polemic that would lead to compensatory masculinity were reacting to profoundly different circumstances: in the West, the enemy was feminism, while in Russia, the enemy was the state, itself at times troped as oppressive mother, at times as the instigator of a social experiment with the "natural order" that was doomed to lead to disaster.[25]

The Russian argument can be found in numerous sources, but it is put most succinctly by V. Vladin and D. Kapustin in their 1991 *Garmoniia*

---

[24] Russian masculinity has also drawn scholarly attention, both in Russia and abroad. See, for example, Sergei Oushakine's collection *O muzhe(n)stvennosti* (*On Mascu[femi-]linity*).

[25] The post-Soviet Russian reassertion of patriarchal values is part of broader phenomenon that encompasses a number of postsocialist countries. See, for example, Joanna Goven's analysis of the situation in Hungary (224–40) and Katherine Verdery's treatment of gender politics in Romania (61–82).

semeinykh otnoshenii (*Harmonious Family Relations*), which I will summarize here. Science has proven beyond a doubt that men are by nature both more rational and more active than women and that they have a biological need to protect their family from enemies and disaster. The family works when there is a clear division of sex roles. Now there is no such division, and in many families, there are no men at all, which leads to the feminization of men and boys. Boys find no male role models close at hand (in school, their teachers are almost all women). The authors' solution is sex-segregated schooling because, thanks to coeducation, "we are crippling our youth, especially the boys. We are raising them to be spineless, and depriving them of the remains of their pride, their feeling of male worth (*muzhskogo dostoinstva*)" (231). Feminization is only the beginning, however: in its worst form, it becomes "infantilization" (*infantalizatsiia*), the watchword for the defenders of male pride. Infantilism expresses itself as "impulsive behavior, irresponsibility, the lack of desire (or ability) to work and make decisions, the inability to explain the reasons for one's actions, to plan these actions, to see the consequences of one's actions, the tendency to easily fall under the influence of other individuals, [and] lack of persistence in the achievement of goals"(231). "A real man," write the authors, "is different from an infantile [man] in that first he makes a decision, then he acts" (233). "Scientists have determined that [infantilism] is not genetically programmed, but develops as the result of improper upbringing" (233). Thus the authors appeal to "natural" roles and the "natural" order while blaming society for corrupting the male essence.

Though Vladin and Kapustin do not make masculinity the subject of their book, their brief discussion of feminization and infantilism contains all the essential elements of this rhetoric but one: alcoholism, which is usually seen as both a symptom and an exacerbating factor in male infantilism. Lina Tarkhova's *Raising a Man*, published in 1992 with a print run of one hundred thousand, makes the same argument: "The former mammoth hunter has become feminized and lost his leadership, no longer a representative of the stronger sex" (23). But Tarkhova widens the scope of the problem, turning it into a disaster for society as a whole: "What is happening with man concerns not only his personal life. Are we ready to admit how serious this is? If there is no real man in the family, the family falls apart. But if there is a shortage [*defitsit*] of real men in society, society falls apart" (67). Tarkhova, a woman writing in the last days of the Soviet Union, perhaps unwittingly builds her apocalyptic rhetoric of social crisis with the most compelling crisis vocabulary of those economically lean times: the shortage. As we shall see, by the mid-nineties, the vocabulary of male inadequacy, now deployed largely by men themselves, will be military rather than economic. Tarkhova's book, along with the numerous articles and pamphlets arguing the same point, paves the way for Erofeyev's somewhat more colorful elaboration of the Russian man's plight. Such works, however, are largely pedagogical, focused on returning traditional male values to the younger generation; these are books for boys and for the teachers of boys.

In 1995, in the sixth issue of *Andrei*, Victor Erofeyev wrote the essay that is the ideological heart of *Men:* "The Flight of the Cloud in Trousers,"[26] supplying most of the material for the book's rather polemical blurb. As printed in *Andrei*, Erofeyev's article is preceded by a garish illustration of a monstrous female head with a woman's symbol hanging from her ear and a long, serpentine tongue sticking out of her mouth; the tongue is curled around the small, rigid figure of a faceless man, the helpless victim about to be swallowed up by this ravenous she-demon. The man's rigid pose could in itself almost be phallic, but the context deprives him of any of the prerogatives of traditional male power; not only does he look like a pawn from a chessboard, but, given that he seems to be staring directly into the eyes of the fishlike woman, he resembles the paralyzed victim of the gorgon's gaze. The cover of *Men* itself presents a far from edifying model of manhood: an unattributed painting of a flabby, bald, naked man sprawled on a chair, his penis pointing directly down.

After a rather typical diatribe against feminism and the controversy over sexual harassment in the West (which, Erofeyev says, may culminate in the executions of former "fun-loving womanizers" for their past "crimes," "like former Trotskyites who were shot in our country"), the author informs us that "Man's fate in Russia looks different but is no less dramatic." Erofeyev's explanation centers on the idea that unites his work with the editorial missions of *Andrei* and *Makhaon:* " "First and foremost, it's a question of consciousness." Though Erofeyev is engaging in deliberate *épatage*, he is also arguing, in a sense, for men's consciousness raising: "A man is a man when he thinks of himself as a man." Thanks to Soviet power (which Erofeyev himself admits was instituted by male Russians), the Russian man has lost the honor and freedom that are the hallmarks of true manhood. Instead, the Russian man has been replaced by a "layer cake" made up of *chelovek* (person), *muzhik* (guy), and *muzh* (husband),

---

[26] Once again, the point of reference is the work of Vladimir Mayakovsky. His 1915 poem "The Cloud in Trousers" takes its title from a phrase that the speaker uses in the prologue: "If you want/ I will be crazed from flesh /—and, like the sky, changing tones—/ if you want—/ I will be irreproachably tender / not a man, but a cloud in trousers!" Erofeyev uses the term to suggest that Russian men have retreated from their natural masculinity.

all of which represent circumscribed, ultimately unfulfilling roles for the potential real man (Erofeev, "Polet" 46).

Erofeyev buttresses his argument by borrowing from the standard arsenal of male metaphors: the language of war. He writes, " 'The person of the gender He,' as Dal's dictionary defines man, is meeting the 21st Century with the white flag of capitulation in his hands" (44). Any woman who is smart enough to give the Russian muzhik an illusory sense of conquest will herself be the victor in the battle that is marriage. The man may think he has won, but his is a Pyrrhic victory: "Then it'll be like what happened 50 years ago: the USSR will win, but Germany will triumph"(46). The persistent militarization of Erofeyev's language, the sense that Russian men have lost a battle, suggests an implicit connection to the fate of his nation as a whole. Not only did the country cease to exist, but it was defeated without firing a single shot. The Soviet national failure comes to resemble impotence writ large.

Erofeyev's essay hints at the specter that haunts Russian masculinity: the specter of Western culture and Western men. If the Russian man is a thing of the past, the Russian woman is entirely real: "Woman consists of necessity. In Russia we have necessity by the ton [neobkhodimosti khot' valiai]. That is why Russia is feminine." It is because she is aware that there are no men in Russia that she is so willing to leave the country and find real men abroad. Once again, this sexual threat is inextricably caught up with an economic one. The Russian man posited by *Andrei* laments the competition with Western men, while *Andrei* itself is haunted both by Russia's competition with American pop culture and by the magazine's own attempts to maintain its market share against the threat of men's magazines imported from the United States, particularly the Russian-language edition of *Playboy*, whose contents differ only slightly from the American version.

The sudden outpouring of sexual discourse in late- and post-Soviet Russia cannot be seen (and in Russia, is not seen) as a self-sufficient, isolated phenomenon. The profound shock of the sexualization of the culture was exacerbated by a kind of gender shock, the perception that, despite the near-total absence of women in leadership positions throughout Russia, despite the feminization of Russian poverty, it was Russian men who had been rendered powerless by the collapse of the USSR. This focus on male incapacity is particularly ironic, because it results in a sexual discourse that is relentlessly masculine in its orientation and assertion of male prerogative while constantly undermining itself through its insistence on a Russian failure of manhood. Nearly all the examples I have cited so far presume that the desiring (and consuming) subject is male, implicitly recapitulating a deeply rooted cultural pattern that posits women as desire's object. Yet the insistence on a traditional gendered hierarchy appears to have a basis in insecurity rather than strength. The sexualization of Russian popular culture becomes part and parcel of dramas of embattled masculinity, of male fantasies of heroism and humiliation. As we shall see, in 1990s Russia, even pornography was tendentiously ideological, and even prostitution, which one would expect to be represented in terms of the plight of women, became yet another testing ground for compensatory masculinity.

Chapter Two

STRIPPING THE NATION BARE

Pornography as Politics

Khrushchev Does Stalin

A Soviet primal scene for post-Soviet times:

Stalin moaned.

Khrushchev carefully unbuttoned his pants, pulled down his semi-transparent black shorts, freeing the leader's swarthy, straining phallus. Spitting on his fingers, the count [Khrushchev] began to tug tenderly at Stalin's nipple and moved his lips down the leader's body—to his blood-engorged phallus. . . .

"Give me your ass, my sweet boy," Khrushchev commanded him softly, gripping Stalin firmly by the balls. . . .

Khrushchev unbuttoned his own pants and took out his long, uneven penis with its bumpy head, its shiny skin tattooed with a pentacle. The count spat in his palm, lubricated Stalin's anus with his saliva, and, falling upon him from behind, started to thrust his penis softly into the leader. . . .

The count's member went all the way into Stalin's anus. Squeezing the leader's balls with his left hand, the count took hold of his penis with his right hand and started to masturbate him slowly.

"You . . . what are . . . you . . . " Stalin lowed. "What's the nice man doing to the boy?"

"The nice man is fucking the boy in the ass," Khrushchev whispered hotly. (Sorokin 257–58).

While it is impossible to know just how many readers have found themselves sexually aroused by Vladimir Sorokin's description of oral and anal intercourse between Soviet leaders, his novel *Goluboe salo* (*Blue Lard* 1999)[1] managed to elicit the other response so often provoked by so-called pornography: outrage and prosecution. In July 2002, the pro-Putin youth group Moving Together filed a criminal complaint with the Moscow prosecutor against both the author and his publisher, as well as organizing a public demonstration that culminated in flushing copies of the novel down a mock toilet in front of the Bolshoi Theater. Over the next seven months, the author faced the politically unlikely, but legally plausible, prospect of two years behind bars on pornography charges.[2] Finally, on April 24, 2003, the Moscow prosecutor's office announced that, after an evaluation of *Blue Lard* by "experts," the Sorokin case was closed "for lack of a criminal offense" (Novikova 8).

Even a cursory examination of the facts reveals complications and contradictions suggesting that the case is more a question of politics than morals. *Blue Lard* had been published to some fanfare in 1999, almost three years before Moving Together took action: why wait so long for a spontaneous manifestation of moral outrage? Though there are laws against pornography on the books and repeated calls for a clampdown, the Russian pornoconsumer can find products catering to the standard varieties of hetero- and homoerotic taste on paper and video, expending minimal effort if not minimal cash. Why target Sorokin, an avant-garde author with "high art" pretensions, rather than magazines and newspapers such as *Miss X, Andrei,* or *Strip*? If pornography has such a negative impact on the morality of an entire nation's youth, why pin the blame on such a difficult novel? The impatient thrill seeker has to wade through over 250 pages peppered with obscure Chinese borrowings and futuristic cyberslang before getting to the famous Kremlin buggery scene; one suspects that if Stalin's anus had been as impenetrable as Sorokin's prose, the author probably would not have been threatened with criminal charges. Moreover, Sorokin seems to revel in putting explicit sex scenes in contexts that would ordinarily defy eroticism, beginning with the novel's name.

---

[1] The particular word for "blue" in Sorokin's title (*goluboi*) is also a slang term for "gay man." Western press reports also cite the novel's title as *Gay Lard, Blue Fat, Blue Back-Fat, Sky-Blue Bacon,* and *Sky-Blue Pork Fat.*

[2] For a detailed, English-language overview of the Sorokin affair, see Gambrell.

Even in a country where pork fat is considered a perfectly acceptable sand-wich ingredient, *Blue Lard* hardly seems like a title designed to arouse pas-sions and stir the blood.[3]

If *Blue Lard* is unabashedly explicit, the Sorokin affair itself is sugges-tive and evocative: its meaning must be teased out. The campaign against Sorokin can be understood only in the context of the flowering of porno-graphic expression that marked the preceding, post-Soviet decade, and in light of the culture's nervous attempts to assimilate or reject it (or even, paradoxically, to do both at the same time). Politically, the Sorokin affair looks like a step backward for a country that had only recently emerged from a self-proclaimed dictatorship; from a Western point of view, charging a novelist with pornography seems almost quaint. In a multimedia age, who cares what novelists are doing? But it is this very quaintness that immediately suggests one lesson to be drawn from the outcry over *Blue Lard*: in Russia, pornography is still a category of mean-ing and content rather than simply form and function. If the West has to be reminded by scholars that pornography grew out of satire during the European Enlightenment, Russia needs no such encouragement to make the connection between pornography and ideas. In Russia, pornography *is* an idea.[4]

Pornography as Knowledge

In 1990s Russia, pornography enjoyed a peculiar status in that it was doubly ubiquitous: not only was the first post-Soviet decade marked by a proliferation of pornographic texts and images on newsstands, televisions, and even shopping bags, but pornography seemed all the more pervasive in that it is featured prominently in the standard litany of woes afflicting post-socialist society. AIDS, prostitution, and pornography were the unholy trinity of both popular and scholarly discussions of Russian life, constitut-ing one of the few things shared by Russians across the political spectrum:

[3] With characteristic bluntness, Sorokin has made this very argument in the press: "Pornogra-phy is a concrete genre. Its chief goal is to cause a reader's erection. I have never pursued that goal" ("Russian Writer").

[4] Indeed, one prominent Russian literary figure, Kornei Chukovskii, would even assert at the turn of the twentieth century that the connection between pornography and ideas was unique to Russia: "Russian pornography is not plain pornography such as the French or Germans produce, but pornography with ideas" (cited in Engelstein 386). Chukovskii made this claim in his review of one of pre-prerevolutionary Russia's most notorious pornographic novels, Mikhail Artsybashev's *Sanin*, a work that shocked its readers with its presentation of cynical, sex- and death-obsessed young provincials rather than with any explicit sexual descriptions.

the common denominator of a common demonology. Feminists in both Russia and the West invoked pornography along with domestic violence, trafficking in women, and the routine sexual exploitation of Russian women in the workplace as examples of a country in crisis, while communists and nationalists pointed to pornography, homosexuality, prostitution, and AIDS as diseases Russia caught from a decadent Europe and America.[5] Pornography in Russia cannot be accepted as a simple, straightforward phenomenon of supply and demand or of stimulus and response. Its widespread dissemination after years of prohibition automatically means that it will call attention to itself, becoming a topic of political and cultural debates. Yet the significance of Russian pornography should not be attributed to novelty alone. After ten years, pornography had already become normalized, to the extent that it simultaneously occupied a discrete, commodified niche (stroke literature aimed primarily at heterosexual men) and had expanded to encompass nearly all aspects of cultural life. The pervasiveness of graphic sexual content in film, television, and popular fiction after years of puritanism suggested a culture "pornographized" nearly to saturation. Both the proponents and opponents of pornography in Russia agreed on one thing: pornography has meaning.

Russian culture has traditionally privileged a conspiratorial epistemology (hoarding and restricting information) that leads to a dogged insistence on hidden meaning, symbolism, and interpretation; it is perhaps no accident that the discipline of semiotics was developed in a culture that is so self-consciously semioticized. Russian pornography partook of this same model of knowledge, creating a system of signs that points to more than just sexual desire. To some extent, Russian pornography showed a stronger connection to the classical porn of the Enlightenment era in that it was overtly political and often could be connected to the satirical tradition. However, Russian pornography's explicit engagement with ideology, which in part stems from the nation's own repressed pornographic tradition, was the result of particular post-Soviet anxieties. Pornography distilled the ideological features that characterized post-Soviet Russian sexual discourse as a whole. Oscillating between the extremes of utopian libertinism and

---

[5] See, for example, Helena Goscilo's "New Members and Organs: The Politics of Porn," the first scholarly article devoted to the contents of contemporary Russian pornography. Her approach, while explicitly opposed to censorship, nevertheless adheres to a feminist definition of pornography as "a practice and presentation of sexual subordination, whereby female submission to male dominance (and violence) is played out in sexually explicit terms degrading to women, for the purpose of arousing a (preponderantly male) audience" (*Dehexing Sex* 142). Goscilo argues that however much the defenders of Russian pornography in the late perestroika period couch their enthusiasm in the rhetoric of liberation, it is a liberation of men at the expense of women.

crypto-fascist nationalism, Russian pornography allegorized the culture's obsession with embattled masculinity, wounded national pride, and the country's perennially fraught relations with the West. It replicated and recapitulated the evolution of popular political attitudes from the heady days of the Soviet collapse to the disenchantment ten years after. Early post-Soviet pornography explicitly aligned itself with liberal-democratic aspirations and a project of postsocialist liberation. But by the end of the decade, pornographic/erotic publications had retrenched behind a reflexive nationalist discourse, often verging on crypto-fascism. Yet it was the right and center right in Russia that also typically sought to repress pornography, and the few instances of selective prosecution consistently targeted liberal authors and publications hostile to a nationalist ideology. One cannot help but wonder: why should pornography be a battleground for Russia's soul? And why should the nation's soul be defined and redefined using sexualized representations of the female body?

Though pornography in Russia undeniably has a history reaching back hundreds of years, the Soviet era amounted to enough of a break in porno tradition that the category of pornography has been largely reinvented in the perestroika and post-perestroika eras. This reinvention was hardly from scratch, and, on the surface, Western models (from glossy magazines to grainy films) were clearly the most immediate source of inspiration; thus the Russian reader and viewer of pornography could be struck by a simultaneous shock of the new, since explicit sexual representation had until then been almost unheard of, and a lingering sense of the secondhand—the first examples of post-Soviet pornography tended to look foreign/Western, even when they were not imported.[6] Scholars in the West have long recognized that porn can provide unique insights about the specters that haunt a given culture. Laura Kipnis writes that "[a] culture's pornography becomes . . . a very precise map of that culture's borders," establishing "a detailed blueprint of the culture's anxieties, investments, contradictions" (164). Or, as Feona Attwood argues, pornography "functions as a 'melodrama' or 'allegory' for a given culture" (91). If pornography is routinely seen as a challenge to established norms even in times of stability, how much more threatening does it become to a country in a state of political, cultural, and economic upheaval? What is true for the West is even truer for Russia, where these anxieties are never far from the surface of the pornographic

---

[6] There has also been a resurgence of highbrow interest in prerevolutionary pornography and erotica, as evidenced by Andrei Balabanov's award-winning 1999 film *Freaks and Men*, a cinematically beautiful, though wholly untitillating, reconstruction of a late-nineteenth- century pornographic photography studio.

text. Pornography is always about limits, charting the boundaries of the acceptable in order to violate them. Russian pornography, whether its definition is limited to low-cultural men's magazines and films or stretched to include sexually explicit high art, is surprisingly self-conscious in its preoccupation with Russia's status as a nation and a culture, allegorizing the fate of the nation through dramas of desire, violation, sexual commerce. Indeed, I argue that national concerns are part and parcel of Russian pornography *by definition*: the pleasure (and the danger) of Russian porn derives from the fact that eroticism and nationalism are offered up for consumption in a single package.

In part, this results from the unusually compressed time frame of post-Soviet porn's development. Brian McNair has argued that the past two decades in the West have seen a "pornographication of the mainstream," in which imagery and themes that would once have been exclusively pornographic have trickled up into everyday culture (24), but in Russia, this process was simultaneous with the (re)appearance of pornography as a distinct category. There was no time lag between the arrival of porn and the pornographication of the culture at large, rendering pornography a privileged locus for worries about cultural change. Pornography as a genre was distinguished from the rest of the mainstream not by its dogged attention to all things genital but by its unwavering focus on the sexually explicit as both an integral part of the nation's culture and an allegory for it. It is this conflation of the sexual with the national that provides the true logic behind the selective campaigns against pornography in the works of certain high cultural figures: where the antiporn crusaders at first look obtuse, they prove actually to be highly perceptive. Even if highbrow fiction containing explicit sexual scenes has an entirely different readership from that of the Russian *Playboy* clones, literary fiction and pornography are constituent parts of the unique discourse that falls under the rubric of post-Soviet Russian pornography: the depiction of sexualized bodies to explore a national idea.[7]

---

[7] The question of a "national idea" has been a vexing issue for both the government and the media since the Soviet collapse. According to a popular school of thought based on readings and misreadings of Nikolai Berdiaev's 1946 *The Russian Idea*, Russia has always been guided by some form of a dominant idea that both unites the nation and defines its mission. After the October Revolution, Bolshevism filled this role, but with Soviet ideology largely discredited, many in Russia now feel that the country needs a new idea or ideology to replace it. Though an ideological void might seem like a less pressing matter than unemployment or rampant crime, the need for a national idea figures prominently in the post-Soviet press and in opinion polls. In 1996, Boris Yeltsin even put together a government commission to develop a new national idea, although the commissions' findings were greeted lukewarmly (Smith 158–72).

Russian Pornography before Perestroika

Only recently has pornography become an even vaguely legitimate object of study for Russianists, who have largely replicated the culture's own reticence on the subject. But something paradoxical happens to Russian pornography when it falls into academics' far-from-sweaty hands: the more it is studied, the more it recedes from view. While there is no doubt that sexual and scatological material has existed in Russia for centuries, recent studies have tended to either interpret pornography so broadly that the term threatens to lose all meaning or to frame it so narrowly as to virtually define it out of existence. Marcus Levitt and Andrei Toporkov's 1999 collection *Eros and Pornography in Russian Culture*, which contained the fruits of the first international conference on the subject, finds pornography in medieval folk woodcuts, nineteenth-century incantations, eighteenth-century bawdy songs, turn-of-the-century philosophy, and recent avant-garde fiction. In its admirable impulse toward eclecticism, the collection sees any text that deals with sexuality or uses foul language as fair game. The very first contemporary scholarly study of pornography in Russia, a 1977 doctoral dissertation by William Hopkins, implicitly identifies one of the problems with discussing Russian pornography: so little of it appears to be designed for erotic appeal. Rather, the early modern texts he discusses fall into the purview of pornography because of their use of forbidden language: it is as much the words as the actions described that are obscene. Thus Hopkins eschews the term "pornography," instead referring to the "genital semantic function," a phrase that accurately reflects the defining characteristics of the genre but that has problems of its own (ix). "Genital semantic function" takes the anerotic character of early modern Russian pornography to its extreme: resting awkwardly between philology and urology, the phrase seems designed to immunize the reader against any possible arousal. The pornographic texts in question are authored largely by reputable men of letters (Pushkin included), and thus they are surrounded with a literary aura that makes any attack on them seem tantamount to philistinism. Tsarist-era censorship saw the struggle against pornography in moral and religious terms, conflating sexually explicit writings with blasphemy and godlessness (Goldschmidt 90–91). As in much of Europe, pornography was a subset of obscenity.

In the West, pornography as a category diverges from obscenity per se when it abandons literary and artistic pretensions and when blasphemy is no longer a relevant issue. In the United States, pornography benefits from First Amendment protections and arguments based on artistic freedom, but it has been a long time since the public failed to distinguish between highbrow fiction with strong sexual content and mass-market masturbation aids. In the visual arts it is another matter, but that is in part because prose is no longer the primary battleground for the souls of impressionable youth. In Russia, a separate, pornographic sphere was only beginning to grow in the first decades before the Russian Revolution (Engelstein 359–86). But the Soviet regime quickly drove pornography underground, although members of the elite *nomenklatura* did have access to erotic publications produced and acquired abroad (Lipnitskii 98). Thus in Soviet times, pornography was at best a theoretical concept, the sort of thing found only in the decadent West, or, in a throwback to the previous century, a charge leveled at writers who broke with accepted standards of decorum in terms of both content and lexicon. Either there was no pornography at all, or the lack of an approved place for pornography meant that any text with strong sexual content could be seen as pornographic.

With the onset of perestroika in the late eighties and the concomitant wholesale lifting of taboos, sexual and lexical license became an integral, if unintended, part of glasnost. The term "pornography" was usually applied to a set of related, but discrete, phenomena: images of naked women (and occasionally men); soft-core, and later hard-core, films on videotape and broadcast television; sex scenes of varying degrees of explicitness in novels, stories and newspapers; and the use of previously unprintable "obscene" language, or *mat* (forbidden words describing the human anatomy, sexual activity, and the rest of the physiological functions that Bakhtin so eloquently ascribes to the "lower bodily stratum"). Though conservative critics of the late eighties and early nineties often failed to distinguish between "literary" or "artistic" erotic representation and mass-market pornography, the phenomena that the word "pornography" was used to describe rather quickly sorted themselves out across the cultural spectrum. It was writers such as Iuz Aleshkovskii, Vladimir Sorokin, and Victor Erofeyev who first broke the taboos by using foul language and describing explicit sex in stories published in the highbrow journals, and a general softening of the linguistic etiquette eventually followed.[8] But fiction that had few or no artistic pretensions—in particular, the incredibly popular mystery and police novels—fiction that *was* oriented

[8] For a discussion of the function of explicit anatomical vocabulary in contemporary Russian fiction, see Goscilo, "Body Talk."

toward the mass reader, tended to avoid the extremes of Russian foul language, as did Russian mass-market pornography itself. When the contents of *Miss X* or *Andrei* are compared with those of their Western counterparts, the tameness of the language is striking.[9] Andrei Zorin notes that the avant-garde writers who broke linguistic taboos were motivated by an urge to be provocative and links this type of language with a kind of aggression ("Legalizatsiia" 139). Zorin's conclusion can be broadened: in Russian, the most extremely obscene words (the equivalents of "fuck," "cock," and "cunt," and all their endless Russian derivatives) belong to the performative category of sexualized aggression rather than sexuality per se.[10] Moreover, the sheer ingenuity of Russian *mat*, which exploits every opportunity availed by the flexibility of a highly inflected language (several Russian jokes suggest that mat comes close to being a full-fledged part of speech), made it appealing to avant-garde and postmodern writers interested in playing with linguistic potential. But outside the rarefied heights of elite prose and the lower depths of street speech and locker rooms, obscene language can seem out of place. Even pornography designed to appeal to Russian men (who are presumed to be the most comfortable with mat) avoided these words entirely, since they apparently fall outside the category of the erotic altogether. No one fucked in Russian porn; they had sex, they "made love" (*zanimat'sia liubov'iu*, a hideous calque that puts sex on an equal syntactical footing with homework and business), or, when, desire overwhelmed lexical restraint, they screwed (*trakhat'sia*).

Both the overindulgence in obscene vocabulary and the pornographers' prim celebrations of sex are understandable consequences of the sudden relaxation of social controls in the last years of the 1980s. After little more than a decade, it is easy to forget how polemical this seemingly random sexual frankness was. To an even greater extent than during the so-called sexual revolution of the 1960s in the West, sexual openness was an explicit sign of personal and political freedom. The only thing more naked than the women plastered on so many publications and advertisements was the ideology that put them there: a naive, largely masculine "liberation sexology" that identified sexual expression with democracy.

[9] Helena Goscilo notes the "slippage into euphemism and periphrasis" in hard-core pornographic publications, an approach to language she calls "canonical rhetoric within soft porn." Goscilo advances a number of convincing explanations for the alternation between coy evasion and clinical vocabulary in Russian pornography, including the need to educate unenlightened readers about anatomy and sexual function (*Dehexing Sex* 157).

[10] The discursive and philosophical implications of Russian obscene vocabulary are discussed in depth by Plutser-Sarno (18–40) and Rudnev (16–33).

Of course, one must be careful when making generalizations about such an amorphous set of publications as Russian pornography.[11] In this chapter, I focus largely on slick magazines, such as the Russian edition of *Playboy*, *Makhaon* (*Swallowtail*), and, most important, *Andrei*. The world of these magazines was, as *Makhaon* put it, a "man's world"; their concern with manhood was encoded in the very titles of *Playboy* and *Andrei* (a Russian name derived from the Greek word for "manly"). Certainly, the label "men's magazine" functioned largely as a linguistic convention, a code to the potential buyer that, if he was looking for sexually explicit material, he would not be disappointed (although the recent Russian edition of *Men's Health*, which steers clear of eroticism, is trying to change this perception). Yet I would argue that *Andrei*'s label ("a Russian magazine for men") was more than merely descriptive; it offered the journal as a bracing tonic to its allegedly weakened audience.

These publications stood in sharp contrast to the other most popular pornographic or erotic publications in Russia, though they shared some superficial similarities: in particular, I have in mind the previously mentioned Russian-language Latvian publication called *Eshche* ("More), and the various magazines and books that made up the empire of *Mister X*, *Miss X*, *Iskushchenie* (*Temptation*), and *Bul'var krutoi erotiki* (*The Boulevard of Hardcore Erotica*). Where the so-called men's magazines defined their role quite narrowly, the world of *Eshche* and *Mister Iks* was accepting and all-inclusive. The texts of the *Mister Iks* publications consisted largely of letters from readers, and the *Iks* anything-goes philosophy is perhaps best exemplified by the regular rubrics under which the letters were grouped: "The Sexual Lost and Found," "The Order of the Knights of Sex," "A Volcano of Virgin Boys," "The Zone of Unspent Love," and, most noteworthy, "The Island of Non-Standard Orientation" and "The Temple of Gay Love."[12]

All these magazines were oriented primarily toward men, and, for the most part, toward heterosexual men.[13] Their reader was assumed to be both Russian and male, and neither gender nor nationality (nor, for that matter, sexual orientation) was an object of extended reflection. The reader of *Mister Iks* was implicitly posited to be secure in both his masculinity and his Russianness; this is not to say that there was any particular standard of

[11] Since I have rarely had the opportunity to view a pornographic film in Russia, in the present study the term "pornography" will refer to print materials only. Unless otherwise specified, the materials to which I refer primarily target the heterosexual male market.

[12] These are letters from prisoners; the title ("The Zone of Unspent Love") alludes to the secondary meaning of the Russian word zona ("*zone*"): prison camp.

[13] I have not included gay porn in the present study. Gay porn was nowhere near as prevalent as straight porn in 1990s Russia; I was able to find only a few examples of it. See Beaudoin (622–38).

manliness or national pride required of the reader but rather that such issues did not play a significant role in the magazines' agenda. Indeed, one might argue that such publications might ultimately have been more reassuring to the male Russian reader than *Andrei*, since he could indulge himself without even contemplating his success or failure as a Russian or a man.

Pornopolitics: Sexing the Nation

In the early post-Soviet years, the proliferation of the naked female form in advertisements could certainly be seen as a function of the market; after all, nothing sells like sex. But at least initially, the market was not a sufficiently strong mechanism to explain the power of the nude. When small, short-lived publications like *Baltiia*, a Russian-language tabloid from the late 1980s championing the cause of independence for Estonia, Latvia, and Lithuania, put a photo of a spread-eagled naked woman on its back cover (rather than on the front), the editors were making a clear connection between the freedom of sexual exposure and freedom from foreign domination. In the post-Soviet years, similar images of supine female nudes could function as part of a discourse of national humiliation rather than pride, but *Baltiia*'s pinup was doubly provocative, a declaration of independence on the part of the men who displayed her. Not surprisingly, in most of the examples discussed here, the naked female form was a weapon of power in male hands; only the weapon's target would change over time.

The ties between sexual freedoms and political liberalization proved to be a marriage of convenience, and a rather short-lived one at that. By the time the first issue of the Russian edition of *Playboy* appeared in 1995, its rhetoric of sexual revolution seemed decidedly dated. The editors wanted to have it both ways: to show that *Playboy* was more than a Johnny-come-lately, that it had always had a connection to Russia, but also to argue that *Playboy*'s Russian edition would further the cause of sexual liberation through its very existence. *Playboy*, we were told, was always a presence in the Soviet Union, at least in the lives of the party elite: in an interview entitled "PLAYBOY in My Luggage," the personal translator to four Soviet leaders admits that he always brought copies of the magazine back with him from his foreign travels (Lipnitskii 97). Artem Troitskii, the editor of the Russian edition, discusses the connection between Russia and *Playboy* as it unfolded over decades, paying special attention to the representation of Russia on the magazine's pages. Troitskii begins his article by noting that Hugh Hefner began *Playboy* in 1953, the same year that Stalin died; elsewhere in the same issue, Vasily

Aksyonov states the connection more boldly: "The new age of the Twentieth Century proclaimed: 'The tyrant is dead, long live PLAYBOY!' " (Aksenov 56). Obliquely, *Playboy* took credit for the relaxation of Russian mores, constantly insisting that the *Playboy* ethic of sexual freedom was the natural ally in the struggle against totalitarianism. Even as *Playboy* offered its reader the best that Western sex has to offer (including nude pictures of Ursula Andress, Bo Derek, Cindy Crawford, and Kim Basinger), it asserted its Russian pedigree. The parade of nude Western actresses was finally interrupted by a picture of Nataliia Negoda, whom the magazine called the "symbol of the Soviet 'sexual revolution' " because Negoda posed for the American *Playboy* back in 1989 (33).

In reality, Russian pornography had already been staking its particular claims to sexual revolution, trying to strike a delicate balance between the need for free expression and the demands of "good taste." Even liberal publications such as *Ogonek*, which, before the late nineties, could normally be counted on to support any attempts at free expression, devoted a cover story in September 1995 to the dismal state of post-Soviet erotica, which had descended into vulgarity and violence (*Ogonek* 39 [September 1995]: 41). When the first Russian men's magazine, *Andrei*, appeared in 1991, the opening editorial argued for a "renaissance" of the long-suppressed Russian erotic tradition, which was so closely intertwined with "literature and art" and "high ideals:" "*Andrei* will fight against the psychology of 'slavish' sexuality—harsh, rude, hypocritical, blind." In other words, *Andrei* was arguing for an eroticism based on liberation, beauty, and morality, of which the intelligentsia could be proud: "The sexual revolution in our country is at a decisive stage. And *Andrei*'s mission is to stand against this 'revolutionary' vulgarity, which has started to appear on the newsstands as calendars, key chains, and postcards. If this elemental trend is not directed toward professionalism, toward beauty, under our conditions it can in the years to come become a monster the likes of which is undreamed of in the West" (4).

By the time the eighth issue appeared, in 1997, the magazine's publisher, Aleksei Veitsler, had taken a more pessimistic view of the sexual revolution:

> Our magazine began as a political action. It was the sexual revolution. The whole intelligentsia was with us—-Aksyonov, Nagibin, Voinovich. The best journalists and artists. But the sexual revolution ended; it was short and stormy, like the beauty of Russian women. Then came the fall. Then came the winter, with its orthodox tendencies, medieval hysteria. Some sort of fundamentalism. Not only here, but throughout the world. And now there's another struggle ahead. (Editorial 39)

The change in the ideological climate becomes clear when an interviewer asks him to describe his potential allies in this struggle: "All honest people. The miners, the army, the militia, and Cuba are with us. All the people who think progressively, but not those screw-ups who could create communism like they were supposed to, and who are now ruining capitalism" (Drobyshev 39).

Without a doubt, something had changed in the politics and ideology of post-Soviet porn. Even *Andrei*, the most liberal of the men's magazines, had adopted a rhetoric of Russian boosterism that, while always present from the beginning, became impossible to ignore. Certainly, the overall disenchantment with the West in general and the United States in particular that followed the early days of post-Soviet Russia explains a great deal. But pornography proved to be a particularly sensitive barometer of the country's flagging enthusiasm for liberalism and growing infatuation with the discourse of nationalism, primarily because the question of national pride and humiliation in Russia was so thoroughly gendered. Without a doubt, even a cursory glance at Russian porn confirms the almost ritualistic objectification and subordination of women, but when the men who produced these words and images reflected on their work, it was the Russian male whom they presented as weak and embattled. In the textual and visual two-dimensional world of the Russian pornographic magazine, Russian men saw themselves as fighting back against national and sexual humiliation.

Magazines such as *Makhaon* and especially *Andrei* represented themselves as the veritable rear guard of Russian manhood. From its very inception, *Andrei* staked out a specific territory on the map of Russian manhood. In its first issue in 1991, the editors write: "The first Russian journal for men is essential today, for it is precisely men who need liberation from stressful aggression and lack of satisfaction more than anything. Their psychological freedom is a prerequisite for the emancipation of society from the crushing complexes of a distorted era" (3).

A similar claim was made by editor L. Konovalov in his opening editorial to the first 1997 issue of *Makhaon*. In part of his ongoing battle against the Russian government's attempts to limit the distribution of pornography, he rejected the "erotic" label for his magazine: "the arts and current-affairs magazine *Makhaon* is not an erotic publication." Instead, he writes, "the path of *Makhaon* lies in the affirmation of a sense of male self-worth (Konovalov, 1). Though the same essay also rejects sexual violence and sadism, some of the more vivid attempts at "affirming male self-worth" in *Makhaon* consisted of articles and photomontages about masochistic women receiving the punishment they crave at the hands (indeed, at the feet) of potbellied, middle-aged men. *Makhaon*'s path to masculine pride consisted of a combination of female sexual submissiveness and extended rants on the evils of Russian "pseudodemocracy." Perhaps nowhere was this strategy better exemplified than by a full-page, color cartoon of a leather-clad Anatoly Chubais, the former government minister in charge of privatization, whipping a blind-folded blonde whose tattoo of a two-headed eagle and white, blue, and red sash suggest that she symbolizes Russia; with gritted teeth, handcuffed wrists, and pierced nipples, this woman turns her rear to the viewer as hundred-dollar bills fall from her vagina into a box marked "Xerox," apparently in response to Chubais's not-so-tender mercies (*Makhaon* 8 (1997): 4).[14]

Though *Makhaon* saw its greatest enemies among the leaders of Russia, it clearly had no love for the West. One article in the fourth issue (1995) blames America for the Chernobyl disaster, while Aleksandr Braterskii's "The Last Virgin in the USSR" describes the collapse of the Soviet Union in terms of seduction and rape, comparing the iron curtain to a hymen. "The people who deflowered the USSR wanted proof of her innocence—they wanted BLOOD" (4). In its disdain for both Russian democrats and Western culture, *Makhaon* was nothing if not consistent. *Andrei*'s attitude to the West was far more complicated, as the editors found themselves embracing certain Western values. The Russian man posited by *Andrei* lamented the competition with Western men, while *Andrei* itself was haunted both by Russia's competition with American pop culture and by the magazine's own attempts to maintain its market share against the threat of men's magazines imported from the United States, particularly the Russian-language edition of *Playboy*, whose contents differed from the American version only slightly. When *Andrei* called itself a Russian magazine for men, the accent was on both "for men" and "Russian," in what seemed to be a deliberate slap in the face of the foreign-derived *Playboy*.

But from its first appearance in Russia in 1995, *Playboy* refused to cede any Russian territory to its domestic competitors. Indeed, the inaugural summer 1995 issue was an overt attempt to bring together two seemingly disparate cultural conventions: *Playboy*'s emphasis on the pleasures of the "finer things" is combined with the most recognizable of Russian cultural icons. The Russian *Playboy* announces its hybrid nature on the cover with a picture that seems to be modeled on an early Soviet coin, perhaps from the 1920s; the sheaves of wheat representing agriculture and the smoke-belching factory on opposite sides of the coin are a classic allegorical representation of the alliance between workers and peasants, while the sun shining from the

---

[14] This cartoon was a satirical response to a recent scandal involving Chubais's aides and large amounts of cash.

bottom of the coin and the open book on the top would both seem to represent the enlightenment brought by the revolution. But the center of the coin, where one might expect to see Lenin's familiar profile, is occupied by that of the bow-tied Playboy bunny. Elsewhere in the issue we find a cartoon showing happy rabbit-eared men and boys marching in Red Square with placards displaying the bunny image.

Yet as the magazine established itself in the Russian market, the editors of *Playboy* relaxed their concern with their Russian pedigree, adding only a thin veneer of Russian content to a largely Western-style publication. By contrast, *Andrei* had intensified its preoccupation with "Russianness," treating Russian and Soviet history as a treasure trove of erotic nationalism. A six-page feature in the sixth issue shows supposedly American porn models surrounded by the props of the Russian/Soviet space program; in this fashion, the magazine compensated for importing exotic American beauties by stressing the accomplishments of one of the few areas of Russian industry that could still be the source of unequivocal pride.[15] Indeed, the English-speaking models are quoted as pronouncing only one Russian word throughout the shoot: "Jessica, Kelly, and Christie responded to the idea of a spaceflight enthusiastically. 'Ga-ga-rin!' they laughed, stretching the costumes of Soviet superheroes onto their American breasts" (Kondakov 10). And in a section suggested by the novelist Vasily Aksyonov but clearly inspired by *Playboy*'s "Girls of the Big Ten," the cover section of the seventh issue features "The Girls of MGU," in which the magazine photographs one naked woman from each of Moscow University's divisions.

Even before *Playboy* appeared, *Andrei* had already begun to stress the Russianness of both its models and their settings. In the introduction to the fifth (1994) issue, the editors lament that Russia has become a lawless, third-world country that is unable to withstand the onslaught of cheap foreign imports such as Snickers and Pepsi-Cola:" Upset? So are we. And that's why we work without days off, and that's why you have before you a new issue of the first Russian magazine for men, one of the few domestic products that isn't "for export" and which is not an embarrassment" ("Intermediia," *Andrei* 5:2). In an editorial in the seventh issue, the writers claim that, unlike the competition, their magazine is respectful of Russian women:

> *Andrei* puts our woman on a pedestal of admiration; unlike invader magazines, of which there are more and more in the kiosks, it does not present her

---

[15] In the following issue an ad by Upjohn makes the rather obvious connection between the launch of a phallic rocket and male sexual response: an injectible medicine for impotence is advertised with a picture of a syringelike rocket blasting off into space.

in an unflattering and biased fashion next to foreign women in order that the
"house" model be MORE sexual and feminine. The invaders' task is simple:
to prove that everything Western is better, more expensive, stronger—and
also to turn our women into a cheap export that is ready for anything. ("*Intermediia*," *Andrei* 7:2)

Not only does the magazine that once identified itself with the allegedly
Western values of freedom and democracy now take on an overtly xenophobic tone, but its vocabulary deliberately evokes the rhetoric of war:
Western magazines, like Western armies, are "invaders" on a hostile mission of conquest.

Though the pictures, stories, and ads in *Andrei* portrayed a free-spending,
luxurious lifestyle available only to the wealthiest of "New Russians," the
magazine's implicit nationalism made itself known throughout. If the letters to the editor are to be believed, the readership responded to *Andrei*'s
pro-Russian boosterism. In the tradition of Soviet-era collective letters, a
group of officers from the Baltic Fleet in Tallinn wrote to *Andrei* in the sixth
(1995) issue, thanking the magazine for mentioning the three hundredth
anniversary of the Russian fleet: "You really are our magazine. Even our national pride, to some extent. Although we've been places and seen many
different men's magazines, *Andrei* is nicer and closer to the heart of our Soviet man" ("Natsional'naia gordost'" 4). The officers' letter is so full of patriotic fervor that it would be easy to forget that they are writing about a
pornographic magazine rather than, say, the launching of a space shuttle.
The anachronistic reference to "our Soviet man" by a group of Russian military personnel based in newly independent Estonia only heightens the
identification of *Andrei* with a nostalgia for Russian greatness.

The officers' nationalistic enthusiasm for an erotic magazine seems excessive only when removed from its context; the issue that prompted their
letter (number 5, 1994) featured a special photospread dedicated to the
three hundredth anniversary of the Russian navy. "The Battleship Marina"
consists of pictures of a female model wearing only a sailor's cap (with the
word "Andrei" on it) as she writhes against the heavy artillery of a gunboat.
Aleksei Veitsler's photos and text deliberately invoke Eisenstein's *Battleship
Potemkin*; only here the film's agitprop message and homoerotic aesthetics
are replaced by the none-too-subtle conventions of the heterosexual pinup:
where Eisenstein's camera lingers on the bodies of Russian sailors, Veitsler's
camera interposes a naked woman between the handsome, seminude men.
Alluding to the incident that sparks the uprising in Eisenstein's film, Veitsler describes the tense scene on a ship in 1905, when the shipmen of the

Potemkin are ready to kill each other over rotten meat: "But here we'd be better off with Professor Freud instead of the student Ulianov [Lenin]." If only, Veitsler writes, the model Marina Pavlova had been on that ship, she would have shouted, "Who wants to try some of my meat?!" ("Bronenosets" 6). Veitsler's fantasy montage climaxes in an imitation of early Soviet propaganda, with a picture of a fully clothed Pavlova, on the shoulders of three of the sailors, raising the Russian flag rather than the banner of revolution. The text makes the utopianism of this scene explicit:

> And everything turned topsy-turvy, as in a fairy tale.
> And the screen was lit in color.
> And it's as if a wave washed off the red from the flag over the ship.
> And there was no decades-long gale.
> And the Crimea is ours.
> And the fleet is Russian.
> Only the riveted battleship has a new name. ("Bronenosets" 15)

Such declarations could not have come at a more politically sensitive time. The much-trumpeted anniversary of the Russian navy took place against the backdrop of heightened tensions between Russia and Ukraine over the status of the Black Sea Fleet and potential Russian claims to the Crimean peninsula. If the 1994 *Andrei* was in part a special issue for Russian sailors, it neatly combined sexual and political fantasy, one where the all-male world of the battleship is mediated by the willing body of a desirable woman, and the coveted Crimea need not be shared with anyone.

Magazines like *Andrei,* whose basic economic task was to sell sexual images of Russian women to Russian men, ultimately returned to some of the fundamental questions of sexual discourse in post-Soviet Russia: how are sex and the marketplace to be reconciled? If sexual metaphors characterized the "free exchange of goods and ideas" between Russian and the West (the source of both the marketplace in general and the very genres of pornography and soft-core titillation such as the monthly newspaper *SPID-Info*), how could the anxieties provoked by the commercialization of sex (the incursions on privacy, the threat of foreign wealth and potency) be allayed? *Andrei* pointed the way by thematizing the anxieties themselves, continually revisiting them in a light-hearted manner. The seventh issue of *Andrei* includes a feature that incorporates exotic locales while turning the threat of the "export" of Russian women into the stuff of comedy: a blonde model is photographed in various locales (and various stages of undress) in Cairo and the Egyptian desert, under the heading "One hundred camels for a Russian girl." Capitalist exchange is replaced by Eastern barter, and the Russians girl's price, for once, is anything but practical ("We sent the camels on their way to a friend in Tashkent. Will they get there?") (Veitsler, "Sto verbliudov" 50). The photo spread depends on a sense of mutual exoticism, as well as a broad parody of cross-cultural kitsch; in the corner of a full-page photo of the naked Russian woman on a camel is a fully clothed Arab woman on a tractor. The contrast between the "backwards" camel and the "progressive" tractor is a cliché of Soviet socialist realist tales of the struggle to civilize the nomads of Central Asia, but where the USSR brought communism, *Andrei* pretends to bring the example of sexual liberation. The caption reads: "The magazine for men was welcomed by a few emancipated women of the East. Out of solidarity with our struggle for the beauty of the body, one of them even climbed up onto a tractor—the symbol of progress" (Veitsler, "Sto verbliudov" 49). The Eastern locale allows Russia to take on a missionary role familiar from the days of communist internationalism, at the same time displacing cross-cultural anxieties by turning Russia into the source of sexual export. Here Russia gets to be the West, raising the sexual question in a mysterious, repressed East.

The implicit ideological agenda of *Andrei* was to compensate for the trauma of the nation's fall from the status of a world power, especially to the extent that this humiliation might be felt by the individual Russian man. The demons of the recent past were to be exorcised through sex. Hence a two-page spread in the seventh issue features seminude women in SS costumes against the backdrop of the Chernobyl nuclear power plant, thus reinterpreting a national tragedy in terms of sadomasochistic games. The cover feature for the third issue (1992) is a woman holding an automatic assault weapon and a grenade as she poses clad in nothing but an army helmet and dog tags; this section, entitled "Conversion," addresses the shock and dislocation entailed by the process of refitting the country's huge military-industrial complex for a new market economy. Veitsler, the section's author, supplies the reader with photographs of the naked and busty Nataliia Sergeeva, purported to be an officer in the Russian army. A life in the army has not prevented her from retaining the "traits of a real woman." Unequaled with both the rifle and the frying pan, Nataliia realizes that it is time for her to leave the army. Her decision combines the personal and the political in that she recognizes the exigencies of a post-cold-war world while heeding the sound of her biological clock ("I want to have a family") (Veitsler, "Konversiia" 82). In the final photo, Nataliia stands on the beach with her back turned to the camera. The text reads: "Sergeant of the Guard Natasha emerges from the boiling iron of war like Aphrodite

from the foam. . . . Transfigured and waiting for happiness. Keep her photograph, as they keep souvenirs made from the shells of intercontinental
missiles. As a memento of conversion" (89) Here conversion becomes
something beautiful and divine, involving both transfiguration and the
birth of new life. At the same time, the attributes of military might (guns,
camouflage fatigues, and army boots) are transformed into sexual paraphernalia. In the new world, the military yields to the pornographic.

A similar process takes place in a truly bizarre section of the seventh
issue, published under the title "Chechnya: What the Soldiers Aren't Saying." Here, pictures of Russian soldiers fighting, eating, and sleeping in
Chechnya are framed by the erotic images of their fantasies, such as Eastern
women in leather fetish garb, wielding whips. A pimply faced Russian soldier stares vacantly at his food, while this photograph is surrounded by
images of naked women caressing phallic-shaped breads. The photos are
accompanied by a prose poem about the unexpressed desires of the Russian
soldier; in the final two pages, the men are shown firing weapons while the
poem describes their eventual return to their "next-door girls with their
firm behinds, whom they will have this way and that way, without extraneous words, upon their return; then [these girls] will bear them children
(Anin et al. 92). The naked woman whose picture accompanies this text
is now far less threatening than the previous models; her expression and
demeanor really do suggest the girl next door, while the gun she holds is
merely a plastic toy. The Russian soldier is thus shown to be dreaming of
returning to a world where war is the stuff of fantasy, while women are the
reality, even as the magazine's reader has both war and sex offered up to
him as erotic stimulant.

Andrei's world of male power and Russian pride thus managed to transfigure the site of the country's greatest post-Soviet humiliation into a
source of ultimately reassuring erotic fantasy: in what might be considered
a postmodern reinterpretation of the biblical injunction regarding swords
and plowshares, the phallic rifle wielded by the young Russian soldier with
such uncertainty is transformed into a long, pink, plastic sex toy caressed
by a nubile Russian beauty. Though the Chechen is perceived as an internal
enemy, the implicit connection made by *Andrei* between men at war and
men's erotic magazines suggests the specific function that such journals
hope to perform in the post-Soviet imaginary: to rally the flagging spirits of
Russian men, surrounded by hostile forces on all sides.

By addressing Russia's post-superpower status within a framework
whose sexual and gendered parameters are so nakedly obvious, pornography insists on a set of metaphors for the nation's fate and future that not

only recapitulate patriarchal values but implicitly exclude any competing subject positions. In this context, Russia can only be a woman, and the drama of her humiliation and potential redemption oscillates between jingoism and sadomasochism. The motherland's weakness is both arousing and embarrassing. Russia as woman is also Russia as object, while the subject who frets over her in nervous excitement is posited as male, if not entirely comfortable in his masculinity. Most of the pornographic scenes examined in this chapter figure the naked woman in situations emphasizing both the beauty of Russia and the primacy of the market, reveling in the commodification of the female form while simultaneously questioning the marketization of the values and virtues for which this form serves as an allegory. Post-Soviet pornography offers up erotic images of Russian women under the guise of sexual liberation and national rebirth, striving to stake a claim for a national purity embodied in the female form even as the boundless proliferation of pornographic imagery suggests a willingness to transform the female body and Russia's virtue into a commodity that can be bought and sold not just locally but globally.

Screwing with Russian Culture

The initial flirtation between pornography and liberalism, replaced by a much stronger union between pornography and nationalism, resulted in ever-stranger bedfellows, with the country's most prominent "erotic" publications staking out a paradoxical position in the post-Soviet culture wars: the rhetoric, imagery, and ideology were strongly reminiscent of the cultural conservatives who so routinely condemned them. Just as Russian pornography eschewed the vulgarity of mat in favor of high-flown language and appeals to the sublime, it assumed the mantle of guardian of the Russian cultural heritage. Though its pervasive bricolage and mixing of genres made contemporary Russian pornography a postmodern phenomenon, its ideology was postmodernism's polar opposite. The contrast between the ethos of postmodernism and the long-standing Russian cult of culture could not have been more pronounced, and practitioners of postmodernism were often portrayed by their ideological opponents as amoral cynics who reveled in the decline of everything that made Russia great. Whereas Russian pornography joined the cultural conservatives in continuing to put the national cultural heritage on a pedestal, the postmodernists continually undercut any reverential attitude toward art, literature, or the

Russian national idea. Thus in Russia, the term "postmodernist" was used as often to describe a particular artist's or writer's attitude toward culture as to characterize his or her artistic technique.

This cultural divide is crucial to any understanding of the highly selective campaigns against pornography in the post-Gorbachev era. After Yeltsin's government used military force to remove the opposition from the country's legislature in October 1993, the press ministry closed down several newspapers that allegedly advocated "fascism" but admitted that one of the publications targeted was guilty of something entirely different:

> As concerns the newspaper *Eshche*, which was in no way involved in the violence in early October, it was openly seeking to deprive its readers of any moral footing. Activity of this kind and calls for the destruction of any morals and morality are deemed to be no less dangerous for society than the calls for restoring the Communist Party of the Soviet Union.
>
> Aggressive amorality with its degrading influence is no less a danger to society than fascism, and we intend to carry on a consistent and tough struggle against it. (Itar-Tass, October 14, 1993, qtd. in Goldschmidt 145.)

The story of *Eshche* is particularly instructive, for it illustrates the way in which post-Soviet Russia has treated pornography as both a political and a cultural threat. The publisher of *Eshche*, Aleksei Kostin, was arrested on October 6, 1993, on pornography charges, only to be released three days later. The prosecutor then proceeded to accumulate further evidence against Kostin and the paper, arresting the publisher once again on February 4, 1994. The newspaper was subjected to several assessments by "experts," who determined that *Eshche* was indeed pornographic (as opposed to "erotic"). The case foundered in legal limbo for over a year, never resulting in prosecution, and the publisher remained in prison the whole time, in violation of Russian procedural law. The newspaper itself emerged none the worse for wear, garnering the support of many outspoken liberals and even upgrading its production values to include color photos as well as black and white.

From the beginning, *Eshche* was an odd choice for pornography charges, since dozens of graphic, hard-core publications were already circulating throughout the Russian Federation without resistance. On the other hand, the prosecutors clearly recognized that *Eshche* was different from most of its competition, and it was this difference that rendered the newspaper so odious. Not only was nearly every possible type of sexual encounter

Figure 3: Logo of *Eshche*, an erotic newspaper that ran afoul of Russian censors in the 1990s.

described in its articles and letters, but anxieties of any kind played little or no role. If the mainstream men's magazines peddled an amalgam of eroticism and nationalism, *Eshche* countered with a parodic, nostalgic transnationalism, using nationalist discourse and traditional calls for international "brotherhood" as grist for its satiric mill. The fact that the magazine was published in newly independent Latvia, a country with a large and restive ethnic Russian population, heightened the irony. Borders were crossed with impunity, and the post-Soviet sexual adventurer was placed on equal footing with his Western counterparts. *Eshche* hardly fits in with the leaden seriousness of the other magazines and newspapers targeted immediately after the 1993 October events—such as the national chauvinist mouthpiece *Den'* (*The Day*), which was quickly reborn with a bit of temporal sleight-of-hand as *Zavtra* (*Tomorrow*)—but its not-yet-fashionable nostalgia for Soviet kitsch did lend it some superficial resemblance to the publications by the loose "Red-Brown" coalition of fascists and Stalinists.

The evaluations made by the experts point to a different reason for the official hostility to *Eshche*: it had a distinct "cleverness and subtleness" that they found troublesome (Goldschmidt 179). As the committee of experts noted repeatedly, *Eshche* included a surprisingly wide range of materials, "artistic works with explicit bedroom scenes," letters from readers, "pornographic" photographs ("when the camera records the minute details of the sexual act or the sexual organs prepared for the sexual act"), and explicit advertisements for sex toys. The experts were concerned about the "consistency" of the publication's "cultural level." As one of the experts noted, popular newspapers like *Mister Iks* were "simple" pornographic works, never attempting to rise from a "low" cultural level, while *Eshche* used "pornographic" pictures to illustrate artistic texts (179–82). Goldschmidt is quick to point out the absurdity of such an evaluation: "*Playboy* would be prosecutable because it could be argued that the text was a trick to get people to open up the centerfold, but a book describing itself openly as a guidebook to child molestation would not be actionable because it did not attempt to hide its intentions" (179). I would argue, however, that the absurdity of the experts' evaluation is quite revealing and is in fact perfectly in tune with the anxieties that certain forms of pornography provoked in Russia in the 1990s. *Eshche* was a threat precisely because it violated the established boundaries between high and low and therefore was potentially as disruptive to the reigning cultural discourse as the overtly fascist *Den'*, if for different reasons. The men's magazines also mixed genres and brought together high and low, but they compensated for their bricolage by ensuring that even their centerfolds were put in the service of patriotism and traditional cultural values. *Eshche* lured the reader with explicit sexual photographs, only to undermine his value system with its unfailing irreverence.

In the 1990s, sexually explicit materials that were easily identifiable as pornography or erotica tended to reinforce the cultural hierarchy, attempting to instill a sense of national pride as well as sexual arousal. Their artistic pretensions may have been an attempt to raise these publications from the gutter, but in the final analysis, these men's magazines knew their place: their appeal to cultural traditions did not contaminate high culture because these publications were so clearly low. A cultural conservative who consumed Russian pornography might be lowering himself, but if he did open up the magazine, he saw his own worldview largely confirmed. Indeed, the fetishization of the classics in Russian glossy men's magazines created the illusion that the hegemony of high culture remained intact in the post-Soviet era: pornography may have been a social evil, but at least the pornographers were still quoting Pushkin.

By 2002, when Moving Together began its crusade for Russian literary purity, Sorokin had been merrily flouting cultural strictures for two decades, with stories of sadomasochism and the entire bouquet of "philias," from necro- to pedo-, more often than not involving figures that were supposed to command respect (party members, Komsomol leaders, government officials). As if that were not enough, Sorokin routinely compared literature to a "narcotic," something habit-forming and presumably harmful rather than uplifting and redemptive. When *Blue Lard* appeared in 1999, it attracted a fair amount of attention and mixed reviews, but nothing in the novel could have come as a surprise to anyone familiar with his work. It was, however, his first full-length novel in several years, which meant that it was initially released to the mass market, rather than printed in a journal, published in an obscure collection, or left to languish in samizdat.

With the benefit of hindsight, the publication of *Blue Lard* now looks like the last gasp of the Yeltsin era, when the outcry against such a novel would have come largely from marginalized extremists. Since then, some of these extremists are no longer marginalized: Alexander Prokhanov, editor of the notoriously racist and anti-Semitic newspaper *Zavtra*, is now an award-winning novelist with at least some veneer of respectability, while Putin has given cultural conservatives a figure to rally around *within* the government, rather than outside it. Putin himself has remained largely above the fray, but his firm, quasi-authoritarian attitude has made him an attractive figure for what the West would call the radical right.[16] When seen as a text for the nascent Putin era (a reading that would be perversely anachronistic were it not for the recent anti-Sorokin campaign), *Blue Lard* does manage to seem at least slightly transgressive. Putin's harsher rhetoric, KGB past, and overall firm demeanor have clearly been a balm to those in Russia longing for the firm hand of a true leader, but the firmest hand in *Blue Lard* is busy tickling the leader's testicles rather than bringing order to the country. As the Russian-American humorist Gary Shteyngart points out, perhaps the biggest offense to nostalgic nationalists is that Stalin is a Bottom rather than a Top (46).

Sorokin's approach to culture and politics is antithetical to the unrelenting earnestness of Moving Together, a group that looks back wistfully to the days when the Communist Youth League provided the nation's young people with both a set of clear and unwavering values and an array of wholesome activities to occupy their time. By contrast, Sorokin is not satisfied with merely tipping over the culture's sacred cows; he has to violate their every orifice. For Moving Together, it is a matter of saving the country's youth from a

[16] Prokhanov also shares a publisher with Sorokin: both his novel *Gospodin Geksogen* (*Mister Hexogen*) and *Blue Lard* were printed by Ad Marginem. Among the many conspiracy theories advanced to explain the Sorokin affair (from a cheap publicity ploy to sell more books to a plot by Putin's enemies to make him look bad) is the hypothesis that the Kremlin is using Moving Together's anti-Sorokin campaign as a way to punish Ad Marginem for publishing *Mister Hexogen*, which asserted that the 1999 Moscow apartment bombings were all part of a plot to bring Putin to power (Zolotonosov 26).

dangerous infection. As their leader, Vasilii Iakimenko, puts it: "Nine out of 15 words are profanities. In Russia, literature has always given people answers they can't find in everyday life. When a young person is just discovering literature and reads Sorokin's vulgarity, it's like showing them a porno film. After Sorokin, they'll think Chekhov is boring and uninteresting" (Sheets and Ydstie). Iakimenko is ascribing to all Russian literature a pedagogical role that Sorokin explicitly rejects; perhaps it is no accident that so many of the teachers in Sorokin's works turn pedagogy into pederasty—both moralists and pedophiles make a fetish of children. Thus *Blue Lard* is actually more harmful to children than a hard-core sex film, since, presumably, young people are not likely to see *The Cherry Orchard* and *Debbie Does Dallas* as equivalent works of culture consumption. The urge to protect children from contamination was expressed even more forcefully by the proverbial man on the street at an anti-Sorokin rally in June 2002: "We would like Sorokin's books in [the] future to be recognized as containing pornography and sold only in plastic covers, like pornographic magazines, in special establishments. We would like the culture minister finally to take some kind of measures against writers like this. Finally, we do not want the kind of society that tolerates this kind of thing" ("Pro-Putin Youth Group"). What he wants, of course, is entirely utopian, since it presumes that contemporary Russia really does enforce rules on pornography's distribution and keeps sexually explicit materials wrapped safely in plastic.

Indeed, even most of Sorokin's defenders were careful to dissociate themselves from his work, repeating the mantra that they disliked *Blue Lard* but defended the author's right to publish. Oleg Mironov, Russia's human rights ombudsman, spoke out against Sorokin's prosecution but was critical of foul language and pornography in the arts: "Writers should speak of the reasonable and the eternal instead of cursing and describing improper scenes" (Gutterman). In other words, they should behave more like the publishers of *Andrei*, *Makhaon*, and even *Playboy*, whose conservative cultural program and persistent nationalism are far more palatable than the disruptive pornographic imagination of Vladimir Sorokin or the irreverence and irony of *Eshche*. Post-Soviet Russia is remarkably comfortable with the conflation of the sexual and the national, with the unspoken notion that Russia's current dilemma and ultimate fate can be conceptualized in sexual terms but only when both sexuality and the "Russian idea" are taken seriously, when each remains on its pedestal. When seen in this light, Russian pornography displays a distinct resemblance to political propaganda, a phenomenon the country has had far more time to assimilate: the consumer must be provoked to the proper response (sexual arousal and ideological agitation, respectively). The dominant, nationalist pornography in contemporary Russia attempts to combine these two goals, to produce the very phenomenon that the post-modern wing would so easily ridicule: excitement that is both sexual and ideological, a proud and patriotic erection.

Chapter Three

PIMPING THE MOTHERLAND

Russia Bought and Sold

In the old days, the boys' ideal was the positive hero: the secret agent, the tank driver, just a good guy, and now they all imitate bandits. And the girls walk the streets. We're becoming cheap labor for "Pepsi-Cola" factories, living merchandise, mail-order brides. The great and mysterious bear has been transformed into a silly Winnie the Pooh with a "Made in China" label.

—Liudmila Petukhova in "Nostalgiia po komsomolke," 117.

As Western ships approached a port in Sevastopol, Ukraine, in late April of 1997, a group of prostitutes lined up to greet them. Given the long-standing connection between shore leave and sex for hire, this was hardly unusual in and of itself, but these women planned a welcome with pickets rather than open arms. The sailors were part of the North Atlantic Treaty Organization's Operation Sea Breeze, a set of practice maneuvers in the Black Sea. NATO could not have picked a worse time or a more troubled spot: the Russian government was outraged over plans for the organization's imminent expansion to include former Warsaw Pact countries, while the Crimea (the largely Russian-speaking region including Sevastopol that was given to Ukraine by Soviet leader Nikita Khrushchev as a "gift" in 1954) had been the focus of a simmering territorial dispute with Ukraine since the collapse of the USSR. On Russia Day, which commemorates the incorporation of the Crimea into the Russian Empire by Catherine the Great, the local Russian-language newspaper, *Krymskoe vremia* (*The Crimean Times*), reported that a group of prostitutes had declared a boycott on NATO sailors: "Let them obtain services from the wives of the officers who let NATO ships into the Black Sea," one of the prostitutes-turned-activists was quoted as saying. "We for our part will shower the uninvited guests with tomatoes and rotten eggs" (Lodge). Her words are almost too good to be true, and one suspects that the reporter might well have fabricated them to spice up his story.[1] Whether real or fabricated, they exemplify the sexualization of boundaries that so often characterizes prostitution as a metaphor for international relations: the prostitute refuses access to NATO sailors, just as the country should have refused them access to its precious and vulnerable warm-water port. Here we have the symbolic counterattack against everything represented by the Jeff Stryker sex toy in chapter 1: the country's metaphorical legs are closed to the invader's foreign phallus. Now the prostitute has become the partisan: *No pasaran!*

In the 1990s, the Russian prostitute was routinely deployed in the symbolic battle for Russia's soul. The collapse of the Russian state, the decline of patriotism, and the absence of a workable national idea shared center stage in the Russian media and culture industry with tales and images of sexually uninhibited young women offering their bodies and their services to paying clients. Just as the media and the culture industry themselves were often pilloried for the boom in prostitution that began in the last years of perestroika, on the assumption that they encouraged young girls and women throughout the country to aspire to imitate the high-priced Russian prostitutes they saw on the silver screen, so were perestroika and the subsequent attempts at economic "shock therapy" blamed for turning the entire country into a nexus of buying and selling, where everything of value was offered cynically to the highest bidder.

At issue here is prostitution as metaphor rather than social phenomenon. Certainly, prostitution and trafficking are very real and serious problems in Russia today. One can scarcely ignore the physical and psychological

---

[1] Indeed, the term "uninvited guests" evokes an ethnic group that is never mentioned in the article but whose absence looms large over any consideration of Crimea's status: the Tatars. As a result of the Mongol invasion and subsequent "Tatar Yoke," the Tatars serve as Russia's archetypal foreign invader and have entered the everyday linguistic consciousness with the extremely common saying *Nezvannyi gost'—khuzhe Tatarina"* ("An uninvited guest is worse than a Tatar"). The Tatars of Crimea were deported to Uzbekistan during World War II and only had their right to return to their land approved definitively in 1988. Thus, the proximity of NATO warships to Crimea could hardly have been more resonant: a Western alliance was seen to be demonstrating its strength off the coast of a region claimed by both Russian and Ukraine, home to a displaced people who are culturally identified with raping and pillaging "Holy Rus'," the birthplace of both nations. See Uehling (37–46).

humiliation suffered by women in the former Soviet Union who have joined the swelling ranks of prostitutes either out of dire economic need or from the mistaken assumption that selling their bodies will give them the "good life." Newspapers are filled with reports of naive young women in the former Soviet Union lured abroad with promises of high-paying jobs, only to find themselves sold into sexual slavery in brothels throughout Europe and the Middle East. But the real-life trials and tribulations of actual prostitutes are beyond the scope of this chapter, whose subject matter is defined in terms of representation and consumption, not daily life or individual psychology. At issue is the way in which Russia, Russian culture, and Russianness (*russkost'*) were constructed in the country's mass media and culture industry for a domestic audience. In Russia, millions of viewers and readers had a strong sense of the chaos into which their country was falling, not only because of their day-to-day experiences but also because the media and culture industry created specific narratives for constructing and understanding that chaos, narratives calculated to appeal to their audience. The plight of actual post-Soviet prostitutes is horrific, but this is not their story.

Indeed, it is not a woman's story at all.[2] More often than not, the network of artistry and ideology that created the metaphorical post-Soviet prostitute functioned like the prostitute herself: its primary target was men. A brief overview of the prostitute's function in Russia's cultural mythology before perestroika will show that the prostitute has rarely been a subject in her own right. Usually, she is a foil for the male hero or an important step in his moral or psychological development. The post-Soviet prostitute was no exception. Burdened with a symbolism that might seem wildly disproportionate to her status, she became a sign of Russian national humiliation— of the desperation of a country forced to sell off its natural and spiritual resources to unscrupulous clients from other lands. Sometimes the scenario was more optimistic, the prostitute representing the nation's enduring pride and moral superiority in the face of hostile enemies. Yet despite this pervasive feminization of the country on the symbolic level, and despite the fact that male prostitution was rarely raised as an issue, the Russian prostitute symbolized national humiliation as male, rather than female,

[2] Nor is it the story of male prostitutes; when prostitutes are deployed as metaphors or symbols, they are almost exclusively female. Isaac Babel's "Moi pervyi gonorar" ("My First Fee," 1922–28) is a rare exception: in this story, an aspiring young writer tells a prostitute that he used to be a "boy for the Armenians," which prompts the young woman to call him "sister" and pay him for his services (Babel 2: 253). For information about male prostitution as a social phenomenon in Russia before and after the revolution, see Healey (233–65).

experience.[3] She represented the anxieties of a post-Soviet masculinity in crisis, where the loss of empire, the onslaught of the market, and competition with a triumphant West were construed as a kind of male sexual humiliation. Even though Russia was embodied by a female prostitute, even though her victimization unfolded within a context of specifically heterosexual violence and commerce, and even though her story fit classical patterns for the heroines of melodrama, in terms of the Russian cultural imaginary, her darkest secret was that, symbolically if not sartorially, she was a cross-dresser. This does not render her story a kind of *Crying Game a la russe*. Quite the contrary: whereas Jaye Davidson's character shocked her would-be lover when she spread her legs to reveal a penis, the post-Soviet prostitute was the perfect expression of the discourse of Russian masculinity because, powerless and alluring, she did not have a phallus at all.

> When out of the gloom of error
> With the hot word of conviction
> I drew out your fallen soul,
> And, full of deep torture,
> Wringing your hands, you cursed
> The vice that had corrupted you.
> . . .
> Believe me: I listened, not unmoved,
> I greedily caught every sound . . .
> I understood everything, unhappy child!
> All is forgiven and all is forgotten.
> And come into my house boldly and freely
> As its full mistress!
> (Nekrasov 101–2)"

The Russian Prostitute and Her Literary Pedigree

All appearances to the contrary, the post-Soviet prostitute of fiction and film had an impeccable pedigree, tracing her ancestry back to classic Russian

---

[3] In her 1993 article entitled "Sex and the Cinema," Lynn Attwood argues that "films about prostitution have one notable feature that sets them apart from the majority of recent films from the former USSR; their protagonists are, inevitably, female. To find women as the centre of attention in films which tackle other themes is increasingly uncommon" (73). While Attwood's assertion is technically correct, focus on the prostitute neither is a guarantee that a film or novel has any investment in a female point of view or in women's experience, nor does it raise the chances that a woman might actually be involved in creating the film. Only superficially do such works deal with the lives of women; their broader themes and concerns tend to concern the fate of the nation itself.

novels, short stories, and verse.[4] The Russian literary tradition is quite tolerant of the fallen woman, who is often treated less as an individual character than as the embodiment of a moral dilemma. N. A. Nekrasov's "When out of the gloom of error" (1845), cited above, establishes a pattern for the literary prostitute that resonates to this very day: the speaker inevitably hears the prostitute's tale of woe, facilitating her redemption by asking her to marry him: "And come into my house boldly and freely / As its full mistress!" In her article "A Typology of Fallen Women in Nineteenth Century Russian Literature," Olga Matich observes that the fallen woman "brings together two major themes of Russian fiction: those of moral integrity and socioeconomic status" ("Typology" 327).

Her words apply equally well to the post-Soviet prostitute, as does her typology itself: examining some of the most important heroines in nineteenth-century Russian fiction, Matich develops a classification system that divides the fallen woman and her "male complement" into four groups: female victim and male victimizer, female victim and male redeemer, female victim-redeemer and male victim, and female victimizer and male victim (327). That the fallen women should be defined in terms of suffering and redemption should come as no surprise to readers of Russian fiction, since these themes are central to the entire literary tradition in general (and to the works of Dostoevsky in particular). Matich reminds us of the numerous attempts by Russian heroes to "save" the prostitute or fallen woman, who is usually depicted as a victim of harsh circumstances: Nekhliudov and Katiusha Maslova from Lev Tolstoy's *Resurrection*, the Underground Man and Liza from *Notes from Underground*, and, of course, Kirsanov's transformation of Nastia Kriukova from prostitute to utopian socialist seamstress in Chernyshevsky's *What Is to Be Done?* The impulse to save such women may be attributed to a variety of motives, from a combination of vanity and a misguided sense of social duty to a selfish need to dominate. Indeed, one might argue that attempts at redemption work precisely in that they sublimate the initial, sexual arousal provoked by the prostitute into a moral one: it is her plight, and not her body, that is so seductive. In 1899, Tolstoy's Katiusha Maslova, the last in a long line of the century's literary prostitutes, so clearly understands her spiritual and sexual status that one might almost suspect she was familiar with Matich's typology. She resolves not to let off so easily the man who seduced her and ruined her life: "she would not give herself to him, would not allow him to use her spiritually as he had used her

---

[4] For a thorough historical study of prostitution before the Soviet period, see Laurie Bernstein; Lebina and Shkarovskii; Engel, *Between the Fields and the City*, 166–97 and "St. Petersburg Prostitutes"; Stites, "Prostitute and Society" and *Women's Liberation Movement* (178–90).

bodily" (259). For the attempt at salvation to be made, the male protagonist must first transform the prostitute in his own mind from a sex object to a moral object.[5]

Yet, as Matich's framework suggests, the prostitute could also be the *instrument* of salvation rather than its object. All but one of Matich's models are predicated on sexual role reversal, in which the man is "socially degraded" ("Typology" 338). Her third model, female victim-redeemer and male victim, is most fully pronounced in the works of Dostoevsky. Although Dostoevsky did not invent the theme of redemption through suffering, it quickly became associated with both his work and the moral imperatives of the Russian literary tradition as a whole; his focus on female sacrifice and redemption played a decisive role in the formation of the image of the self-sacrificing Russian heroine. In the aforementioned *Notes from Underground*, the narrator's fantasy that he will "raise up" the prostitute Liza is a parody of the utopian idealism of similar scenes in Chernyshevsky's *What Is to Be Done?*; by the end of the story, Liza, aware of his degradation, "assumes the role of redeemer in a redistribution of power and an inversion of the classical redemption model ("Typology" 339). Sonya, from Dostoevsky's *Crime and Punishment*, is certainly a victim to the extent that she turns in her passport for the prostitute's yellow ticket in order to save her family from destitution. Yet her primary role in the novel is to facilitate the hero's rejection of the path of sin, hubris, and murder. As Matich and numerous others have noted, "it is Sonya who is the Christlike savior in the novel ("Typology" 340).[6]

Although the suffering woman as both victim and redeemer would stubbornly persist into the Soviet period (with Solzhenitsyn's Matrena being one of the most famous examples), after the 1920s she was only rarely a prostitute. Certainly, prostitutes would be found throughout the literature documenting the Russian Revolution and civil war, from Kat'ka in Aleksandr Blok's "The Twelve"—the prostitute who had disrupted the comradely harmony of the revolutionary soldiers, a harmony that would be restored only after her death—to the camp followers of Isaac Babel's *Red Cavalry* stories. During the New Economic Policy, the prostitute resurged as a social and cultural phenomenon: the prevalence of prostitutes both

---

[5] This brief overview of the nineteenth-century fictional prostitute should by no means be considered exhaustive; a more complete discussion would have to include Aleksandr Kuprin's *Iama* (*The Pit*, 1908–15), a novel about a brothel whose inhabitants and clients bring together every cliché and motif connected with the representation of the Russian prostitute. For more on Kuprin, see Matich 1983 and Zholkovsky.

[6] For more on the attempts to "save" the literary prostitute, see Siegel (81–107) and Zholkovsky (317–68).

responded to the newly restored market forces and, in literature and film, reflected them.[7] Now prostitution was treated as a social problem to be eradicated through labor and reeducation rather than romantic idealism; if anything, the role of redeemer was now co-opted by the state and by doctors who were acting in the name of "enlightened science."[8] By the 1930s, victory was declared in the war on prostitution, and the category officially ceased to exist. The prostitute vanished from the horizon, reappearing only after Gorbachev's perestroika was well under way. Of course, women continued to perform sex for hire in train stations, hard-currency hotels for foreign visitors, and by special arrangement for the party elite. Yet if there is ample evidence that prostitution actually persisted as a social phenomenon, it vanished as a discursive one: it was no longer a subject fit for literature and art.

Making that film is tantamount to actually luring women into prostitution. It should be prosecuted under the law. A Moscow policeman, 1989 (Belova 44).

Perestroika Prostitutes

The prostitute's disappearance from Soviet discourse was necessitated by the supposed eradication of prostitution as a social ill, but her loss of currency also points to more fundamental characteristics of Soviet culture before glasnost. In a society where money and market relations were not the dominant means of exchange, the metaphorical power of prostitution was diminished. Even when the country was represented as feminine, Mother Russia's problem was not that she was selling her services to foreign customers. In World War II, clearly the Soviet Union's greatest international

[7] Indeed, the prostitute in NEP Russia functioned as a kind of shorthand for the moral and physical diseases brought on by the partial return to a market economy. Mikhail Bulgakov's infamous stage play *Zoikina kvartira* (*Zoia's Apartment* 1929) is only the most famous example. In their article on the evolution of the Russian procuress, Julie Cassiday and Leyla Rouhi also discuss a 1926 film by O. Frelikh called *Prostitutka/Ubitaia zhizn'iu* (*A Prostitute/Crushed by Life*), which associates prostitution with the evils of the past and provides a happy ending, thanks to the enlightened policies of the state (413–31). In her study of Russian public health posters in the 1920s, Frances L. Bernstein observes that the prostitute's image serves to personify the threat of syphilis and other sexually transmitted diseases: she is both temptress and disease vector ("Envisioning Health" 191–217). For more on the Soviet fight against prostitution in the 1920s, see Waters, "Victim or Villain," and Wood.

[8] As part of the public health campaign known as "sanitary enlightenment," Soviet doctors under NEP attempted to redeem prostitutes through labor, establishing special clinics to cure their ailments and teach them a trade (F. Bernstein, "Prostitutes and Proletarians" 113–28).

crisis, Mother Russia had to be protected from rape by a violent invader rather than seduction by a rich exploiter. When forbidden by law, prostitution is a classic example of a victimless crime: no direct harm comes to anyone as a result.[9] The resolution of moral dilemmas under Stalin (and even Brezhnev) did create victims: prostitution is a woefully inadequate metaphor for denouncing of friends and neighbors to the authorities. The dominant metaphor for "selling out" in Soviet times was Faustian rather than whorish: avoiding the mediation of the cash nexus entirely, one sold one's *soul* rather than one's *body*. One of the challenges faced by the art of the Thaw was to address not just the victims of Stalinism but those who actively colluded to ruin people's lives.[10]

Among the oppositional intelligentsia after Stalin, selling out to the authorities or to the crushing dictates of Soviet life was a matter of either submission to blackmail (denial of basic rights or privileges if one failed to go along) or invidious compromise (a series of small concessions that led one down the primrose path to total capitulation). The man who conveyed this dilemma the best—indeed, the undisputed master of the genre—was Brezhnev-era author Yuri Trifonov; his 1976 novel *Dom na naberezhnoi* (*House on the Embankment*) tells of a perfectly normal and likable young man who betrays his teacher during the Stalin era, while his 1969 novella *Obmen* (*The Exchange*) shows the more mundane deals with the devil made during Brezhnev's "period of stagnation": step by step, a man parts with his principles in order to swap his tiny apartment for a larger one.

With the advent of perestroika, the dominant metaphors changed. Not only did the state rapidly lose much of its ability to force its citizens into ethical compromises with the system, but the system itself quickly became preoccupied with issues of money and market relations. One of Russia's most prominent, and most controversial, fiction writers appeared to have

[9] The use of the term "victimless crime" is not meant to imply that prostitutes never suffer as a result of their work but rather that they do not cause harm to third parties. Where prostitutes themselves are considered victims, the crime in question is pimping rather than prostitution (see Cassiday and Rouhi). Prostitutes in Russia and elsewhere have faced legal prosecution for offenses related to their profession, such as spreading venereal disease to their customers (F. Bernstein, "Envisioning Health" 205–7).

[10] For example, Pavel Rusanov, the party hack in Solzhenitsyn's *Rakovyi korpus* (*Cancer Ward*, 1967–1968), is appalled at the prospect that the people he sent to the camps might return and demand their jobs and apartments back, not to mention justice and reparations. Yuli Daniel's haunting novella "Atonement" (1963) presents the Kafkaesque dilemma of a man who finds himself shunned by his circle of friends after one of them returns from the gulag; the narrator discovers that this man holds him responsible for the years spent in the prison camps, even though in actuality the returnee had been denounced by someone else entirely. By the story's end, the narrator nonetheless accepts his guilt, if not for this particular crime, then for his failure to speak out when his friend was caught up in the machinery of the Terror.

anticipated this shift earlier than most: between 1980 and 1982, Victor Erofeyev wrote a novel called *Russkaia krasavitsa* (*Russian Beauty*), which would be published in the USSR only in 1990. The novel's obscene language (which was unprintable before the late 1980s) and graphic descriptions of sexual violence did not exactly endear it to the Russian intellectual readership, while its stream-of-consciousness narration was a bit too daunting for those who were simply looking for titillation. *Russian Beauty* tells the tale of Irina Tarakanova (her last name means "cockroach"), a beautiful, high-class slut who, although not strictly speaking a prostitute, services the communist *nomenklatura*, artists, and various hangers-on. As the female embodiment of a debased and mercantile Russia on the cusp of perestroika, Tarakanova is perfect: at a time when connections and favoritism can make or break someone's life, Tarakanova implicitly sells her services without taking cash. She is not a prostitute, but she is a whore. As in so much of Erofeyev's work, underneath the modernist narrative techniques and scandalous four-letter words of *Russian Beauty* are themes resurrected from the literary classics: in this case, the suffering, beautiful female "fallen woman" as a symbol of Russia's salvation. Erofeyev is one of Russia's most self-conscious stylists, and his approach to the theme is easily identifiable as parody: as Helena Goscilo has noted, Irina clearly represents the new Russia ("two fates were to be decided: Russia's and mine" [*Russian Beauty* 227]; Goscilo, *Dehexing* 43). She is convinced that she will be Russia's spiritual savior because "beauty will save the world" (Prince Myshkin said as much in Dostoevsky's *The Idiot*, so it must be true).

Ultimately, it would not be "high art" like *Russian Beauty* that would establish the image of the perestroika prostitute; that honor would fall to a novel and movie called *Interdevochka* (*Intergirl*). Viktor Kunin's 1988 novel and Petr Todorovskii's movie of the following year tell the melodramatic story of Tania, a nurse's aide by day and foreign-currency prostitute by night. Although Tania uses her ill-gotten income for luxuries and fine clothes, her main concern is the welfare of her friends and her mother, a middle-aged woman of poor health. After many trials and tribulations, Tania marries one of her clients, a Swedish businessman who takes her away from both mother and motherland to install her in a house with all the modern conveniences of Western suburbia and all the warmth of a Scandinavian winter. Tania's relationship with her husband rapidly deteriorates as she is overcome by boredom and homesickness; her only solace is her friendship with the Soviet truck driver who is her one link to her past life. By the story's end, the truck driver has lost his job for consorting with Tania, her mother has discovered her secret life and committed suicide, and a distraught Tania dies in a car accident.

This wildly successful potboiler simply begs for a political reading. In her discussion of Todorovskii's film, Lynn Attwood argues convincingly that the prostitute is a symbol of Soviet society as a whole: "everybody is forced, metaphorically, into prostitution" ("Sex and the Cinema" 72).[11] Katerina Clark offers a more provocative interpretation of the perestroika prostitute: such works as *Intergirl* highlight the intelligentsia's anxiety over the fate of culture in the era of the international marketplace ("Not for Sale" 189–205). As Goscilo observes, "the dominant lexicon of *Intergirl* is that of economics (not sex)" (*Dehexing* 144). The novel itself, which was published along with a brief foreword by the prominent Russian sexologist Igor Kon praising Kunin's work for its social utility, is remarkably chaste in its language, containing neither obscene words nor explicit descriptions of sexual acts (the American Motion Picture Association would be hard-pressed to give it an R rating). In *Intergirl,* Goscilo discovers a prurience of a different sort: a "preoccupation with various brands and names of commodities, which relentlessly repeat themselves whenever clothes, cars, makeup, perfumes, etc., are mentioned. Needless to say, these are all Western imports, weapons with which the corrupt materialist West invades innocent Russia to tempt and degrade it" (*Dehexing Sex* 144). Of course, crucial to all these readings of *Intergirl* is the fact that Tanya is a *foreign-currency* prostitute, one who disdains mere rubles in her quest for dollars and deutsche marks. Indeed, Tanya meets her death in a foreign car whose name seems to point back to the body parts with which she earned her keep: a Volvo. When we recall the frequent recourse to female symbols to represent Russia, Tania's melodramatic story becomes a transparent allegory of Russia's relationship with the West: rich in natural beauty, Russia sells herself to foreign suitors only to be overcome by nostalgia and regret.[12]

Although *Intergirl* was, on the one hand, just a novel and movie, the work represents a turning point for the social construction of the Russian prostitute. Contemporary reviewers of the movie feared that its depiction of its star, Elena Iakovleva, decked out in foreign clothes and enjoying imported luxuries, would prompt millions of young Soviet girls to follow in

[11] When Tanya's mother expresses her horror at the thought that her daughter is "selling herself," Tanya replies: "Correct. But how many of us do *not* sell ourselves?" (Attwood, "Sex and the Cinema" 73).

[12] The fact that Tania meets her demise in Sweden of all places is also worthy of note. On the level of plot, Sweden is clearly meant to embody the West at its coldest: an efficient land where any act of spontaneity is greeted with suspicion and any expenditure of money must be counted to the last decimal. Symbolically, Sweden still functions as one of Russia's oldest and weakest European enemies, the country whose army was defeated by Alexander Nevsky in 1240, by Peter the Great (most notably at Poltava in 1709), and by Alexander I in 1809.

her spike-heeled footsteps.[13] And although the media are too easy a target to blame for all contemporary social ills, it is true that the number of prostitutes in the former Soviet Union began to skyrocket in the years following the movie's release. Unquestionably, there are clear socioeconomic reasons for this phenomenon that have nothing to do with the corrupting power of film and fiction, but the movie did provide an easily digested narrative for becoming a prostitute that could have exacerbated the situation.[14] Over a decade later, *Intergirl* is still routinely blamed for Russia's prostitution problem. The May 1999 issue of *Kino-Park*, a popular movie magazine, featured an article called "How *Intergirl* Was Accused of Prostitution" in which professors, policemen, and even prostitutes themselves make the case that, despite its tragic ending, Todorovskii's film is to blame for luring girls from the path of righteousness. Curiously, the metaphor of prostitution is used to explain how a film about prostitution led real girls and women to turn tricks for a living: the movie's producers are essentially accused of pimping the Russian public.

> There are nations and cultures that simply *know how* to sell and buy women . . . In theory, Russian *high* culture [*kul'tura*] couldn't stand that. Buying and selling gave her [culture] convulsions. She was uniquely unmercenary. Without investigating the matter thoroughly, she declared woman priceless. That's why Russian culture's attitude toward prostitution was so strained.(Erofeev, "The Price of the Prostitute," *Muzhchiny* 108)

After 1991: On the Market

Intergirl appeared only two years after the paradigmatic moment when sexuality reemerged as an important part of Russian discourse, the 1987 declaration "We have no sex!" These words functioned as a call to arms: in the decade that followed, Russia had been doing its best to prove this notion

[13] Igor' Kon cites a 1989 survey of high school senior girls in Riga and Leningrad claiming that foreign-currency prostitution "had become one of the top ten most prestigious professions," as well as a survey in which prostitutes ranked higher than journalists, diplomats, and academics among prestigious and lucrative professions admired by Moscow schoolchildren (223). Survey results in the former Soviet Union are notoriously unreliable and should be viewed with a healthy dose of skepticism; nevertheless, the appearance of such survey results in the Russian mass media has been important in defining the role of the prostitute in contemporary Russian sexual discourse. At the very least, the surveys have created the *impression* that prostitution is considered a desirable profession.

[14] For information about the rise in prostitution during the perestroika era, see Sanjian (270–95) and Waters (133–54).

wrong. Since Russian culture can be said to have undergone both a market revolution and a sexual revolution simultaneously (although both claims are problematic), the discourse of sex became inextricably linked with the discourse of economics. The result was a commodification of women's bodies and female sexuality that was unprecedented in Russian history. Want ads casually announced secretarial vacancies for attractive young women who were *bez kompleksov* or "uninhibited," a none-too-subtle code for explaining the secretary's horizontal duties. And just as American and European commercials use beautiful women to sell cars and beer, Russian ads routinely featured half-naked, sexually available beauties to promote the most unlikely of products A 2001 billboard for a copy machine had a sexy woman lying on top of it, with the slogan *ona ne otkazhet* (a play on words suggesting that the copy machine would not break down and the woman would not say no). Equally evocative was a 1999 billboard for "West" cigarettes: in it, a beautiful stewardess sat next to a handsome male passenger, smiling broadly as her breasts, barely covered in a black lace bra, spilled out of her unbuttoned uniform. Although the man was looking her in the eye, the cigarette's logo pointed straight to her cleavage, while the slogan above their heads proclaimed: "Everything is possible."

This last ad is particularly significant, since it brings together female sexual commodification and the tortured relations between Russia and the West. The man's clothing and the women's face strongly suggest that both are Russian, but the artifact responsible for their unlimited possibilities is packaged as foreign: the color scheme is a rip-off of that used in ads for Marlboros, which had been the undisputed favorite among Russia's smokers with the money to pay for them, while the product's name speaks for itself. West presents a relatively uncomplicated connection between sexuality, Russian male sexual success, and Western consumer culture. But as the 1990s drew to a close, this utopian idyll was more the exception than the rule. Here again, the figure of the prostitute played a central role: repeatedly standing in for Russia as a whole, she sold her services, herself, and often her pride.

Post-Soviet Russia's drama of international prostitution was always played out in a number of arenas simultaneously: on the empirical level, there was the unchecked growth of highly paid call girls serving New Russians and foreign businessmen, the boom in Russian mail-order brides, and the notorious trafficking in women from the former Soviet Union throughout the world; allegorically, the export of Russian women was inevitably compared with the shortsighted marketing of the country's oil reserves for Western consumption. The Russian woman had become part of a constellation of symbols for

Russian anxieties over commodification. The prostitute who catered to Western clients served much the same function as the baby adopted by American and European childless couples or the victims of kidnapping in popular urban legends about organs harvested for the underground transplant market. In each case, something that might normally be considered intimate or even sacred was thrown to the tender mercies of the postsocialist international market, turning Russia into a depot for human spare parts. Rita Prozorova, the heroine of Sergei Pugachev's 1999 novel *Ty prosto shliukha, dorogaia!* (*You're Just a Slut, My Dear!*) flees from sexual slavery in the provinces only to be lured into a black-market organ-harvesting scheme in the capital. She escapes only because she has heard enough news stories on TV to recognize the imminent danger: "Some millionaire in Chicago's heart valve fails him, and a man in Moscow or Petersburg disappears. She'll disappear the same way, so that her kidney can process American urine somewhere in San Francisco. To die, just to piss in San Francisco? Screw that!" (296). Rita's escape from the organ harvesters parallels her escape from prostitution: refusing to be a victim, she does not hesitate to commit murder herself.

Rita's story is unusual, however, in that she herself is the action hero and that she is also an irredeemably unattractive character. Nor is she a professional prostitute. The professional prostitutes in Russian popular narrative were usually far more appealing, and their stories were calculated to arouse numerous conflicting feelings in the male audience. On the sexual level, the Russian prostitute's story contributed to a growing complex of inferiority and insecurity among Russian men, one that was amply demonstrated by the numerous publications and broadcasts aimed primarily at male consumers. Indeed, the very existence of men's magazines and soft-core pornography in Russia inevitably pointed back to the threat of foreign competition: no matter how hard they might try to be unique, male heterosexual erotica and pornography in Russia betrayed their foreign origins. *Andrei* made such anxieties crystal clear in a cartoon in its very first issue. Two prostitutes display their wares on a Moscow street: the first, a Russian woman standing under the M of the metro sign, looks on in horror at a black woman leaning against the M of a McDonald's sign (*Andrei* 1: 27). Such publications trumpeted the virtues of Russian women, repeating the male mantra that women in Russia are the most beautiful in the world; but they also reinforced the threat that these women would attract the attention of rich foreign men (through associated projects such as *Andrei*'s own website).

How, then, did Russian popular culture attempt to exorcise itself of the sense of humiliation and betrayal as symbolized by the prostitute, who shamelessly crossed borders and exchanged bodily fluids? By appealing to a tired cliché of prostitute narratives while adding a nationalist twist: the desirability and value of the prostitute was proven by the fact that the West was willing to pay, but her spirituality, and the ultimate superiority of Russian men, was demonstrated when she performed her services for love rather than for money. By and large, the prostitute was mercantile only with her foreign johns, bestowing her gifts on the Russian hero for free.

Indeed, the moment when the prostitute stops taking money can be tantamount to the validation of the hero's Russian credentials. In 1993, director Ivan Shchegolev and screenwriter Lev Korsunskii produced a rather ham-handed comedy called *Amerikanskii dedushka* (*American Grandfather*), the last film starring the beloved actor Evgenii Leonov. Leonov plays an émigré who returns from Brooklyn to his native Russia in order to buy a cemetery plot, plan his funeral, and die at home surrounded by loved ones. These same loved ones, however, have far more mercantile ideas. Through the inexplicable logic of film comedy, Leonov has gotten rich in America (after all, that is what America is for), and so he is soon the target of various hangers-on who hope to squeeze as much money out of him as possible before he takes to his grave. Along the way, Leonov goes to a hotel restaurant and meets a Russian woman whom the viewer has little difficulty identifying as a prostitute (she wears the uniform of high heels, fishnets, miniskirt, and garish makeup). Incredibly, Leonov fails to realize she is a professional: after all, he has been away from Russia so long, he does not know that the country is now swarming with call girls. Apparently his experience in America has not given him the street smarts to recognize a hooker; instead, prostitution is implicitly identified as a post-Soviet Russian phenomenon. This being a comedy, and one with the word "American" in its title, it has to have a happy ending; and so the tragic finale of the funeral is replaced by the celebration of Leonov's wedding to the prostitute, who is now pregnant. Leonov has come home to live, not to die.

There is much to unpack here: at the very least since the Russian Revolution, emigration and exile have been symbolically linked to images of death, with the foreign countries standing in for the land of the dead.[15] Indeed, *Intergirl* itself makes use of this tradition, turning Tania's new home into a land that virtually buries her alive and ultimately kills her. Leonov's happy end is the mirror image of *Intergirl*'s tragedy: the prostitute finds happiness by marrying a foreign john who turns out to be a Russian; she helps reconcile him

---

[15] Mikhail Bulgakov's 1928 play *Beg* (*Flight*) and Yuri Olesha's 1931 melodrama *Spisok blagodeianii* (*A List of Assets*) present emigration and death as either virtually equivalent (the émigrés are the living dead) or a matter of cause and effect (even considering emigration leads to the hero's death). See Avins, *Border Crossings* (79–90, 101–16).

with his greedy relatives, and the newlyweds remain in their native land to raise children rather than move abroad to die. Here the prostitute facilitates reintegration with Russia and a reassertion of "family values" rather than exile and the soul-crushing dominance of market relations.

The foreign-currency prostitute plays a similar function as the guide back "home" in Rudol'f Fruntov's 1997 action film *Vse to, o chem my tak dolgo mechtali* (*Everything We Dreamed About for So Long*), although its end is tragic. A young man is tricked by his old army buddy into running drugs from Western Europe into Russia, not realizing that he is being set up to be caught and killed. Although he is told to drive nonstop, he is lured by the bright lights of a German city and makes his way to a strip club, where he is immediately attracted to a platinum blonde exotic dancer who he is convinced is a "real German." Naturally, when he arranges to pay for her services, she turns out to be a Russian (named Natasha, no less—Russian prostitutes throughout Europe and the Middle East are routinely referred to as "Natashas"), and mayhem ensues. He finds himself in jail, and Natasha, who at first disdained him as just another raggedy Russian, soon finds herself in an all-too-familiar role for women from the ex-USSR: she brings him packages in prison. Eventually, she meets up with him after he breaks free, following a kickboxing struggle to the death with a fellow prisoner while clad in nothing but a loincloth and silver body paint. Natasha turns out to be a foreign-language graduate who was lured abroad with promises of work as a translator, only to have her passport seized and her body sold into sexual slavery. Thanks to her, the hero turns his life around. She brings him to a Russian Orthodox Church, where, overwhelmed by the power of the icons, he faints. He returns and is baptized into the faith of his fathers, as a more modestly dressed Natasha looks on, smiling beatifically. Soon she gets pregnant, and the couple starts to make plans for the future. Before she and the hero can start a new life together, however, she is shot by gangsters.

Everything We Dreamed About for So Long is a prostitute melodrama in the Dostoevskian mold, where the heroine facilitates her lover's salvation.[16] But here these hackneyed themes are transposed to the realm of international commerce and national disenchantment. When the hero was still in the army, he and his friend dreamed of the good life, the kind available only in the West; but when he arrives in Germany, the West for him is nothing but a prison. His status in life is both typical for so many young Russian men, who leave the army aimless and disillusioned, and symbolic of Russian manhood in general; where once he belonged to something, to an organization of

[16] On the film's Dostoevskian subtext, see Hashamova ("Post-Soviet Film" 60–62).

comrades that gave some sense of purpose, now he must try to find a place for himself in a harsh and unfamiliar world. As for Natasha, she charges foreign men for her sexual favors but gives herself to the hero for free, facilitating his reintegration into traditional Russian spiritual values.

A prostitute named Natasha is also crucial for the redemption of the hero of Viktor Dotsenko's best-selling series of action novels, Savelii Govorkov, nicknamed "Mad Dog" (*Beshenyi*).[17] The fifth novel, *Mest' Beshenogo* (*Mad Dog's Revenge* 1998), begins at the funeral of Savelii's latest dead girlfriend, Natasha. Virtually all of Savelii's lovers quickly turn into beautiful corpses to be avenged by Mad Dog, with the exception of the underage Rozochka, whom Savelii eventually marries. Right after the ceremony, he meets a beautiful young prostitute who shares his beloved's name and marvels at the rather unremarkable coincidence of knowing two Russian women named Natasha. This is Natasha's day off, but when she looks into his eyes, she realizes what he needs. She is no stranger to loss, since her small daughter was killed by a drunk driver three years before, and the sight of the other Natasha's funeral brings back memories of her own daughter's death: "In a purely womanly way, she felt that he needed help, that something tragic had happened to him." (25). She takes him home, where they have numerous shots of cognac, including a toast to the fallen Afghan veterans. Soon enough, they fall into bed together, and the experience is redemptive for both of them. The all-too-experienced Natasha is as nervous and excited as though she were with a man for the first time, while Savelii reaches an epiphany that is unparalleled in modern literature: crying out her name, he enters her rectally and communes with the spirit of his departed lover, while the living Natasha experiences the first orgasm of her life (30–32, 39). Now Savelii is able to return to his mission, saving Russia from its enemies, while anal sex with Savelii has transformed Natasha entirely. "Her soul was joyous and calm: for the first time in many long years, she felt pure and immaculate" (34).

By the late 1990s, the prostitute with a heart of gold was once again such a ubiquitous feature in popular culture that she easily lent herself to satire. Victor Pelevin's 1997 novel *Zhizn' nasekomykh* (*Life of Insects*), a postmodern animal fable in which nearly all the main characters are insects navigating the absurdities of contemporary Russian life, uses the trope of the prostitute to lampoon one of the author's favorite targets: the ultranationalist and pseudo-pseudomystical discourse of Russia's fate. One of the

---

[17] Literally, his name means "rabid." I have chosen "Mad Dog" because it strikes me as a more plausible name in English.

novel's main characters, a visiting American businessman, Sam Sucker, is actually a mosquito who has come to Moscow to sample the local cuisine (that is, Russian blood).[18] Soon after his arrival, he meets a young fly named Natasha, whom Sam's Russian companions immediately recognize as a prostitute. Here Pelevin manages to send up both *Intergirl* and Kornei Chukovskii's classic children's poem, *Mukha-Tsokotukha* (in which a female fly is rescued by a male mosquito). Like Tania from *Intergirl*, Natasha is a disappointment to her sick mother (in this case, a housebound widow who consumed the remains of Natasha's father as nourishment while waiting for her eggs to hatch), choosing to sell her body in exchange for a better life. After she and Sam have sex in the pristine countryside, Natasha whispers a naive question to her foreign lover: "Sam . . . is it true that America has lots of shit?" (223). Sam nods indulgently, reassuring her that he really is from the land of plenty. But, as with so many of her predecessors, Natasha's story ends in tragedy. She has been so certain of Sam's love that she has even been practicing her English in preparation for their eventual departure ("Please cheese and pepperoni"), but Sam intends to leave her behind. Grief-stricken, Natasha commits suicide, hanging herself on a strip of fly-paper (348–49).

Nympho: The Prostitute as Spiritual Barometer

I had a country I was proud of. My country was betrayed, ruined, and raped, like the cheapest of sluts. They just let it be desecrated. What's now called the Russian state can't make you proud, only ashamed. The country is a prostitute who lies down under any scum who happens by! And she even eats her young like a pig! All right, enough. Let's go on. I had ideals. They weren't subtle ideals, but still they were respected by any normal person. Now these ideals are mocked, slandered, smeared in shit, any cowardly bastard can publicly spit on them, where before he wouldn't even have dared make a sound! When I see this sort of thing, I want to kill! But I'd have to kill too many people. . . . (D. Shcherbakov, *Nimfomanka: besposhchadnaia strast'*, 8–9)

---

[18] Sam's encounters with ordinary Russians inevitably revert to a parody of Russian chauvinism. After getting drunk on a Russian man's vodka-infused blood, Sam attacks his Russian mosquito hosts: "Admit it, *bliad'* [whore]. . . . Don't you suck Russian blood?" (167). Later on, a driver launches into a tirade about the enemies of Russia while Sam quietly sucks the man's blood from behind: "We've been sold. . . . And all our rockets and our navy. They've drained us of our life's blood . . ." (217).

So laments Sever Belov, the hero of Dmitrii Shcherbakov's lurid pot-boiler *Nimfomanka: Besposhchadnaia strast'* (*Nympho: Merciless Passion* 1999), the second book in a trilogy describing the adventures of a sex-crazed but highly moral woman and her superpowered husband as they fight Russian and Chechen organized crime. Sever certainly knows whereof he speaks: not only has he spent the best years of his life trying to save a country that doesn't want to be saved, but his wife Mila is a career prosti-tute whose "disease" (her physiological need to be gang-raped and humili-ated) continually drives her back to the brothel after each rescue from the clutches of the latest in a long line of pimps. He is telling his story to his best friend, the surgeon Pavel Kuzovlev, whose dedication to the Belovs led him to retrain himself as a psychoanalyst in order to try to cure Mila of her nymphomania and Sever of a "reactive psychosis" that has led him to at-tempt suicide. The good doctor's response to Sever's tirade? "You've been watching too much television!" (9).

All three parts of Dmitrii Shcherbakov's "Nymphomaniac" trilogy (*Nympho, Nympho: Merciless Passion,* and *Nympho: A Hooker's Love* [*Li-ubov' putany*]) date from the late nineties, and, while there is no evidence that they will ever attain the popularity of *Intergirl*, taken together they form the post-Soviet prostitute text par excellence. All of the themes dis-cussed above are present: border crossings, a feminized Russia and the West, the prostitute as symbol of Russia's natural resources, the focus on the male hero, and, most notably, the prostitute as Christlike redeemer. The first novel is the story of Sever and Mila, both of whom have lost their memory after a car accident. When they meet again, they do not even know that they were lovers before, but they are immediately united by passion. And by something more: each of them has phenomenal powers. They can project an aura that prevents people from remembering what they look like; they possess super strength and an iron will; Belov can kill dozens of people with his bare hands and soon teaches Mila to do the same. But Mila has one additional ability: through her erotic dancing, she can drive men and women into a sexual frenzy.

After their accident, Sever finds work as a mechanic and eventually is employed by the local mafia. Mila becomes the most coveted prostitute in an elite brothel, and as much as she despises herself for her work, she cannot give up prostitution. For reasons that do not become clear until the end of the first novel, she has an insatiable need to be gang-raped and abused, both verbally and physically. Belov's doctor friend even describes her nymphoma-nia as physiological: if her brain does not receive the essential impulses it gets when she is gang-raped, it will literally self-destruct. When Sever and Mila fall in love (for what turns out to be the second time), their relationship is seriously undermined by the fact that, even though Sever's superhuman abilities extend to the bedroom (he usually has sex with Mila throughout the night), he is never enough for her.

All of this unfolds in a context of virulent racism and offhand disdain for democratic reform. Sever's enemies in the first novel consist largely of Chechens and Georgians, whom he routinely dismisses as *chernozhopaia mraz'* ("black-assed scum") and *chernomazy*, one of the Russian language's strongest ethnic slurs. Sever's solution to the Chechen problem is simple: exile all Chechens from Russian territory and close Chechnya's borders forever. His judgment of Yeltsin's government is equally uncompromising, if a bit less heated: the narrator casually refers to the year 1991 as the time when "American agents of influence" took over the Kremlin. Sever's nationalist credentials, which are established early on, are further strengthened when the reader discovers that, in his past life, Sever was a border guard who devoted all his efforts to preventing the theft of Russia's mineral resources. This detail is particularly important in light of Sever's problems with Mila: even after he rescues her from the brothel, she still has a physiological need to be abused, and by more than one person. His only solution is to form a brothel of his own, in which Mila plays the starring role and Sever provides the protection. Of course, it is a kinder, gentler brothel, a whorehouse with a human face: Sever and Mila greatly improve the lives of the prostitutes who end up working for him.[19] But Sever, the strong Russian action hero, ends up in the position of pimping for the woman he loves.

By the end of the first novel, Sever's friend Pavel, the surgeon-turned-psychoanalyst, discovers the root cause of Mila's nymphomania. Before the accident, her love for Sever was so strong that it was like a drug; she could not do without him. While she is in the hospital following the accident, an unscrupulous doctor, who is in the habit of pushing her female patients into prostitution, injects her with an aphrodisiac to determine her erotic potential. Unfortunately for Mila, a group of young criminals is being treated in the hospital for minor wounds at the same time, and they gang-rape Mila while she is under the influence of the aphrodisiac. Against her will, she is aroused by the experience, but meanwhile she hates herself,

---

[19] Sever's brothel resembles a parody of Vera Pavlovna's sewing cooperative in Nikolai Cherny-shevsky's *What Is to Be Done?* Where Vera Pavlovna rescued young prostitutes from a life of shame and redeemed them through labor, Sever gives them a better life without actually changing their profession.

knowing that somewhere out there lives her beloved, whose name she cannot recall, and she is betraying him. Subconsciously, she decides she is not worthy of him and that the world is a terrible place filled with evil people who do evil things. Her only possible value in life could be to let herself be raped and abused, thereby sparing other women her fate. As the doctor puts it, "Mila's system has become a kind of barometer, reacting to the spiritual atmosphere of society. If there is too much evil surrounding her, she tries to reduce its quantity . . . in the only way she can" (*Nimfomanka* 493). Moreover, Mila is uniquely attuned to her native country. Before she and Sever meet again after the accident, Mila is taken to France to dance in a Parisian nightclub. But she has to be flown home immediately because she nearly dies of a literal form of homesickness. She cannot leave Russia because "Russia is the land of sincerity, and evil here is also sincere, open, with no pretensions to false morality. In the West it's different. The West is hypocritical to the marrow. Evil is everywhere there, but it clothes itself in respectability. The West is soulless in both good and evil. It lives only for a sense of advantage, which usurps any other moral values. And Mila is too sensitive an instrument" (494). Nor can she go to the East, since people are animals there, lacking any sense of good and evil.

Mila is the lowbrow apotheosis of the prostitute as redeemer: her libido is the cross she has to bear. In these novels, it is not beauty but nymphomania that will save the world. Her status is a source of inverted pride: she is far more moral than almost anyone around her, and her beauty is unsurpassed. Even her humiliation has a higher purpose. But her humiliation is ultimately shared by her man. Sever is in a bind, as both lover and patriot: the object of his affections is as beautiful as ever, but it wallows in filth and seems unlikely to recover.

The sheer overindulgence in psychosexual nationalist horror exemplified by the saga of Mila and Sever proves to be surprisingly optimistic, suggesting that overkill can have a purpose. By wedding the Russian Orthodox tradition of redemptive suffering to the lurid melodrama of post-Soviet pulp, the narrative of prostitution imbues chernukha with meaning. Here we have a moral universe that incorporates all the everyday atrocities so meticulously catalogued since the advent of glasnost while rejecting the nihilism and anomie that could easily attach themselves to tales of moral and national collapse. Perestroika reintroduced the prostitute as a social problem, while the nineties transformed her (back) into a metaphysical one. During perestroika, the prostitute embodied anxieties about the market in a context of novelty that rested on the implicit binary opposition between the market and its absence. A decade later, neither the market nor the lowbrow culture it facilitated could realistically be rejected out of hand. The choice was no longer between chernukha and an uplifting culture of chaste restraint but between pointless overkill and ideologically meaningful excess. The answer to chernukha is not purity but more chernukha, while humiliation is to be embraced for its redemptive power.

Chapter Four

TO BE CONTINUED

Death and the Art of Serial Storytelling

Nonetheless, she found a way out of the dead end in which she
was trapped: leaving for the next world.

—Dar'ia Dontsova, *A Kiss, Execution Style* (*Kontrol'nyi potselui*)

Violent crime in popular entertainment is first and foremost a question
of storytelling. On the most basic level, violence demands more story than
does sex. Consider, for example, the extreme cases in popular entertainment directed at roughly the same demographic (men): in pornography,
storytelling is kept to a minimum, since anything that is not overtly sexual
is simply a distraction, and thus sex scenes can be strung together with the
flimsiest of narrative threads ("Is that the delivery boy?"). In stories of violence, there is no precise narrative equivalent to pornography, as graphic
violence tends to be much more motivated by plots involving suspense or
adventure, however schematic such plots may be.[1] Pornography also relies
on a particular kind of novelty to make up for the limited variety of action:
if new positions and perversions are unlikely to be found, at least the audience is treated to a constant flow of ever-changing participants.[2] Ironi-

---

[1] The world of gaming perhaps provides an exception, as computer games such as *Grand Theft
Auto* are notorious for their nonstop bloodshed. But computer games are a distant cousin to storytelling, a hybrid involving roleplaying. As active participants, gamers are not the audience of a developing story.

[2] In his study of "formula stories," John G. Cawelti notes the similarity between serial storytelling and pornography, arguing that pornography "arouses an excitation so intense and uncontrolled that it tends to force immediate gratification outside itself" (14).

cally, the very iterability of sexual acts creates a demand for disposable participants as a hedge against monotony.[3] Pornography does not lend itself to serialized, never-ending stories of beloved heroes; presumably, the last thing the pornoconsumer wants is for his imagination to be monogamous.[4]

This is not the case with violence. The most popular genres of violent entertainment rely on the lure of the familiar rather than the novel: many of the most successful murder mysteries, thrillers, and adventure tales are parts of series whose beloved heroes are always ready to reprise their roles. In the best of all possible worlds (which, admittedly, is not a claim anyone is making for post-Soviet Russia), sex is a much more common part of everyday adult experience than violence. If a story involves contests of physical force, it usually features professionals in violence, whether criminals, police officers, or soldiers; even in the extremely popular stories whose hero is a novice to violence (the everyday man or woman accidentally drawn into a bloody mystery or battle), part of the appeal depends on the ordinary person's *interaction* with inhabitants of a persistently violent world. As a matter of narrative economy, the relative rarity of violence as opposed to sex would encourage an initial effort to develop the scenario for believable violence, to which the author could then return in subsequent episodes. If we are to begin to examine the role of violent crime in post-Soviet popular culture, we must first try to understand it in terms of the narrative form that returned to prominence at roughly the same time that crime became the predominant theme. In today's Russia, serial narrative and the thematics of violent crime are inextricably linked. It is violent crime that has made the serial form philosophically acceptable in the Russian context, while seriality in turn fuels the culture's construction of violence as a cyclical, never-ending phenomenon that establishes the contours of the post-Soviet world.

What does it mean for a story to have no end? This question calls to mind the work that has been left unfinished by the author's untimely demise, waning interest in the subject matter, or descent into madness (*The Mystery of Edwin Drood*, *Dead Souls*, "Egyptian Nights"); if anything, such texts call attention to the role of the ending only through its absence. The missing conclusion looms large over the eternal fragment, inevitably encouraging speculation as to the author's intent (how was the story "supposed" to end?)

---

[3] The other option is to escalate the transgression and "perversion" in which the participants indulge. Yet this is a risky strategy, since the audience will shrink as the sex becomes kinkier (pornography easily accommodates niche markets).

[4] There are, of course, exceptions, but they tend to fall more into the vague category of "erotica" and are also more friendly to a female audience (such as the series of French novels and movies about *Angelique*, which remain popular in Russia today).

Conversely, by way of provocation, a finished work can end on a note of permanently frustrated suspense ("The Lady and the Tiger," *The Crying of Lot 49*); the text is complete even if the plot is unresolved.[5] The question of completion is even more problematic in the realm of popular entertainment, where market forces and perceived audience expectations can have a more direct effect on narrative form. The rise of mass communications and cheap reproduction and distribution has facilitated a growing reliance on a type of storytelling that rejects the very notion of completion, a form of fiction that flirts with our customary tragic sense of the inexorable progression of time while satisfying a deep-seated need to capture the present, freezing it or at least slowing it down to lull us with intimations of immortality in a mortal world.

This would seem to be a narrative conundrum: painting, sculpture, and lyric poetry have long served as snares for the fleeting moment, at least in part because they are virtually devoid of a temporal element. But once we turn to stories that at least pretend to recapitulate real time, we are immediately confronted with duration, and hence mortality. In what Bakhtin would call our "novelized" world, in which our stories are populated largely by mortals like ourselves and not set in a closed-off, epic past, it is all too easy to read (or view) a story in terms of its apparently inevitable ending.[6] Emma Bovary is immortal to the extent that she "lives" every time we open Flaubert's novel, but she also dies each time we finish it. In contemporary literature, this narrative death drive is most obvious in the works of authors who insist on making sure the reader knows how their characters die, even if the deaths take place decades after the novel closes (either parenthetically, as in the case of Muriel Spark's *The Prime of Miss Jean Brodie*, E. Annie Proulx's *Accordion Crimes*, and Louise Erdrich's *Last Report on the Miracles at Little No Horse*, or in epilogues, as in John Irving's *The World According to Garp* or the final episode of *Six Feet Under*).[7] Walter Benjamin argues in

[5] Though the ending of a fiction can easily be confused with the ending of the story's action, Paul Ricoeur notes that the realist novel also recognized a "law of good form" that parallels poetic closure. The criterion of good closure is complicated with the onset of modernism, where "the ending of the work is the ending of the fictive operation itself." Thus an unexpected and even unsatisfying conclusion can be appropriate: "An inconclusive ending suits a work that raises by design a problem the author considers to be unsolvable" (21–22).

[6] See Gary Saul Morson's *Narrative and Freedom*, in which he discusses the "diseases of time" that so often beset the novel, including the "desiccated present" that results from either eschatological narration or the "exhaustion" of "epilogue time" (when the writer treats his characters as if their stories are already over) (189–201).

[7] Kurt Vonnegut highlights this problem by playing with his reader's attachments to his (mortal) fictional characters in his novel *Galapagos*. Here the narrator declares that it is unfair of authors to make their readers grow fond of the heroes only to watch them die unexpectedly, so he softens the blow by placing an asterisk before the names of characters a few pages before they die.

"The Storyteller" that the opportunity to share in the hero's experience of death, and therefore to partake in otherwise unattainable wisdom, is the source of the novel's appeal, yet many post-Victorian novels close with the fact of the protagonists' deaths rather than with any connection to an interior life.[8] One has the sense that these novelists are not satisfied until all their characters are safely dead and buried.[9]

Yet the world of popular entertainment has long offered an alternative to the novel's capitulation to mortality: the serial. Serial narrative puts off the conclusion as long as possible, in some cases avoiding completion altogether. There are obvious economic reasons for such never-ending stories, reasons that help consign them to the world of low art: why kill a cash cow if it can still be profitably milked? Though the idea of serial narrative can be traced back far enough to include *The Thousand and One Nights* (and, even further, the oral traditions the book evokes), its rise to prominence is clearly tied to the rise of the market; thus it should come as no surprise that, despite the serial's roots in both parts publication and the French feuilleton, the serial form now looks so fundamentally American. While other cultures have created serials of their own, it is the United States that has developed them most pervasively as forms of popular entertainment, particularly in the formats that are indisputably the invention of our culture industry: the soap opera, the situation comedy, and the superhero comic book. Countries around the world have adapted these serial forms with varying degrees of success, but nowhere is the serial's flirtation with timelessness and immortality more problematic than in Russia.

While serial narratives were not entirely absent during the Soviet period, they were a marginalized form. Ironically, since most serial narratives available before the advent of television were prerevolutionary foreign works published in Russian translation, serials existed in pre-Thaw Russia only to the extent that they were already complete: Sherlock Holmes is dead by definition. With the reintroduction of the profit motive, the market economy has provided a new stimulus for recurring characters and drawn-out stories. It is a truism that most of the recent cultural imports to post-Soviet Russia fit uneasily with the country's traditions, but I would argue that serial narrative is particularly alien to Russia, less because of subject matter

---

[8] "The reader of a novel actually does look for human beings from whom he derives the 'meaning of life.' Therefore, he must, no matter what, know in advance that he will share their experience of death. What draws the reader to the novel is the hope of warming his shivering life with a death he reads about" (Benjamin 100).

[9] Recall Henry James's ironic comment about such conclusions: "a distribution of the last of prizes, pensions, husbands, wives, babies" (Kermode 98).

than because of questions of form and philosophy. Frank Kermode argues that modern life is characterized by the "sense of an ending," the saturation of history and the everyday with an eschatology that now transcends the linear chronology that initially defined it. When the apocalypse becomes domesticated in the form of pervasive, never-resolved "crisis," the end of the world is now always with us. Never falsifiable and eternally postponed, the end is just around the corner, and the end times are always now: according to Kermode, the apocalypse is no longer imminent but immanent (112). Fiction simultaneously relies on and frustrates teleology by working the reader's generic expectations into the text: the reader eventually reaches the anticipated end, but satisfaction comes from the unexpected twists and turns (peripeteia) that prolong the journey.[10]

Kermode was speaking broadly about modern Western culture, yet his findings are particularly apt in the Soviet context. Soviet ideology consistently devalued the present in favor of both a mythic past (the triumphs of revolutionary movements; the heroic victory in World War II) and a radiant future (the triumph of communism just beyond the ever-receding horizon). The present became an impoverished field characterized by sacrifice, for which both the past and future served as justification. For a culture that had been eschatological long before communism elevated teleology to axiomatic status, what does it mean to adopt narratives whose purpose is to postpone the end as long as possible? Some of the most popular forms of serial narrative are the product of a culture that is notoriously obsessed with the present, eternal youth, and the denial of death, a culture that places a high premium on optimism. How can these forms be reconciled with a culture that has typically devalued the present, focused on long-term goals, and never shied away from individual mortality? How does Russia embrace the serial form without accepting the ideology behind it? All these questions rest on the connection between death and narrative: as Eco argues, serial fictions are a compromise allowing the heroes to move forward in time without being "consumed" by the narrative and hence brought closer to death. In post-Soviet Russia, the prominence of crime fiction as a virtually hegemonic genre allows the culture to confront this problem metonymically: preserving the primary characters for future stories while sacrificing the secondary figures both to the exigencies of the plot and as a kind of ritual offering, surrounding the near-immortal, virtually "unconsumable" hero with corpses at every turn.

---

[10] As Kermode writes, "Now peripeteia depends on our confidence of the end: it is a disconfirmation followed by a consonance, the interest of having our expectations falsified is obviously related to our wish to reach the discovery or recognition by an unexpected and instructive route" (82).

Previously...

Continuing sagas frequently engage in extended exposition in order to bring the audience up to speed; by the same token, any discussion of post-Soviet serials requires an examination of their native antecedents (both Soviet and prerevolutionary) as well as the foreign models on which they are based. Even more crucial is the question of definition: what exactly does "serial narrative" mean? Given its broadest possible interpretation, serial narrative could be any story that, in the telling, is parceled out in time and/or space: a single novel whose first appearance is stretched out over years by parts publication; a set of timeless stories about recurring characters that can be told and retold in virtually any sequence (like the wonder tale, or Mickey Mouse cartoons); a set of discrete novels, stories, comic books, plays, TV episodes, or films about recurring characters, in which sequence is followed but not absolutely essential, and which can be either finite (the miniseries) or open-ended (most American television comedies and dramas); or, at the far extreme, the North American soap opera, which, as opposed to its biggest worldwide competitor, the Latin American *telenovela*, hews as closely as possible to real, biographical time, stretching endless plotlines over the course of decades.[11] There are art forms or media that are even more timebound than the soap opera, but they veer so far in the direction of recording minutiae as to abandon all pretense to serialization and even narrative itself. Whether or not webcam sites are fascinating is a matter of individual taste, but they are so continuous as to be virtually timeless: they are chronicles rather than histories, and there are no episodes to miss or ongoing plotlines to follow. In serial narrative, it is the episode form that provides the artistry, shaping time and plot into digestible portions rather than simply recording them.

The defining feature of the type of serial narrative at issue here is *continuity*: the implicit recognition that events in one episode can have repercussions in the episodes that take place after it (and here I am using the term "episode" generically to refer to any discrete, freestanding part of a serial narrative). When continuity is at work, episodes are not entirely autonomous but interconnected, allowing for intricate plot entanglements and references to prior events. In serials, continuity runs the spectrum

---

[11] Thus Tania Modleski argues that the North American soap opera constructs a "fantasy of immortality" that is based on constant deferment: "truth for women is seen to lie not 'at the end of expectation,' but in expectation, not in the 'return to order,' but in (familial) disorder"(88; emphasis in the original).

from the enormously high and agglutinative to the virtually nonexistent. On the low end of the spectrum, both folklore and myth rely on forms of time that have little resemblance to our own quotidian world. Folktales often take place in an eternal present, where each tale is thoroughly isolated from all the others. If Baba Yaga is killed by Ivanushka the Fool in one story, that does not prevent her from trying to cook him for dinner in another, and the conventions of the genre condition us so that we find nothing remarkable about what would otherwise be considered paradoxical. Japanese and American monster movies of the 1950s and 1960s followed a similar Proppian schema: Godzilla may be a dangerous monster who is put to death at the end of one film, but he can be a force for good in the next one, with no reference to his defeat by the combined efforts of Tokyo's armed forces and aesthetically challenged giant robots. The children's cartoons of Disney and Hanna-Barbara have, at least until recently, typically taken place in a similar eternal present, although now this lack of continuity is such a cliché that ironic shows such as *The Simpsons* (where baby Maggie has been sucking wordlessly on her pacifier for well over a decade) or *South Park* (where the boys have advanced one grade level in eight years without failing their classes) routinely poke fun at the convention.[12] The other extreme in American popular culture is usually found in the worlds of fantasy, science fiction, and superhero comics, whose fans are notoriously obsessed with narrative coherence.[13]

None of the examples of post-Soviet serials discussed here will reach such an obsessive level of consistency, at least in part because until recently Russia's exposure to high-continuity extended forms had been limited. Russia, like Europe and the United States, had been accustomed to parts publication of novels in the nineteenth century, providing readers with suspense and cliffhangers that, with the advent of separate editions, have since been forgotten. As William Todd's work on the serialized version of *Anna Karenina* shows, Tolstoy's contemporary readership got to

[12] The low levels of continuity in genres and media typically associated with children become particularly apparent when one looks at the exceptions to the rule. Newspaper comic strips, for example, tend to treat their heroes as timeless and ageless; the decades-long series *Gasoline Alley* was noteworthy precisely because its protagonist, Skeezix, started out as a child and reached middle age in real time. More recently, Gary Trudeau synchronized his characters' biological clocks with historical time after a sabbatical from *Doonesbury* in the mid-1980s, while Lynne Johnston, in *For Better or for Worse*, has been allowing her characters to age for years.

[13] The letters pages in the back of comic books used to feature nitpicking screeds about whether issue 286 of *Fantastic Four* could be reconciled with what happened in issue 137 of *The Uncanny X-Men*, while the hard-core *Star Trek* fan's preoccupation with continuity descends into self-parody almost effortlessly. In other cases, continuity makes promises that the producers fail to deliver. Fans of the 1990s hit television show *The X-Files* could only throw up their hands at Chris Carter's muddled mythology by the time the series hobbled to a close.

watch Anna indulge in her passion for two years before her plotline and the train line so tragically intersected (160).[14] Given the demands and peculiarities of the book market in the USSR, such parts publication remained a far more significant component of the average reader's experience than it did in the United States. The primacy of the "thick journal" in Soviet times meant that, even as late as the 1980s, readers of both highbrow and mass fiction followed serialized novels as a matter of course.[15] But parts publication is of limited relevance; for the most part, the serial aspects of a serialized novel are ephemeral, disappearing without notice once the installments are collected. The intention is clearly to create a unified work, and thus the serial experience is almost impossible to reestablish once initial publication is completed: the work is seen only as a book. Granted, comics may be collected in trade paperback editions, and a season of a popular television show may be released as a DVD boxed set, but in both cases, the serial form is still dominant: the basic unit of narrative is still the episode (or issue), while the overall story is conceived of as an arc.[16] It is almost a question of platonic forms: a television season on DVD is still a collection of episodes, while a novel, even if it is first serialized, is almost always equated with a book.

Yet in late-nineteenth-century Russia, as literacy rates increased, the novels serialized in the boulevard press began to resemble the serial forms that dominate popular culture today. It can be argued that these novels were conceived in a much more serial fashion, with their agglutinative, picaresque plots and fast-paced composition and publication suggesting that the authors had only a vague sense as to how long their stories would actually go on. Their very length militates against conceiving them as books first and foremost: Anastassiia Verbitskaia's best-selling prerevolutionary potboiler *The Keys to Happiness* (1909–13) is too big to fit comfortably in

---

[14] Tolstoy also has several works featuring a character named Nekhliudov, most famously the novel *Resurrection*, but these works share no continuity and are not part of a recurring-character story cycle.

[15] In postwar America, the serialization of novels has been confined largely to the realm of "genre" magazines, particularly those devoted to fantasy and science fiction. Stephen King made headlines in 1996 for a publishing "innovation" that was actually a return to a very old practice, serializing his novel The Green Mile in six separate paperbacks over as many months, thus singlehandedly dominating half of the paperback fiction best-seller list.

[16] Here, too, economic changes can and do result in artistic decisions that shift the balance away from seriality: as the comics industry increases its reliance on the trade paperback format, readers of the monthly series have begun to complain that the individual issues no longer read as episodes in themselves and are therefore less satisfying. By contrast, the traditional plot recapitulation at the beginning of each issue becomes tedious when reprinted in book form, which is why DVD collections of television series usually do not include the half-minute "Previously, on . . ." segments that often introduce the episodes when they are first broadcast.

one volume, and the reader actually loses something by approaching it continuously rather than in episodes—it quickly becomes tiresome.[17]

In the two decades before the revolution, Russia experienced a minor boom in serial entertainments. In addition to these popular serialized sagas, Russians also fell in love with cycles of stories and novels centered on recurring characters, most notably in translation (the Pinkerton detectives, the adventures of Tarzan, Fantomas, and Sherlock Holmes). Such cycles are predicated on a level of continuity that is logical and consistent without being stifling or off-putting: the Sherlock Holmes of "The Hound of the Baskervilles" is the same detective who can be found in "The Red-Headed League," but one can read the stories in virtually any order with no appreciable loss. The "recurring character" model is the dominant one in Russia today, but it was something of a rarity during the Soviet years; under Brezhnev, a writer as popular and ideologically trustworthy as Julian Semenov had the leeway to create a series of novels featuring Isaev, secret agent extraordinaire, but one can also argue that the very paucity of recurring characters and ongoing story lines made Semenov stand out and contributed to the success of his work, on both the printed page and the silver screen.[18] Back in the 1920s, both hard-line Bolsheviks and fellow travelers were contemptuous of prerevolutionary penny dreadfuls, and the attempts to create "Red Pinkertons" were short-lived.

On the face of things, there is no reason that socialist realism, whose centrality to revolutionary culture had been proclaimed indisputable by the time of the 1934 Congress of the Union of Soviet Writers, had to be incompatible with serial narrative: it does not require a great stretch of the imagination to picture a Soviet superhero, professional spy, or dauntless soldier whose ongoing exploits could have both dazzled and edified the masses, yet this is clearly the road not taken.[19] Three explanations immediately suggest themselves: first, the aforementioned absence of a profit motive meant that

---

[17] The tensions between the reader's suspenseful expectations and the writer's work pace can be seen in the case of Alexander Kuprin's sensational The Pit, a serialized saga about a brothel. Kuprin took so long producing the final part that the conservative popular novelist Count Amori wrote the conclusion in his place, prompting the outraged author to compose his own ending and publish it as quickly as possible. See Boele (99–126) on the political and aesthetic motivations behind Count Amori's repeated fictional hijackings of other authors' works.

[18] One exception is the works of science-fiction writers Arkady and Boris Strugatsky, who, starting in the 1960s, recycled their characters through several novels and stories. One can, however, argue that the appeal of these stories was not what Eco describes as the lure of the "iterative scheme," in which one of the rewards of reading the latest Nero Wolfe story is being exposed once again to the detective's familiar and beloved "tics" (339). The Strugatskys' work is driven more by ideas and plots than by characters.

[19] Instead, the most famous recurring military heroes live in a mythic or folkloric time frame, such as Andrei Tvardovsky's soldier Vasily Terkin.

there was no compelling financial reason for keeping a fictional hero alive endlessly. Second, if one follows Katerina Clark's model of the socialist realist novel as the ritual enactment of the movement from spontaneity to consciousness, there is no room for sequels because the hero's story is so teleological that the end is final, even when the hero physically survives. Indeed, the problem of sequels resembles the problem of utopianism itself: what comes next? After the hero has achieved consciousness, he cannot lose it, and therefore his story is all told; otherwise, in narrative terms, we would be treading on dangerous Trotskyite territory: characters would be subject to something tantamount to permanent revolution.

Finally, Stalinist culture and its heroes were built on a mythic conception of time. Once the audience or readers learned of the accomplishments (and often death) of a particular hero, said hero achieved iconic status. The record-breaking Aleksei Stakhanov did not need to have multiple adventures in order to be inspiring; instead, his story could be told and retold, and his image would be disseminated widely in order to make people want to be like him. In a sense, the audience was supposed to provide the sequel to Stakhanov's story by adopting his role (and thereby possibly even serving as additional mythic models, supplementing the original Stakhanov himself). Soviet heroes disappeared into timelessness as soon as their stories were told, at least in part because so many of them were martyrs (Pavel Korchagin, Chapaev). Also, the very nature of their heroic deed was often such that while it could and should be repeated by the masses, it was unrepeatable by the heroes who originated it. Even if the story of Pavlik Morozov, who turned in his parents as anti-Soviet traitors, had not ended in his death, what was he supposed to do for an encore? Turn in his uncles and aunts? Repetition would transform this particular act of heroism into its own abject other, revealing the horror that lies just below the surface.

Even when the popular imagination resurrects them for subversive purposes, as in the endless anecdotes about Chapaev, Petia, and Ania the machine gunner, these heroes dwell in a continuity-free folkloric time: Chapaev never grows or changes; he is always already dead. One need not know all the previous Chapaev jokes to get the latest; at most, one need only know the canonical Chapaev story itself (usually the film rather than the novel). The few exceptional serials were so anomalous as to go virtually unrecognized: Babel's Red Cavalry cycle of short stories has enough internal consistency to require a continuity-based reading, and yet the structural paradoxes (it has three stories that can be read as the ending) suggest that the author's civil war saga could have gone on almost endlessly; as with

*M*A*S*H*, *Red Cavalry*'s serialization lasted longer than the military conflict it described.[20]

Serial narrative made a limited comeback in the post-Stalin era thanks to the rise of a new medium: television. As critics in a 1975 special issue of *Sovetskii ekran* noted, the miniseries, or "multi-episodic production," was the most "organic" form for the small screen, allowing viewers to fit small doses of story into their daily lives (qtd. in Prokhorova 12).[21] A 1967 survey of Leningrad TV viewers ranked miniseries as the third most popular form of televised entertainment, after feature films and KVN (competitive variety shows) (Powell 9–10, qtd. in Prokhorova 42). In her remarkable dissertation on the rise of the Soviet miniseries, Elena Prokhorova argues that this new form of mass entertainment required significant alterations to the socialist realist masterplot: "The miniseries diluted the structure of canonical narratives because of their fragmented, episodic structure, focus on dialogue, and multiple narrative lines" (41). Early Soviet miniseries were basically extended films that relied on predictable narrative tricks to delay the resolution of the plot, which, thanks to the choice of well-known historical events such as the civil war and World War II as backdrops, was always a foregone conclusion running few ideological risks (192, 203). Nonetheless, despite the politically correct framework, unhappy endings were still the rule: in keeping with the Soviet ethos of self-sacrifice, the heroes' success was often at great personal cost.[22]

As the miniseries genre developed, it began to privilege contemporary plots and police procedurals over epic sagas and war stories; the 1973 series *17 mgnovenii vesny* (*17 Moments of Spring*), directed by Tatiana Lioznova, was a notable exception. In 1979, *Mesto vstrechi izmenit' nel'zia* (*The Meeting Place Cannot Be Changed*), directed by Stanislav Govorukhin, became a cultural landmark, revisiting the postwar era and questioning Soviet conventions of justice and honor. Yet it cannot be said that the Soviet television industry fully capitalized on the miniseries' popularity. Given the frequency with which these beloved shows are invoked in the culture to this day, it is clear that they only whetted the public's appetite for ongoing stories. Indeed, only one Soviet program resembles the Western model of an ongoing series: *Sledstvie vedut znatoki* (*The Experts Are in Charge of the*

---

[20] For more on *Red Cavalry* and the serial form, see Borenstein, *Men without Women* (chap. 2).

[21] These miniseries coincided with the development of the Soviet *detektiv*, which did lead to the resumption of stories about recurring characters (Olcott).

[22] It can be argued that Russian viewers had long been conditioned to unhappy endings. See Iurii Tsivian's argument that early Russian filmgoers developed a taste for such endings because they identified death and loss with the values and aesthetics of high culture (7–8).

Investigation) ran from 1971 to 1989, but over that eighteen-year span its producers filmed only twenty-two episodes (Prokhorova 122).[23]

On the whole, the miniseries genre did little to change the temporality of Soviet popular entertainment. The case of *17 Moments of Spring* is particularly instructive; a runaway success when it was first broadcast in August 1973, this twelve-part drama became a staple of Soviet and post-Soviet reruns.[24] Over the years, those who missed it the first time (including many who would have been too young to follow the story) had frequent opportunities to view it later, but anecdotal evidence strongly suggests that viewers who had seen the program before happily watched it again. In reruns, *17 Moments of Spring* only reinforced the finite character of the Soviet serial, as it quickly became an extended but closed narrative whose outcome was always already known. That is, the paucity of Soviet serials, combined with the repeated rebroadcasting of the few that were available, made the miniseries historically discrete, providing no real threat of an open-ended present to challenge Soviet teleology. Such a challenge, if it had emerged, would have been a question of form rather than content: there could have been no question of a Brezhnev-era miniseries overtly disputing the current party line, but an open-ended narrative would have been disruptive on an entirely different level. Never-ending stories challenge not the nature of the goal but the insistence on the goal itself.

Instead, *17 Moments of Spring* parted ways with Soviet teleology in a much less radical form. The undercover Soviet agent Stirlitz (in reality Isaev, the hero of many of Semenov's novels), quickly joined Chapaev and company in the realm of Soviet jokelore. The miniseries lent itself particularly well to jokes, in no small part thanks to the hokiness of the omniscient, voiceover narration, but one can also look at Stirlitz's folkloric afterlife as an expression of the popular desire to get more of a beloved story, to hear further adventures. Moreover, this is despite the fact that related stories were available— about Isaev and not his more popular secret identity as Stirlitz.[25] Indeed, the eternal, iterative present of the Russian anecdote seems to be the default

[23] Sledstvie was also the only production that was entirely contemporary, showing cases that took place in the viewers' own environment (Prokhorova 123). An eight-episode sequel was broadcast on the First Channel in February of 2002: *The Experts Are in Charge of the Investigation: Ten Years Later* (Oushakine 431).

[24] In *Tot, kto znaet* (*The One Who Knows*, 2001), Aleksandra Marinina's love letter to the serial form, the premiere of *17 Moments of Spring* is one of the many cultural turning points the author references in order to give her historical chronicle a sense of verisimilitude: one of the novel's young boys is fortunate enough to be home to watch the entire series and spends the next several months retelling the story to his friends) (1: 109–12).

[25] Given that the story takes place in World War II, where the final outcome can never be in doubt, the miniseries is surprisingly open-ended: we never see Stirlitz die, be captured, or escape. If the story had been told by Hollywood and had been anywhere near as popular as it had been in the Soviet Union, it would probably have developed into a franchise.

mode for recurring characters, suggesting a traditional preference for archetypal figures that can be injected into virtually any situation rather than a
continuity-based, ongoing pseudobiography This preference even holds true
for characters based on real people who are still alive today, such as the
Leningrad/St. Petersburg Bohemian "Mit'ki" circle, whose authors have long
since become the protagonists of their own urban folklore; the characters live
timeless lives that are virtually independent of any events that may happen
to their real-life prototypes, not to mention any stories that have already
been told.

Such folkloric heroes, who face no threat at all of narrative consumption
by continuity and the passage of time, live in a world that does not function
according to Soviet teleology, but the thoroughly timeless nature of their
stories is a weak antithesis to the official time frame. Their eternal present
in no way resembles lived experience, while Soviet sagas do mimic biographical time. Only with the advent of perestroika would serial narrative
develop an open-ended chronology that would be antithetical to Soviet
teleological discourse.

Attack of the Clones

In the declining years of perestroika and the early days of independent Russian statehood, the mass audience was reintroduced to Western serial
forms, most notably on television. Three different species of continuing
drama grabbed the attention of the national viewership, each with its own
distinct temporality: the American soap opera *Santa Barbara* (1984–93),
the 1987 Mexican telenovela *Los ricos también lloran* (*Bogatye tozhe plachut*,
or *The Rich Also Cry*), and David Lynch's *Twin Peaks* (1990–91). Their virtual simultaneity is one of the many ironies of the post-Soviet flood of
Western cultural imports, especially since *Twin Peaks* was a deliberate parodic response to the soap opera genre, as witnessed by the inclusion of
Invitation to Love, the fake daytime drama the townspeople are always
watching on TV during the first season. *Santa Barbara*'s time frame was by
far the most jarring for Soviet television habits: announcers would inform
viewers that tonight they would be treated to, say, episode 1,249 of the
American serial *Santa Barbara*, as though they couldn't wait to get to the
last one (there were 2,137 episodes in all).[26]

---

[26] Viewers clearly had a different idea. When the RTR television network stopped broadcasting
Santa Barbara in November 1998 (the bank failures two months earlier left the network short of
funds), fans took to the streets to protest (Zolotov; Heller 71).

Though *Santa Barbara* had many fans, it was *Los ricos* that turned the country into soap opera addicts.[27] Not long after the show first aired, the network moved to broadcasting it twice a day so that the country's already hobbled economy wouldn't be devastated by people neglecting their jobs in order to watch the latest adventures of the downtrodden but spirited Marianna. Clocking in at a mere 248 episodes, *Los ricos* followed a time frame that is typical of the telenovela: the first half told the story of Marianna's life as a young woman, while the second skipped ahead almost two decades to include the romantic (and near-incestuous) entanglements of her son Beto. Like American soap operas, *Los ricos* was extended and padded—in one episode, several minutes of narrative dead time were filled by watching a femme fatale do her daily gymnastics routine—but it also hurtled forward in historical time at what by *General Hospital* standards would be breakneck speed, aging the characters overnight and thereby bringing them that much closer to death. Though the telenovela genre does not demand the deaths of its protagonists, neither does it depend entirely on their longevity. The characters are masks donned by the shows' biggest stars, whose show-business careers are the real overarching narrative. Thus Latin American soaps provide a closure that the North American variety assiduously avoids. If North American soap operas use continuity of plot to guarantee long-term revenue, the telenovela depends on a recycling of the actors rather than the characters: fans of Veronica Castro as Marianna are expected to tune into her next star vehicle, *Dikaia roza* (*Rosa Salvaje*, or *Wild Rose*).

Twin Peaks opened up a wealth of new narrative possibilities for American prime-time drama, paving the way for shows that were both quirky and self-consciously intellectual, as well as requiring fairly tight continuity. But for the Russian audience, *Twin Peaks,* despite its iconoclasm, is a case study in the strengths and pitfalls of the American serialized drama.[28] *Twin Peaks* introduced Russia to two important standard aspects of Western serialized broadcast narrative, both of which are functions of economics: outliving the premise, otherwise known as "jumping the shark" (was there really any need to continue the show after Laura Palmer's killer was identified?), and

---

[27] These Mexican soap operas were preceded on the Russian screen in 1989 by the international Brazilian hit *Escrava Izaura* (*The Slave Izaura*, or *Rabynia Izaura* in Russia) (1976). Though this show was extremely popular, Los Ricos is usually credited with beginning the post-Soviet soap opera boom.

[28] The impact of *Twin Peaks* may be seen in the most unexpected places: in Maks Frai's "Chronicles of Echo" fantasy series, when Frai returns to the otherdimensional land of Ekho from an extended sojourn in our world, he brings back his video library and his ex-girlfriend's VCR to introduce film and television to a land that has never seen it. His boss immediately takes several days off from work so that he can watch *Twin Peaks* nonstop (*Volontery* 593).

premature cancellation (what happened to Agent Cooper and Bob? Will Annie every be rescued?).[29] The fact that *Twin Peaks* was prey to such seemingly opposite vices makes it all the more exemplary: the viewer is frustrated both by the less convincing later plotlines and by their indefinite suspension. The audience is left wanting more but not necessarily convinced that more would be all that satisfying. *Twin Peaks* also shows why the reflexive episode counting of the Russian *Santa Barbara* announcer is so inappropriate: at least until recently, ending an American serial has been tantamount to an admission of failure.[30] As long as a show remains popular, artistic reasons alone do not usually warrant cancellation.[31] This is not the case with Latin American and European models and certainly not the case with post-Soviet Russian serials, where endings are consummations devoutly to be wished.

Nonetheless, the popularity of *Twin Peaks* makes sense when the show is examined in the context of the Russian serials that would follow it. While the tone and quality of Lynch's drama had arguably little effect on post-Soviet television and fiction, the genre-crossing *Twin Peaks* gave Russian audiences a credible backdrop for the interpersonal melodramas that drive soap opera narrative. Despite the overwhelming popularity of foreign-made soap operas and romance novels in the Russian Federation, the first post-Soviet decade saw only tentative steps toward russifying romance: the domestically produced soap *Melochi zhizni* (*The Little Things in Life*) (1992–95) was far from a runaway hit, while the flood of cheap translations of Harlequin romances was virtually uninterrupted by Russian names. *Twin Peaks*, which insisted on highlighting its soap opera origins during the same scenes that featured violence and horror (again we recall the TV in the background showing "Farewell to Love"), showed that romantic drama could become believable in Russia as long as it took place against a backdrop of murder

[29] *Twin Peaks* also played its part in a growing segment of the Russian book industry: the quick TV/movie tie-in. All of the fiction related to *Twin Peaks* published officially in the United States made an immediate appearance in unlicensed Russian translation (*The Secret Diary of Laura Palmer*, among others).

[30] Soon enough, Russian audiences would become familiar with the sorrows of cancellation in something closer to real time, such as when the Fox TV show *The Pretender* was canceled in the States while viewers in Russia were still watching the second season.

[31] In America, the situation has begun to change, with a growing recognition that a show might be better off bowing out while it is still good. In adventure/science-fiction dramas, *Star Trek: The Next Generation* made television history when its producers chose to end the popular show with its seventh season, thereby inadvertently setting up the seven-year life cycle as the standard for the genre (*Star Trek: Voyager, Star Trek: Deep Space Nine,* and *Buffy the Vampire Slayer* all followed the show's lead; fans experienced the 2004 cancellation of *Buffy's* spin-off *Angel* at the end of its fifth season as a betrayal, at least in part because they had been conditioned to the seven-year life span). Economically, a show need last only five seasons to be profitable in syndicated reruns.

and crime.[32] It was easier to suspend disbelief for the mysticism of *Twin Peaks* than for the carefree wealth and privilege of daytime drama.[33]

Return of the Native

When post-Soviet Russia began producing its own serials, it clearly picked and chose from the available models, borrowing only what seemed to resonate most with local narrative traditions and perceived audience expectations.[34] For the most part, the open-ended model of the American soap opera was avoided, though the soap-opera inspired 1994 advertising campaign for the MMM pyramid scheme was a notable exception.[35] Economic realities certainly conditioned this choice, since scarce funding means that one can hardly count on a show lasting for years.[36] But with the exception of the aforementioned *Santa Barbara*, even the American serial narratives broadcast in the early post-Soviet days were anomalous in their native context: in the realm of science fiction, for example, instead of the relentlessly optimistic, open-ended *Star Trek*, Russian viewers were treated to *Babylon 5*, a series whose overall, five-year narrative arc was planned from start to finish and whose dominant mode was decidedly tragic (interstellar civilization is saved, but nearly every character is trapped by a miserable fate).[37] Russian serial narratives borrowed more heavily from the experience of such tragic, downbeat, and—most important—*finite* series. Pessimistic storytelling is unusual for American popular culture, while in Russia, the Anglicism *kheppi-end* is routinely used to ridicule Hollywood's insistence on positive outcomes. American audiences are conditioned to suspend disbelief and even demand a positive resolution to the plot, whereas Russian audiences, for whom the enforced optimism of the Stalin years was decidedly

---

[32] This point has also been made by David MacFadyen, who notes the prominence of romantic themes and love stories in Russian crime drama: "It had to involve criminals, said one journalist, since nobody would believe a tale of honest policemen and their love-lives."

[33] It is also possible that the travails of wealthy people in foreign countries could inspire empathy, while rich Russians could only be the objects of resentment and envy. Pesmen notes a long-standing hostility toward those who "live better than others" (142).

[34] One popular American television genre that went nowhere on the Russian airwaves was the sitcom. Despite the popularity of shows such as *Friends* and *Grace Under Fire*, the few attempts at developing Russian sitcoms in the 1990s were commercial and critical failures (Heller 60–72).

[35] See Borenstein, "Public Offerings: MMM and the Marketing of Melodrama."

[36] Indeed, domestically created serial narrative in the 1990s was much more a phenomenon of print than of television; it was only after the banking crisis of August 1998 that television companies found it cheaper to produce shows than to import them (MacFadyen).

[37] Even though an individual *Star Trek* series eventually ended, it was usually replaced by another entry in the franchise. Taken together, the five live-action *Star Trek* series consist of 686 episodes.

anomalous, have come to equate misery, failure, and suffering with truth value. Heroes can succeed, and good can even triumph over evil now and then, but only at great cost: a Russian happy ending has to be bittersweet.

The key to this tragic tonality is, as I suggested at the beginning of this chapter, death. Open-ended American serials distrust both death and endings, relying on an optimism implying that our televised friends will never leave us and our television producers' profits will never cease (the common practice of reruns only adds to this sense of immortality). Serial storytelling easily lends itself to metaphors of both sex and death, teasing the audience to increase pleasure and forestalling an ending to a narrative that is tantamount to the characters' demise. *The Thousand and One Nights* makes both connections explicit, as Scheherazade resorts to nightly cliffhangers in order to sustain her lover's interest and arousal and oblige him to refrain from beheading her at least long enough to find out how the story ends.[38] Contemporary serial narrative in the West also flirts with death (thus keeping us on the edge of our seats) but avoids it as much as possible (the story must go on). Courting and avoiding death are most easily accomplished in the realm of fantasy and science fiction, where characters' lives can be prolonged indefinitely almost as a matter of course.[39] Superhero comics, which provide the illusion of the passage of time while keeping characters young for decades, handle the death question through the motif of resurrection, or, as comics fans call it, the "revolving door of death": if a member of the X-Men hasn't died and come back at least twice by now, she hasn't been really trying. Again, the reasons are primarily economic: as Disney's success in extending copyrights shows, life is short, but corporate trademarks may well be eternal.

If, at least until recently, Russian storytelling conventions have not been so thoroughly conditioned by the profit motive, and if open-ended narrative is a poor fit with a tragic, fatalistic outlook, how do contemporary Russian serials reconcile this conflict? Russian serials make their own compromise with death, one that is facilitated by the fact that the dominant themes for Russian entertainment today are violence and crime. Bakhtin argues that the novel as master genre of the modern era "novelized" other genres (such

[38] Her stories are always told after their nightly lovemaking, reinforcing the evident connection between storytelling and sexuality: her storytelling technique parallels female rather than male sexuality (serial climaxes).

[39] The motif of extended longevity and even immortality is so entrenched in science fiction and fantasy that it often functions as an aside in plots with very different concerns, or as an easily accepted plot device allowing for the story to encompass an extrahuman time frame while still following the same characters. Recent examples include Nancy Kress's trilogy about the Sleepless, which began with *Beggars in Spain*, and Kim Stanley Robinson's acclaimed Mars trilogy, which began with *Red Mars*; older examples include Frank Herbert's Dune series).

as lyric poetry and drama); by the same token, in today's Russia, the supreme status of crime fiction, an offshoot of chernukha, is so unassailable that it colonizes the other genres, criminalizing them, as it were: even fantasy and science-fiction stories tend to have a "police procedural" framework, solving supernatural, mystical, or high-tech crimes (as in Luk'ianenko's *Night Watch* series or Maks Frai's ten-volume *Chronicles of Ekho*). The combination of chernukha and serial narrative inevitably leads to high body counts. When we looked briefly at socialist realism, we saw that the iterative structure of the serial was incompatible with the teleological drive of official Soviet art; yet it is this very insistence on repetition that makes the serial and chernukha such a perfect fit. Serial narrative provides a comfortable home for the serial killer. What could be more dismal and horrifying then the story of a bloody, violent murder? An endless story where each gruesome killing is followed by an even more appalling atrocity. The 1990s Russian serial is almost Aztec in its demand for blood (if not for virgins), exchanging teleology and eschatology for an open-ended present that is covered in the blood that otherwise would have been reserved for the apocalypse.

Russian crime narrative has two main models for serialization: first is the cycle of novels, films, or television episodes about recurring central characters, while the second is the creation of a small fictional world in which continuity is predicated on a shared setting and shared action rather than on an ever-present primary character. In each case, a thanatropic drive is both postponed and satisfied, serving up no small share of victims while holding out the possibility of a sequel. In the *detektiv* (murder mystery) genre, the most popular example of the recurring-character type is Aleksandra Marinina's dozens of novels featuring police detective Nastia Kamenskaia. The central recurring figure in the other main crime genre, the *boevik* (action/adventure tale) is Viktor Dotsenko's *Beshenyi* ("Mad Dog"), who has starred in twenty novels so far.[40] The Mad Dog books are exemplary when it comes to the question of death, since after the first novel, *Srok dlia Beshenogo* (*Mad Dog in Prison*), a pattern is quickly established allowing for death to be ever-present while still leaving the cycle open-ended. Mad Dog begins nearly every novel recovering from the physical and psychological traumas inflicted on him in the previous story. Yet despite the sadistic and grotesque murders that punctuate every Dotsenko novel, one senses an unsatisfied demand for the hero's own demise. Mad Dog undergoes clinical death at the beginning of the second novel, *Tridtsatogo—unichtozhit'!* (*Number Thirty Must Be*

[40] As Marinina and Dotsenko are the focal points of the next two chapters, discussion about them here will be brief.

Destroyed!), only to be resurrected by his Tibetan teacher. A few novels later, Mad Dog's secret service bosses decide to stage their agent's death, and Savelii Govorkov (Mad Dog's real name) is given a hero's funeral, while Mad Dog himself undergoes plastic surgery and is given a new name (Sergei Manuilov) to go with his new face. By 1999, Mad Dog faced a different kind of extinction: cancellation. In *Voina Beshenogo* (*Mad Dog's War*), Dotsenko included a postscript saying that his publishers had the feeling that the public was tired of his hero and begged his readers to initiate a letter campaign to save Mad Dog from his economic enemies. Apparently, the appeal worked, since *Mad Dog's War* was only the eleventh entry in this continuing series, but Mad Dog's near-death experiences continue to be an essential feature in this ongoing series. He is lost on a desert island and presumed dead, essentially missing in action for an entire novel, before he is rescued by his disciple and potential replacement, the eponymous *Uchenik Beshenogo* (*Mad Dog's Pupil*), in a book called *Mad Dog Lives!* (*Beshenyi zhiv!*).

Other authors hedge their bets against death through the creation of their own fictional worlds. This need not require the grand, epic scale of Tolkien, nor does it have to have anything to do with fantasy and science fiction (although Maks Frai, Mariia Semenova, Nik Perumov, and Luk'ianenko exploit the concept of the fantastic fictional world quite successfully). In crime serials, it can be a matter of creating a fictional city, as is the case with Aleksandr Bushkov's *Wolves* series, his *Mad Bitch* novels (*Beshennaia*), and his tales of the Piranha, all of which take place in the imaginary provincial town of Shantarsk.[41] More provocative are projects in which the city is real enough, but the events and characters that populate it constitute a parallel, fictional world with its own continuity, which shadows real life. Here the prime example is the extremely popular series of novels that became an even more successful set of televised miniseries: Andrei Konstantinov's multivolume *Banditskii Peterburg* (*Bandit Petersburg*).

Repeat Offenders: *Bandit Petersburg*

Everything about *Bandit Petersburg* straddles the line between real life and fiction, starting with the title. Konstantinov's first book-length project was a sprawling, nonfictional study of the same name, covering three centuries

---

[41] Imaginary worlds are Bushkov's specialty, as he writes both *boeviki* and science fiction. Bushkov is the author of a popular series of novels about Stanislav Svarog, a late-twentieth-century Russian paratrooper whose last name just happens to be that of an ancient Slavic pagan God. Svarog's adventures take place in a pseudomedieval, parallel future world.

of crime in the former capital.[42] When he turned to fiction, the name followed him and quickly became the umbrella title for a series of novels whose count reaches anywhere from nine to fifteen, depending on the criteria for inclusion. Konstantinov adopts a shocking, disruptive strategy for a serial, one that creates an unusual level of suspense: he is not at all shy about killing off his protagonists. Hence the hero of the first two novels, Sergei Chelishchev, who one would assume is the protagonist, dies at the very end of *Sud'ia* (*The Judge*), along with nearly every other character we might have cared about along the way. A few do remain alive, however, and the narrative focus shifts to them. The third novel inexplicably goes back a decade in time, to describe the Middle Eastern adventures of Sergei's old friend, the future journalist Andrei Obnorskii-Seregin (to whom Chelishchev gives important documents right before his death). The Petersburg plot is resumed in book four, where Andrei is now clearly the hero.[43]

From this point on, Seregin will follow a pattern much like Mad Dog's: near death, followed by recovery, followed by near death. But Konstantinov and his subsequent coauthor, Aleksandr Novikov exploit the remaining ensemble cast both to give the reader a break from Seregin, or perhaps give Seregin a respite from the tortures to which the authors put him, and also to develop long-term characters who will eventually die in later episodes. Toward the end of the fourth novel, *Vor* (*The Thief*), a woman named Lida, who has been caught up in a very complicated set of criminal machinations, asks him to explain what is going on, but he refuses, saying: "Behind my

---

[42] Konstantinov's other documentary projects include Corrupt Petersburg, *Corrupt Petersburg 2*, and *Swindler's Petersburg (2000)* (Baraban 168). His first book, The Criminal World of Russia (1992) was coauthored by the Swedish author Malcolm Dickselius and is clearly the model for the joint project Seregin developed with his Swedish colleagues in the sixth novel, Vydumshchik (The Fabricator).

[43] When transformed into a set of six televised miniseries (roughly thirty hours of viewing pleasure), *Bandit Petersburg* becomes a relatively straightforward story, introducing its overall hero (the journalist Seregin) and virtually unbeatable villain (Antibiotic) in the first series (*Baron*), based on Konstantinov's fourth novel. Chelishchev, the initial protagonist of the novels, only arrives on the scene in the second series, *Advokat* (*The Attorney*). As a result, his death on screen is less jarring; Chelishchev's death in the books might have called the future of the entire project into question, but the miniseries never relied on him in the first place. The remaining three series detail the elaborate plot by Seregin, Katia, and, eventually, a new hero (the disgraced policeman Zverev) to put an end to Antibiotic's criminal empire. Only some of the stubbornly slow temporality of the novels is retained in the films, largely in the titles: Antibiotic's "fall," announced halfway through the sequences of miniseries, is only truly accomplished in the final episodes. The films' producers simplify the often contradictory nomenclature used by the books as they moved from publisher to publisher, along the way jettisoning or condensing all the plotlines that take the heroes far from the title city. In the successful adaptation of *Bandit Petersburg* to television, the producers turned it into something with a much greater resemblance to a conventional serial.

story, there's death" (405).[44] His statement is true on every level, as his story is lethal to nearly everyone except the readers. In a typical example of Konstantinov's overkill, the last woman to whom Seregin tells his story dies a few pages later in an explosion but only after she has been burned with a cigarette and doused with gasoline. Indeed, it could be argued that the primary focus of these books is not the ultimately disposable heroes but the seemingly undefeatable villain, nicknamed "Antibiotic," who continues to cling to power over the course of eight novels despite the heroes' best efforts.

Designating the most powerful criminal boss in the city "Antibiotic" inverts the standard political metaphors of a healthy society. From the time of Plato's *Republic*, the equation of the city with the human body has been a commonplace, further facilitated by the notion of the body politic. Campaigns against moral, economic, and culture corruption, in Russia and elsewhere, are easily couched in terms of pernicious disease and harsh remedies (purges). In *Bandit Petersburg*, Antibiotic marshals the forces of social pathology against the attempts to institute a noncriminal rule of law; the "bacteria" he so handily destroys are the novels' heroes. Govorov's nickname is by no means a misnomer: Antibiotic is the strong medicine that keeps Bandit Petersburg functioning, protecting it from the parasitic forces of law and justice that might otherwise compromise its immune system. Antibiotic is proof against hope, the guarantee that any utopian talk of cleaning up the streets will remain mere words. Antibiotic ensures the long-term survival of Bandit Petersburg, never failing to supply the steady stream of corpses that the series requires.

The fact that so many different books and films (and, eventually, even authors) find a home for themselves under the "Bandit Petersburg" rubric suggests that the organizing principle at work adds an extra dimension to the concept of the serial. The umbrella title is more than a mere declaration of the topic; rather, it is a full-fledged chronotope: Bandit Petersburg identifies a particular representation of space and time. Konstantinov's initial nonfiction study is devoted to a centuries-long history of St. Petersburg crime, but the larger series that it inaugurates inevitably partakes of an equally well-established cultural tradition, that of the "Petersburg myth."[45] Established by imperial fiat in total disregard for climate, the environment, and human life, Peter's capital has long been represented as an unreal city,

[44] The television version drives this point further home. Seregin tells Lida that he is cursed: "There is death on me." The miniseries ends with a drunken Seregin standing on a bridge, recalling all the people who have died because of him (shown to the viewers in a montage sequence).

[45] Jennifer Ryan Tishler argues that St. Petersburg's reputation as the "criminal capital" relies at least as much on the Petersburg myth as it does on actual (and dismal) crime statistics (127–29).

at once hyperrational in its attempt to overlay a distinctly un-Russian urban grid over the swampy, chaotic landscape and [phantasmagorical thanks to the non-Euclidean geographies that were the result.] By the mid-nineteenth century, Nikolai Gogol had firmly established Petersburg as a city of magic and danger, of deception and allure, exemplified by the treacherous main thoroughfare, Nevsky Prospekt.

On the face of things, *Bandit Petersburg* is entirely different: beautiful women are not in danger of being swept away in the wind, and imperial statues stubbornly fail to come to life. Yet Konstantinov's Petersburg is no less uncanny than Gogol's: this black hole of criminality warps its fictional space-time continuum, creating a world in which ultimately everything depends on, results from, and even facilitates crime. Crime structures both space and time in *Bandit Petersburg*, facilitating abrupt shifts to the past and even drastic changes in locale but somehow resulting in an essential unity of action. *Bandit Petersburg* is so powerful that it can even encompass a story set in Africa during the last years of the Soviet regime because the intrigues and characters introduced there inevitably make their way back to Russia's criminal mecca.[46] *Bandit Petersburg* is a complex, apparently unending set of disparate narrative units, all interconnected in space and time even as they defy conventional expectations about sequence and location. If Konstantinov's project is successful, then he owes it all to crime. Konstantinov has crossbred the myth of Petersburg with the myth of Chicago (still frozen in the Russian consciousness as the land of Al Capone): both are "second cities" that are the capitals of crime, and both can dominate a narrative even at a distance. The gangster period piece *The Road to Perdition* is all about Chicago, even when the protagonists are traveling across the country: the town of Perdition is their ostensible destination, but Chicago was a metaphorical hell even before they left it. By the same token, all criminal roads lead to Bandit Petersburg.

In the preface to the 2001 edition of the 1992 documentary study that lent its name to the bulk of Konstantinov's subsequent fictional work, the author is at great pains to insist that he is not slandering his beloved city: "[W]hen I write the book's name—'Bandit Petersburg'—of course this doesn't meant that I think all of Piter is criminal (*banditskii*). I'm writing about only one sphere that does, unfortunately, exist in my city" (5). In the 1998 afterword, Konstantinov insists that he is not a pessimist: "Once I wrote that the darker it gets, the sooner the inevitable dawn will come. At the same

---

[46] Considering the Russian verbal habit of using Africa as an example of the most extreme antithesis to everyday life ("even in Africa"), the fact that *Bandit Petersburg* can be expanded to include African locales suggests that nothing falls out of the criminal capital's scope (Pesmen 285).

time, I did not imagine that the night would turn out to be so long and dark. Nonetheless, we have to grit our teeth, keep our heads up, and work. And then the dawn we've been waiting for will have to come"(537). There is something disingenuous about this assertion of optimism, as is his ritual claim in the preface that he hopes the book will be "useful" rather than simply "entertainment" (6). The intervening five hundred pages, with their chronicles of three hundred years of organized crime in the country's northern capital, are a litany of murder, theft, and extortion that, like the photograph of a bloody corpse in the middle of the book, clearly cater to an appetite for shocking details. The book's cover features the photograph that embodies the book's contradictions. The man pictured may well be taking Konstantinov's inspirational advice: he is gritting his teeth and holding his head high, but he is also pointing a gun directly at the reader. Whatever messages the book might be transmitting, "Don't panic" is certainly not among them.

The Antibiotic arc of Bandit Petersburg novels is insistent on imminent (and perhaps immanent) death and is so attached to the replaceability of its characters that it suggests a cross between Propp and Lacan. Like the almost interchangeable characters in Russian fairy tales, the heroes and villains of *Bandit Petersburg* can have contradictory functions from one story to the next.[47] The central female character, Katia, fits this pattern best. Her frequent betrayals of the men in her life at first look like a character flaw, but by the seventh book they resemble a reliable alternation of narrative tropes: first Katia (re)creates her man, whether helping Chelishchev transform himself into a respectable gangster through the acquisition of the requisite wardrobe,[48] or nursing a nearly broken Seregin back to health; then she abandons them (in the first case, at Chelishchev's own request). By the same token, all the relationships that revolve around Katia are love triangles involving two male rivals, each of whom at times claims pride of place in her bed. Ultimately the rivalries are less personal than they are positional: who will play the paternal role in Katia's conjugal bed? The *Bandit Petersburg* books are variations on a constant theme of loss and betrayal.

It is not the case that *Bandit Petersburg* has no continuity—far from it, the events of a given installment can and do have various repercussions for

---

[47] *Bandit Petersburg* also relies on specific character types that can be called on to play a predictable plot function. For example, the novels feature several examples of the commonplace figure in police narrative, the "one good cop" (Kudasov, Markov), but usually only one of them is active at a given time.

[48] Elena Baraban notes that Chelishchev's mobster makeover, which is even more dramatic on television than it is in the novel, is a matter of acquiring yet another professional "uniform," replacing the one he previously wore at the prosecutor's office (191–92).

Figure 4: Cover of Andrei Konstantinov's *Bandit Petersburg.*

the rest of the cycle. Yet these repercussions are just as likely to move backward as to go forward, retroactively affecting parts of the story with which we are already familiar.[49] Katia's love triangles are emblematic of the novels'

[49] The repeated excursions into the past in order to expand upon or revised the backstory, or even the plot itself, employ narrative techniques that Morson calls "sideshadowing" and "backshadowing." Their extensive use by Konstantinov and Novikov puts *Banditskii Peterburg* in the company of particular types of popular narrative that rely on such games with time: the soap opera, which brings back dead characters with predictable frequency, and the superhero comic book, which often employs retroactive continuity—or "retconning"—to bring past events in line with the present.

sticky temporality, which is almost as iterative as that of Propp's fairy tales. Like the proverbial criminal, *Bandit Petersburg* always returns to the scene of the crime. If we accept that *Bandit Petersburg* begins with its first published fictional installment, *Advokat* (*The Attorney*) (rather than some of the subsequent volumes that serve as prequels), a remarkably regressive pattern becomes clear. The preface to the novel begins in a cemetery with a death that proves to be figurative rather than actual: Sergei Chelishchev and Oleg Zvantsev drink to the memory of Katia Shmeleva, who had been the center of an intensely passionate but unconsummated three-way friendship. Katia has betrayed them both by marrying an unknown third man and leaving Petersburg behind. Sexual betrayal is thus immediately framed in terms of death, and when the plot itself begins, years later, the cemetery framework is mirrored by the deaths of Chelishchev's parents in the first chapter. Chelishchev, now a divorced police detective, is confronted with a perverse juxtaposition of the crime scene and the primal scene: his father lies dead in the doorway, while his mother's throat has been slit in the bedroom. Thus the two central triangles in Chelishchev's life are disrupted in the first twenty-five pages of the novel, and the remainder of the first two books is tantamount to a quest to restore the irrevocably broken.[50] Chelishchev's desire for vengeance is frustrated by a thoroughly corrupt police force, leading him to the paradoxical resolution that the only way he can destroy the criminal band responsible for his parents' death is to infiltrate it. For all intents and purposes, he must become a criminal to fight crime.

Chelishchev joins the "mafia" because of the loss of the two people closest to him in the world, but he also regains the other two people whom he had written off so long ago. Both Katia and Oleg also work for Antibiotic. Where Katia had been metaphorically dead to Chelishchev, Oleg's physical demise in Afghanistan had been publicly announced long ago. The resumption of their triangle inaugurates a motif that will run through the rest of the *Bandit Petersburg* novels, in that most of the characters are leading essentially posthumous lives.[51] Chelishchev learns that Katia had been rescued by Oleg after her husband, a corrupt businessman, had been killed by a rival gang. But even the husband's death proves to be no more permanent than Oleg's: the readers discover that her husband, Vadim, had escaped to

[50] In the miniseries, when Seregin sits in his parents' kitchen during the days after their funeral, he looks out his window and wistfully recalls Oleg and Katia, rather than his father and mother.

[51] Both Katia and her first husband are at times presumed dead, living abroad under assumed names and Israel passports. Seregin is left for dead on a number of occasions, while his sojourn in a prison camp during the ninth novel, *The Prisoner* (*Arestant*), and subsequent release in the tenth, *Cop* (*Ment*), tap into a narrative of imprisonment and resurrection that dates at least as far back as Dostoevsky's *Zapiski iz mertvogo doma* (*Notes from the House of the Dead*).

Europe years later with the proverbial "Communist Party gold." In terms of the overarching plot, Vadim's retroactive survival was justified by the new adventures it brought to the main heroes. Vadim himself is quickly killed again, a death that is presumed to be permanent.[52] Such posthumous lives have a complicated effect on the overall narrative, one that recalls the tension inherent in serial storytelling. The frequency with which characters come back from the dead suggests the possibility of, if not immortality, then at the least the restoration of something considered irretrievably lost. The key plot point of the novel *The Thief* and the film *Baron* is thematically crucial here: the painting that has been stolen is either Rembrandt's *Aegina* or an excellent copy, but in either case, both the original and the copy are at least in part the work of a master restorer, who saved the painting after it was nearly destroyed with acid by a mentally unbalanced man in 1985.[53] The fate of Rembrandt's painting is evocative of the theme of loss that pervades so much post-Soviet culture; in this case, the national treasure that could be stolen from the people is neither mineral resources nor beautiful women but a work of art of foreign provenance, which itself is suggestive of St. Petersburg's own status as a preserved national treasure built on decidedly foreign lines.[54] But by the same token, the "resurrected" characters, like the restored paintings, are no longer exactly themselves. They change careers (Seregin, Chelishchev) and names (Seregin, Vadim, Katia), they are arrested and released (Seregin, Oleg, Katia, and Antibiotic), and they even gain a new perspective on life: Antibiotic finds religion, however hypocritically, while Seregin, after one of his many "deaths" fails to take, develops limited psychic powers that alert him when he or his friends are in danger.

On the other hand, the afterlives in *Bandit Petersburg* ultimately reinforce a sense of impermanence, since most of the characters who are resurrected are eventually killed again. While the characters' return from the dead might be reassuring, the fact that their subsequent deaths are usually more gruesome (and more permanent) suggests a bloodthirsty repetition compulsion. *Bandit Petersburg* uses and alters the serial format in order to put the characters through hell. If there is a kind of immortality at work, it

---

[52] Vadim's second death, unlike the first one, takes place "on camera." In *Bandit Petersburg*, characters whose deaths are portrayed for the reader rather than recounted secondhand tend to stay dead.

[53] Konstantinov's point of departure is a real event, but the defaced Rembrandt painting is called *Danae*, not *Aegina*. Rembrandt's *Danae* did inspire Jean-Baptiste Greuze's *Aegina*, which depicts another of the many conquests Zeus/Jupiter made in nonhuman form. Presumably, this substitution allows the author to be more cavalier with the painting's final fate (it is destroyed in an explosion).

[54] The replacement of an original with a copy can also be tied into one of *The Thief*'s running themes, the degradation of the criminal world as the old-style thieves are replaced by amoral, bloodthirsty bandits. This topic is investigated more thoroughly in chapter 7.

is the immortality of damnation: like Prometheus, condemned to have his liver eaten by an eagle each time it grows back, Konstantinov's heroes endure so much torment that permanent death becomes welcome. Even in the cases of the episodic characters, it is not enough that they are simply murdered by criminals; again and again, they are brutally tortured, dismembered, and (in the case of the women) sodomized and raped. Most of the prominent characters in *Bandit Petersburg* have doubles, who lead parallel lives or take over for each other after one dies. But even here, the result is rarely a matter of long-term survival—Seregin is the only one who really does get the chance to finish what his dead friend began)—but rather an excess of death. *The Thief/Baron* features two women named Irina, one of whom was the Baron's common-law wife; Seregin, in searching for clues about the missing Rembrandt painting, finds the wrong Irina, accidentally leading Antibiotic's henchmen to her. She is subsequently beaten, burned with cigarettes, raped, and finally nailed to a piano keyboard by her hands. But the real Irina does not survive much longer: she dies in an explosion at the story's end.

The entire cycle of *Bandit Petersburg* is driven by such doubling, substitution, and overkill; with grim consistency, the hopes raised by the double's existence (an excess of life) are dashed through murderous repetition (an excess of death).[55] Again, the novels' initial triangles are instructive, since they so successfully reproduce themselves through a substitution facilitated by doubling: the Chelishchev-Katia-Oleg triangle, renewed after Vadim's apparent death, relies on an interchangeability between the two men that is based on their physical and psychological complementarity. It is Oleg who first gets the nickname "Attorney," even though Chelishchev is the one with the legal education; once both men share the criminal limelight, the dark-haired one becomes "Black Attorney," while the fair-haired one becomes "White Attorney." In Russian, as used here by Konstantinov, these terms suggest not race but chess, with the attorneys as analogues to bishops or rooks, protecting the all-important queen (Katia, naturally). By the end of *The Judge*, Katia is pregnant, with both men claiming, if not biological paternity, then equal concern for the life of Katia and her children (Katia is carrying Chelishchev's baby, but she has also secretly given birth to Oleg's son years before). Hence the two old friends die together in a hail of gunfire, content that their lover and offspring will survive: they can expect to be replaced by yet another triangle but this time one based on biological ties.

---

[55] The television adaptation of *Bandit Petersburg* adds another layer of doubling: over the course of six miniseries, Katia is played by three different actresses (although, in a departure from the novels, the "Katia" of *The Fall of Antibiotic* is revealed as an impostor in *The Detainee*).

Katia and her two children become an inverted replica of the family triangle shattered by the murder of Chelishchev's parents, evoking the connection between seriality and reproduction that is at the heart of a different kind of serial narrative, the family saga.

Katia's story is far from over, however, and eventually she gets involved with Seregin, another double for both Chelishchev and Oleg. With Chelishchev's death, the narrative continues metonymically, passed along to Seregin together with the incriminating dossier Chelishchev has complied on Antibiotic. Seregin is the new Chelishchev, for it is he who is now Antibiotic's sworn enemy, but Seregin is also the new Oleg—typically for *Bandit Petersburg*, Chelishchev, in addition to Oleg, had a spare long-lost boyhood friend (Seregin) to whom he could turn in his hour of need.[56] When Seregin joins forces with Katia to take revenge on Antibiotic and the two become lovers, he is taking both Oleg's and Chelishchev's places. Such doubling and replaceability combined with such a high mortality rate are reminiscent of the temporality and continuity of the Soviet fiction and propaganda about World War II: when one comrade falls, he is never entirely dead, since another warrior takes up his weapon and continues the fight (Borenstein, *Tekst kak mashina smerti*). But *Bandit Petersburg* inverts this heroic temporality, indirectly suggesting the limits of the popular metaphor of a "war on crime." The soldier's immortality is the function of the war's teleology, where future victory justifies present-day sacrifice, but in *Bandit Petersburg*, a final victory is impossible.

Cliffhanger

In the absence of happy resolutions to story lines involving rape, torture, and murder, serial narrative becomes one of the many late- and post-Soviet cultural products involved in an endless loop of negativity and pessimism, feeding the consumer a steady diet of misery that sits well with a pervasive sense of "complete disintegration" (*polnaia razrukha*).[57] One can argue that the cultural resistance to never-ending stories is related to a long-standing distrust of the everyday, the desire to transcend *byt* (the daily grind) and escape from a pointless "bad infinity" (*durnaia beskonechnost'*). Yet the post-Soviet serial trades bad infinity for "evil infinity," a concept

[56] For Seregin himself, the role of "spare friend" is played by his old friend Zhenia Kondrashov, an ex-cop who is murdered almost as soon as Seregin involves him in the case.

[57] In her study of conversation during perestroika, Nancy Ries identifies complete disintegration as a folkloric genre fueled at least in part by the mass media (*Russian Talk* 46).

that is actually featured as the subtitle in one of Aleksandra Marinina's best-selling novels, *Smert' radi smerti: Beskonechnost' zla* (*Death for Death's Sake: The Infinity of Evil*). Marinina's recurring heroine, Nastia Kamenskaia, discovers that an ex-KGB laboratory is using radio waves to control people's minds, turning one neighborhood into a collection of law-abiding citizens while having the unfortunate side effect of driving another neighborhood into a frenzy of violence and murder.[58] The usually dispassionate Kamenskaia is herself driven to unprecedented peaks of emotion, but in her case, it is outrage at a government that treats its populace as guinea pigs, as well as despair about ever really solving such problems definitively. The ex-KGB experiment is an obvious symbol of Soviet utopian scheming, but it can also be seen as a metafictional cue: Kamenskaia "lives" in the world of serial crime fiction, whose generic laws drive their characters to bloodshed again and again (as the title suggests, it really is "death for death's sake"). No one cares about what happens in the "good" neighborhood, and we presumably do not want to read about it.

Given the popularity of foreign-produced soap operas and translated family sagas, the monopolization of the serial form by the thematics of crime, death, and despair is all the more noteworthy. Thanks to its reliance on iteration and substitution, serial narrative proved to be a particularly hospitable site for the exploration of post-Soviet malaise. The serial form easily became the narrative embodiment of overkill, for serials never seem to know when to stop. Open-endedness allowed the horrors of the 1990s to be hypertrophied: what better way to convey or inculcate a sense of hopelessness about the state of the country than to tell stories in which a lasting improvement is impossible by definition? Eventually, Russian serial narrative would evolve and take tentative steps toward optimism and away from violent crime, but such efforts during the Yeltsin era were few and far between.

---

[58] As Goscilo notes, distrust of unrestrained scientific experimentation is a recurring theme in Marinina's work ("Big-Buck Books" 13).

Chapter Five

WOMEN WHO RUN WITH THE WOLVES

No one who had ever seen Catherine Morland in her infancy
would have supposed her born to be an heroine.

—Jane Austen, *Northanger Abbey*

Smart Women, Foolish Choices

At first glance, the blood-soaked landscape of 1990s popular entertainment
would appear numbingly monotonous. How many different ways can people be beaten, assaulted, and killed in the course of fifty minutes or four
hundred pages? The cultural hegemony of violent crime in virtually all
media (prose fiction, television, and film) creates a self-perpetuating confidence in the corruption and criminalization of both the country and its
representations, a hyperreal projection of a terrorized populace consuming
narratives about their criminal state. However novel the myth of the criminal state might be in content, it is immediately familiar in form, replicating
the false totality posited by socialist realist culture. In this case, all of society, from top to bottom, is mobilized by and for crime. But just as official
Soviet culture could sustain its monolithic rejection of all things anti-Soviet
only through a growing syncretism (Epstein, *After the Future* 156–61), the
predominance of violent crime in 1990s Russian culture bred variety as
well as conformity. No doubt the conditions of the new market economy
were of crucial importance, for if post-Soviet readers and viewers had few
alternatives to violent entertainments, they had far greater latitude in the
kinds of violent entertainment available for consumption. These are the
choices that commodity capitalism facilitates, and they arguably reduce

freedom and initiative to insignificant options. But they are effective precisely because they build and reinforce a broad consumer trend through stratified niche marketing. If all the violent storytelling in Russia really had been the same, it could never have dominated the cultural scene as it did in the years immediately following the Soviet collapse. For violence to succeed, it had to come in different flavors.

Violent entertainment in the 1990s quickly generated its own system of genres and modes, coinciding only in part with the products' marketing. Roughly speaking, violent crime narratives can be sorted out across two different axes, according to gender and mode. By no means am I proposing a strict typology; the boundaries among the categories are far from distinct. Mode defines the kind of violent entertainment discussed in chapter 7: the amoral pessimism of bespredel crosses genres with impunity, with no fixed, recognizable position in the taxonomy of post-Soviet entertainment. The division according to gender is harder to ignore and has been successfully exploited by publishers and producers. Action tales of heroic melodrama and graphic violence are explicitly marketed for men, while the increasing feminization of the most popular fiction genre in the 1990s, the detektiv, was widely recognized. The detektiv's role as a "female" genre gives it a unique status in a culture industry dominated by violent crime, resulting in a mutual accommodation between traditional feminine sensibilities and the harsh, masculine world of guns and grit. The women who write detektivy adapt crime for a female readership without challenging the hegemony of violent entertainment or irrevocably undermining established notions of gender. Quite to the contrary, the detektiv guarantees a predominance of violent entertainment that would have been impossible if half the population were absent from the target audience. The detektiv succeeds at being congenial to women readers, if not to all its female characters (who are just as likely to end up as crime victims in stories by women as they are in stories by men). Though women in the detektiv are constantly in danger, the genre pulls off a remarkable feat: the detektiv makes violence safe for women.

No doubt there are numerous pitfalls in approaching the detektiv in terms of gender. As the functional equivalent of the Anglo-American murder mystery, the detektiv by rights should be conceived more broadly. The genre, which dates back to pre-Soviet times, was extremely popular during the Brezhnev years, with an established canon that did not include a single female author. Nor is there any evidence that women were a clear majority of detektiv readers in the sixties and seventies. Though the subject matter was decidedly masculine (involving the police, army, and intelligence services), the genre itself was not marked as either masculine or feminine. The two best-selling foreign mystery writers of the perestroika era were a man and a woman, James Hadley Chase and Agatha Christie, and the initial domestic response to the late-eighties detektiv craze was to publish new books by the few (male) authors who had already been writing detektivy in the Brezhnev years, both in the USSR and in emigration (Nikolai Leonov, Friedrich Neznanzky, Edward Topol). But not long after new writers appeared on the scene, the major role played by women as both producers and consumers of detektivy could not be ignored. By the mid-nineties, it was common to distinguish between "men's" and "women's" detektivy. In a 1998 interview with the *Sankt-Peterburgskie vedomosti*, the undisputed queen of the genre, Aleksandra Marinina, agreed that the two subgenres were vastly different:

> Male authors are more dynamic and "hard-boiled' [*kruty*]. They're into chases, fights, bare naturalism, violence. Naturally, this gives the text a certain edge [*ostrotu*]. But the heroes of "men's" detektivy" are often loners, supermen who lack motivation and logical thinking.
>
> Women don't write like that. They go into detail about what the hero was thinking when he was deciding to take this or that step. There's a lot more psychology in women's detektivy. There's always a lyrical, romantic plotline. And as for chase scenes, fights, and bloody shoot-outs, those are kept to a minimum. (Gondusov)

If the division between men's hard-boiled detektiv and women's psychological approach grew throughout the nineties, it is arguably the women who were keeping with the traditions of the Soviet-era detektiv more than the men. As Anthony Olcott argues in *Russian Pulp*, one of the features that distinguished the detektiv from the murder mystery was the emphasis on the motivation behind the crime rather than on the logical investigation that led to its solution (43). Moreover, the Soviet detektiv was simply not as bloody as the "men's" detektiv that would follow it, both because of the strictures on such content in Soviet times and because of the simple fact that the crimes that were investigated were often nonviolent. Though some post-Soviet male writers, such as Andrei Kivinov and even Konstantinov in *Bandit Petersburg*, did imbue their detektivy with the psychological richness that Marinina so highly values, men's crime writing in the 1990s generally came closer to the orbit of the boevik (action story) than the detektiv.

The other danger in examining women's detektivy in terms of gender is that the novelty of female crime writers in Russia makes such an approach all too obvious. Marinina's work has already sparked a significant body of criticism, and the continued focus on gender could suggest that there is little else in her work that might be of interest. Nor is her status as a woman writer overlooked by the post-Soviet media that have lavished coverage on her for over a decade.[1] In interview after interview, Marinina is obliged to explain, with barely concealed exasperation, that despite her unshakable epithet "Russia's Agatha Christie," the only traits she shares with the British mystery writer are her popularity and her biological sex.[2] Marinina's work is far from Christie's genteel drawing rooms and railroad cars; if Miss Marple were to wander into a Marinina novel, it would only be because she was guilty of disemboweling her neighbors. Nonetheless, in the post-Soviet entertainment marketplace, gender *is* genre. Or rather, gender is to genre in the world of violent crime as biological sex is to gender in the world at large: gender in Russian cultural marketing is the largely unquestioned, naturalized base on which a corresponding superstructure is built. In a culture that finds the assertion of "natural" gender differences reassuring rather than problematic, the stark labeling of certain forms of entertainment as men's or women's makes as much sense as men's and women's clothing. Yet it also yields the possibility of a cultural transvestism that is not restricted merely to creators (women writing under male pseudonyms). The hypermasculine boevik, for example, clearly posits a male reader. This is not to say that women cannot or do not read them, but that the boevik all but requires that the reader identify with the male characters; women in the boevik are underdeveloped to the extreme, functioning as objects of sex and violence (seduction or rape, salvation or murder). The lack of psychology in men's crime fiction, when combined with the power fantasies that animate so many of the stories, leaves virtually no space for any kind of female subjectivity.

By contrast, the women's detektiv opens up the world of violent crime, allowing the female reader to imagine her way into the plot as something more than just a victim. Not that victimhood is abandoned—on the contrary, the threat of violence against the heroine and other female characters is always present. But if the boevik allows men to take control of an imaginary violent

---

[1] Irina Savkina notes the tendency of Marinina's critics to place her work in a particular female context, usually marked by a predictable set of patriarchal assumptions (5–16).

[2] When a reader asked her in 1999 how she felt about the comparison, Marinina responded: "I find it laughable. If they call me 'the Russian Agatha Christie,' considering that I'm just as beloved and just as popular, then of course it's nice. But as for the rest, I write completely differently! First of all, my works are longer, more like a novel. Second, my detectives work for the state" (Belyi et al.). Catharine Nepomnyashchy considers the "persistent invocations of Agatha Christie by the critics" to be little more than the assertion of a "'brand name' identifying Marinina as a woman writer of puzzle murder mysteries" (171). Goscilo finds that Marinina's work more closely resembles that of Ruth Rendell and P. D. James ("Feminist Pulp Fiction" 15).

scenario through violence itself (revenge fantasy, gang wars), holding out the possibility of survival thanks to greater strength and fortitude, the detektiv carefully manages women's encounters with violence. Even the women who investigate crimes tend to hover above the fray, relying on their wits and on the support of the positive male characters who can fight and kill on their behalf. In the boevik, men win by fighting. In the detektiv, women triumph either by manipulating violence or by carefully extricating themselves from the scene. Their involvement in the struggle against crime can stretch conventional notions of a woman's role, but the way in which they get involved ultimately upholds the reigning sex/gender system, keeping as far from the despised label of "feminist" as possible.

The Russian book market is flooded with detektivy written by women. In this chapter, I look at the most popular detektiv writer of the 1990s, Aleksandra Marinina (Marina Alekseeva, writing under a pseudonym), whose leading status on the best-seller list was all but unchallenged in the 1990s.[3] Marinina exploits the possibilities for reader identification and ongoing interest inherent in the serial form, creating a heroine and supporting cast whom the readers (and eventual viewers) visit like old friends. The individual novels function as episodes in the ongoing chronicle of the life of Nastia Kamenskaia. But Marinina also forgoes the emotional excesses and high drama of the soap opera and family saga, both by explicitly defining her heroine according to her impressive intellect but deliberately limited emotional range and by choosing not to create an ongoing story arc that links the novels together (as in *Bandit Petersburg*, for example). Nastia's life does change in the course of the books but usually not because of the cases she investigates; the murders and kidnappings that drive a given book's plot have few long-term repercussions, whether for Nastia's own personal life or for future cases.[4] The ongoing story of Nastia Kamenskaia is about her home and her office, while her cases are self-contained stories that show her using her professional skills.

Marinina is one of the central figures in Russia's emerging canon of 1990s popular culture. Her prominence in the bookstores, her ubiquity in the popular media, and the disdain heaped upon her by highbrow critics

---

[3] By 1999, Marinina had sold over 15 million copies of her books (Goscilo, "Big-Buck Books" 12).

[4] Occasionally, one of Nastia's cases involves someone from her past, as in *Stilist* (*The Stylist*), or a member of her family—her unfounded suspicions about her beloved stepfather in *Muzhskie igry* (*Men's Games*). Two criminal bosses have recurring roles, one as an adversary—Arsen in *Ukradenyii son* (*Stolen Dreams*) and *Za vse nado platit'* (*Everything Has a Cost*)—and the other as a friend—Denisov, whom Nastia meets in *Igra na chuzhom pole* (*Away Game*) and continues to consult until his death in *Men's Games*. But these are examples of Marinina's expansion or deployment of her cast of characters rather than an ongoing, multinovel plotline.

would all make her worthy of note, even without the question of gender. Although her plots are contrived and their action constitutes a jarring hybrid of crime solving, espionage, and mad science, her books were the closest thing to the ideal of the "well-wrought work" in Russian crime fiction until the rise of Boris Akunin. Her plots wander, but the books display a strong thematic coherence, so that even when the combination of disparate plot threads defies all credulity, their juxtaposition still develops her overall thematic concerns. Russian critics complain of the formulaic character of the women's detektiv, but the formula described bears little resemblance to the work of Marinina,[5] the first woman to break into the genre, as well as its most accomplished practitioner. As a retired police officer and best-selling crime author, Marinina is preoccupied with her status in both of her chosen fields of endeavor, as well as with the state of the fields themselves. In each, she looks to the ideals of professionalism as her guide. Her heroine overcomes the obstacles faced by a woman in law enforcement, both internal (her distaste for violence) and external (institutionalized bias) but still struggles to find a way to be a consummate professional and complete human being. The characters who represent authorship are in an even greater bind: the greater their professional acumen, the stronger the threat of turning into self-hating, crippled hacks in a literary marketplace with little room for originality.

Professionalism is more than just a theme in Marinina's work. As an ideal for both women writers and women police officers, professionalism allows Marinina to maintain a female subject position in a world of violence without doing violence to the construction of femininity itself. Wary of overkill in all its manifestations, Marinina has little interest in the two obvious extremes of female subjectivity taken by other women in her field. On one end of the spectrum are novels featuring tough, aggressive women who are comfortable on men's turf: superspies and sleuths such as Maria, the heroine of Nataliia Kornilova's series of novels called *Pantera* (*Panther*). Trained by the last sensei of a forbidden Japanese sect, Maria has peerless physical and extrasensory abilities: she is virtually invulnerable and has the strength and speed of a panther. Though she now works for a private detective agency, her powers and her background are more characteristic of the boevik, rendering her the female equivalent of Dotsenko's Mad Dog. Moreover, she keeps her abilities a secret from her

---

[5] See Anna Orlova-Novopol'tseva's "Kak sochinit' krutoi zhenskii detektiv" ("How to Write a Hard-Boiled Women's Detektiv"). Some of her comments are applicable to Marinina (the heroine's great intellect, for example), but the insistence on a love plot is more appropriate to Dashkova.

employer and coworkers, all but creating a superhero's secret identity. So far removed is Maria from the role of girl victim that she practically leaves the genre of detektiv behind.

On the other extreme one finds the flirtation with victimhood. Russian women crime writers of the 1990s did not share their male colleagues' propensity for treating female characters as beautiful sex objects destined to become beautiful corpses, but the amateur heroines who populate the work of such competitors as Polina Dashkova trace an arc that should be familiar to consumers of Hollywood criminal melodrama.[6] In each novel, Dashkova invents a heroine from a sheltered and cultured world, a virgin in the ways of violence who must quickly find her way in unfamiliar, dangerous territory (usually with the help of a kindly male love interest met along the way).

In content, Dashkova's tales of terrorism, gang wars, and murderous cults are gothic romantic adventures, but the basic plot structure is the one perfected by Alfred Hitchcock, with Dashkova's hapless heroines playing the Jimmy Stewart role. Her characters, if not exactly "everywomen," are recognizable as clever, well-educated "good girls" who never would have imagined themselves looking down the barrel of a shotgun.[7] Behind the thrills and terrors of the actual adventures themselves is the frisson of slumming, the heroine's and narrator's self-consciousness about falling down the rabbit hole and surviving in a wonderland of violence. Yet because of Dashkova's formula, her heroines see far more action in one book than police detective Nastia Kamenskaia sees in twenty-five. Rather than imagining either herself or her female audience in the world of professional violence, she takes advantage of this presumed distance, building much of her drama and emotional impact on the use of heroines who can function as the stand-in for her readers. Dashkova's female characters are not victims per se, but they narrowly avoid *becoming* victims. Dashkova relies on the fact that her heroines are in the wrong place at the wrong time, and their survival is a matter of good luck, strong wits, and the help of a conveniently available Prince Charming with a background in police work or espionage. Even if Dashkova were not adamant in her hostility to series with recurring heroes, it would only stand to reason that she finds herself inventing new protagonists for each new novel: once a heroine has been exposed to violence, she has been "consumed" by Dashkova's plots

---

[6] Boris Tukh notes in 2002 that the total print runs of all Dashkova's books to date were close to 15 million copies (127).

[7] Tukh provides a detailed typology of Dashkova's heroines and their evolution in *Pervaia desiatka* (122–61).

and cannot be trotted out for a repeat performance.[8] By no means passive, Dashkova's female characters nonetheless reinforce the reigning gender paradigm rather than undermining it, for their brief adventures in the world of violent crime inevitably usher them back into a world of domesticity and successful romance.

Eschewing both the amateur heroics of Dashkova and the aggressive superheroics of Kornilova, Marinina focuses on professionalism to lay claim to a middle ground in terms of both gender and genre. Nastia's approach to crime mirrors her creator's approach to crime fiction: each is an intellectual and psychological exercise, a response to violence without engaging in violence. With a few notable exceptions, Nastia manages to avoid both the feminized role of victim and the self-conscious role reversal that constitutes the gun-toting, kickboxing superwoman. Marinina's novels feature Nastia's brain rather than her body, in an attempt to create a fully realized heroine whose exceptional gifts both defy and confirm gendered expectations. Relatively safe from the violent world that is the object of her beloved profession, Nastia proves vulnerable to the contradictions between her status as a professional and her capacity to sustain an emotional life. Though Nastia never worries that she is becoming masculine, she is haunted by the fear that she has lost her essential humanity.

The Seven Habits of Highly Effective People

In a post-Soviet publishing industry flooded with action novels, mysteries, sword-and-sorcery epic fantasy, and quick-and-dirty translations of the latest Western thrillers, Marinina was a phenomenon unto herself. As the decade drew to a close, if an urban commuter was reading a novel on the bus or subway, the book in his or her hands was probably written by Marinina. Her success in the Russian marketplace was due to the features that made her stand out from her competitors: complex, interwoven plotlines that, though often straining credibility, usually come together into a coherent narrative organized around a single, overarching idea; a set of easily recognizable and engaging protagonists; consistent attention to the psychology and motivations of her characters; a keen understanding of the nature, appeal, and limitations of serial narrative; frequent references to the literary classics and high culture in general; and a readable, individual prose style

---

[8] The heroine of her first novel, *Krov' nerozhdennykh* (*Blood of the Unborn*), is brought back in her second, *Legkie shagi bezumiia* (*The Light Footsteps of Madness*), but this is the only exception to Dashkova's rule.

that, although subject to easy caricature, was far superior to that of the average Russian mystery and potboiler. Since 1999 Marinina no longer dominates the best-seller lists to the same extent that she did in the nineties, in part because the competition has become more fierce, and in part because she has not sustained the same breakneck writing pace that characterized her output in the mid-1990s (she now averages one book per year, as opposed to the eight new novels she published in 1995, the peak of her production).⁹ But the adaptation of her work into television films (all of her novels either have been made into movies or are slated for production) ensures an ever-broadening audience for Marinina's stories.

Her first solo effort, *Stechenie obstoiatel'stv* (*A Set of Circumstances*) (1992), introduced the reading public to Nastia Kamenskaia, an exhausted, lazy woman in her thirties struggling to get out of bed. Kamenskaia's unwillingness to wake up in the morning and her endless cups of coffee become, in the course of the series, a touchstone that helps define and redefine the character and welcome the reader back into her world. Unlike most of her colleagues in the Moscow Police Violent Crime Unit, Kamenskaia has a university education, relatively refined tastes, and a familiarity with five foreign languages (English, French, Italian, Portuguese, and Spanish). Her skills as a polyglot are of little help to her at work, but they do enable her to supplement her small police salary through translations of foreign mystery novels. If the invocation of Agatha Christie is hackneyed and inaccurate, a more appropriate comparison would be between Kamenskaia and Nero Wolf. Kamenskaia never carries a gun, wears a uniform only under duress, and does her best to avoid leaving her office. She prefers processing numbers and statistics, generating analytical reports for her supervisors and avoiding actual crime solving.

With the benefit of hindsight and a familiarity with the two dozen-odd novels that follow it, *A Set of Circumstances* proves to be an impressively organized, compact introduction to the characters, themes, and motifs on which the Kamenskaia novels are built. Marinina's debut novel, a cat-and-mouse game between the police and a top-notch hit man, is all about professionalism. As is usually the case in a Marinina novel, the book starts out with the killers and victims, rather than with the heroes. From the moment the killer is introduced, Marinina insists on his consummate professionalism, describing his unique talents in painstaking detail. The killer, nicknamed "Gall," is motivated entirely by logic, and therefore he knows that

---

⁹ According to Marinina, at least four of these novels each took only a month and a half to write (Tukh 192).

there is always a risk to his work: "[S]ooner or later either he would make a mistake, or a set of particularly unfavorable circumstances would come about; he was philosophical about it. He was not a sadist and got no pleasure from his work. He simply performed it well and found a realm in which there was a demand for this work" (10).

Gall's sober attitude toward his work is stressed as a counterpoint to his clients' anxieties, but Marinina's unrelenting emphasis on Gall's professional qualifications is a sign of more than just a beginning writer's lack of subtlety. Right out of the gate, Marinina sets up a murder based on logic, skill, and a work ethic, rather than any crimes of passion (those would come later). Luck and the eponymous set of circumstances will play their role, but Gall's ability to turn everyday household appliances into hidden murder weapons suggests a world devoid of accidents, since seemingly random events are actually the work of a highly skilled guiding hand. The first case Marinina offers her readers is a struggle between professionals: those who are best at what they do will win.

If the professionalism of the killer is never in doubt, Marinina has to fight an uphill battle to establish similar credentials for the forces of law and order. The second half of the chapter tells us how Gall's intended victim, Irina Filatova, makes her way from the airport back to her apartment (where she is to be killed). Filatova is given a ride by Dima Zakharov, a limo driver whose adherence to his professional code of ethics is introduced in his first lines upon arriving at the airport, when he refuses a tip from his passenger: "For us the best gratitude is when our company gets repeat customers" (11). Driving Filatova home, Dima serves as an efficient plot device to get her talking. Filatova reveals that she is a jurist who works in the militia but that none of her colleagues take her analytical work seriously. Her tirade lasts a page, but Dima does not respond. Instead, he is remembering his own ten years in the militia, when he, too, laughed at analytical work, but his superiors' incompetence and his own low salary prompted him to leave law enforcement for the world of "commercial security." The narrator informs us that Dima's silence indirectly seals Filatova's doom. If he had shared his own experiences, their discussion "might have become more professional and more confidential," and they would have struck up a conversation and even an acquaintance that could have led somewhere, perhaps even preventing Filatova from returning to the department where her death awaited her. But the plot requires Filatova to talk and Dima only to listen.

Filatova's encounter with Dima is doubly significant. First, it establishes a context in which present and former police officers cannot count on the same level of professionalism that a hit man expects as a matter of course. More important are the parallels between Filatova's (and, to a lesser extent, Dima's) experiences and those of the novel's heroine, Nastia Kamenskaia. Nastia and Filatova enjoy a kind of narrative complementary distribution.[10] With Filatova presumably dead by the end of the first chapter, chapter 2 finally introduces the reader to Nastia as she tries to force herself awake in time to go to work. Later we learn that Nastia actually knows ex-militiaman Dima Zakharov, the last person to see Filatova alive. Marinina is at great pains to have the reader accept this coincidence as believable; Nastia patiently tells a younger colleague that after enough time in police work, everyone knows everyone else (and in any case, in her subsequent novels Marinina demands a far greater suspension of disbelief where coincidences are concerned). Dima and Filatova meet, fail to share their common experience, and go their separate ways, but he and Nastia end up in bed together. Toward the end of the novel, Nastia's scheme for capturing Gall involves sitting alone in an apartment with the hired killer, setting herself up, like Filatova, as a potential victim. Nastia's role as bait for the killer, so typical of a certain type of mystery novel involving female protagonists, proves to be the exception rather than the rule as the series develops.

In point of fact, Nastia's behavior with both Gall and Dima is equally anomalous when compared with her actions in the subsequent Kamenskaia novels because both are instances where Nastia's involvement in her case necessitates that she act as a sexual being.[11] Yet this rather trite motif (the female detective as a locus of sex and danger) succeeds in *A Set of Circumstances*. The doubling between Filatova and Nastia restores the agency so often lost by female characters (and the implied female readers) in tales of violent crime: the novel starts with the archetypal girl victim but ends with a heroine's triumph, thanks to her superior professional acumen. Nastia's victory is doubly sweet revenge, asserting both the superiority of intellectual work (Nastia's careful calculations catch a murderer previously considered unstoppable) and the ability of a woman to prosper in the man's world of law enforcement. Nastia proves that Filatova's colleagues were wrong on both counts, at least theoretically. Small wonder that she should take such a strong personal interest in Filatova's case—in the most important respects, Filatova's case is Nastia's own.

What is it, then, that allows Nastia to succeed and become a heroine, while her less fortunate sister is left dead on the kitchen floor? Nastia's great

---

[10] Nepomnyashchy notes that Filatova is "clearly an alter ego" for Kamenskaia (173).

[11] According to Nepomnyashchy, Nastia is much more likely to become a potential victim when she is playing the role of a "sexually alluring female"; otherwise, she is rarely at risk (175).

fortune is that she lives and works in a rarefied hothouse of professionalism and respect. Viktor Alekseevich Gordeev, the division head of MUR (the Moscow Criminal Investigation Department) and Nastia's boss, is repeatedly praised throughout the series for creating a unique working environment that allows every staff member to realize his or her professional potential. Like all the characters Marinina sets up for admiration, Gordeev is systematic to a fault—or, rather, to the point of faultlessness, since Marinina's characters have the preternatural knack of taking theoretical knowledge they have learned from their studies and putting it to its proper use, a triumph of utopianism on the local level.

Gordeev finds the path to success in "American books on the theory and psychology of management," and when he achieves the post of MUR division head, he "put into practice all the interesting discoveries that he had unearthed in his smart books" (25). Gordeev has begun his MUR experiment in 1987, when he immediately sees the forthcoming consequences of the early perestroika discussions on instituting the rule of law: people will be barely acquainted with the new ideas that will have to govern their new practices, and the process of transforming law enforcement will take at least a generation ("There was no time to cultivate professionalism"). Gordeev concludes that the only way to compensate for this terrible lack is to cultivate specialization, choosing fifteen people, each with his or her own particular talent: "So that in the end they would be like one good professional" (250).[12] Kolia Seluanov has a phenomenal visual memory and a savant's detailed knowledge of Moscow's topography. Misha Dotsenko is a master at working with witnesses, guiding them to mnemonic feats that rival Seluanov's natural abilities; a typical Dotsenko scene starts with a witness honestly protesting that she remembers nothing and ends with her praising the officer for helping her recall details she never knew she had noticed. Volodia Lartsev was a psychologist before joining the militia, while Nastia herself has unparalleled analytical talents.

Thus Gordeev's division is filled with people who excel at one skill, and the narrator discusses each of their skills in every installment of the Kamenskaia series, along with all the habits and character traits that make them immediately recognizable—Gordeev's chewing on the ends of his glasses, Nastia's hot-and-cold-showers and morning coffee. The result is extremely schematic and, like so much in Marinina's novels, could be interpreted as self-referential: Gordeev assembles fifteen narrowly defined

---

[12] Gordeev's no-nonsense approach to problem solving, which often involves breaking a conundrum down into its constituent parts, suggests that the phonetic resemblance between his last name and the "Gordian knot" (*gordiev uzel*) is at least appropriate if not necessarily intentional.

coworkers to create one good professional, while Marinina distributes her virtues and quirks among her supporting cast rather than create one well-rounded character. But, viewed more charitably, Marinina's and Gordeev's insistence on specialization and individualization amounts to a progressive political stance within the Soviet context and also constitutes a compromise between the idealization of crime-fighting heroes and the need to show them as human, flawed, and therefore worthy of our emotional investment and identification.[13]

Professionalism and systematic thinking are clearly interrelated in Marinina's world, and their centrality is made all too obvious by the fact that characters on both sides of the barricades share a basic understanding of these key concepts. Like her heroes' fondness for protracted, uninterrupted explanation, this tacit agreement among all her characters about the fundamental terms of their debates suggests that Marinina's tendency toward the monologic is not limited to her weakness as a scripter of dialogue. Despite their primary function as entertainment and diversion, Marinina's books share the flaw common to so many tendentious or ideological novels: on a purely lexical level, everyone uses the same vocabulary (the characters all speak alike), while on a philosophical level, the opposing sides never challenge the shared framework that structures their ideological disputes.[14] Marinina's monologism may be aesthetically detrimental (at least for readers who notice it), but it helps drive her point home all the more assuredly.

Marinina's heroes are not the unbelievably versatile superspies of the Stirlitz era, nor are they the unstoppable, multitalented warriors of the boevik. They are unbeatable but only in their own particular fields of strength. Gordeev's own unique talent lies in his ability to manage other people's talents, using his office as an effective laboratory for the proper management of skilled professionals. But the larger world of Marinina's crime fiction is so replete with confident professionals that her work at times borders on self-parody. When expanded far enough to include a more generalized perfectionism, nearly all of Marinina's characters are past masters at something. Even Irochka, the relative, friend, and housekeeper to Tatiana (Tania) Tomilina, turns out to have a carefully conceived system for shopping for Tania's clothing. In *Igra na chuzhom pole* (*Away*

---

[13] Cf. Eco's discussion of the superhero as a compromise between the epic distance of the tales of the gods and the quotidian stories of average mortals (330–32). In the golden-age superhero comics, it was the Clark Kents of the world who made the Supermen emotionally accessible.

[14] In her later novels (after 1997, when her pace of production slows), Marinina devotes more time and care to the creation of distinct narrative voices: *Soavtory* (*Coauthors*), *Sed'maia zhertva* (*The Seventh Victim*), and especially *Kogda bogi smeiutsia* (*When Gods Laugh*).

Game), the plot hinges on the fact that even snuff films need classically trained, conscientious composers to write the movies' score and that even a drug-addicted dwarf with a musical education can listen to the score and realize that it culminates in murder. Marinina's preoccupation with the virtues of such rational, systematic thinking often takes its toll on the narrative; her characters tend to indulge in elaborate, multipage monologues in which they explain exactly how something works. On the metatexual level, Marinina's enthusiasm is understandable: not only was professionalism arguably all too scarce throughout Russia in the 1990s, but it was also a sore point for both of the author's own chosen careers, as a member of law enforcement and as a producer of popular entertainment.

In the first novel, Marinina wastes no time establishing Nastia's analytical abilities and her adherence to systemic thought. The narrator describes Nastia's reluctance to get out of bed in the morning, one of the many character beats taken up in novel after novel, but spends far more time depicting the process she uses to get her brain working again. Rather than summarize, it is worth citing the entire passage, since the overly methodical detail is precisely the point.

> Nastia got in the shower, turned on the water, first hot, then cold, and began to wait patiently for her system [*organizm*] to wake up. This usually took about ten minutes. Sluggishly setting up her toothbrush, Nastia tried to multiply thirty-seven by eighty-four. She got it wrong. Her sleepy brain refused to perform the simplest operations. She changed the figures and tried again. It worked. She began to multiply three-digit figures. The process of awakening was going well, because she got the result right the first time. The final test: recalling ten words in Swedish. This time Nastia recited words for kitchen utensils. She had never really studied Swedish the way she had learned so many other languages, but she liked to memorize words, as she herself admitted, for mental gymnastics. Nastia knew around fifty words in all the European languages. The thing is that her mother was an unparalleled specialist in creating programs for computerized language instruction, and Professor Kamenskaia tried out and developed all her ideas and methodological discoveries on her daughter.
>
> On the tenth word Nastia felt that she was freezing—the water turned out to be too cold. She strained her memory, drew forth from its depths the Swedish synonym for "sieve," and quickly grabbed a towel.
>
> Half the job was done; her brain was now in working order. Now it was time to get her body moving. (*Stechenie obsotaitel'stv*, 19–20)

The actual substance of Nastia's mental gymnastics is almost aggressively irrelevant—readers need not anticipate a plot twist in which the successful resolution of the case depends on the investigator's familiarity with the finer points of Scandinavian kitchenware. Instead, Nastia is simply exercising her brain the way a more active detective would exercise his body, keeping her mental reflexes sharp and encouraging her thoughts to move along systematic lines. Only later in the novel does her morning ritual become self-reflective and didactic. This time she stands under the showerhead translating the phrase *Vo vsem nuzhen poriadok* ("There must be order in everything") (136).[15]

Cinderella and the Glass Ceiling

At least once in every novel, Nastia calls herself a "walking computer" or a "computer on two legs," an accurate description of the specialized skill set she brings to Gordeev's division but a potentially dehumanizing way to conceive of one's own personality. To borrow Lady Macbeth's famous phrase, it also "unsexes" her, revealing the tension that always threatens to topple Marinina's literary edifice even as it is the probable source of much of her success. How can a woman succeed in the world of violent crime (fiction) without sacrificing either her femininity or her agency? The Kamenskaia novels toe a fine line between railing at the sexism that is a repeated obstacle in Nastia's path and upholding a standard of traditional feminine difference. Marinina engages in a complex set of strategies that allow her to assert Nastia's undeniable intellectual superiority while acknowledging both her "womanly" weakness (her fear of blood and violence, for instance) and her weakness as a woman (the emotional inadequacy that is discussed below). Nastia is a consummate professional, but, in keeping with Gordeev's own definition, she falls far short of being "universal," both as a specialist and as a human being. Marinina's solution eschews activism in favor of particularism, thereby distancing her work from those varieties of feminism that offer a political program or utopian solution. In keeping with the general post-Soviet skepticism toward political or social change, neither Nastia nor the other characters have any hope or interest in modifying attitudes, the law, or the workplace. Nastia is perfectly aware that, as a woman, she has no chance of promotion to a leadership position,

---

[15] This particular exercise is quite felicitous for Nastia. Her long musings on the various translations of the Russian word for "order" allow her to solve a conundrum involving Filatova's papers.

but since she lacks "male" ambition, she does not care.[16] In Marinina's world, traditional notions of gender are largely correct and need not be challenged; if anything, the exceptional cases, such as Kamenskaia's, prove the rule. The important thing is to recognize the exception when one sees it, and not allow prejudice to get in the way of an outstanding specialist at work.

Nastia's exceptionalism is never described as masculinization, which would probably have limited her appeal as a heroine.[17] Instead, she oscillates between "woman" and "not-woman," rather than "woman" and "man." Again, the designation "walking computer" is appropriate; while the Russian word *komp'iuter* is grammatically masculine, the emphasis here is on Nastia's strong intellect and nearly absent emotions and passions. Nastia is quite capable of being feminine: in fact, her cat-and-mouse game with Gall depends on her ability to transform herself from a "gray mouse" into a seductive vamp.[18] For Nastia, "being a woman" is not her default state. As she says to Dima Zakharov, "I'm not a normal woman. I'm not a woman at all" (172), to which he eventually responds, "Enough with being smart [*umnitsei*]. Just be a woman, if only for a little while . . ." (*Stechenie obsotaitel'stv*, 184).

On the most basic level, Nastia is always ontologically female, and the minor differences between Nastia and her male colleagues are noted repeatedly; but "being a woman" entails an added effort: Nastia can "be a woman" as a performance. She has a closet full of elegant clothes that she never wears to work, but she loves to try them out every now and then in front of the mirror (*Igra na chuzhom pole*, 167). While on vacation in *Away Game*, Nastia decides to play the vamp again: "I'll try being a WOMAN" (57, emphasis in the original). Her performance of femininity could almost be considered a drag act, except that in Nastia's case she is performing what is, or should be, "natural" for her. Nastia plays with the classic Cinderella trope of revealing an inner beauty hidden by domestic dirt, with a crucial difference that can be chalked up both to Nastia's character and to the open-ended nature of the serial form: her transformations are never perma-

[16] Marinina herself was quite sober about her own prospects for advancement within the militia. On the eve of International Women's Day (2000), the time for the annual ritual of highlighting women's issues before forgetting them for the rest of the year, Marinina was one of many famous women polled about sex descrimination by *Kommersant"-vlast'*" "If I was moved along the service ladder, then it was definitely downwards. I was sort of given a new position, but a lower one. While the men were moving up. What can you do, a broad [baba] is a creature of a lower order, after all" ("Vas ushchemliali").

[17] Elena Trofimova argues that Marinina is "trying to create a new, modern strategy for representing the feminine," without simply making Nastia "masculine" (27).

[18] Such transformations are a recurring feature in Marinina's novels, leading Nepomnyashchy to speculate that this "fairy-tale motif" could account for some of Marinina's popularity with female readers (171).

nent. The true Nastia is not the beautiful woman hidden beneath the professional demeanor but rather the professional woman who always has the potential to become a knockout if the situation demands it.

Nastia's exceptionalism is both a handicap and a source of strength. She has a great deal of patience with the numerous men in law enforcement who initially assume that a woman cannot be an equal colleague because she does not see her own status as a challenge to gender norms. Even though her forays into womanliness are performative, Nastia's transformations are posed as an argument *against* social construction rather than for it. Alexandra Marinina is no Judith Butler. In keeping with the dynamics of masculinity and femininity discussed in chapters 1–3, Nastia essentializes gender so thoroughly that it becomes an abstraction that supersedes biology itself. Russia in the 1990s still operated according to masculine and feminine principles that date back at least as far as the Silver Age (1890–1920), when Russian poets and philosophers assumed essential notions of gender that could distribute themselves differently among specific, biologically sexed bodies. Thus there is no need to alter our definitions of femininity even in the face of a specimen such as Nastia Kamenskaia: the principle is observed in the breach.

In fact, Nastia herself evaluates the people she encounters according to the very same standards that so often bar her way. At one point in *A Set of Circumstances,* she is investigating an acquaintance of Filatova's, to whom she takes an immediate dislike. Aleksandr Pavlov, like Gordeev, is the head of an investigative unit (in this case, within the UVD, the Internal Affairs Directorate), but he is the first of many unsatisfactory doubles for Nastia's boss. Pavlov got his position by rising through the party elite, and therefore has a poor understanding of detective work, which earns him one of the harshest epithets in Marinina's lexicon: "He's not a professional" (*On—neprofessional*) (165). His lack of professionalism is exacerbated by a curiously feminine flaw:

> He's a boss by specialty. But in his way of thinking, he's a typical "broad in trousers" [*baba v shtanakh*]. Nastia loved Arkadii Averchenko's wonderful story "The Lie," and reread it often. Life has shown that the well-known satirist was right: in order to cover up an insignificant little nothing, a woman will raise a veritable Eiffel Tower of lies, and will do it so clumsily that the construct threatens to fall apart any minute, and she props it up with even more lies, getting mired in deception like a fly in a drop of honey. While masculine thinking is distinguished by the fact that they prefer telling the partial truth [*nedoskazannuiu pravdu*] and don't risk being unmasked for nonsense. (165)

Nastia's reasoning can only make sense within a system of such unshakable gender absolutes that even counterexamples pose no threat to the system's basic assumptions. Pavlov displays a style of reasoning that Nastia associates with women; therefore, he is basically a woman in men's clothing, which proves everything Averchenko wrote about how clumsily women lie in the absence of male restraint. The circularity is absurd, and if the results of her reasoning did not reinforce the reigning definition of femininity, one could easily imagine Marinina's male characters citing it as an example of the inadequacy of feminine logic. And if Nastia herself does not suffer from the failings she ascribes to the womanly Pavlov, this is because she herself deviates from true femininity and not because the idea of femininity might need to be reassessed.

Nastia's ability to dismiss Pavlov's failings as feminine while never doubting her own effectiveness as a law enforcement professional is one of the very qualities that makes Marinina's heroine exceptional. Thus on the one hand, she is not bothered by disparaging comments that neither interfere with her work nor disparage her basic abilities; quite to the contrary, she does not hesitate to invoke feminine stereotypes when they work in her favor. In *Away Game*, the 1993 novel that addresses these issues most directly, after a long tirade about how the local militia in the resort city where she is recuperating from back trouble refuse to take her seriously, she tells her colleague and close friend Yuri Korotkov to make some minor decision: " 'You're the man, after all,' said Nastia with a conciliatory smile." To which Korotkov responds: 'Oho! Now you remember! And you're the first to get offended when you're considered a woman! There's something wrong with your logic, my friend [*podruga*]!" (250) Thus Marinina puts the maximum distance between her heroine and the Russian caricature of the feminist as humorless bluestocking: sexual difference is to be emphasized and enhanced as long as it is playful and productive but not when it gets in the way of professional work.

Though Marinina includes such playful banter in many of her novels, its deployment in *Away Game* seems strategic, as a counterbalance to Nastia's outrage at her poor treatment by her provincial counterparts. A murder has been committed in the same resort where Nastia has a room, but the detectives on the scene treat her with condescension and mild contempt. "From the very beginning in this City they didn't take her seriously, not disguising the general sense that a woman in criminal investigation is utterly ridiculous" (193). Nastia's response is an interior monologue that takes up five pages in the paperback edition, of which only the highlights are cited here.

Humanity is divided into Men and Women. This banal truth, rather than simply affirming a biological fact, slowly became a rule, a guide to action, on whose basis humanity began to construct its wobbly social sphere. To the extent that this "construction" advanced, the rule was expanded somewhat. Thus alongside the basic categories were added the, shall we say, elective categories of Effeminate Man and Mannish Woman.

Guided by this basic rule, wise humanity began to come up with games that vary according to their complexity: some just for men, some just for women, some for mixed teams. And it got so carried away with the process of social-sexual segregation that it failed to notice how the borders, which at first were somehow unreal [*nevzapravdashnimi*] and were more of a ritual, a part of the game, were suddenly transformed from playful to absolutely real, concrete, impenetrable by even the most advanced mind or the most perfect weaponry. (188–89)

Goscilo argues that this passage "might have been extracted wholesale from a feminist handbook," but the broader context of Marinina's treatment of men and women would suggest that feminist theory, much like the provincial town in which the novel takes place, is not Nastia's home territory ("Feminist Pulp Fiction" 16). As Goscilo herself comments elsewhere, the "moderate feminism" featured in Marinina's novels is "piecemeal and intermittent, operating within the parameters of a changing but established system" ("Big-Buck Books" 13). Nastia has no problem with the categories of gender but rather with their rigid application (hence her dismissal of Pavlov's feminine weakness). Masculinity and femininity are perfectly acceptable concepts as long as they are treated playfully rather than axiomatically (as in Nastia's banter with Korotkov).

This is why the novel's title works so well—Nastia is forced to play an "away game" because she is not on her home territory, but the local militia play with such limited imagination that they cannot even accept her as a participant: "Here Nastia once again was on foreign turf [*na chuzhom pole*—part of the Russian title] where they played their usual game according to the old rules" (192).[19] Yet the local cops who dismiss Nastia out of hand are wrong ultimately not because of a general principle of equality but because they have allowed their narrow-mindedness to get in the way of the crucial elements needed for their work—professionalism and specialization: "Everyone must do what he does best. If you're good at shooting

---

[19] Marinina returns to these sports metaphors in a 1997 novel that touches on Nastia's status as a woman in law enforcement, *Men's Games*.

and running fast—catch criminals. If you know how to work with information, then work, not just for yourself, but for the common cause, for each of your colleagues. And it shouldn't matter what letter your sex starts with, 'M' or 'F' " (191). Nastia never claims that she would be as good as men at street-level police work; rather, her specialization demands talents that are not at all sex-linked. The problem is a double lack of imagination, in that both women police officers and analytical work are denigrated, leaving no possibility of respect for Nastia. Again we recall Irina Filatova, who had the misfortune of working for a much less enlightened boss than Gordeev. And again Marinina reminds the reader of Gordeev's managerial gifts: "In his division, [Gordeev] gathered together people who all could do something well" (191–92). The narrator launches into the same inventory of police talent provided in *A Set of Circumstances* but this time ends with Nastia herself: "If at first Gordeev's division was skeptical about her, since besides [Gordeev] they all continued to play by the usual rules, now they not only loved and valued Nastia, they were ready to kiss her feet [*s nee pylinki gotovy byli sduvat'*]" (192).[20] But when Nastia ventures outside her familiar territory, she is obliged to fight the same battles over and over again.

Such moments of frustration, which highlight Nastia's always exceptional role as virtually the only female in a masculine world, suggest an otherwise unlikely homology with the novels of Dashkova. In Dashkova's works, the heroines could not be more alien to the world of violence, because of their educated and cultured background as well as their gender; changed as they may be by their experiences, all of them return to the everyday world from which they came. Since they are not the protagonists of serial novels, they presumably never repeat their adventures in violent crime. Serialization would make this "virginal" scenario unworkable, and thus the heroine must be a professional if some sort if credibility is to be maintained.[21] Nastia Kamenskaia is undoubtedly professional, but the repeated emphasis on her difference as a woman and the lack of respect she so often encounters render her enough of an outsider to function as a surrogate for the female reader and author.

[20] The television version of *A Set of Circumstances* shows us a bit of this process of acceptance, since the producers chose to make Nastia new to Gordeev's team for the first episode.

[21] Here I am stretching the word "professional" to include those "amateurs" who are not paid for their investigative work but who eventually earn a reputation as crime solvers: Miss Marple, Darya Dontsova's heroines, and the Angela Lansbury character from *Murder, She Wrote*. They may not be on the police payroll, but neither can they be expected to be easily shocked by the crimes they encounter.

Our Dead Bodies, Our Dead Selves

Nastia may well be proud of her abilities as a walking computer, but Marinina shows that they come at a serious cost, for, at least in the first dozen novels, Nastia is painfully aware that something is lacking in her compartmentalized, carefully controlled persona. One almost has the sense that Marinina anticipated criticism that her heroine was not a full-fledged, complicated human being, incorporating Nastia's emotional and psychological limitations as one of the ongoing themes of the novels. Paradoxically, this may be Marinina's greatest success in developing Nastia as a changing and maturing heroine of an ongoing series. If Nastia starts out as the somewhat schematic, overly intellectual protagonist of cheap genre fiction, over the course of several books, she struggles with her own limitations, essentially trying to skip several rungs up the literary hierarchy and transform herself into the heroine of a realist novel. In the very first book, she tells Dima Zakharov that she has no "fire" in her. Her brief fling with Zakharov is an attempt to light this flame, but the long-term effects would take years to be felt. By the second novel, *Ukradennyi son* (*Stolen Dreams*), Nastia has begun the litany that she will repeat for the next several years: "I'm a moral freak" (*Ia—moral'nyi urod*), cut off from human emotions (141); "Her soul was filled with cold. Permafrost and great boredom. She was interested only in intellectual work" (55). She can't even bring herself to be jealous when she realizes that Alesha Chistiakov, the man with whom she has lived for years, is having an affair: "Lord, don't I have any feelings at all? Why am I made of stone [*tverdokamennaia*]! Can I really only feel two things: hurt and fear? An analytical machine, deprived of normal human emotions" (274).[22] The point here is not the cheating—Nastia herself had an affair in the first novel, and the narrator makes it clear that she and Chistiakov have an understanding. But this very understanding becomes nothing but cold, inhuman logic if Nastia does not experience even a twinge of jealousy.

Nastia's struggle with her own coldness becomes the main serial subplot that is developed from novel to novel. What little suspense Marinina cultivates regarding her heroine's own story has the external trappings of soap opera. Will Nastia finally marry Chistiakov? And when she does, can they truly find happiness together? Yet the events themselves are virtually devoid of melodrama, precisely because of Nastia's increasing alienation, which is

---

[22] Nastia's last name, "Kamenskaia," also suggests "stone" (kamen').

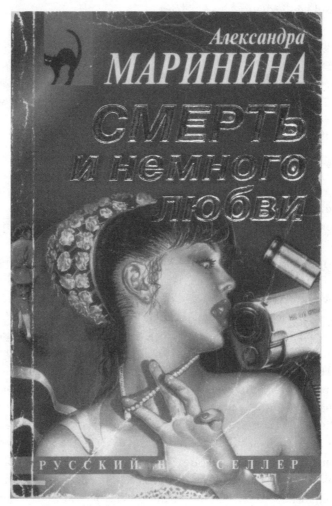

Figure 5: Cover of Aleksandra Marinina's *Death and a Little Love*, about a murder committed at a marriage registry.

her real character arc through 1997. Nastia does love Chistiakov, her childhood sweetheart, and they do get married, but the event itself is appropriately casual for a relationship that has already lasted decades. The marriage advances Nastia's story, but the wedding itself serves as the excuse for a murder case in a wonderfully novel setting: the ZAGS, a Soviet-era institution for the solemnization of matrimony that manages to be pompous, bureaucratic, and crass at the same time (*Smert' i nemnogo liubvi* [*Death and a Little Love*], 1995).

Nor does marriage help Nastia with her emotional distress. By the time her midlife crisis comes to a resolution in the nineteenth Marinina novel, *Ia umer vchera* (*I Died Yesterday*) (1997), Chistiakov has moved out of her apartment, ostensibly to take care of his sick father but fundamentally because the couple are on the verge of divorce. Appropriately enough, it is an encounter with Zakharov, the man with whom Nastia had a fling back in *A Set of Circumstances*, that forces her to reassess her values and change her outlook on life. Dima wants to pick up where they left off, invoking the happiness and freedom to be found in a casual relationship, but Nastia cuts him off firmly, reaffirming her distaste for soap opera clichés: "Zakharov, don't take advantage of the moment, it's tacky [*poshlo*]. Getting a woman into bed because she has a conflict with her husband" (41). Nastia successfully avoids tawdry melodrama, but Dima cannot escape from the coincidences of a Marinina crime novel: immediately after she refuses him, Dima dies, the victim of a bullet intended for her.[23]

Nastia deals with death every day and has become accustomed to the sight of dead bodies—she is, after all, a professional. If at times she blames her coldness on the nature of her job and on her hypertrophied intellect, this is the only long-term spillover she has from the office to her home. As we established earlier, *A Set of Circumstances* is anomalous in that Nastia herself is a target for murder; considering how often female detectives find themselves in personal danger, Marinina uses this motif sparingly. Now Nastia's near-death experience, combined with the unintentional sacrifice of a man with whom she once was close but has just rebuffed, removes the emotional constraints under which she has been suffering for years.

> The fear was gone. That very fear that grabbed her by the throat and prevented her from talking with her husband and her parents. It all seemed so shallow and insignificant. She suddenly understood that the bullets that had killed Dmitrii only missed her by a miracle. She was a hair's breadth away from death. And the only thing that really meant anything was that she was still alive. The fear of death is the only thing that needs to be addressed. Everything else is foolishness, nonsense, and sniveling [*rozovye sopli*]. (*Ia umer vchera* 47)

---

[23] Tukh sees this episode as an example of Marinina's moralizing tendency: the author saves her heroine from doing wrong by eliminating the temptation, even if there is no compelling motivation in the plot for Dima's murder (169–70). Tukh also considers Nastia to have been left unmoved by Dima's passing (181). I believe Tukh is missing the point: Dima is crucial for Nastia's character development and not for the crime story on which *I Died Yesterday* is constructed.

Her emotional barriers finally down, she calls Alesha, volunteers to help with his sick father, and eventually extracts a promise from him that he'll move back home. Nastia's great revelation is disappointingly anodyne.

> It can't be said that everything in life is wonderful, but problems and un-pleasantness are a common and normal thing. Lesha will come back. That's the important thing. Everything else can be attached to that from various sides. In this life, one has to be able to separate the important from the sec-ondary, there is real wisdom in this. But why does it come to people so late, when all sorts of thinkable and unthinkable mistakes and idiocies have already been committed? (133)

Ironically, Nastia resolves her emotional inadequacies precisely when the compartmentalization of her life breaks down and she narrowly avoids be-coming a case for someone else to investigate (another Irina Filatova). Her emotional life is the one puzzle that her cold intellect and impeccable pro-fessionalism cannot solve. It is important that she has not been able to re-solve her personal problems on the stage of domestic melodrama—Stanley Cavell's "comedy of remarriage" is not for Nastia Kamenskaia. Marinina works hard to create detektivy that contain the relative psychological com-plexity, or at least interiority, of romance fiction, but, unlike Dashkova, she refuses to wed the murder mystery to the romance plot. Nastia's emotional and romantic problems have to be resolved with the clichés of violent crime tales or not at all. The extent of Nastia's emotional (and even profes-sional) growth becomes clear years later, after her beloved Gordeev retires, to be replaced by the dull-witted Afonia, whom Nastia recalls as an unin-spired C-student in their college days. Afonia is a typical Soviet manager; like most of the bosses depicted in Russian crime fiction and film, his meth-ods are based on voluntarism: everything is possible if people simply work hard enough. If a job is not getting done, the solution is to yell at one's sub-ordinates in order to get them to improve their work. At first Nastia tries to find a way to work with him, but at the end of *Nezapertaia dver'* (*The Un-locked Door*), she realizes that she is a grown woman and a free agent and has other options than simply suffering in silence under Afonia's arbitrary rules. She tells him:

> You're a good cop [*oper*], I'm sure, otherwise you wouldn't have been moved up the service ladder. But a good cop and a real cop are two entirely different things—one big, one little. A good cop is a tough pro, but a real cop is a per-son. Afonia, you're a pro, but you're not a person. People are dirt for you.

For you, their lives and suffering are only an excuse for getting ahead at work. Maybe I will work under your management. But I will never respect you. Just sign the requests, and I'll leave. (410–11)

As she exits Afonia's office, she is no longer terrified at the prospect of changing her life: "Beyond the door was life, maybe a different one, maybe one she wasn't accustomed to, but not a frightening one. There were people who lived that life, ordinary people just like Nastia. And who said that she couldn't live like them?" (412)

What to Expect When You're Expecting

As a character, Nastia embodies the virtues and vices of professionalism in the world of violent crime. Thanks to her particular skills and great intellect, she is able to transcend gender without ignoring it. It takes little imagination to see that Nastia is a stand-in for Marinina herself, an idealized version of the author as heroine.[24] Nastia also shares Marinina's tastes in art and literature, often serving as a mouthpiece for the author's aesthetic pronouncements. Where they diverge, of course, is in their professional relationship to literature itself. Nastia has not followed in her creator's footsteps to become a best-selling author, but in the first several books, she supplements her substandard police income by translating mysteries from the five languages in which she is proficient. Nastia's status as a translator evokes Marinina's own role as, if not a translator, then a mediator between pop cultural traditions. On the one hand, we know from Nastia's own reading habits that Marinina looks favorably on the old-style Soviet detektivy of Nikolai Leonov but that she is also a big fan of the police procedurals of Ed McBain and the thrillers of Sidney Sheldon. As the author who single-handedly did more to lure the Russian reading public away from cheap translations of Western crime fiction than all of her initial competitors combined, Marinina deserves credit for striking an appealing balance between local traditions and Western imports without slavishly imitating the most popular Anglo-American authors on the post-Soviet book market. More to the point, she did not try to be a Russian Agatha Christie, no matter how resilient this label has proved. She

---

[24] Marinina makes no secret about her resemblance to Kamenskaia: "My heroine has no real prototype, although ninety percent of her basically comes from me. Only I know just one foreign language and can't drive a car. Otherwise we're a lot alike—we're both fantastically lazy, have great difficulty getting up in the morning, drink a lot of coffee, are always freezing, and prefer comfortable footwear with low heels" (A. Shcherbakov).

re-created the detektiv to maximize its appeal to both women and men, maintaining the Russian tradition of professional investigators rather than private detectives and creating a heroine who excels in the context of "men's games" while remaining aware of her own unusual status.

In developing Nastia and becoming a successful writer, Marinina inevitably adds a metafictional element to Nastia's special status.[25] If Nastia can always be seen as something of an outsider in the context of law enforcement, despite her years of service, what does that say about Marinina's own role in the world of crime fiction? Many of the Kamenskaia novels are extremely self-conscious about their own status as genre fiction and about the role of the Russian writer in a hybrid international tradition. Nastia's gender dilemma becomes a genre dilemma, highlighting an uneasiness about being both an interloper and a runaway success. Where Nastia as detective triumphs thanks to her professionalism, the question of literary professionalism for Marinina's authorial stand-ins is fraught with anxiety. If professionalism in the militia is a quasi-utopian goal attainable thanks to the magic touch of Gordeev, such high standards are even more problematic within the context of the post-Soviet publishing scene. In Marinina's hands, publishing offers the same mélange of intrigue, corruption, and scandal as the world of crime and law enforcement that provides so much grist for the literary mill.[26] Writing and publishing under the new market conditions are always haunted by the specter of adulteration, compromise, and plagiarism.[27]

Virtually all the numerous writers, translators, and publishers that populate Marinina's work have a vexed relationship to their literary productions. Nepomnyashchy, citing Gilbert and Gubar's famous suggestion that the pen is a metaphorical penis, connects the female detektiv author's anxiety with that of the female detektiv protagonist (who, in Marinina's case, refuses to carry a gun) (180). Her approach makes perfect sense, but I would extend it further, for Marinina's trouble with her literary progeny suggests metaphors of reproductive capacity as much as sexual potency. Marinina's author figures are midwives to freakish progeny whose genealogy is never straightforward, at times even serving as doubles to the mad scientists whose tampering with the natural order is at the root of so many of her plots.

---

[25] Marinina often uses her novels to comment on the states of Russian popular literature. Her characters argue about whether or not authors such as Eduard Topol' or Dean Koontz write "trash" or produce works of value (Goscilo, "Big-Buck Books" 13).

[26] Here we should recall Gordeev's nickname, *Kolobok* (a round loaf of bread, which the rotund Gordeev resembles). In Russian folklore, the kolobok is the equivalent of the Gingerbread Man—he runs away from everything, and nothing can touch him or stop him.

[27] Nepomnyashchy also highlights Marinina's anxieties of authorship and gender, paying particular attention to *A Set of Circumstances*, The Stylist, and *Another's Mask* (180–81).

As Claude Lévi-Strauss argues in "The Structural Study of Myth," one of the fundamental questions hovering over the passage from "nature" to "culture" is that of origin. The Oedipus story, with its series of mistaken identities, incestuous entanglements, riddles about the human life cycle, and confrontations with chthonic beasts, makes both paternity and maternity a mystery (314). In several of Marinina's novels, Nastia's feats of detection focus on literary parentage: who is the author of a disputed text, and what exactly does authorship mean? The biological metaphor implicit in the relationship between author and text is highlighted by Marinina's constant fascination with fractured and blended families whose genealogical charts are initially baffling. Nastia herself is the product of broken marriage, and claims a stronger relationship with her half-brother and stepfather than with either of her biological parents. She even asserts with Lysenkoist certainty that, since her stepfather is a lifelong police detective, law enforcement is "in her genes": "You're the one who raised me" (*Stechenie* 79–80). Marinina's second double, the criminal investigator (*sledovatel'*) Tatiana Obraztsova who writes detektivy under the pseudonym "Tatiana Tomilina," has gone through a string of husbands before settling down with private investigator Stasov, the father of a daughter conceived late in life. Along the way, Tatiana has added to her family a young woman named Irina, whose connection to Tatiana is so convoluted that she simply calls her a "relative" (Irina is the sister of one of Tatiana's ex-husbands). Marinina eventually completes her substitution of proximity for biological heredity in her 2001 family saga, *Tot, kto znaet* (*The One Who Knows*), in which true family ties are based on the shared experience of living in a communal apartment, rather than on bonds of blood.[28] Just as Marinina's characters can easily claim more than two parents, the books that are at the center of so many of her plots are the products of multiple authors, for whom literary maternity or paternity is a source of both pride and shame.

From the very first Kamenskaia novel, texts tend to be of uncertain parentage and pedigree, kidnapped or extorted from their rightful authors and claimed by others with shady agendas. Filatova's murder in *A Set of Circumstances* can be traced back to a literary scandal: the underpaid police researcher agreed to sell the doctoral dissertation she had been writing in exchange for much-needed cash, renouncing authorship in order to find

---

[28] Revelations of unexpected biological bonds prove to mean much less than lives spent together under one roof. When Irina discovers that the old lady who took such a strong interest in her upbringing was actually her grandmother, the news has little impact.

the funds to buy her own apartment.[29] Meanwhile, Nastia's sideline as a literary translator is also introduced in this novel, which carefully establishes parallels between Kamenskaia and the murder victim. Italian aphorisms about translators and traitors aside, Nastia is performing honest, remunerated labor, yet subsequent novels reveal that the task of the translator is never straightforward and is rarely honest. In *Stolen Dreams*, the mystery revolves around the works of a popular French writer, Jean-Paul Brisaque, who turns out to be as much a fiction as his novels: a sinister publishing cabal has found a way to funnel second-rate thrillers by underfed Russian graphomaniacs to be whipped into shape by a team of underfed French translators using Brisaque's name. As unlikely as this scenario may be, it plays into the post-Soviet anxieties over both the brain drain of Russia's intellectual elite and the export of the motherland's natural and metaphorical treasures (as discussed in chapter 3); hence the term "raw materials" (*syr'e*) for the manuscripts smuggled out to France. As in the other versions of this particular national myth (including the Western demand for Russian wives and adoptive children), the Brisaque case can function as a source of pride as well: even on the international literary market, whose flows seem largely unidirectional (the flood of Western best sellers into Russian bookshops), Russia's hidden wellspring of untapped talent is in great demand. This scenario helps counter the whiff of illegitimacy that clings to Nastia's own translating work (denigrated by an aging intellectual in *Away Game* 55) and, by extension, Marinina's entire literary project.

Marinina revisits this international anxiety of authorship in *Stilist* (*The Stylist*), which uncovers a scenario that is a variation on *Stolen Dreams*. Here the wealthy Russian translator of Japanese thrillers, Vladimir Aleksandrovich Solov'ev, has a dirty secret that would be unimaginable in a book market that valued native talent: the original Japanese novels are virtually unreadable. Solov'ev calls himself a translator, but he actually rewrites the novels completely, fleshing out the bare bones of the plot with his rare stylistic elegance. Solov'ev, like so many of Marinina's intellectual heroes, is a crippled talent, a demiurge who can do wonders with someone else's raw material but cannot create from whole cloth. Solov'ev's character is a condensation of motifs suggesting impotence and sterility surrounded by material comforts that can never make him happy. When Nastia was still in college, Solov'ev was both her mentor and her lover, but now he is a middle-aged man, partly paralyzed and chair-bound after an automobile accident

[29] Nepomnyashchy notes an important parallel between Filatova's ghostwriting and her murder, in that the term *zakazchik* ("customer") describes the man who ordered both her dissertation and her murder (180).

engineered by his crooked publishers. Solov'ev still feels attracted to Nastia, but Kamenskaia will not play Jane Eyre to his mangled Rochester. Rounding out the portrait of the artist trapped in a dead end (he is also estranged from his son), Solov'ev is suspected of raping and murdering nine young men with nearly identical Semitic good looks. Innocent of this crime, Solov'ev is nonetheless tainted once again with suppositions of perversion and frustration (murder aside, his alleged homosexuality could never be seen as a mere neutral fact in an overwhelmingly homophobic culture). *The Stylist,* in which literary parasitism rather than murderous homosexuality is the suspect's dirty secret, shows the life of the post-Soviet literary professional to be dangerous, dishonest, and thoroughly ungratifying.

In other cases, the ostensible author really is the writer of his works, but there is still a residue of scandal and, in the figure of a possible coauthor or double, the return of the repressed. *Chuzhaia maska (Another's Mask)* focuses on Leonid Praskevich, another stand-in for Marinina in that he is an extremely popular writer who has crossed gender lines (in his case, he is the author of best-selling Russian romance novels, a genre that had yet to take off at the time Marinina was writing). Throughout the novel, Praskevich oscillates between being a fake murder victim and a real author or a fake author and a real murder victim. After his apparent death, Praskevich's wife, Svetlana, reveals that she was the real writer but that the books were published under her husband's name in order to create more of a sensation. As the novel progresses, the reader learns that Svetlana's claim is false and that Leonid is still alive—the couple had simply plotted a way to make his next books sell even better owing to the "posthumous" scandal of their authorship. The body presumed to be Leonid's was actually that of his long-lost twin brother, who had been taken from their unknowing mother as part of a Brezhnev-era plot by a corrupt obstetrician to perform cesarean sections on mothers who did not know they were having multiple births. The "extra" babies were stolen and sold on the black market. Again authorship is associated with deception, theft, and trafficking in freakish progeny. This is perhaps Marinina's most explicit connection between popular authorship and mad science, a motif to which she returns repeatedly.

Where does this strange preoccupation with authorship, experimentation, and reproduction come from? On a general level, Marinina is concerned with questions of the fate of cultural patrimony in a globalized literary marketplace. Her works are generic hybrids that owe at least as much to foreign models as they do to Soviet-era antecedents, and even when she is acknowledged to be Russia's best-selling author, it is in the context of a facile and inappropriate comparison ("the Russian Agatha

Christie") that emphasizes her status as a woman writer. More personally, Marinina herself has been dogged by persistent rumors about her legitimacy as an author. The incredible pace of her literary output in the mid-nineties suggests an almost superhuman productivity, which is in turn more grist for Marinina's metafictional mill. The plot of *Za vse nado platit'* (*Everything Has a Cost*) hinges on an experimental compound that allows gifted scientists and artists to achieve their maximum potential but at the cost of a drastically foreshortened life span. Certainly, the work of multiple literary hands would seem more plausible than appealing to Marinina's mad science for an explanation. If Alexandra Marinina actually were a literary factory rather than a single author, this would not be an unprecedented phenomenon—a number of best-selling authors are commonly assumed to be brand names rather than individuals.[30] In her interviews and public appearances, Marinina has repeatedly denied allegations that she employs "literary negroes" (*literaturnye negry*, originally a French term for ghostwriters in which Russians detect no particular racist overtones). The texts themselves provide little reason not to take Marinina at her word: the consistency in characterization, along with the author's preference for certain locutions and patient, detailed monologues, are all indicative of a single authorial voice. Nonetheless, the authors who populate her novels again and again threaten to turn into collectives rather than individuals—one detects a residual sense of loss or anxiety over the now-disclaimed original "Aleksandra Marinina," which Marina Alekseeva admits was originally a name she shared with another writer.[31]

Authorship for Marinina is the one professional sphere where professionalism fails her—if she publishes too many books, she runs the risk of being either a hack or a fraud. When she slows down, her detractors wonder whether she has lost her touch. Within her novels, most of the professional writers suffer from a variation on Nastia's midlife crisis: they cannot function as complete, well-rounded human beings. Only Marinina's second fictional stand-in, the writer/investigator Tatiana Obraztsova, manages both her personal and professional life, but it is quite telling that she is the only author figure whose actual books are never really discussed. Tatiana is the embodiment of Foucault's author-function—she exists to be a character who is also the author of books, but the books themselves are of no interest.

---

[30] For example, the *Blind Man* (*Slepoi*) series of action novels is credited to Andrei Voronin, but the tone, style, and even content vary so much from one book to another that it is easy to identify the moments when a new writer has joined the team.

[31] Marinina's situation is analogous to that of Maks Frai, another female author who retains sole propriety of a pseudonym formerly shared with a man.

Instead it is Nastia, rather than Tatiana, who truly exemplifies Marinina's anxieties of authorship: what could be more indicative of the plight of the hyperefficient, popular writer than a fictional double whose impeccable professionalism masks a lack of emotional depth? Thus it makes perfect sense that Nastia overcomes her own emotional limitations at the same time that Marinina drastically scales back on her literary output. *I Died Yesterday* was written in 1997, one of only two novels produced that year (as opposed to six in 1996 and seven in 1995). These novels also began Marinina's new tendency to write longer books, to the point that they could no longer be reprinted in single-volume paperbacks. From this point on, Marinina begins to experiment with new characters, voices, and even genres (though never leaving Kamenskaia for very long), while Nastia herself has been rewarded with a more confident maturity, surviving shake-ups in her office, taking on a temporary posting elsewhere in order to finally get a promotion, from major to lieutenant colonel in *Prizrak muzyki* (*The Specter of Music*). Both Kamenskaia and her creator are now seasoned veterans of a cutthroat world to which they initially appeared ill suited. More than a decade after Marinina began the reinvention of the detektiv genre, she has allowed her heroine and her novels to settle into a comfortable, well-rounded middle age.

Middle age in fact proves to be the happy goal toward which both Kamenskaia the character and Kamenskaia the series have been moving all along. As a walking computer, Kamenskaia has never been comfortably embodied, observing her own actions from a distance and remaining ironically detached from her own occasional transformations into an alluring vamp. Her lack of interest in having children is always a given but rarely discussed; at the same time illegitimate authors and freakish progeny proliferate unabated in the Marinina novels. Freakish reproduction haunts Marinina work of the nineties as both a symbol of authorial anxieties and a poignant return of the repressed. The sheer literary fecundity represented by Marinina's breakneck publishing speed constitutes an excess, even if the books themselves avoid overkill in most of its manifestations. Despite the baroque plots, Marinina's novels make a virtue of restraint, avoiding the overindulgence in blood and gore characteristic of men's crime fiction while also steering Nastia clear of the soap-opera plots that a female protagonist could so easily inspire (as is usually the case in Dashkova's novels). Marinina the author reaches an equilibrium only after she slows down her frenetic output, devoting more time to the craft of writing. Nastia, the consummate professional, turns out to suffer from an excess of restraint, cutting herself off from her emotions while excelling as one of the few women in a violent milieu. The evolution of Marinina's work shows the woman's detektiv as a genre that lends itself to a holistic examination of virtually all aspects of the characters' lives, rather than simply the extreme states of violence, arousal, and death that dominate the action-oriented fiction offered as men's entertainment. It takes years for Nastia to follow through on the implicit promise that Marinina's early novels made to her readers, balancing the demands of her profession (and genre) with the imperative of living a fully human life.

Chapter Six

MEN OF ACTION

Heroic Melodrama and the Passion of Mad Dog

Deep down I wanted to create a hero who was like I saw myself in
my dreams. To endow him not just with unbeatable strength, swift
thinking, and an unbending will, but also tenderness and a
vulnerable [*ranimaia*] soul. He must be unconditionally loyal to
his friends and merciless to his enemies. And honesty and justice
are as natural to him as breathing…. Intuitively I understood that
I needed a hero the sight of whom would inspire the fair sex to fall
in love, men to believe in their own strength, and children to want
to become just like him.

—Viktor Dotsenko, *Mad Dog's Father* (*Otets Beshenogo*)

Readers of the first volume of Viktor Dotsenko's memoirs, *Mad Dog's
Father* (2000), had to wait over four hundred pages for the author to describe the turning point in his life: the birth of his fictional son, Savelii
Govorkov, better known as *Beshenyi* ("Mad Dog").[1] Dotsenko's paternal
pride fits a common model of male authorship, but it is particularly noteworthy in Mad Dog's case, for both specific and generic reasons. Dotsenko's public proclamation of paternity is ironic and appropriate in that
Savelii himself, like so many action heroes before and after him, is an
orphan. A ward of the state after his parents' tragic demise, Savelii takes
the well-trod path from orphanage to army, finding surrogate fathers at

---

[1] Literally, his name means "rabid." I have chosen "Mad Dog" because it strikes me as a more
plausible name in English.

every turn.[2] But his only mother is the motherland itself, the country he constantly protects from its conniving internal and external enemies. Indeed, the passage that serves as this chapter's epigraph comes from a four-page sequence that is tantamount to the series' primal scene, when the reader sees exactly how Mad Dog was conceived: by the solitary father, fantasizing about the heroes of the past (from folklore, Jack London, and Robert Louis Stevenson) while dreaming of inspiring greater love for the motherland and increased respect for its army. Though the erotics of male creation often suggests masturbation (unless there is a female muse to inspire and bed), Dotsenko presents a case of nonstop ideological autoeroticism, a fixation on the hero he strives to pass on to the audience. He conceives Mad Dog while pondering a parade of idealized types, in the hopes of creating not so much a hero but an image (*obraz*), an ideological pinup to stir his readership's blood.

Mad Dog may be Dotsenko's sole literary child (as opposed to the numerous biological offspring Dotsenko scattered around the former Eastern bloc),[3] but Dotsenko's paternity arguably extends to an entire genre: the highly profitable, much-maligned boevik, or action story. Though the term existed before Mad Dog made his film and prose fiction debut, it is Dotsenko's hero who set the standard for those who followed.[4] I do not wish to make too great a claim for Dotsenko's originality, not least given the influence of an already popular Sylvester Stallone hero. But if Dotsenko himself has conflicting feelings about calling Savelii the "Russian Rambo" (a term that appears in virtually every newspaper article about Mad Dog and that was also used in Vagrius's promotional campaign for the series), recognizing the connection does not mean that Mad Dog can be simply dismissed as a Rambo clone. In creating the most popular and recognizable Russian action hero of the 1990s, Dotsenko no doubt showed fortuitous timing, for in retrospect the idea of a Russian Rambo seems simple and obvious. Like Rambo, the hero of the boevik is appealing precisely because he is a study in contrasts. His unbelievable endurance and overwhelming physical strength are the armor that cannot always cover the psychological wounds that

[2] In what may well have been the first scholarly article on the Russian boevik (1996), Boris Dubin notes the prevalence of orphans among action heroes, connecting the protagonists' fatherlessness with their need for mentor figures later in life, as well as with the genre's emphasis on the hero as lone warrior ("Ispytanie" 253–55).

[3] Dotsenko had five children with various women over a thirty-year period. As his memoirs draw to a close, he strikes a sentimental yet defensive note: "If my older children [two boys and a girl] read this book of my revelations, understand it, and try on their own to find me and end up coming and saying, 'Forgive us, Papa! We didn't know all of this, and so we were wrong!' then my happiness will be simply boundless" (*Otets Beshenogo* 498).

[4] By 1996, Dotesnko's books had sold more than 2.5 million copies (Shevelev 68).

refuse to completely heal. Dotsenko's contribution is significant in that he did more than simply replace Rambo's Vietnam with Mad Dog's Afghanistan. With Mad Dog, Dotsenko developed the Russian boevik as a highly productive model of post-Soviet heroism, bolstered by a complex (indeed, often contradictory) ideology and a set of standardized, but effective, plot devices. The Russian book market is flooded with such heroes cut from Mad Dog's mold, usually identified by a nickname that, like Savelii's, happens to be a substantivized adjective: *Mechenyi* ("Scarface"), *Liutyi* ("Wild Man"), and *Slepoi* ("Blind Man").[5]

The boevik, along with the broader genre I call heroic melodrama, provides a systematic, and ultimately reassuring, approach to chaotic, post-Soviet reality. The Manichaean world of the boevik has clear distinctions between heroes and villains, answering both of Russia's eternal questions: Who's to blame? What is to be done?. The villains are responsible for virtually every social ill that has befallen Russia, while the heroes actually have the power to fight evil and, if not transform the country (even fantasy has its limits), at least prevent the motherland from sliding further into the abyss.

There has been a tendency to treat the boevik as a subset of the mystery genre, the detektiv, because both are based on foreign models, because the Russian versions rose to prominence at roughly the same time, and because they share a preoccupation with crime and are distributed by the same publishers, However, as the Russian market for popular entertainment has developed, both publishers and reviewers have become more conscious that the boevik and the detektiv are discrete genres. A close look at works in the two categories shows some of their obvious differences. Though each tends to include no small amount of violence, blood, and murder, in the detektiv, most of the drama is based on the intellectual thrill of the hunt and the psychological complexities of the crime. In the boevik, the conflict between the forces of good and evil is resolved primarily through violent physical combat. Moreover, if the foreign model for the Russian detektiv is primarily textual, the closest analogues to boevik film and fiction are audiovisual: American and Hong Kong action movies, the American and

---

[5] The nicknames given to boevik heroes are so recognizable a cliché that they become an easy target for parody. Mikhail Ukspenskii, one of the better-known authors mining the Terry Pratchett vein of lighthearted parodic fantasy, has his hero Zhikhar' browse the offerings of a *lubok* ("chapbook") stand, only to discover half a dozen novels about a hero called *Soplivyi* ("Snot-Nose"): "*Snot-Nose's Conspiracy, Snot-Nose's Reprimand, Snot-Nose's Agreement, Snot-Nose's Slander, Snot-Nose's Sentence,* and, finally, *A Hanky for Snot-Nose*" (Uspenskii 65). The Russian titles emphasize the lack of creativity in a way that the English translation cannot, since they all contain minor variations on the root *govor* (*Zagovor, Vygovor, Dogovor, Nagovor,* and *Prigovor*), suggesting the creation of new books entirely by rote.

Italian Western, and the Japanese tale of the wandering *ronin* or rogue samurai in live-action film, *manga* (comics), and *anime* (animation).[6]

Finally, as these comparisons suggest, the detektiv and boevik are clearly *gendered* entertainments, at least in terms of their marketing and production. Though many detektivy are written and read by men, the most prominent authors are women, and their works are a proven success with their female audience. Boeviki in film and fiction are geared primarily toward men, and their authors and producers are almost exclusively male. If the detektiv discussed in the previous chapter gives the female reader access to the alien yet thrilling world of violent crime, the boevik and heroic melodrama develop fantasies of compensatory masculinity that are packaged specifically for a male audience. Violent crime is consumed and assimilated through engaging in virtual combat, not only with the fictional enemies posited by the novel but also with the sense of powerlessness and despair inculcated by the daily paper and the nightly news. This fight, however, is never easy, demanding constant sacrifices enacted in a mechanistic drama played out on the hero's own body: inevitably Christlike, the hero of the boevik must undergo a series of ritual deaths and rebirths in order to bring salvation to a benighted world.

Mad Dog's World

The first question that must be addressed in any examination of the boevik is terminological: what, exactly, does *boevik* mean to the Russian cultural consumer? In this book, I have tried to keep my special pleading on behalf of Russian terms to the bare minimum (chernukha, detektiv, and bespredel), but it is particularly noteworthy (and ironic) that boevik should have no equivalent in English, since the genre and phenomenon are seen as an American product. When action movies such as *Rambo*, *Die Hard*, and *True Lies* were brought to Russia, boevik was the word typically used to describe them. Yet the term is broader than any possible English analogue, immediately suggesting several important features of the genre. Even if the Russian boevik is inspired by Western models, it is definitely the product of cross-cultural fertilization rather than cultural importation. Given that both the detektiv and the boevik deal with crime and crime fighting, there is considerable slippage between the two terms. Nepomnyashchy parenthetically calls

---

[6] Cf. Dubin: "The models for the regular episodes of combat scattered through the text are probably drawn from American action films" ("Action Hero" 113).

boeviki "thrillers" (166), which, while close to the mark, does not accurately convey the type of plot and hero that the genre puts forward.

The heroes of thrillers can be either professional specialists in violence or seemingly random men and women off the street, while the (usually male) protagonist of the boevik is almost always an accomplished warrior, even when his involvement in the plot's violence is initially unmotivated. He may be a former soldier drawn back into the world of mayhem against his will, but in the boeviki created and marketed as uncomplicated mass entertainment, he is never a hapless, mundane Jimmy Stewart. Moreover, if Western thrillers were initially billed as boeviki now they are simply marketed as *trillery*, suggesting a growing differentiation between the two genres. Nepomnyashchy treats the boevik as a subgenre of the large detektiv, which is consistent with the popular understanding in post-Soviet Russia. Olcott sees the two as distinct subgenres, with the detektiv focusing on crime solving and the boevik emphasizing "Rambo-like action" (3). Emphasizing the superhuman abilities of the typical boevik protagonist, Olcott defines boeviks as "wish-fulfillment tales" (144), which he compares to superhero comics. Even this analogy is unsatisfactory, however. Unlike the classic superhero, the hero of the boevik is usually the product of the security and law enforcement apparatus; even when he functions as a lone wolf, his outlook and priorities reflect their origins in the worlds of the military and espionage.

In Russian popular culture, the term *boevik* was originally used simply to designate a wildly successful example of a given genre, whether in film, fiction, or the theater, acquiring a generic meaning only toward the end of the century.[7] This dramatic shift in meaning is not, however, unmotivated. The word literally means "fighter" or "warrior," implicitly referring to the hero rather than the story itself. This suggests that, at least initially, the genre was defined largely in terms of the characters who populated it rather than the events that comprised the plots. While the situation is actually much more complicated (the boevik as genre is far more than simply a story that has a fighter as its hero), the expansion of the term *boevik* from American action movies to Russian films, books, and television programs can be seen as a transplantation first and foremost of character: the boevik genre switches media by taking its fighters with it. American popular culture has its own rich tradition of superheroes, who themselves jump from medium to medium, and pulp heroes, a dying breed most notably represented by

---

[7] Baraban finds evidence for the original usage as far back as a 1935 Soviet dictionary and cites personal correspondence with Jeremy Dwyer attesting to the term's evolution in the 1970s (156n105).

Doc Savage and the Avenger and resurrected on screen in the figure of Indiana Jones; but the action movie, as the term itself suggests, has remained largely within the confines of film (and, where budgets permit, television). In the American context, this makes a great deal of sense, since the action movie is first and foremost a postliterate spectacle: we watch it to be dazzled. The action movie provides a particular visual and visceral thrill that cannot be reproduced in prose, and, for the most part, the American publishing industry does not even try.[8]

By contrast, in Russia the boevik as a locally created product made its mark primarily in book form; though Dotsenko's work first attracted broader attention with films of the first two novels, *Po prozvichshchu zver'* (*Nickname: Beast*) and *Tridtsatogo unichtozhit'!* (*Number Thirty Must Be Destroyed!*), Mad Dog is essentially a prose phenomenon.[9] At least one of the reasons is clearly economic. Particularly in the early post-Soviet years, the Russian film industry was in dire straits. Raising enough money to make an action film that would not seem like a cheap imitation of Hollywood blockbusters was all but impossible. Novels were another story: inexpensive to produce and distribute and therefore sold at a price that all but the most impoverished could afford, paperback books were an attractive alternative to celluloid (even without making allowances for Russia's logocentric culture and traditionally voracious reading habits). Thus the boevik is an example of an unusual generic evolution: the movement from fiction to film is as old as cinematography itself, but it is rare for a genre to be born on screen only to flourish later on paper.

The boevik initially makes more sense as a phenomenon of marketing rather than artistry, for *boevik* is a term used to position a product for a particular imaginary audience. Thus the packaging of the boevik is at least as revealing as the contents of a given film or novel. Quite simply, the Russian consumer knows a boevik when he sees it, and the entertainment industry makes sure that the salient features of the boevik are always readily apparent, as a brief examination of Russian videocassettes sold and packaged as

---

[8] If prose fiction is less than hospitable to transposed action movies, the same cannot be said for comics. With the vastly improved production values in comics and graphic novels over the past decade (combined with an aging readership and a gradual rejection of the restrictive comics code), the aesthetics of the action movie have been embraced in so-called widescreen comics (particularly those written by Mark Millar and Warren Ellis, such as DC/Wildstorm's The Authority or Marvel's The Ultimates).

[9] In 1997, Izvestiia reported that the ORT television channel was planning a 120-episode series based on the Mad Dog novels, but the project was never completed (Selivanova). Mad Dog may yet become a film success story; Dotsenko began filming a third movie, *Number Thirty Returns* (*Tridtsatyi vozvrashchaetsia*) (Nikolaev and Lyshchitskaia 16), thanks to funding from the Moscow city government ("Chto dlia vas" 1).

boeviki shows. I have selected three videos that, taken together, provide a clear picture of the genre's themes and tropes. The cover of the case for the 1994 joint Russian-Polish film *Psy: Posledniaia krov'* (*Hounds: The Last Blood*) (directed by Wladyslaw Pasikowski) shows three men holding locked and loaded guns, all pointed erect and ready; behind them is the image of a dog's open maw, with bloody fangs hanging over their heads. The back cover contains five stills from the film itself, two showing men pointing guns, two with men covered in blood, and one with a blood-soaked man holding a knife to another man's throat. The back cover blurb also accentuates the violence: "War on Earth never stops, even for a day. Every day terrorists' explosions resound, crippling and killing innocent people, while the gunshots of hired killers rip open the silence, cutting short thousands of lives."

The violence of the film's images is thus enhanced by the film's description, adding a silent soundtrack (the silence is ripped open) and providing something of a political context.

A similar strategy is evident on the cover of the videocassette for the *Afganets* (*Afghan*) (1991, directed by Vladimir Mazur); here we have a military collage, complete with helicopters, gun-toting Muslims, and the bloody, decapitated head of a Russian soldier. The context for *Afghan* is clearly political, highlighting the genre's recurring theme of patriotism and betrayal.

> A simple Soviet guy, after suffering a painful ordeal and the cruelty of captivity, can't imagine his life without the motherland, but it greets him with gang wars and blood, and the people around him show only incomprehension and indifference. How is he supposed to go on [*zhit' dal'she*] with a soul wounded by the horrors of the Afghan war, what path is he to choose. . . .

Finally, we have the "new *super*boevik" *Krestonosets* (*The Crusader*) (directed by Aleksandr Inshakov and Mikhail Tumanishvili, 1995), a more lighthearted entry about stuntmen making a movie set in the Middle Ages, while also fighting the "narcomafia" that threatens to halt the film's production. Both the film and its back-cover blurb depend upon a conflation of the values of medieval knighthood with the heroism needed to fight against the mob: "He [the Crusader/Stuntman] looks danger in the eye with professional composure. . . . One against all. . . . He survives and triumphs."The film's violence is more stylized, as is the video's packaging. Rather than showing blood and gore, most of the still shots emphasize the potential for violence, particularly on the cover, where the star's face is doubly framed by the crusader's cross and the crosshairs of a rifle.

While it is difficult to say how consciously the producers of these films manipulated certain themes and motifs in their particular boeviki, the videos' packaging highlights the genre's paramount concerns: violence (both redemptive and spectacular), the pathos of Russia (and, in the case of *Hounds,* Poland as well), the frustrations of the hero's return (often linked to the death/resurrection motif mentioned earlier), and the superhuman valor of the lone wolf encircled by implacable enemies. Taken together, these themes constitute a powerful imaginary reconstruction of an always already lost ethos of masculine heroic honor, a point that the marketing department of the largest publisher of boeviki in print makes abundantly clear. The term "men's novels" (*muzhskie romany*) was already industry shorthand for the broad panoply of crime-related fiction thought to appeal primarily to men, but Vagrius took this gender marking even further, with a series that apparently began in 1998.[10] *Men's Business* (*Muzhskoe delo*) presents itself in terms of gender and moral philosophy, for here the calling of the "real man" is to fight those very forces of evil that would drag the world into total chaos if not for the efforts of the hero: "When the law is powerless, they are the judge and jury [*oni vershat svoi sud*]—superdetective, elite fighters, just people driven to despair by criminal *bespredel*. This is their choice, this is *men's business* . . ."[11] Vagrius's marketing campaign defines the hero rather well, for despite the fact that he is a specialist in violence, he is rarely portrayed as a thrill seeker. Instead, circumstances compel him to act, for, as a professional warrior and real man, he can do nothing less.

Mad Dog's Birth

The Russian literary hero is typically the protagonist in two overlapping dramas: the finite story in which he is ostensibly the star and the ongoing saga of the culture's quest to find or create an inspiring, positive protagonist who is presumed absent almost by definition. For at least two centuries, Russian heroism has suffered from a periodic crisis of representation, in which the most salient feature of the Russian hero is his scarcity or impossibility. The

---

[10] I have no evidence of books published in the series earlier than this date.

[11] Emphasis in the original. Text taken from the back cover of Il'ichev's *Psikh protiv mafii.* Vagrius calls *Muzhskoe delo* "the best Russian_detektivy and boeviki," thereby undermining the distinction between the boevik and the detektiv that I have been so careful to make. Yet the selection of the books included in the series, and the fact that Vagrius publishes plenty of other mysteries that are not part of the *Muzhskoe delo* line, suggests that Vagrius is including only a certain kind of detektiv in the genre of boevik: the action-packed, macho adventures that the publishing house assumes will have a greater appeal for men than for women.

mid-nineteenth century saw endless debates about the passivity of the Russian (male) protagonist, often called the "superfluous man" by way of convenient shorthand. In his 1860 essay "When Will the Real Day Come?" the radical critic Nikolai Dobrolyubov lamented the paucity of what would now be called positive role models in Russian fiction: the Russian hero, rather than being the captain of his fate, was indecisive and weak-willed to the point of near-immobility, more reminiscent of the incompetent heroes of the Russian wonder tale (*skazka*) than the larger-than-life *bogatyri* (knights) of the folk epic.[12] After the revolution, socialist realism attempted to create a panoply of heroic types for readers' and viewers' emulation. Here, too, though, the task was not an easy one, as writers often found their protagonists critiqued in the press for lapses in revolutionary consciousness or rugged strength. And even the most successful socialist realist heroes displayed an uncanny drive to sacrifice and self-destruction. From Ostrovskii's perpetually moribund Pavel Korchagin through Polevoi's legless aviator, Soviet novels and films demanded martyrs, with plots functioning as infernal machines that mangled the heroes fed to them as fodder.[13] If, broadly speaking, the nineteenth-century discourse of heroism was animated by the hero's absence, Soviet ideology insisted on his presence but also on his suffering, death, and rebirth. Presumably, the pedagogical and mimetic impulses of Soviet culture at least in part explain this dynamic. Rather than allowing the reader to be the passive witness to the ongoing adventures of a seemingly deathless Superman, Soviet narratives stressed the mortality of the individual hero along with the immortality of the heroic type. It was up to the reader to pick up the baton dropped by the dying protagonist.

The Russian hero, both in his own plots and the cultural plot about him, is not, therefore, always waiting in the wings or on patrol looking for evildoers. He must be summoned, whether by individuals or organizations needing his aid (in books and films) or by voices within the culture decrying a perceived crisis of values and lack of positive models for emulation. His is a command performance in the service of an explicit ideology (as in Soviet times) or as a response to a vaguer, but no less pressing, sense of the threat of an ideological void. Thus it is only fitting that the post-Soviet hero of the boevik is often an initially reluctant warrior who thought that his

[12] When the hero of the typical Russian *skazka* encounters a problem, his first response is usually to sit down on a hot white stone and cry until a magical helper appears.

[13] Victor Pelevin's debut novel, *Omon-Ra* (1992), turns the Soviet ethos of sacrifice into devastating satire: at a special aviation training camp, would-be pilots have their legs amputated in imitation of the hero of Boris Polevoi's *Story of a Real Man*. For more on the function of the wounded male in the discourse of Soviet masculinity, see Kaganovsky (577–96).

days of struggle were behind him, since this is precisely the role he plays in the current cultural dynamics. Throughout the perestroika era (and arguably longer, starting with the Brezhnev years), the positive hero was, if not defunct, at least on the decline; his return was prompted by the disaster that has befallen his country and his culture. Once again, Dotsenko's description of his creation of Mad Dog is paradigmatic: not only must Dotsenko's hero be admirable and entertaining, but the tales of his heroic deeds must redeem the nation's collapsing military-industrial institutions and, like the Stakhanovite hero of Stalin's time, set the reader and viewer on the path to heroism in their own lives.

Savelii Govorkov's birth as a literary hero was as torturous as his own fictional biography was tragic. Dotsenko spent years trying to interest both publishers and filmmakers in his project, in a series of false starts that is mirrored by Savelii's own frequent setbacks and rebirths. Though Savelii's life story is told in the series' first installment, *Srok dlia Beshenogo* (*Mad Dog in Prison*), it is not until the second book that Dotsenko develops a comfortable pattern for his Mad Dog stories. The first, anomalous Mad Dog entry functions essentially as a prequel, providing a backstory that will be referenced in subsequent novels while built on a plot that little resembles the later works. Most of the important information we need to know about Savelii's past, though initially presented in *Mad Dog in Prison*, is boiled down to a paragraph in the forewords that precede each of the Mad Dog novels starting with the seventh, *Zoloto Beshenogo* (*Mad Dog's Gold*): "Savelii Kuz'mich Govorkov was born in 1965, and was orphaned at the age of three.[14] The orphanage, workers' dormitory, army, *spetsnaz*, the war in Afghanistan, some wounds. Later he was convicted and deprived of his freedom, rehabilitated" (*Zoloto* 3).

Mad Dog in Prison gives us the birth of a hero but not the birth of a genre; while we learn much about Savelii's past, the bulk of the story belongs to a particular subset of men's crime fiction, the prison drama, or "zone" story. It is the novel's flashbacks that provide Savelii's history, establishing a pattern of heroism and martyrdom that will only be intensified in the books to come. Essentially, his life so far has been a series of betrayals, often by women. When he is given to a family for adoption, the mother beats him so much that he begs to be returned to the orphanage ("I'd rather be beaten here!") (286). Already rudderless from his experience in Afghanistan (he is one of his regiment's few survivors), Savelii is convicted of a financial crime that he did not commit, thanks to his girlfriend's treachery.

---

[14] Actually, according to young Savelii's own testimony in a flashback in the first novel, he was two and a half (*Srok* 283).

These betrayals punctuate the overarching pattern of Savelii's life, in which the intervals of routine, daily existence grow shorter and shorter while extreme, near-fatal encounters occur with increasing frequency. It is not enough that Savelii is left an orphan; toward the end of the novel, a flash-back describes the immediate aftermath of the car crash that killed his parents and little Savushka's grief and fear as he struggles to overcome the physical pain caused by the accident. "You can take it, you're a man!" an old man tells him, as if supplying the motto for his subsequent adventures and travails (283). From this point on, Savelii is both the eternal warrior and the eternal orphan, never wavering in the fight to protect those weaker than he, yet so often beaten and tortured that he passes out from exhaustion, only to be taken in and cared for by any one in a series of big-hearted (and usually short-lived) women.

Eight (fictional) years pass between the first and second novels, time enough for Savelii to be thoroughly transformed into a nearly superhuman action hero. In the second chapter of *Number Thirty Must Be Destroyed!* we discover that nearly all of the action of the first novel has become irrelevant[15]—Varia, the woman who saved him after his escape from the prison camp, conveniently kills herself not long after the previous novel's close, as it turns out that she cannot live with the memories of the gang rape and torture she suffered at the villains' hands. As if to reinforce the sterility of the previous plotlines, Varia's suicide note informs Savelii that she had been pregnant with his son at the time of the rape, after which she lost not only the baby but her capacity to conceive.[16] Savelii's grief helps motivate his unexpected return to Afghanistan, which leads to his subsequent adventures. But this second tour of duty has another function beyond its role as mere plot device. It is as though Dotsenko realized that he had given Savelii's Afghan experience short shrift and now was taking the opportunity to dwell on this personal and national trauma at much greater length. When Andrei Voronov, Savelii's closest friend, recalls his Afghan tour of duty in the third novel, he thinks:

> Of course, the biggest event that bound them [Voronov and Savelii] together was the war in Afghanistan. A strange war, where you feel vulnerable from all sides. Those who stayed in this war almost from the beginning, like him and

---

[15] One apparent throwaway character does return to assume a surprisingly prominent role, but only much later. An eight-year-old girl named Rozochka will eventually grow up to become Savelii's child bride.

[16] How she knew the child's sex is never explained, but the assumption of a male heir is thematically consistent—she was to produce the next generation of heroes.

Savelii, quickly understood the insane pointlessness of this "war of liberation." They understood it, but couldn't do anything about it: they were SOL-
DIERS, they were doing their DUTY, subordinate to only one commander:
their OATH. (*Vozvrashchenie* 128–29; emphasis in the original)

For Voronov, and, by extension, for all the Afghan veterans who populate
Dotsenko's novels, the war experience was a tempering process that left the
surviving soldiers with superhuman survival skills and an unwavering
moral code: "Captain Voronov understood one thing: those who had gone
through the war in Afghanistan and those who had not were entirely different people. No, he didn't idealize the former at all: among them were scum,
wheeler-dealers, scavengers, and traitors, but such people made up only a
small percentage" (*Vozvrashchenie* 129).[17]

This time, there can be no doubt that Afghanistan is a transformative experience.[18] Not only does Savelii hover on the brink of death (again), but upon
his revival, he is granted the superhuman powers that will become so crucial
in his never-ending fight against evil. Wounded in battle with the treacherous
Afghan rebels, Savelii is delivered into the care of a mysterious Tibetan
Teacher (*Uchitel'*) and revived by an order of monks. In an abrupt break from
the action of *Mad Dog in Prison*, the second novel begins with a chapter entitled "Initiation," in which Savelii is now prepared to undergo a rite of passage
that will change him forever. This is the culmination of a five-year process that
began with Savelii's healing. The Teacher conveniently summarizes Savelii's
accomplishments in the first of many monologues, all of which are rendered
in entirely capital letters, as if to impress the reader with his gravitas:[19]

[17] Voronov's primary concern about Afghan war veterans is based on the American experience
in Vietnam: he knows that post-traumatic stress disorder is likely to strike many of them and
laments that the country is doing nothing to prevent this disaster (129).

[18] Dotsenko was far from alone in making Afghanistan central to the boevik genre, nor was he
the first to do so. Boris Kvashnev's 1991 film *Ameriken boi* (*American Boy*) also tells the tale of an
Afghan veteran on a crusade to avenge a fallen comrade. Though *American Boy* played an important role in the development of the Russian boevik, I would argue that it was something of a rough
draft for works that would prove to be central to the canon. Particularly anomalous is the hero's
own lack of patriotism. Nikolai Naidenov, like Mad Dog, is the product of both the Soviet orphanage and the Soviet army, but when circumstances allow him to become an American citizen and
start a new life, he does so with nary a backward glance. His adventures upon his return to Russia
reconnect him with the motherland but are not enough to make him abandon his pregnant American wife. His refusal to remain in Russia is understandable within the context of the film itself but
separates Naidenov from the typical boevik hero (whose periodic despair over the state of the
country never detracts from his patriotism).

[19] Though to the American eye this sort of capitalization for emphasis looks more like something out of Internet spam or a direct-mailing campaign, it is an accepted convention in Russian
publishing. However, I know of no Russian author who uses capitalization anywhere nearly as
much as Dotsenko does.

"I HEALED YOU. I PUT MY SOUL IN YOU . . . I TAUGHT YOU TO CONTROL YOUR BODY, AND NOW IT IS PROTECTED FROM THE DESTRUCTIVE EFFECTS OF POISONS, FIRE, AND IRON" (*Tridtsatogo* 8–9).[20] Savelii is branded with the "Son Mark," which must always radiate warmth; if he ever meets someone whose mark is cold, he will know that this man has betrayed the brotherhood and serves evil.

This rite of passage sets the pattern for Savelii's relationship with the men in his life for the next twenty novels: his connection with his teacher, his "brothers," and his comrades in arms will always be depicted as more spiritually intense and morally significant than his relations with women.[21] As Savelii tells his teacher: "For five years, you replaced my father, friend, and brother. Now you're more than simply a mentor [*nastavnik*], a teacher, more than a father. It's too bad that we are not of the same blood, but our Spirit is one!" (11). In fact, it is the blood that must be shared to bring the rite to its completion: Savelii and his Teacher drink each other's blood in order to become one, which provides the rational explanation behind the subtext-heavy greeting that Savelii will always exchange with the Teacher and his other followers: "You are in me, and I am in you!" Though the ritual itself is reminiscent of rites of blood brotherhood, in this case the exchange of fluids cements their relationship across the generations: the Teacher (who always addresses his followers as "my sons") is the father Savelii never had, the father who is responsible for his second birth.

Indeed, adventures aside, the emotional heart of Mad Dog's story is his success in re-creating a family of men, compensating most directly for his loneliness as an orphan but also ideologically for the abandoned status of the soldier returning from Afghanistan. The Teacher is the only member of his new male family who is not a battle-seasoned veteran of a military structure. When *Number Thirty Must Die!* flashes back to Savelii's second tour of duty in Afghanistan, we see his close bond with fellow soldier Andrei Voronov. Though they were childhood friends, it is the war experience that bonds them: "It was not even friendship, but something bigger, something that can't be conveyed with simple words. Each of them said of the other . . . 'He's more than a brother to me!' " (*Vozvrashchenie* 128). They share secrets that they would tell no others, and, of course, save each others' lives. After they both return to the "Big Land" (the Soviet soldier's

---

[20] This is only the beginning; over time, Savelii also develops limited telepathic abilities.

[21] Dubin notes that the boevik hero is always a loner, resembling a "monk in the ascetic tradition." Yet by the same token, the hero is also "a representative of a warrior caste, even of a holy order"—that is, a lone wolf who can still identify with a pack (Dubin, "Action Thriller" 106).

slang for the USSR), Andrei becomes Savelii's trusted partner in the fight against evil. Their bond is repeatedly emphasized throughout the series, a cross between brotherhood and friendship that at times seems both mystical and erotic, as in this scene, when they meet each other while undercover:

> Their eyes met literally for a moment. A bystander would think that two strangers quickly looked each other over and immediately forgot each other. In actuality they invested so much information in these gazes that the uninitiated couldn't possibly understand.
>
> They said that they missed each other and worried about each other, that Andrei had completely despaired of ever finding Savelii, but that he never gave up hope for a successful outcome, that Savelii couldn't send word of himself, but would tell everything later, that now he needed help, but that they had to be very careful, that he had prepared a letter for him and was ready to send it, to which Andrei answered in kind. These gazes contained a great deal more than could be told on paper. (*Vozvrashchenie* 253)

Both Savelii and his "adopted brother" (*nazvannyi brat*) work for another heroic warrior, General Bogomolov, a state security officer who makes no secret of his paternal feelings for Mad Dog. For his part, Mad Dog is well aware of the importance of substitute father figures for his moral development.

> Yes, Savelii's parents laid a powerful foundation, but you need to work hard to have a durable house. And he was lucky with his teachers: the Japanese Ukeru Magasaki, the old general Porfirii Govorov, finally, his wise Teacher. Savelii was very grateful to these people. If not for them, he could have become an entirely different person, directing all his power and skills for evil. (*Zoloto* 298)

By extension, Savelii's musings on the importance of guides and role models in his own development as a hero highlight the pedagogical mission that Dotsenko himself attributes to Mad Dog's adventures: powerful male authority figures are all that save a rudderless youth from a wasted life of crime. Savelii will continue to collect fathers and brothers over the course of his adventures, including even FBI agent Michael James. But most of the men with whom Savelii forges strong bonds are also Afghan veterans, united by common sorrows. These soldiers are usually credited with a heightened sensitivity to danger and a strong moral code whose imperative is defending the weak, even if this defense involves the physical extermination of those who prey on them.[22]

The ideological and emotional power of Dotsenko's affiliative male families should not be underestimated. Dotsenko appeals to an old and powerful fantasy of military brotherhood that facilitates the submerging of self in a group identity and the inflation of self through heroic deeds. The hero can bond with a band of brothers who share common values and ideals, living essentially as an equal; by the same token, he can prove himself through solo missions or by rescuing fallen comrades.[23] This compromise between self-sufficiency and horizontal group identity also has a vertical parallel, providing the brothers with idealized father figures. In Dotsenko's case, Mad Dog benefits from the wise counsel and strong support of Bogomolov and also periodically receives affirmation from paternal figures of almost demigod status: over the course of the first ten novels, Mad Dog meets and is decorated by Yeltsin, Prime Minister Viktor Chernomyrdin, and even Bill Clinton (before the 1999 NATO bombing of Yugoslavia shifted the American president into the "villains" category). Such a blessing of the hero by a great leader is a familiar pattern, both from world literature in general and from socialist realism in particular. If socialist realist protagonists inevitably made their way to the "center" and met with Stalin or Stalin-substitutes, the boevik hero is equally favored. One must also recognize that this kind of relationship with patriarchal authority manages to retain only the positive aspects of the father-son dynamic, enacting a submission to the father that is empowering rather than castrating. The key is that these encounters are brief and relatively infrequent. In the Mad Dog books, even Savelii's meetings with Bogomolov serve primarily to get him back out into the field, where he is his own master.

The boevik is unmistakably a man's world, predicated on male fantasies of power and control that leave little room for the female reader's imaginary identification with characters. With the exception of the occasional, idealized Beloved (to whom we will return later), women in the boevik serve distinctly functional roles. As Boris Dubin notes, their defining feature is sexual availability (253), in part reflecting a common understanding about women's semiofficial duties in the new world of Russian *biznes*.[24]

---

[22] Even popular writers as distant from this genre as Aleksandra Marinina occasionally avail themselves of the "magic Afghan" archetype. In *Chernyi spisok* (*The Black List*) an Afghan veteran's sixth sense for danger saves the heroes on a number of occasions.

[23] Male comradeship was a cardinal virtue of Soviet culture. See Borenstein, *Men Without Women*, and Zimovets.

[24] On the masculinization of the Russian business environment (and the concomitant sexualization of women in the workplace), see Yurchak, "Muzhskaia ekonomika."

When Mad Dog (or any other boevik hero) encounters a young woman who works in an office, she is inevitably a long-legged beauty whose generosity with her sexual favors seems to be part of her job description. Despite longstanding Soviet and Russian attitudes toward female promiscuity, in the boevik such women are not usually condemned as sluts, or seen as degraded by what not infrequently amounts to sexual servitude. Instead, they seem to be fulfilling their "natural" roles, trading in the gifts and talents they have. Hence, the damsel in distress can give herself to her savior without qualms but without expectation of a long-term relationship because she is giving the hero something that defines her basic value and function.

In the Mad Dog books, it is a rare sexual encounter that does not lead to the woman's satisfaction. All the women scream with pleasure almost as soon as they are penetrated, begging the men to go deeper. They all reach orgasm with the greatest of ease, ejaculating a "nectar of love" (*nektar liubvi*) in response to his "powerful stream" (*sil'naia struia*). The reassurance to the male reader is self-evident: female sexual physiology, rather than being mysterious or threatening, proves to be identical and in sync with the male's. The man's success in bed is a function not of technique (there is none), but rather of his manliness itself. The woman responds to male strength and forcefulness, to a primal masculinity that gives her exactly what she needs. Indeed, virtually every female character who populates Dotsenko's fiction is submissive to a quite literal phallic authority. When a young woman in the eighth novel, *Mad Dog in Love* (*Liubov' Beshenogo*), tracks down her lover's killer to his hospital bed, she discards her plans for revenge in favor of frantic sexual coupling upon her discovery that his penis is even larger than that of her dead lover (*Takoi penis!* ["What a penis!"] a nurse tells her before she sees it for herself). Arkadii Rasskazov and the other villains engage in orgies quite frequently, and their female partners, as well as the male readers, inevitably learn that while Rasskazov's top henchmen are well endowed, it is Rasskazov who is cock of the walk. Mad Dog is also no slouch in that particular department, but since he rarely indulges in group sex (and in any case, never with the villains), there is less opportunity for comparison.

Only occasionally does Mad Dog encounter a female antagonist, such as the sadistic nightclub manager Lolita, who tortures a man who once raped her, having sex with her boyfriend while the rapist slowly bleeds to death (*Vozvrashchenie* 26–28). If most of the women in Mad Dog's world provide constant support for male strength and power, Lolita is their nightmarish opposite. The fact that she castrates her rapist makes her symbolic role grotesquely literal. Throughout the Mad Dog books in particular (and boeviki in general), women are either raped, threatened with rape, or simply used sexually without much forethought or concern. Indeed, Russian men's crime fiction often indulges in the male fantasy that legitimizes sexual violence by rendering it consensual after the fact. The man begins to use force, but soon the woman stops resisting, enjoys herself, and falls in love. Only three situations seem to make heterosexual coercion undeniable rape: when torture is involved, when the woman already "belongs" to a positive hero (such as Varia in *Mad Dog in Prison*), or when the aggressor is from the Caucasus (sex between "dark" men and Russian women is framed as rape almost by definition).

To this rosy view of sexual coercion, Dotsenko adds a sustained apologia for pedophilia: Mad Dog's main opponent, Arkadii Rasskazov, has a marked taste for underage girls, a passion he satisfies with a harem of preteen Thai prostitutes he calls his *kurochki* ("chicks"). Though they are initially afraid of him, he showers them with gifts, gives them Russian names, and teaches them to love him "like a father." The situation would be at least somewhat ambiguous if it were only the villain who had this propensity, but the great love affair of Mad Dog's life, the relationship that makes him a complete and happy human being, is with a sixteen-year-old girl who fell in love with him when she was eight: the orphaned Rozochka first encountered in *Mad Dog in Prison*. Rozochka is not only pure, good-hearted, and innocent but also the beneficiary of the kind of good fortune that usually befell orphaned girls in turn-of-the-century melodramas. After inheriting a great deal of money, she moves to America, where she studies at Columbia University. Savelii returns her love when they meet again but resists the temptation to sleep with her until she finally begs him to "make her a woman." During that same encounter, two things happen to her: she learns of Savelii's real work (which involves no small share of murder) and she becomes pregnant with his child (naturally a son, naturally named Savushka). Though at first she is horrified by Savelii's revelation, she quickly realizes that his way is right and soon learns martial arts and psychic tricks from a sensei of her own. Just as Rasskazov's "chicks" find the love and paternal care that they lacked in their impoverished homeland, Savelii's own nymphet is transformed by his love into an adult, self-confident superwoman who can eventually battle at his side. By this point, both Savelii and the author seem to have forgotten the long-dead Lolita, whose own encounter with an older man ruined her life and transformed her into a castrating villain.

Mad Dog's Metaphysics

Instead, the best women in Mad Dog's world participate in the series' over-arching paradigm of near-death and mutual redemption. Once Savelii's Teacher breathes new life into his all but lifeless corpse, Mad Dog will find himself on the verge of death with surprising regularity, usually to be revived by a woman (thus returning to the pattern established with Varia, his rescuer-turned-beautiful-corpse from the first novel). Many of the *Mad Dog* novels begin with Savelii lying in bed, on the mend after surgery or personal loss, thus allowing him to reenact a national myth of trauma and recovery, of the transition from passivity to aggression in a ritual that becomes as familiar as his infiltration of enemy compounds and the Schwarzenegger-like catchphrase he growls at his antagonists again and again: "Live . . . for now . . ." ("*Zhivi . . . poka . . .*") Whatever the means of his recovery, whether it be a new call to action, faking his own death and arranging a complete course of plastic surgery and a chance to begin a new life, or a mystical experience during anal sex with a prostitute (see chapter 3), the key to his physical and spiritual renewal lies in decisive action. The sixth novel, *Mad Dog's Gold*, begins with an enactment of Savelii's death in an automobile accident in order to throw his enemies off his trail. While his friends and acquaintants attend his funeral, Savelii is in an elite hospital undergoing plastic surgery, whereupon he will have not only a new name (Sergei Manuilov) but a new face (matched by a new model for the covers of his paperback novels). Mad Dog's new secret identity is eventually all but discarded, by which point the author once again subjects him to a fictional death: at the end of the fifteenth novel, *Ostrov Beshenogo* (*Mad Dog's Island*), Savelii is held captive off the shores of Nicaragua by the mysterious Shiroshi, and in the next novel, *Sled Beshenogo* (*Mad Dog's Trail*), his double is killed before his wife's very eyes. The book ends with "Savelii's" funeral (the second in the series), whereupon his wife, now convinced that Savelii is actually alive, goes to search for him in a novel from which Savelii, now incapacitated by Shiroshi's mad science, is all but absent (*Mad Dog's Pupil*).

In Dotsenko's novels, Savelii must be repeatedly broken and mended, lost and found, with a regularity that suggests something on the order of the mythic or the compulsive. The pattern of redemptive suffering and spiritual rebirth is an old one for Russia, an assumption of the Christ narrative most famously enacted in the works of Dostoevsky. But it also has its roots in the boevik's foreign antecedents, most notably in John Rambo's repeated brushes with death, wallowing in obscurity, and returns to the

Figure 6: Cover of Viktor Dotsenko's *Mad Dog's Reward*, one of the author's many novels about the heroic Savelii Govorkov.

sites of American national trauma. Given the frequency with which post-Soviet popular heroes lament their country's humiliating subordinate position vis-à-vis the world's one remaining superpower, it is particularly ironic that the very pattern Dotsenko borrows in order to enact and work through Russia's trauma is itself a partial borrowing from an adversarial culture. It is not enough that Mad Dog be brave and strong; he must also be vulnerable, subject to the same crises and despair that afflict his country.

Again, the pedagogical dimension emerges, in this case with distinct religious overtones: Savelii must descend into misery in order to show that one can rise above the horrors of the everyday. Mad Dog does not quite die for our sins, but we would do well to accept him as our personal, gun-toting savior.

Though the Mad Dog series does not read as if Dotsenko were following a long-term plan, the contours of Savelii's life suggest a kind of repetition compulsion In the early novels, Savelii keeps coming back to Afghanistan, making a third trip in *Komanda Beshenogo* (*Mad Dog's Team*), a book that once again begins with a bed-ridden Savelii's recovery from his latest wounds. Predictably, Afghanistan soon gives way to Chechnya, where the ongoing military conflict provides seemingly endless possibilities for Mad Dog's heroism. By the time Kosovo is thrown into the mix (*Pravosudie Beshenogo* [*Mad Dog's Justice*]), the pattern could not be clearer: in the best traditions of the Slavic epic (which extols Slavic heroism in battles that end in defeat), the Mad Dog books always return to the site of Russia's failures, inserting Savelii into the battles in order to turn them into qualified successes.

It is this identification between the hero and his country, this preoccupation with the fate of Russia, that, on the one hand, makes Mad Dog so typical of the boevik genre but, on the other hand, goes to such an extreme as to put Dotsenko's works in a category of their own (perhaps thereby explaining the series' particular popularity). As we saw in our examination of the *Nympho* series in chapter 3, the action-packed boevik provides a surprisingly comfortable backdrop for off-the-cuff philosophizing about Russia, morality, and the role of God, mysticism, and fate in human life. This combination of soft-peddled nationalism, back-to-basics Manichaeism, and the aggressively masculine but fundamentally wounded hero is pervasive in the genre. In film, it can be found in the 1997 quasi-Dostoevskian gangster and gladiator drama *Everything We Dreamed about for So Long* (discussed in chapter 3); the truck-driving crusader for vengeance in *Vultures on the Road*; the Christlike martyrdom of the karate expert and Afghan veteran in the 1994 *Russkii tranzit* (*Russian Transit*) (directed by Viktor Titov); and the 1999 sophomoric, soft-core porn comic parody *Superkhirurg* (*Supersurgeon*) (directed by Andrei Badin), in which a hard-drinking, hard-fighting surgeon is kidnapped by the mob in order to perform a penis transplant on the once well-endowed mob boss, only to take over as leader after beating the bad guys and proving his phallus is the biggest of them all.

We meet Fox, the hero of Daniil Koretskii's novels *Antikiller* and *Antikiller-2* (both turned into very successful films with high production values and no small share of gore), when he, like Mad Dog, is a righteous man waiting to be released from prison (in Fox's case, he is in the special prison zone for corrupt police officers in Nizhnii Tagil). But where Mad Dog earns his freedom through heroic action and by proving himself innocent, Fox is technically guilty: he killed a man in order to protect an innocent witness. Moreover, he engineers his release by falsifying evidence. Nonetheless, we are clearly meant to see Fox as correct, since the corrupt criminal justice system cannot protect the innocent. Hence Fox becomes an "antikiller," that is, a hit man for the cause of justice (the Russian word "killer" is narrower than the original English, always referring to a hired killer).

The *Antikiller* books and movies bring home a point that might not be clear from reading Mad Dog alone: most boeviki are decidedly pessimistic. Yes, the hero wins his particular battle, but not before being convinced yet again that the world in general, and Russia in particular, is becoming an increasingly grim and hopeless place. Fox's short-term successes and strong moral (as opposed to legal) framework still keep his adventures within the category of the boevik, but the situations in which he finds himself, and the particularly amoral enemies he fights, bring *Antikiller* into the mode of bespredel. Fox is the apotheosis of the betrayed, lone hero who still fights for his country. The film version of *Antikiller* both begins and ends with a close-up of the protagonist reciting his oath of service while twisting his lips and gritting his teeth so emphatically that, without the benefit of context, one might imagine that the induction into the militia had been combined with his physical in order to save time ("Recite your oath, bend over, and cough"). Indeed, given his betrayal by everyone around him (the second iteration of the oath comes while Fox's head is squarely within a marksman's sights), the comparison is rather apt.

By contrast, despite the seemingly overwhelming forces of evil Savelii fights, despite the proliferation of global conspiracies victimizing Russia, Mad Dog's world is an unusually optimistic one. Unlike Fox, and unlike many of the Mad Dog clones that populated bookshelves in the 1990s, Savelii rarely compromises with the forces of evil, nor does he need to: there are enough good, uncorrupt people around that Mad Dog does not need to suffer in the morally ambiguous world of Western spy fiction or Russian bespredel tales. True, he does occasionally meet, and even help, old-fashioned gangsters who still play by the Soviet-era rules of organized crime, but his sympathy partakes of the long-standing Russian tradition of empathy for "good criminals"(Brooks 175). Savelii is by no means happy about what has happened to his country, but his experience leaves him hope for the better. Wherever he goes, he meets "salt of the earth" Russians who are still guided by a moral compass. This is in keeping with the surprisingly liberal politics Dotsenko espouses in the pre-1999 Mad Dog novels, both via his more positive characters and through direct authorial address: for Dotsenko, Yeltsin is a hero who is honestly attempting to transform the country for the better, and therefore, unlike the majority of authors and directors who work in the genre, Dotsenko does not transform the words "reform" and "democracy" into terms of abuse. Indeed, Russia is fortunate to be guided by men who truly love the country and care about its fate, including Boris Yeltsin himself, who, like the prototypical Russian "good tsar," is an honest man deceived and betrayed by his close advisers.[25]

The optimism of Mad Dog is part and parcel of the series' particular form of nationalism. While Dotsenko makes it clear that Russia is assailed by an astounding array of international conspiracies and hardly turns a blind eye to the sufferings of the nation, he does not cultivate the despair that characterizes narratives of bespredel. Instead, he continually points out signs of hope in his idealized portrayal of Russians and Russianness. In the Mad Dog novels, the dedication, generosity, and resolve of the Afghan veterans are Russianness itself, distilled and purified in the crucible of war. The magic power of these soldiers, symbolized in an extreme version in Savelii's own superhuman abilities, is shared by all Russians, or at least it can be. When Mad Dog's American friend Michael is shocked at his accomplishments, he asks, "What, are you a wizard [*volshebnik*] or something?" Savelii replies: "In our country, everyone's a wizard!" (*Nagrada Beshenogo* [*Mad Dog's Reward*] 138). When a stranger helps Savelii regain his passport and return to the motherland, Savelii thinks: "No, only a Russian person could do that!" (*Tridtsatogo* 104).

Before the 1999 NATO bombing of Yugoslavia, the Mad Dog books implicitly advocate a relatively liberal nationalist ideology, one that puts duty to country first but calls for tolerance and understanding among peoples. Indeed, the relationship between ostensible content and ideology in the Mad Dog novels is perhaps unsurprisingly similar to the role of ideology in pornography (discussed in chapter 2): the recurring philosophical digressions about the fate of Russia, the plight of "sexual minorities," and the need to respect the military and rebuild the country add heft to an otherwise

---

[25] Savelii first speaks with Yelstin in the seventh book, *Nagrada Beshenogo* (*Mad Dog's Reward*), when the president personally congratulates him and calls him a hero (159–61). In the thirteenth novel, *Kremlevskoe delo Beshenogo* (*Mad Dog's Kremlin Case*), Yeltsin personally approaches Savelii to have him investigate allegations that his advisers are corrupt. When the president's suspicions prove to be founded, Yeltsin takes the only honorable course left to him: resignation.

lightweight narrative, at the same time raising the suspicion that the story itself at times becomes an excuse for indulging in philosophy. Evidently, Dotsenko wants to be the Tolstoy of the boevik set: just as *War and Peace* alternates battle and homefront scenes with authorial tracts on the nature of history, novels such as *Mest' Beshenogo* (*Mad Dog's Revenge*) always make time for extended discussions of the meaning of life.

Though I have called these monologues "digressions," the term is not entirely apt, since they seem to play an integral part in the rhythm and composition of the Mad Dog books. Dotsenko's novels do not work exactly like typical adventure stories, or at least like well-wrought ones: plotlines are begun and abandoned, while villains are discarded, replaced, and revived, all in the course of one book. The plotting itself seems more agglutinative than anything else, as if it were a matter of achieving the requisite four hundred-odd page count in paperback and calling it a day. Just as the detektiv is rarely a classical whodunit, the secret to the novels' composition does not lie in suspense and resolution. In fact, the chapter titles typically give away most of the revelations (and are sometimes accessible in the table of contents): "The Police Commissioner's Death" (*Mad Dog in Love*), "The Downfall of the Robot of Death" (*Mad Dog's Reward*), "Mushmakaev's Capture" (*Okhota Beshenogo* [*Mad Dog's Hunt*]). Instead, Dotsenko builds his novels through a sequence of beats that the reader comes to expect: a regular alternation of graphic sex, equally graphic violence, soulful male conversation, and short philosophical tracts punctuated by at least one telepathic conversation between Savelii and his Teacher.[26]

The philosophy itself is unapologetically anodyne, as evidenced by the Teacher's main message during Savelii's Initiation: "ALSO REMEMBER: GOOD ALWAYS CONQUERS EVIL!" He continues: "YOU MUST NEVER REGRET ANYTHING, MY BROTHER! IF IT WAS BAD, THEN IT'S BETTER NOT TO RECALL THE BAD, AND IF IT WAS GOOD, THEN PEOPLE DON'T REGRET THE GOOD" (*Tridtsatogo* 11). The simplicity of the message sums up the appeal of the Mad Dog books themselves, and perhaps of the entire optimistic wing of the boevik genre. At the same time, the source of these words calls our attention to the convoluted undercurrents of this surface simplicity: the reflexive, unexamined syncretism of Dotsenko's boevik philosophy. Savelii and his comrades value Russia above all, and Dotsenko's caricatures of the series' non-Russian villains often cross

---

[26] Dubin sees the alternation between sex and action scenes as an organizing principle of the boevik: "One way or another, these are all scenes of ordeal." He notes that the covers of the sundry boeviks published by boevik all contain "advertising photos of the heroes in precisely these two key states: aggression and orgasm" ("Action Thriller" 114).

over into open racism. Yet Savelii himself is the lucky beneficiary of knowledge and skills that initially seem to be a kind of canned "wisdom of the East" but ultimately replicate the New Age omnivorousness that often begins with Westerners' uncritical borrowings of poorly digested Eastern philosophy. Savelii's Teacher is not really a Tibetan at all: he is actually one of the aliens who crash-landed at Roswell in 1948, on a mission to raise human consciousness to the level of the "cosmos." Such syncretism serves a number of functions, but the most important one for the boevik is its ability to invite complexity, encompassing many diverse and apparently conflicting ideologemes in a single system, essentially transforming daunting complexity into reassuring simplicity.

Mad Dog's Irony?

By now it should be clear that Mad Dog's world is an irony-free zone. There is little room in it for nuance or ambiguity; indeed, in Dotsenko's deliberately black-and-white world, ambiguity of any kind might well be considered Mad Dog's greatest enemy. Witness the author's ham-handed caricature of Russia's most popular postmodern writer, Victor Pelevin, a master of irony who is a common whipping boy for disgruntled cultural conservatives. In *Voina Beshenogo* (*Mad Dog's War*), "Viktor Poverin" becomes a superficial, narcomafia-connected propagandist of drug use, whose prose, rather than striving for Pelevin's typical faux Zen irony, is straightforward to a fault.

> Like a lover waiting to meet his beloved, incapable of parting from her, thinking of her every minute, day and night, so does the drug addict [*narkoman*] love his high [*kaif*] and wants to get it more and more often. And not because of banal physiology, but because a high is not only a particular psychosomatic state, it is something greater, it is the boundless, universal Love that can and must take the place of the entire world" (*Voina Beshenogo* 125).

Of course, Dotsenko gets Pelevin entirely wrong, but it is his very incapacity to understand Pelevin enough even for the purposes of broad parody that reveals so much about the limitations and worldview of Mad Dog's creator. If Pelevin's narrators and characters engage in naked philosophizing, it is either in the realm of parable and koan (as in *Zhizn' nasekomykh* [*The Life of Insects*]), the language of marketing (*Homo Zapiens*), or, more often, as an obvious parody of national chauvinist discourse (the drunken ramblings of Sam Sucker or the cab driver in *The Life of Insects*). Dotsenko, however, is an incorrigible monologist, and hence his parody of Pelevin resembles nothing more than Dotsenko's own writing, with the normal value system inverted. Dotsenko is like a missionary who can only understand paganism as Satanism (inverted Christianity): his syncretic but fundamentally binary discourse assimilates anything of which he approves into the category of the good while rejecting everything else as anathema.

There is humor in Mad Dog's world, but it is as broad and simple as his worldview. Savelii and his friends take particular satisfaction in repeating clichés, catch-phrases, and quotes from popular films as though they were expressions of genuine wit: "Mukhtar postaraetsia!" ("Mukhtar will try!") and "Let's get back to our rams" (the Russian translation of the French "Revenons à nos moutons") are particular favorites. Less optimistic boeviki are another matter: in the novels of Bushkov, Koretskii, and the revolving door of writers using the pen name Andrei Voronin, sarcasm abounds. The hero of Bushkov's popular *Na to i volki* (*That's Why They're Called Wolves*) series has nothing but amused contempt for anyone involved in political activity, whether "democrats" or "red-brown," has a healthy skepticism about the West. He refers to the American dialect of English as a debased *mova*, a Ukrainian word adopted in Russian to denigrate alleged dialects that dare to call themselves languages (*Na to i volki* 54). But even here, we are less in the realm of ironic ambiguity than that of sarcastic rejection: the entire world is worthy of scorn, and if the heroes rise above their surroundings, it is not because they are paragons of morality like Savelii but because they have no tolerance for cant.

As the genre of the boevik took root, however, it also began to mature. Even by the mid-1990s, crime fiction and film had become such an unavoidable feature of the cultural landscape that writers and filmmakers of middle- to highbrow aspirations saw the potential for a more nuanced, sophisticated, and ironic action story. On the lower end of the spectrum, following the wildly successful adaptation of Andrei Kivinov's *Ulitsa razbitykh fonarei* (*Broken Streetlights*) series of detektiv novels and novellas as the hit show *Menty* (*Cops*), in 1998 the producers adapted the action/humor format for the boevik, with the series *Agent natsional'noi bezopasnosti* (*National Security Agent*). The plots of the first season's episodes cover tropes familiar to readers of *Mad Dog* or *Blind Man*: evil, brainwashing cults, fights with thugs in bars and nightclubs, and sensitive, top-secret assignments that can be entrusted only to Aleksei (Lekha) Nikolaev, an actor/secret agent. The difference is that Lekha, unlike the grim heroes of classic boeviki, is clearly having fun, and the plots are played more for humor than for suspense or thrills. Much of the comedy involves the contrast between the manly, confident Lekha and Sergei, his girlfriend's ex-husband, a stereotypical, glasses-wearing, overeducated intellectual (also a regular in the cast). Sergei is no doubt a useful plot device—he can be counted on to supply the necessary exposition and esoterica that serve as background to whatever fiendish plot Lekha is attempting to foil, but he also serves as the conflation of both Soviet and American popular culture's disdain for intellectuals. In socialist realism, the intellectual hero was typically hampered by indecision, passivity, and even cowardice, rendering the opposition between Lekha as "regular guy" and Sergei as effete intellectual all too familiar.[27] Sergei's usefulness must be weighed against his total inability to function in the real world, or to understand the difference between intellectual trivia and matters of life and death. When Lekha is investigating a case involving a transvestite who calls himself "Makhaon," Sergei turns out to be a font of information, since his grandfather was a famous entomologist ("Perhaps you've heard of him?"). Sergei explains that a makhaon is a kind of butterfly and later calls Lekha with the urgent information that this particular breed eats lots of dill ("Makhaon").

But the portrayal of Sergei also plays into the self-congratulatory hegemony so prominent in certain forms of American popular entertainment, which insist on turning anything associated with "high culture" (intellectuals, classical music, difficult novels and films) into figures of fun or oblige the caricatured eggheads to pay respect to the superiority of pop. In the third episode of the first season, Lekha investigates the disappearance of a Stradivarius, a MacGuffin that places the conflict between high and low firmly on center stage. Now Sergei is important as Lekha's ambassador to the world of fine arts, but the people they meet are even more ridiculous than Lekha's egghead sidekick, particularly a fat, unattractive female violinist who, though presented as a figure of fun, also turns out to be the villain of the piece (she tries to strangle Lekha's girlfriend with a violin string). Meanwhile, the Strad itself is found in a Twix bag traced to a factory that employs drunken former musicians, while the episode's Led Zeppelin-inspired theme song makes sure that the trappings of high culture are always kept within an appropriately popular frame.

Though played almost entirely for laughs, the conflict between the intellectual and the man of action does point us in the right direction for examining the boevik's emergence as a more sophisticated, self-reflexive genre.

---

[27] Here the series is continuing the traditions of Soviet comedies, where the awkward intellectual is dragged into outrageous adventures by a charming yet aggressive lout.

What if the intellectual were the one forced to play the role of action hero? In the beginning of this chapter, I claimed that the boevik typically chose as its heroes natural-born killers guided by a strong moral compass, and that if the detektiv could highlight stories of ordinary, educated women confronted by a world of extraordinary violence (Dashkova's trademark), this was not the case for the male protagonists of the boevik. Yet it is the very primacy of the natural man of action as boevik hero that opens up the potential for generic self-consciousness by attempting to replace the action hero with a thoughtful, unaggressive intellectual. If so much of the entertainment aimed at men projects a fantastic ideal of male potency and power, what does that mean for the consumer of this fantasy who really has nothing to do with this violent world at all?

Thus by the late nineties a small but noteworthy subgenre of the boevik began to emerge: tales of the accidental hit man. Initially, the key figure behind this new kind of tale was Andrey Kurkov, a Russian-born writer living in Ukraine. In 1996, Kurkov published a largely unnoticed short novel called *Smert' postoronnego* (*Death of a Bystander*), which garnered some international attention, first with a German edition, then in a 2001 English translation as *Death and the Penguin*. The hero of the novel is Viktor, an unemployed writer who has adopted an emperor penguin named Misha from the financially strapped Kiev Zoo. Viktor eventually stumbles into a very lucrative, if not quite ethical, business: he is hired by a local newspaper to write long, meditative obituaries for important Ukrainian public figures who are still very much among the living. But one by one, the subjects of his "obelisks" (the slang term his newspaper uses for obituaries) are killed by hit men and political rivals, leaving Viktor with the growing suspicion that his writings are somehow responsible.

Throughout the book, Misha the penguin watches his master with silent melancholy, a somewhat absurd counterpoint to Viktor's own impenetrable emotional detachment. In Kurkov's hands, the penguin as Viktor's double serves as a constant reminder of the protagonist's displacement: the intellectual Viktor has no business being involved in the gang wars and turf battles of Ukraine's mafioso political elites, just as Misha's heavily insulated body is ill adapted to southern climes (and one cannot help but wonder if the penguin's plight is not also representative of that of the author, himself a transplant from icy St. Petersburg to balmy Kiev). Both Misha and Viktor suffer from failing hearts. In Viktor's case, the problem is figurative: though he has become accustomed to living with the four-year-old Sonya, left in his care by a casual acquaintance who quickly becomes the victim of his own criminal connections, and the twenty-something Nina, Sonya's nanny and eventually Viktor's lover, he cannot muster any real feelings for them. Nor does Viktor concern himself all that much with the victims of his increasingly dangerous prose. Misha's heart problem is literal: if he does not receive a transplant from a human child, he will die before Viktor can use his blood money to return the penguin to the Antarctic.

The success of the novel's German translation prompted a Russian reprint in 2001, this time under the title *Piknik na l'du* (*Picnic on Ice*).[28] The book's front-cover picture and back-cover blurb clearly position Kurkov's penguin story as crime fiction, an odd choice from a literary point of view but a reasonable one from a marketing standpoint. Though *Death and the Penguin* seems to have little in common with potboilers such as the Mad Dog series, whether in tone, characterization, or address, the novel makes far more sense when considered within the context of contemporary Russian crime fiction. The theme of the intellectual's confrontation with the criminal world is an emerging subgenre in popular and middlebrow post-Soviet entertainment. The 1997 film *Priiatel' pokoinika* (*A Friend of the Deceased*) (directed by Leonid Boiko and Viacheslav Khristofovich) covers much of the same territory as *Death and the Penguin*, which perhaps should not be a surprise, given that Kurkov wrote the screenplay. Anatolii, the protagonist of *Friend*, shares Viktor's anomie but takes it one step further, for his lack of involvement in the world around him leads him to the brink of suicide. In each case, the intellectual hero has only a dim sense of the connection between his words and the resulting actions. The writer Viktor initially takes no responsibility for his apparently self-fulfilling obituaries, while the underemployed translator Anatoly is used to eliding the aggressiveness inherent in words, rather than accentuating it.

We first meet Anatolii when he is interpreting at a negotiation over a shipment of oranges, translating not just the spoken language but the commercial cultures involved: when the Ukrainian businessman threatens to cut off his new business partner's head if the fruit arrives rotten, Anatolii simply renders the threat into English as a gentle admonition to "deliver the fruit in good condition." After Anatolii is abandoned by his wife, an old friend of his with mafia connections suggests that he order a hit on his wife's lover. Contacting the hit man depends on a complicated, impersonal mechanism, involving anonymous letters and post-office boxes. Such arrangements are a tried-and-true feature of crime fiction (Marinina describes them in great detail), but here they are exploited for their thematic

---

[28] In 2002, Kurkov also published a sequel, *Zakon uliki* (*The Law of Evidence*), which appeared two years later in England as *Penguin Lost*.

potential. As in *Death and the Penguin*, murder for money is removed from the realm of street violence and decisive action; the passive intellectual kills with his casual words. In Anatolii's case, this impersonal violence is directed at the "inaction hero" himself. Anatolii leaves the killer his own photograph rather than that of his wife's lover, thereby retreating as far from the laws of the boevik as possible: not only does he not take violent action into his own hands, but he turns himself into a victim rather than a savior.

If Dotsenko's own rationale is to be believed, the boevik is intended to raise spirits rather than to crush them, inspiring its jaded readership to action. Kurkov, in both film and fiction, takes a much more nuanced route to roughly the same result. Both his heroes are overeducated, refined, and, in the chaotic postsocialist world, useless: unemployed and unwanted, they are redundant in virtually every sense of the word. They are not born warriors, and they are not moved by crime and injustice to take up arms in defense of the weak. Viktor and Anatolii embody the very crisis of post-Soviet masculinity for which so much of popular culture tries to compensate: Anatolii's humiliation is particularly gendered in that he is betrayed by his wife, who has managed to adapt to the new economic reality far better than he. With the same educational background as his, she works in an advertising agency while he scrapes by giving English lessons to repulsive businessmen who cannot be troubled to find dollar bills small enough to pay him.

Yet both Viktor and Anatolii do manage to regain their self-respect and even become action heroes of a sort, and in each case their recovery depends on their being needed by others. Viktor is brought out of his isolation by his new responsibility for a young girl, for the woman who starts out as her nanny and becomes his lover, and, of course, for his penguin, while Anatolii rediscovers his love of life thanks to the attentions of a helpful prostitute (a stock figure we have already seen in the boevik). Meanwhile, Anatolii has inadvertently become responsible for the death of the hit man he hired and now has to care for his orphaned son and take over the killer's job. In Kurkov's stories, action and violence are secondary, yet the result is still an ironic boevik that creates the imaginary space into which an intellectual (male) reader/viewer can project himself. If the mainstream boevik adapts the tropes of adventure literature and socialist realism for postsocialist consumption, Kurkov seems to be looking slightly further back: what if Isaac Babel had written a boevik? His heroes are the fin-de-siecle descendants of Babel's tormented intellectual who tries to adapt to the warrior culture of Red Army Cossacks, but who lack the ideological underpinnings that could justify the attempt to overcome their nonviolent nature. Instead, they can commit violence only indirectly, verbally, and if they become protectors of the weak, it is only because their hypertrophied consciences oblige them to take care of the people their victims leave behind (in Viktor's case, quite literally: his contact from the newspaper leaves his daughter with Viktor and then disappears for good). Though Kurkov's heroes are far from warriors, the intellectual's post-Soviet dilemma is essentially the same as that of the military veteran: each has skills that could still be considered valuable but must be channeled in new directions, both for the heroes' survival and for the general improvement of the world around them.

Both Anatolii and Viktor depend on words for their livelihood, but in the harsh world of robber capitalism they succumb to the temptations of using words on behalf of organized crime. In Anatolii's case, his work as an interpreter degenerates into self-parody. Instead of translating from one language to another, he becomes something akin to a ventriloquist's dummy, uttering other people's phrases and repeating their instructions. The words he now deploys for money are virtually devoid of content, functioning as performative speech acts that lead to specific, predictable results, whether in court (when he agrees to perjure himself for a rich man's money, claiming to have slept with the man's wife in order to force her to grant her husband's divorce petition), on paper (when scribbling dates and times on the backs of the photographs of the hit man's next victims), or behind the scenes of the hit man's transactions (telling his prostitute friend exactly what to do in order to a hire a hit, then telling the second hit man where to find the prostitute's instructions). Gone is the moral clarity of the Mad Dog books or even the cynical yet ultimately righteous context of Bushkov's Shantarsk novels: Kurkov's world is unimaginable without moral ambiguity.

A Friend of the Deceased was released in 1997, which turned out to be something of a banner year for the unlikely-hit man genre. First Polish director Juliusz Machulksi made a splash on the film festival circuit with his comedy *Killer*, a story about a taxi driver mistaken for a hit man, who finds unexpected pleasure in his new role (the film was a success both on the international festival circuit and on video in Russia). But the undisputed champion of this minor genre was Aleksei Balabanov's film *Brother* (*Brat*), also released in 1997. Though Balabanov's protagonist is as far removed from Kurkov's intellectual heroes as possible, *Brother* does the most thorough job of both subverting and reinforcing the standard tropes of the Russian action story, saturating the boevik with so much irony and ambiguity that the film invites its audience, reviewers, and (as we shall see when we look at the sequel) its director to take it seriously as a Russophile ideological statement.

Figure 7: Still photo from Aleksei Balabanov's *Brother*, a popular film that presented a new take on the "hit man" genre.

Danila Bagrov, the hero of *Brother*, is neither the battle-scarred veteran of Russia's failed wars nor the reluctant intellectual spurred to action. Rather, Danila is an eternal naïf who can engage in redemptive violence without reflecting at all on his vague and unformed worldview, a Candide without the optimism nurtured by Pangloss's education (or any education to speak of). A closer antecedent for Danila is Chauncey Gardner from Jerzy Kosinski's *Being There*; like Chauncey, Danila stumbles from one situation to another, as incapable of understanding nuance as he is uninterested in making the attempt. But where Chauncey meanders his way into political prominence, Danila's exploits inevitably involve violence and murder.

When *Brother* begins, Danila has recently been demobilized from the army, but the filmmakers reject the pathos that typically accompanies this scenario. Danila is neither embittered nor battle-scarred and looks like an unlikely candidate for post-traumatic stress disorder. He gets into trouble with local law enforcement but only for inadvertently disrupting the filming of a music video. In one of the film's recurring motifs (if not jokes), nearly everyone Danila meets asks him where he did his military service, and Danila always replies: "At headquarters," sometimes adding that he handled paperwork. When pressed, he claims that his shooting experience was limited to exercises on the rifle range.[29] Again, Balabanov is giving us the antithesis of the boevik veteran, since Danila lays no claim to any of the martial skills that prove invaluable to the hero once he is obliged to resume combat on the domestic front. Yet when Danila, at his mother's prompting, leaves the countryside to join his brother in St. Petersburg, Danila proves to be an expert shot with nerves of steel, a natural-born killer who is a much better hit man than the brother who brings him into the business.

Once he reaches Petersburg, Danila embarks on a series of escapades familiar to readers and viewers of the boevik. He becomes a champion of the weak (protecting innocent women from men who abuse them); he is nursed back to health after a bullet wound by a simple, ordinary young Russian woman who becomes his lover; he defends honest Russians from "uppity" dark-skinned predators (when the trolley inspector is confronted by Caucasians who refuse to pay a fine); and he gives money away rather than holding on to it for himself. Nonetheless, all these standard topoi are undermined. Out of pity, his lover takes the side of the husband who beats her, throwing Danila out of the house. The money goes to some good causes (supporting Danila's impoverished German friend) but is also given to a carefree drug dealer he befriends early in the film. Finally, the confrontation with the Caucasians on the trolley, while clearly functioning as a satisfying urban revenge fantasy (when the men refuse to pay the fine, Danila pulls a gun on them), hardly reaches the epic proportions of Sever's fight against the "black-assed" Chechens in the *Nympho* series or Dotsenko's demonization of Chechen terrorists in the Mad Dog novels. Rather, Balabanov is giving us the daily, domestic racism that only has the potential to explode into full-fledged racial violence (as it does in the sequel).

What truly separates *Brother* from the boevik mainstream is the metaphysical and ideological void embodied by Danila himself. Even the cynical heroes of Bushkov and Voronin, let alone Mad Dog, are ultimately fighting *for* something; Mad Dog consistently advances a specific patriotic agenda. Danila's patriotism and xenophobia are laughably knee-jerk: at a party, Danila informs a Frenchman (who does not speak Russian) that his "American music" is "shit," and that "soon your America is gonna get it" (*vsia vasha Amerika—kirdyk*). Danila, who cannot pass by someone being victimized

---

[29] A scene in the film's sequel, *Brother-2*, suggests that Danila saw much more action in the army than he admits.

without trying to help, arguably has the instincts of the action hero, but the main item on his agenda is tracking down a hard-to-find rock album by Nautilus Pompilus.[30] A year before *Brother* was released, Boris Yeltsin established a National Idea Search Commission, whose task was to develop an ideology to fill the void left by discredited communism (McLaren).[31] While it is easy to ridicule the attempt to inspire the country by committee, Danila could have served as the commission's poster child: look what happens to our youth when they have nothing to fight for. Yet Danila's own ambiguous status as a basically sympathetic hero who is nonetheless more ignorant than his implied audience renders any attempt to frame *Brother* as a "social problem" film (like those of the perestroika era) seem as naive as Danila himself.[32] *Brother* may be a boevik but only to the extent that *Don Quixote* is a chivalric romance: it participates in an emerging genre that parodies and interrogates a preexisting set of generic conventions. The film's use of parody and irony not only makes it fit company for Kurkov's work but also ties it to Western films and television shows that cast an ambiguous light on the conventions of crime drama, such as *Prizzi's Honor, Grosse Point Blank, The Sopranos,* and, of course, *Pulp Fiction.*

At least this is the case with the first *Brother* film. In 2000, Balabanov released *Brat-2 (Brother 2),* which reunited Danila and his treacherous brother, sending them on a new adventure. *Brother 2* is a sequel but not a straightforward one. Its relation to the first film is much like that of *Rambo* to *First Blood*: *Brother 2* is the sequel not to *Brother* but to the reception of *Brother* by a sizable portion of the audience that missed most of the film's irony. The first film ended with Danila's disappointment in St. Petersburg. As he tells his German friend, "You said that the city was power, but everyone here is weak." So Danila goes to try his luck in Moscow, where the second film begins. But soon Danila must go to the United States to help out the brother of one of his fellow veterans, a hockey player who has gotten into trouble with the mob. Danila ends up in Chicago, a city whose sole association for Russians is the gangsters of the Al Capone era. For the boevik genre, Chicago looms large as the criminal equivalent of a cross between

---

[30] Admittedly, given Nautilus's high status in Russian rock culture, this is a rare sign of good taste on Danila's part; he is not chasing down music by popular prefab bands such as Na-Na or Strelki. Larsen argues that Danila's transformation into a hard-core Nautilus fan is just as significant as his metamorphosis into a hired killer, offering "an idealized version of the relationship between the post-Soviet producer of culture and its consumer" ("National Identity" 508).

[31] The commission was established in July 1996, right after Yeltsin's reelection.

[32] No doubt Danila's aura of "innocence" is bolstered by the relative paucity of graphic violence in the film, which Daniil Dondurei ascribes to the film's rejection of cherukha (66). As Igor' Mantsov points out, much of the violence happens between the scenes (63).

Mecca and Disneyland, while for the *Brother* films, it also brings to mind a line more commonly associated with New York City. If Danila can make it there, he can make it anywhere.

Danila overcomes all the obstacles he faces in the United States except one: the heavy ideological agenda of the film itself. For Danila, in crossing the ocean, has made a concomitant journey from one end of the boevik spectrum to the other. *Brother 2* takes place in the same irony-free zone as does Mad Dog, only with higher production values and a better sound-track.[33] Following in the footsteps of Hollywood sequels, *Brother 2* retreads many of the main plot points of the original but with little of the charm or inspiration: again journeys are made by car and truck, with friendly drivers helping him out along the way. Again a wayward brother must be rescued. And again Danila tries to help out the weak. But this time there is no question about what Danila is fighting for: his motherland. Even in America, he is beset by representatives of the national minorities that figure so prominently in right-wing Russian demonologies: a predatory Jewish émigré who tries to sell him an overpriced car while telling him, in stereotypically accented speech, that "We Russians have to stick together" (a line that is immediately humorous in the original, since Jews are not "Russian" by definition); Ukrainian crooks who fail to appreciate everything Russia has done for their country; and, perhaps most perniciously, African Americans, who are consistently portrayed as hostile, violent criminals preying on defenseless white (Russian) women. Danila saves a Russian émigré prostitute named Dasha from her abusive black pimp, after which Dasha explains that American blacks are stronger and more primal, which is why white people fear them.

If in the previous film, Danila's intellectual simplicity and reluctance to speak at length made it possible to see him as an ethically ambiguous figure, now he is a model of morality and patriotism. He explains to Dasha that he has to help her, since "Russians never give up on their own." The people he fights are the epitome of evil, extorting money from the innocent, forcing women into prostitution, and even producing snuff films. After rubbing out a dozen evildoers in a scene that is remarkably reminiscent of a "first person shooter" video game, Danila trudges up several flights of a fire escape to confront the American who is the source of all the vice shown up to now. As he walks, he chants a poem about the motherland, one

---

[33] Here I agree with Yana Hashamova, who argues that the ambiguity of the first film is absent from the sequel (*Pride and Panic*). Lipovetsky comments that the declamation of a poem by Lermontov in the beginning of *Brother-2* raises the possibility of irony but that Balabanov chooses to emphasize action and clarity instead ("Vsekh liubliu" 56).

that he heard declaimed earlier in the film by the son of one of his intended victims, and when he has the villain in his sights, he asks him, "Tell me, American, does power come from money? I think the person who has the truth [*pravda*] is the more powerful one." The film's ending brings together many of the tropes of the ordinary boevik: not only does Danila triumph over evil, but he redeems the prostitute Dasha, bringing her back to Russia—when a ticket agent tells her she will never be able to come back to the United States, she gives him the finger. Dasha's gesture is emblematic of the film as a whole (which ends to the tune of the perestroika rock classic "Goodbye, America"). Having regained her national pride, she gives America an unambiguous sign, using a gesture that was only recently imported from the United States. *Brother 2* uses the conventions of the boevik (many of them lifted from American models) to militate for a resurgent Russian national chauvinism, going back to the mythical wellspring of organized crime as entertainment (Chicago) in order to prove that the pupil has far surpassed the teacher.

With *Brother 2*, Balabanov's exploration of the boevik comes full circle. Having toyed with an ironic, polyvalent approach to a genre that is otherwise deadly earnest, the director returns his hero to the boevik's ideological wellsprings. In America, Danila fights a battle against an enemy whose evil is reinforced by the film's execrable racial politics: the boevik's world is literally a struggle between black and white. The trappings of irony remain (the friendly neo-Nazis Danila meets in Moscow, for example, or the jokes about smuggling contraband pork fat into the States), but they fail to undermine the high seriousness of the film's overt nationalism.[34] Nonetheless, as Danila shows us in a quest that brings him to America only to return him home, a round trip is still a journey traveled. Films such as *Brother* and *A Friend of the Deceased* are a sign that the boevik, like the detektiv, has sufficiently matured to include works that call into question some of the genre's premises without actually violating them. By the same token, *Brother 2*, in retreating from the ambiguity of its predecessor, reinforces one of the primary functions of the boevik: the violence and degradation of chernukha

[34] Mark Lipovetsky makes the intriguing argument that much of the popular culture of the post-Yeltsin era borrows from socialist realist models while rejection the parody and irony that characterized Sots-Art, an earlier attempt by the avant-garde to deconstruct Soviet mythology. The resulting "Post-Sots" features unambiguous struggles between good and evil, heroic archetypes, a military context, and minimal participation for women ("POST-SOTS" 359–62). Post-Sots is a highly productive model when applied to post-Yeltsin popular culture in its broadest manifestations (including the unironic revival of Soviet kitsch). In the case of the boevik, however, the category of Post-Sots may well be redundant. All the features Lipovetsky ascribes to Post-Sots hold true for the entire boevik genre.

are shown to be pervasive but not unbeatable. In fighting back, the boevik hero not only gives a purpose to the violence in which he engages but retroactively endows with meaning the violence he combats. Chernukha in the boeviki we have examined is not random and pointless but rather a metaphysical evil to be kept at bay by the noble warrior. The hero fights on two fronts simultaneously, defeating his opponents through greater strength, skill, and, above all, virtue while also fighting against hopelessness and despair through the power of his example.

Chapter Seven

OVERKILL

Bespredel and Gratuitous Violence

Rita once again examined the premises where this woman had
decided not just to live, but to live in harmony with herself and
with the whole world. There was nothing pathetic or wretched in
what she saw there—the pathetic or wretched remained up there,
where Rita had come from. Here the usual standards didn't
work—this must be how the different understandings of life and
death, of good and evil, of beauty and ugliness, fall apart, when a
person steps over the borders of earthly existence and the real
essence of life opens up before him.

But can this essence really open up to a person only in a forgotten
sewer, on a pile of filthy rags and old cardboard Coca Cola boxes,
ten meters from a pipe pouring out a turbid stream of shit and
fuel oil, infecting the atmosphere with miasmas?

—Sergei Pugachev, *You're Just a Slut, My Dear!* (*Ty prosto shliukha,
dorogaia!*)

In 1999, the reading public was treated to a new addition to the emerging canon of Russian pulp fiction: a potboiler by Sergei Pugachev entitled
You're Just a Slut, My Dear! Even in a market where lurid paperback covers
are taken for granted, *You're Just a Slut, My Dear!* stands out for its explicit
sexualized violence: a man smiles as he holds a beautiful woman by the hair
and forces her to suck on the barrel of a gun. When the novel begins, a
young woman, Rita Prozorova, has just been fighting with her mother,
whom she holds in utmost contempt. So naturally Rita kills her with a

blunt object, slaughters a nosy neighbor who stumbles upon the scene, and sets fire to her apartment, all in the first chapter. The body count does not stop there; if anything, Rita becomes an even more prodigious killer as the novel wears on, leaving behind a trail of corpses stretching like bread-crumbs from her native provincial town of Pskov all the way to Moscow. Fairly early on, her long-lost fiancé's criminal associates turn her into a heroin addict and gang-rape her, launching her on a quest for vengeance that culminates in a bloodbath. But the road to revenge is not easy: Rita is constantly obliged to avoid the many predators who want a piece of her— literally. When she arrives in Moscow, she barely escapes a ring of kidnap-pers who lure young provincial women to their home, drug them, and then sell their organs to rich Americans and Europeans who need transplants. At times, Rita wonders how such things can happen. After all, she has seen nu-merous films where justice triumphs and where legal procedure steps in to facilitate the determination of guilt and innocence. Then she remembers: "But that's not how it is in our country. That's what she saw on video. That's in America. But we're not America; we have no laws" (31).

It is fitting that Rita compares her own lived experience to the stories about America that she has seen on TV, since *You're Just a Slut, My Dear!* posits an imaginary Russia as a counterpoint to the hyperreality of near-perfect order embodied by American police procedurals. One of the most likely sources of her knowledge of the rights and privileges of American crime suspects is the long-running television show *Law and Order*, which Russian viewers could watch twice a day at the time that Pugachev's novel was pub-lished. In its Russian translation, *Law and Order* (*Zakon i poriadok*) had the ring of a cruel joke, since domestic television and the print media were quite effectively constructing a crime-ridden Russia in which neither law nor order was anywhere to be found. In fact, the world in which Rita Prozorova fights for survival is defined precisely by their absence: the world of bespredel.

Though the bloody backdrops of the detektiv and the boevik are evi-dence of each genre's preoccupation with violent crime, neither of them can match bespredel for sheer sensationalism or pessimism. Even Konstan-tinov's multivolume saga of murder and betrayal allows for some hope that the forces of good can at least survive, if not triumph, while the forces of evil have the reassuring virtue of being understandable and even logical— nothing illustrates the economic doctrine of "rational choice" better than the self-interested actions of organized criminals. Indeed, the cardinal virtue of organized crime is the very fact that it is organized. At its most ex-treme, bespredel inspires horror precisely because it is chaotic, random, and without motivation. If organized crime is powerful thanks to its stran-

Figure 8: Cover of Sergei Pugachev's *You're Just a Slut, My Dear!*

glehold on corrupt law-enforcement agencies, that means it relies on the functioning (or well-planned dysfunction) of an overall system. Bandit Petersburg is a far better place to live in than lawless Russia.

Bespredel is a particularly difficult word to render in English. Literally meaning "without limits" or "without boundaries," this noun is used freely and fluidly in contemporary Russian discourse, accruing new contents and contexts over time. Bespredel is an evolving concept; one of the few features that unite all its various uses and definitions is that it is always something to be lamented and decried (even when this disapprobation barely conceals the exploitation and sensationalism that keep the thematics of bespredel alive). My use of it as a rubric for the purposes of this chapter might not strike a Russian speaker as intuitive, but my approach is informed by the broad, varied, and at times contradictory manner in which the term is deployed. A number of English words suggest themselves as possible equivalents but only for particular aspects of bespredel as it is understood by the various constituencies that invoke it. As it stands today, bespredel is an important Russian discursive category but a far from scholarly one. Rather than settle on any one of several English synonyms, I prefer to use all of them and none of them, keeping *bespredel* as an umbrella term to preserve its polyvalent strangeness but using the English words to highlight the concept's key features.

The term *bespredel* seems to originate, appropriately enough, in the world of organized crime and the national prison camp system (the zone). In this context, Vadim Volkov defines it as the "unjustified use of violence" (195), the violations of the norms of the criminal world. Here bespredel, with its literal lack of boundaries, actually functions to delineate the limits of proper lawlessness: the declaration that an enemy is engaging in bespredel effectively makes him an outlaw among outlaws. By violating the rules of good criminal conduct, the *bespredel'shchik* (the person who commits bespredel) in effect also suspends these rules as they relate to him. Reminiscent of Agamben's "state of exception," the ability of organized crime to identify and punish those who threaten to *dis*organize crime constitutes the criminal leaders' authority (9). Bespredel is the mathematical limit of violence, always to be approached but never reached. When invoked in film and fiction, bespredel also transposes a nostalgia for the orderly days of Soviet power to the context of crime: the "good" thieves respect the laws of the criminal fraternity, while the gang leaders of today are simply scum who do not know the meaning of the word "respect." Ironically, this criminal generation gap replicates the central anxiety of perestroika discussed in the introduction: what is wrong with kids today?

Bespredel proved to be far too evocative a term to be limited to gangland misbehavior, and, as Volkov notes, the word has become a part of Russians' everyday vocabulary, particularly in the realm of politics. Thus the Russian defense minister decried the 1999 NATO bombings of Yugoslavia as bespredel, while Vladimir Putin, in one of his early speeches as acting president of Russia, used the word to describe the alternative to his infamous "dictatorship of law" (Volkov 82). The term's political meaning preserves its criminal roots, since it is applied when politicians and world leaders overstep their bounds. Even more broadly, when invoked as part of a conversational litany of post-Soviet evils, the boundlessness of bespredel means total chaos, describing a state of pure and utter lawlessness, with crime and corruption running rampant. In this context, bespredel is a post-perestroika variation on what Nancy Ries calls a "perestroika epic": tales of "complete disintegration" (*polnaia razrukha*). This "folkloric genre" contained many of the features of bespredel, particularly the emphasis on blood, gore, and violence (*Russian Talk* 44–47). Yet bespredel differs in two crucial ways. First, I would argue that it is not the source of the twisted Dostoevskian pride that Ries discovers in complete disintegration. Complete disintegration, a variation on the Russian tale, sets up Russia as an anti-Disneyland that unites people in their common experience and shared suffering, suggesting a particularly Russian strength in adversity that no other nation could hope to match (Ries, *Russian Talk* 50). Bespredel may be fascinating, but it is not heroic: bespredel puts the ordinary person in the position of victim. This leads to the second point, which is the question of agency: though tales of complete disintegration could (and mostly likely did) lead to the eternal Russian question, who's to blame? the focus was on collapse itself, not on those who took advantage of postsocialist chaos. Bespredel, with its implicit focus on the lack of limits, is all about the actions taken by people who recognize no strictures.

Bespredel is horrifying because it is chaotic. The violence of bespredel is unnecessary by definition: it is popular culture's gratuitous violence decried by critics throughout the world. This gratuitousness is crucial, defining both the aesthetics and the philosophy of bespredel. Aesthetically, bespredel is clearly about overkill in that it literally denotes a slaying that continues long after life has expired: no violence can be too much, no detail can be too graphic. Reminiscent of the ultraviolence of Anthony Burgess's *Clockwork Orange*, bespredel's aesthetic certainly found common cause with the films of Quentin Tarantino (especially *Reservoir Dogs*). Philosophically, bespredel is a Dostoevskian nightmare world in which the absence of God turns men into beasts. Or rather, bespredel gives a demonic twist to early-twentieth-century French thought, which put a different value on the gratuitous: *l'acte gratuite* (the gratuitous act). Demonstrating the principle that true human freedom could be expressed only in an action that had no motivation and no purpose, the most famous literary examples of *l'acte gratuite* were instances of murder: Lafcadio, the hero of André Gide's *Les Caves du Vatican* (*The Cellars of the Vatican*), who throws a man off a train with no warning and no consequence, and Merseault, the narrator of Albert Camus's *L'Étranger* (*The Stranger*), whose fatal shooting of an Arab is maddening in its apparent randomness. Bespredel posits a limitless, irresponsible human freedom that can take shape only in senseless violence.[1]

Finally, I apply the word *bespredel* to an important component of post-Soviet mass culture that is not usually covered by the term but that makes the actions and consequences of bespredel its central theme: the media representation of "true crime." This includes the sensationalistic and lurid reports on criminal violence in newspapers and on television, as well as the documentary books and even novels (such as *You're Just a Slut, My Dear!*) that find their primary purpose in the graphic depiction of violence. The audiovisual representation of violent crime comes as close to the aesthetic of pornography as violent entertainment can get (short of the snuff film), while the transformation of true crime into narrative entails choices that result in quite different stories from those found in the detektiv or the boevik. True-crime narratives lack positive heroes, focusing almost entirely on the criminals who, in other genres, would be the object of disapproval. Here the story is all about the crimes themselves, with only a minimal moral framework and little hope of redemption. Violence in true crime cannot be redemptive, for it cannot have meaning. It is, to borrow the title Marinina used in a different mode, "death for death's sake," violence that is fascinating simply because it is violence. The pleasure to be found in consuming this particular type of bespredel narrative is in the secondhand, guilt-free enjoyment of the acts themselves and in the reassurance of identifying with the performer of violence rather than with the victim. The external moral context is, of course, one of disapproval, but the reader's or viewer's shock at real violence only adds to the thrill of identification with the fictive violence, all the while confirming the basic message of bespredel in all its forms: we live in a world of unmitigated, but fascinating, horror.

Honor among Thieves

Bespredel is an untidy term, but its messiness is helpful to anyone interested in the discourse of Russian violent crime, its evolution, and its growing hegemony over the culture at large. The word manages to be conversational and neutral (available to any speaker who cares to invoke it, without violating linguistic etiquette) and clearly marked; its origins in the Russian

---

[1] Thus I take issue with L. D. Gudkov's observation that "mass literature" deals entirely in absolutes (95). His argument may well hold true for the boevik, but it has limited applicability to the detektiv and fails to account for bespredel.

prison camp culture and its relevance to contemporary gangland culture have not been forgotten. The very fact that grandmothers and government officials use the word routinely is evidence that the once rarefied *blatnoi* ("criminal") culture has moved beyond not only its initial isolation but also its Brezhnev-era status as the source of an added piquancy to the daring songs of the Russian bards, who appropriated the slang of the zone in their own stylized, pseudocriminal songs. The first years of Russian independence saw a minor boom in dictionaries, encyclopedias, and ethnographic studies of the zone;[2] with the benefit of hindsight, their publication seems almost prescient, as though the editors foresaw that the smart cultural consumer of the 1990s would have to acquire a basic literacy in organized violence. Now the helpful glossary at the back of Dotsenko's first Mad Dog novel (*Mad Dog in Prison*) looks touchingly quaint, if not embarrassingly uncool: what Russian reader does not know that *nishtiak* means "good," or *bazar* means "conversation"? (414–15) The same decade that witnessed an obsession with the mastery of English for career advancement and edification—with audiocassettes, guides for self-study, and ads for special classes on nearly every urban street corner—saw a subtler (and probably more successful) drive for linguistic competence: by the end of the 1990s, everyone knew how to speak crime.

In his *On the Other Side of the Law: An Encyclopedia of the Criminal World* (1992), Lev Mil'ianenkov includes an entry for *bespredel*: "lawlessness, arbitrariness [*samoupravstvo, proizvol*]; a thief who has left the world of thieves and ceased his criminal activities" (84). Thus Mil'ianenkov associates bespredel with the traditional ways of Soviet-era crime, but its rise as both a linguistic term and a discursive phenomenon is the result of the drastic changes that have shaken Russian traditional culture just as surely as they have transformed the culture at large. The word *bespredel* has escaped the bounds of the prison camp and thieves' gang precisely because its culture of origin has been threatened by the lawlessness that the word describes.

The Soviet underworld was one of the many subcultures that sprang up in opposition to officially sanctioned culture, and, like so many of them, it mirrored the structures that it purportedly opposed. Hence the Russian tendency to speak of such subcultures as "antiworlds" (*antimiry*), since they are by no means independent of official influence. The product of a

---

[2] The list includes, but is by no means limited to, Baldaev et al., *Slovar' tiuremno-lagerno-blatnogo zhargona* (*The Dictionary of Prison-Camp-Criminal Slang* (1992); Edvard Maksimovskii, *Imperiia strakha* (*Empire of Fear* (1991); and Lev Mil'ianen'kov's *Po tu storonu zakona: Entsiklopediia prestupnogo mira* (*On the Other Side of the Law: An Encyclopedia of the Criminal World* (1992). For an analysis of the material presented in these books, see Condee ("Body Graphics").

fundamentally binary culture, they are to Soviet culture what Satanism is to Christianity: a deliberate inversion that wears its influences on its sleeve.[3] This criminal fraternity is truly *organized* crime, for it is just as fundamentally systemic as the Soviet Union itself. It arose, appropriately enough, within the Soviet labor camps and prisons during the 1930s, and the power of its leaders and its cultural codes is well documented by political prisoners from the purges onward, who were obliged to tread lightly around their nonpolitical (and hence more ideologically trustworthy) inmates.[4] The leaders of the Soviet underworld were known as *vory v zakone*, which is usually rendered as "thieves-in-law," an unfortunately literal translation that in English suggests an extended family (*Married to the Mob*) rather than a particularly authoritative status. I will follow the convention adopted by Volkov (to whom I am also more generally indebted for my discussion of the *vory v zakone*) and simply call them "thieves," a shorthand commonly used in Russian as well.[5]

This thieves' subculture was highly ritualized, with a strict hierarchy of subordination and control, and behavioral codes that regulated life both in and out of the zone. Thieves were forbidden to cooperate with the state in any fashion (even military service, which was theoretically mandatory for all adult men, prevented a criminal from rising in the ranks). Nor was a thief allowed to be gainfully employed, since honest physical labor (so idealized by the Soviet regime) was beneath his dignity. Devotion to the underworld left no room for any conflicting loyalties, resulting in a "criminal fraternity" truly worthy of the name: thieves had to break off all contact with biological relatives and were forbidden to marry or have children. Thus the thieves abided by a code that was quasi-monastic in that it segregated them entirely from the "secular" world of both government and family, even if it did not celebrate the total self-denial required of true monastic orders (sex was fine, but heterosexual attachment was not; robbery was essential, but luxury was proscribed). The result was akin to a warrior brotherhood, like the mythic Cossacks celebrated by Nikolai Gogol, and was also far from antithetical to the masculine ethos perennially celebrated by official Soviet ideology.[6] Indeed, the thieves' world relied on a collectivist spirit that, in other contexts, a true Leninist could not have helped but admire: all

---

[3] This is particularly evident in criminal tattoos, with their "blasphemous" caricatures of Brezhnev, Stalin, Lenin, and Marx (Baldaev 477–90).

[4] See, for example, Solzhenitsyn (2: 38).

[5] See Volkov's detailed description of thieves-in-law (54–59). See also Olcott (136–39) and Humphrey (115–18).

[6] See Borenstein, *Men Without Women* (1–42).

thieves had to tithe their earnings into a central set of communal funds (the *obshchak*) that functioned as a social safety net for criminals during their frequent periods of imprisonment, supplying food, drugs, tobacco, and bribes to make zone life bearable (Volkov 54–58).

The details of the thieves' code are less important for my purposes than the mere fact of the code's existence, the reliance on a strict hierarchy and unbendable rules. Thieves' culture was systemic through and through, betraying the influences of Soviet ideology, the military, and the prison camps— institutions to which thieves' culture was hostile by definition. The thieves' code literally inscribed itself on its adherents' bodies, with tattoos of images and slogans that both reminded criminals of their most important precepts and alerted them to the status of their interlocutors. Whatever the source of the term "thief-in-law," it is perfectly appropriate, even if the juxtaposition of "thief" and "law" sounds paradoxical. These are criminals who, when faced with the dehumanizing conditions of prison camps, do not revert to a state of nature, nor do they descend into a Hobbesian nightmare of total chaos. Quite the contrary, the thieves' world can be seen as reassuring evidence of a human tendency toward order and control, which is part of the thieves' mythic appeal. On the one hand, they are outlaws, but on the other, they follow their own rules and are thus predictable.[7] An ordinary person's encounter with a thief could be easily survivable because a thief is not a blood-crazed sadist. Just as the orderly old-fashioned horror stories and monster movies are only minimally threatening (vampires cannot enter your house if you do not invite them in), the thief represents violent crime that is understandable and manageable precisely because it is always being managed.

Also important is the primacy of zone experience for the thieves' world; as Volkov argues, "prison life was its ultimate system of reference" (55). Thus the thieves' code was formed in a context in which total freedom of action was excluded by definition. The limits were always visible: they were the barbed wire surrounding the camps and the armed guards keeping watch over the inmates. The thieves' code implicitly accepted these boundaries, for the goal was to improve life in prison rather than to escape.[8] The

---

[7] Nancy Ries notes that in her fieldwork in 1990 and 1992, the mafia was often invoked by Russians as "the supreme symbol of evil and terror"; four to five years later, "the terror the mafia provided was sometimes represented as the means by which avarice and corruption might be reined in" (" 'Honest Bandits' " 305). She argues that mafia served as "both the *destroyer* of any hopes for justice and social order and also the most likely potential *source* of justice and order" (278, emphasis in the original). See also Verdery on the "conceptual mafia," or "mafia-as-symbol" of anxiety over the market economy and the post-socialist power vacuum (219).

[8] In fact, prison sentences were an integral part of the thief's experience; one could not become a true thief-in-law without spending time behind bars.

thieves' code, rather than fighting against the limits on freedom, multiplied them: the barbed wire of the zone became metaphorical and portable, structuring criminals' conduct.

It is in this context that the notion of bespredel makes sense. A culture built on accommodation with incarceration cannot accept a state of pure lawlessness. Bespredel is about more than simply transgression (the concept implicit in the Russian word for crime, *prestuplenie*); it is about not recognizing the existence of any boundaries to transgress. The thieves' insistence on orderliness and systems and their Foucauldian assumption of self-surveillance and self-discipline make bespredel the worst possible crime: it is the crime that no longer recognizes itself as crime. Punishing a criminal for violating the thieves' code was already serious, but a declaration of bespredel meant that the offender had placed himself not merely outside the law but outside the *outlaw*. Thus bespredel could be fought only by eradicating it at the source, since the offender could no longer be incorporated into the (anti-)social body. Bespredel is abomination.

The rise of bespredel is connected to the pathos of the thieves-in-law, who are something of a dying breed in the post-Soviet era. Volkov contrasts the thieves with the modern breed of "bandits," who have a stranglehold on the economy in major metropolitan areas such as Petersburg and Yekaterinburg: "The thief's income comes from the illegal secondary redistribution of property and consists of the appropriation, by illegal means, of the private possessions of other citizens or of state property. The bandit aspires to receive a share of other entrepreneurs' income, which, as he claims, has been produced under his patronage or with the participation of the organized group he represents"(Volkov 60). As pure abstractions, thieves and bandits represent polar opposites, though the two groups have reached something of an equilibrium in recent years. The thieves' way of life is a product of the zone, while the bandits are firmly rooted in civilian life. Bandits reject the monastic form of the thieves' code, marrying and having children, although their attention to physical fitness and propensity to ban alcohol and drugs make the thieves look almost hedonistic (Volkov 60). If the bandits look upon the thieves as living relics, the thieves scorn the bandits for their refusal to follow the code. The bandits, whose ranks are filled with veterans of Russia's military conflicts and former participants in sports clubs, are seen as disrespectful and unnecessarily violent. If the concept of bespredel has spread beyond the world of organized crime, it is in part because the development of bandit culture has led to more and more instances of what the thieves consider bespredel. From the point of view of the thieves' code, much of banditry is bespredel, or it would be, if it were committed by thieves.

Two opposing tendencies have facilitated the spread of bespredel as a phenomenon and as a concept: the first is the generational conflict between these two broad segments of the Russian underworld, and the second is their gradual reconciliation. As thief culture and bandit culture have grown together, the thieves have relaxed some of their strictures, while the bandits have adopted many of the trappings of thief culture, even insisting on undergoing the "coronation" ritual that installs a new thief-in-law. And they have also inherited the concept of bespredel: accusing a rival gangleader of bespredel is fighting words. What constitutes bespredel for a given criminal formation is less important than the fact that bespredel remains an operative concept. Even a bandit world still recognizes its own rule of law.

In contemporary Russian narratives about organized crime, bespredel sparks anxiety among the criminals themselves, for it is only people who belong to the underworld who can determine what behavior is considered out of bounds. When bespredel is presented as a result of the rise of bandits and the fall of thieves, such stories invariably side with the thieves, for reasons that are immediately comprehensible. The thieves stand for restraint, tradition, and honor, while the bandits are corrupt even by criminal standards. The political implications are never far beneath the surface: the old-fashioned thieves, often played by beloved Soviet-era actors on screen, take pride in their dying world just as their counterparts in law enforcement and the military might lament their motherland's loss of great-power status. The fact that the thieves are criminals by definition only makes the comparison stronger, containing an implicit recognition that the lost great power itself was hardly angelic or perfect. But organized crime narratives present both the thieves and Soviet power as inherently ideological, which is viewed positively when compared with Yeltsin's government, "wild" capitalism, and mercenary bandits. These post-Soviet phenomena represent the triumph of capitalism exactly as it is portrayed by its opponents rather than its boosters: all values are rendered valueless if they cannot be expressed in the cash nexus. For the new generation of criminals, as well as for the businessmen they extort and the state officials they bribe, everything is fungible: money, property, and human life. For the thief, such indifference is the essence of bespredel.

This particular formulation of bespredel is expressed most clearly in Konstantinov's *Bandit Petersburg*, particularly the fourth book, appropriately entitled *The Thief* (*Vor*)(which was filmed as the first miniseries, *Baron*). As discussed in chapter 4, *The Thief* is focused on the conflict between an old thief-in-law bearing the noble nickname of "Baron" and the slippery bandit leader nicknamed "Antibiotic." The reader's and viewer's sympathies are aligned from the very beginning with the Baron, who, as is fitting for the representative of a dying era, is pulling off his last heist before succumbing to terminal cancer. The Baron is educated, eloquent, and even gentle when circumstances allow, and Konstantinov's story gives him several occasions to philosophize about the state of Russia and the underworld. Readers and viewers first meet the Baron when the story begins, as he is breaking into an apartment, but only the novel includes his meditation on Russia's criminal mayhem:

> If in the old days, a [thief] with rotten tendencies took a long time to turn bad . . . after the triumph of democracy in Russia, which opened the gates to the road into the radiant capitalist future . . . formerly decent thieves and movers and shakers went savage and turned into scum, for whom walking through blood was just as simple as stepping over a puddle. . . . Why even talk about the young people, if even respectable bosses [*avtoritety*] no longer tried to resolve arguments and conflicts peacefully? Who needs words if a bullet, knife, or grenade can always easily compensate for the lack of fair arguments? Whoever is stronger is right. Of course, it was just like that before, but human life was more respected in the criminal world. . . . No question, serious people were killed before, only it wasn't today's low hits, but the execution of sentences—and everybody knew for what. . . . While bloodthirsty, trigger-happy *bespredel'shchiki* could be found and punished by the thieves' world more quickly and effectively than by the cops. . . . But that was before, and now was the time of the collaborators [*ssuchennykh*], who twisted the thieves' law like card sharks at a casino. (10–11)

Later the Baron laments the corruption of the country brought on by the new-style bandits who, unlike thieves, work with the state authorities, leading to a complete collapse of both state and underworld law: "[T]his was awful, because it gave rise to bespredel, which is unavoidable in an organization whose ideological basis was collaboration [*ssuchennost'*], lack of principle, and treachery in the name of power and money. . . ." (147).

It is only when the Baron gives an interview to the journalist (and authorial stand-in) Andrei Seregin that he gets the chance to explain his views in depth, this time in both the film version and the novel. His entire monologue is a requiem for the thieves' world: "Our world is fading. . . . Now there's nothing but bespredel" conducted by complete "morons" (*debily*), whose underdeveloped brains know only food, sex, and fear. In the old days, criminals lived according to the "rules" (*poniatiia*), murdered only when necessary, and never killed cops, but for today's thugs, murder is always justified if it can lead to greater profits (167–68). This is more than just a criminal matter, for the Baron insists that bespredel is useful to Russia's enemies: "I can only tell you one thing: a strong criminal world, with its own laws and rules, with traditions and without bespredel, is only possible in a strong country. And who needs a strong Russia? [The West] needs a weak Russia" (168).

One of the intrinsic problems caused by the new world of bandit crime, which is impossible to disentangle from "legitimate" business and the business of state, is that it is becoming coterminous with Russia itself ("I always felt that the criminal world should be small, and not all-encompassing . . ." [168]). Here we return to the geographic metaphor implicit in bespredel: crime must have boundaries and must know its limits. The criminalization of Russia is, in this sense, the apotheosis of one of Russia's central myths, the notion of the motherland's "boundlessness" (*neob"iatnost'*), its wide-open spaces (*prostory*) that in turn define the expansive national character (Pesmen 66–68).[9] If *bespredel* were not such an irredeemably marked term, *Rossiia bespredel'naia* would sound like just another variation on national boosterism. Bespredel is a demonic inversion of everything that is good in Russia's own mythic self-conception.

Even as the West shares some of the blame for the mayhem of the 1990s, Western countries also have the most to lose by a postsocialist Russia that has succumbed to bespredel. Like the troika at the end of Gogol's *Dead Souls*, bespredel Russia is a terrible force with which the rest of the world will have to reckon. "You know, sometimes I think that there's going to be a new iron curtain, only this time it will be the West that establishes it out of fear of our bespredel" (168). Or perhaps bespredel is the criminal manifestation of Dostoevsky's nightmare scenario in *Demons* (*Besy*): once all traditional authorities have been overthrown, the country will descend into a Boschian nightmare that could eventually sweep up the whole world in its wake. An old thief presents just such a view on his deathbed in one of the novels in Evgeny Sukhov's *I Am a Thief-in-Law* series:

> Proper [*pravil'nye*] thieves are being replaced . . . by *bespredel'shchiki* . . . Yes, before there was fear. And there was the law—harsh, strict, but fair. Everything was held together by fear in Soviet life. And in thieves' life—by the law.

---

[9] This myth, which was touted so successfully by Gogol (the troika scene in *Dead Souls*, his representation of the Cossacks as the embodiment of Russia's boundless frontier spirit) was taken up by Stalinist culture as well, most notably in the "Song of the Motherland" made famous in the film *Circus*: "Broad is my native land / So many forests, fields and rivers! / I don't know any other such country/ In which man can breathe so freely."

And now there's nothing left. Neither fear nor the law. Freedom and anarchy. And in Rus', freedom was always called liberty [*volia*]. *Vol'nitsa* [wild liberty]. Russian liberty gone wild is a terrible thing. Wild liberty is . . . merciless and bloody. Pointless cruelty. . . . (*Oboroten'*)

If I invoke Gogol and Dostoevsky in connection with thieves-in-law, it is not to appeal to a prophetic literary tradition but to put bespredel in the context of perennial Russian laments and jeremiads about the country's fate (hence the Baron's conclusion that only cruelty on the part of the state can counter the cruelty of criminal bespredel [169]). In the pre-Soviet context of political upheavals and dissent, such fears of chaos were often part of a generational conflict, the older liberals watching in horror as their offspring militated for radical solutions. Post-Soviet bespredel is also troped as a generation gap, in this case decrying the moral degeneracy of younger criminals who do not know the meaning of the word "respect." Bespredel takes the anxious hand-wringing over the younger generation that was so prominent in perestroika and ups the ante significantly, for the question of total honesty, idealism, and integrity is no longer even on the table. The very fact that the latest iteration of panic over wayward youth is situated in a context that takes criminality for granted is itself a sign of all-pervasive bespredel.

This generational conflict is set in even starker relief in Daniil Koretskii's 1995 novel *Antikiller*, a book that gained far more attention when it was turned into a big-budget movie by Egor Mikhalkov-Konchalovskii in 2002. *Antikiller* follows the familiar plot of the lone avenger's struggle with a world of evil (as discussed in the previous chapter), and this type of plot is often closely linked to bespredel: if the country were not in such chaos, if the institutions of law enforcement were not thoroughly corrupt, there would be no need for vigilantism. The avenging vigilante is not like the superhero; he does not seek out crime wherever it happens to take place, nor is he a secret agent, accepting assignments from his handlers. Instead, his story is profoundly personal, and if his crime-fighting task expands to include the struggle against an entire criminal structure, this is part of the search for the true villains who gave the orders for the initial incident that set the hero on the path of vengeance, as a result of complications that arise in his quest for vengeance.

Antikiller is the story of Fox (*Lis*), an honest cop who was sent to the zone through the machinations of a mob boss. Upon arranging his release, Fox sets in motion a complicated plan for revenge, getting involved in a number of tangentially related adventures along the way (by sheer chance, he even foils an attempt to assassinate the president, a plotline not included in the film). *Antikiller* is based on a complicated, at times contradictory, notion of the law. As mentioned in chapter 6, the film is structured around Fox's recitation of his oath of service, highlighting an honest policeman's ideals and the impossibility of their application within the rule of law. In the novel, we see that Fox was a vigilante even before he was sent to jail: he did, indeed, commit the crime for which he was convicted, methodically planning and implementing the murder of a man who was undoubtedly going to kill a witness Fox had promised to protect. Fox is caught because the mob boss, Shaman, used his crooked police contacts to capture Fox's crime on video. Fox was set up, but he was not innocent.

Yet in *Antikiller*, Fox is clearly one of the few good cops left (another, Litvinov, is that great cliché of Russian crime fiction, the honorable Afghan war veteran). Fox is fighting a rearguard battle against crime and corruption, and besides his two trusted comrades within the force, his most reliable ally is . . . a thief-in-law. Fox's quest for vengeance ends up involving him in two interconnected plotlines that highlight the generational conflict within the Russian underworld, in which the old-fashioned, honorable thief Cross (*Krest*) matches wits with amoral bandits and loses all patience with a small group of degenerate punks who murder, rape, and torture for sheer pleasure.[10] The conflict between bandits and thieves plays out along the same model as in *Bandit Petersburg*, but the fact that the hero is an avenging ex-cop makes the parallels between law enforcement and crime even clearer. Fox recalls the good old days: "Back then everything was clear: the thief steals, the detective goes after him. A thief is a thief, and a detective is a detective." The police were harsh in Soviet times, but the thieves respected them and took care never to kill cops, but now everyone is corrupt and ready to kill at the drop of a hat (238). Cross, in turn, must deal with the new breed of bandits who want to take on the trappings of thieves without actually respecting the thieves' code: his enemies are "quick-ripened oranges" [*skorospelye apel'siny*], slang for men who have managed to get themselves crowned as thieves-in-law without a proper criminal biography (they served in the army, or married, or never spent time behind bars) (150). Cross and Fox have a common enemy in Shaman, who authorizes dismemberment with little forethought and almost no justification. As a representative of a group that was the target of Shaman's indiscriminate violence puts it, "First of all, it wasn't his zone. Second, you have to sort

---

[10] The irony is not lost on Fox: "Now I've seen it all! . . . Criminals are complaining about bespredel!" (442).

things out first, not just attack. . . . Third, you can't just cut someone's hands off! That's bespredel!" (126).

Despite the convoluted plot and underdeveloped characters, *Antikiller*, in its allocation of blame and innocence and its bloody resolution of violent disputes, shares the preoccupation with the establishment of justice that characterizes ancient Greek tragedy. But where *The Oresteia* resolves the dilemma of vengeance and guilt through the establishment of a legal system, Koretskii's novel moves in the opposite direction, demonstrating the complete bankruptcy of every Russian institution and the total identification of the country with bespredel; the only possible solution is to ignore the law entirely and rely on one righteous man to mete out justice: the Antikiller. As a question of plot, it makes little sense that Fox should find himself at the confluence of so many seemingly unrelated campaigns of violence, adding new missions to his original plan for personal vengeance thanks to coincidence and metonymy. Shaman is connected to Cross, both of them are having trouble with the young punk gang, and Fox's girlfriend just happens to be sleeping with the hit man who is about to try to assassinate the president of the Russian Federation (who happens to be visiting Fox's imaginary provincial hometown of Tikhodonsk). But these multiple converging plotlines are a perfect fit thematically, establishing bespredel at every level of Russian society. Mikhalkov-Konchalovskii was wise to eliminate the presidential assassination plot from his already action-packed film, choosing instead to invoke the story's larger political ramifications through the scenes of Fox's recitation of his police officer's oath. The resulting film is more streamlined, but its very lack of messiness and its more narrow focus on the provincial underworld requires that the viewer infer the ubiquity of bespredel, whereas the novel makes the case by involving Fox in bespredel on the highest levels of state. Shaman may have put Fox in jail, but it was the corrupt system that forced Fox to break the law in the name of justice: "Fox ground his teeth in fury . . . at those who threw the country into fear and bespredel" (238).

If bespredel can be found everywhere (that is the nature of bespredel), it is exemplified in its purest form by the youngest characters in the novel, who never got the firm moral education that presumably molded older generations of good cops and honest thieves. In *Antikiller*, these punks are so wild and violent that even the bandits are appalled: the only thing the bandits, thieves, and Fox all agree on is that something must be done about them.[11]

---

[11] Hulk and his gang are examples of a particular criminal type called *otmorozhennye* ("thawed out"), whose wanton cruelty and lack of common sense make them anathema to more "orderly" criminals. See Humphrey (114–16).

Fittingly, the novel starts with them, rather than with Fox: the mentally defi-
cient Marik Rynda, the weak-willed punk whose mohawk earned him the
nickname "Parrot," and the charismatic sociopath who serves as their
leader, Hulk (*Ambal*). If nearly all the young criminals in the novel perform
acts of gratuitous violence and sexual sadism (Rynda forces a young woman
to have sex with him, strangling and killing her as he reaches orgasm), it is
Hulk who is the face of degenerate young Russia. Everyone wants him dead
after he and his friends steal guns from local gang members, kill them for
fun, murder one crimelord, and threaten another. But Fox goes after Hulk
for more personal reasons: first, Hulk's gang kills an honest cop trying to
save a young woman from rape; then Tamara, a prostitute with whom Fox is
friendly, actually tries to hire him to kill Hulk, who burned her genitals with
cigarettes before having sex with her. She offers Fox three thousand dollars
for the job, but he refuses: "No, my dear! I'm an antikiller! If I take out that
Hulk of yours, it won't be for money" (334). In the novel, Fox and Litvinov
make quick work of Hulk's gang, with little description of the actual fight,
but the film lingers on the spectacle of their torture and execution, with the
insane Hulk laughing as Litvinov eviscerates him. Fox does not approve of
torture and simply executes the thugs. He suffers pangs of conscience ("We
killed children"), but Litvinov gets the final world: "Not children, mutants."

    Antikiller is a model of the most common narrative representation of
bespredel: the vigilante hero provides the moral framework for bespredel's
condemnation, thereby allowing the reader or viewer to indulge his or her
prurient interest in the details of bespredel in good conscience. This is not
the struggle between good and evil found in the boevik but rather a battle
between order and chaos. The forces of order are always embattled and
outnumbered, since order is clearly an outmoded concept, a holdover from
the days of either strong Soviet power or honest, authoritative thieves.[12]
Nonetheless, the sheer fact of the heroes' existence saves these tales of
bespredel from total pessimism; presumably, as long as one righteous man

---

[12] The generational politics of bespredel reaches its apotheosis in Stanislav Govorukhin's film
Voroshilovskii strelok (*The Sharpshooter*) (1999). When an innocent young girl is gang-raped by
three young men whose political connections shield them from the law, it is her veteran grandfather who uses the skills he learned on the battlefield to punish them (castrating one, nearly killing a
second, and driving a third insane). If the Afghan war veteran in the boevik is morally superior to
those who did not serve, he cannot hold a candle to the veteran of the "Great Patriotic War" (World
War II), a conflict that is portrayed with none of the moral ambiguities surrounding the Soviet in-
tervention in Afghanistan. Nineteen ninety-five was the fiftieth anniversary of the victory over the
Nazis, and the official commemoration helped reinforce the popular sentiment that veterans of
that generation are honorable and incorruptible. (See, for example, the *Liubit' po-russki* (*Russian
Love*) film trilogy, in which a collective farm is saved from the predations of corrupt New Russians
thanks to the leadership of a World War II veteran and a cache of weaponry hidden since the days
of the German invasion.)

remains, there is still hope. When bespredel is loosed from the confines of the boevik and the detektiv, however, the heroic context is abandoned, and all hope must be abandoned with it.

The News from Hell

In 1997, two overeducated and underemployed young Americans living in Moscow founded a satirical newspaper, the *eXile*, which combined the gonzo journalism of Hunter S. Thompson with an unabashedly frat boy sensibility. Never shy about giving offense, the editors included their own version of a crime diary called "Death Porn" in every edition. Death Porn featured pithy, irreverent descriptions of murder, cannibalism, and dismemberment, accompanied by grotesque photos of mutilated bodies with cutlines such as "Hey, pal, can you lend me a hand? And a leg? And a head?" (Ames and Taibbi 71), or "Whyn't you guys go on ahead? I'll catch up with you in a sec, I promise! Don't wait up!" (80). The section was accompanied by a helpful graphic called the "Death Porn Legend," a guide to the fourteen symbols that were used to categorize the crimes:

> Each Death Porn story came affixed with little cartoon pictures, which told you what kind of story elements to expect in the tale you were reading: a Far-Side-ean screaming old woman to indicate "Cries For Help Ignored," a piece of Swiss cheese to indicate "Riddled With Bullets," a turkey for "Carved Up Like a Turkey." Worse still, the stories were narrated with an unabashed voyeuristic glee that even the most progressive of our readers couldn't endorse publicly. Whoever was writing this stuff clearly got off on what he was doing. (71).

The Death Porn section of the *eXile* did not spring from nowhere, but it was hardly the product of American investigative reporting. Quite the contrary, it was based on clippings compiled from Russian newspapers. As the editors explain, "There was no shortage of material, of course. Russia was a yellow journalist's dream. Not only did it have one of the highest crime rates in the world, it was simply overrun with Dostoevskian lunatics who were constantly outdoing one another in their efforts to be more disgusting, more bloodthirsty, and more disturbingly, ingeniously evil" (Ames and Taibbi 71). Unfortunately, this description of Russian crime is one of the few points at which the editors of the *eXile* fall victim to the same assumptions that they find so outrageous in articles by mainstream

Western foreign correspondents: they identify the "facts" presented in yellow journalism as indicative of Russian reality. ("They were killing and raping and eating one another at an alarming rate. It was mayhem. Absolute nihilism.") (71). Behind the daring and tasteless mockery of human suffering in Death Porn lies the earnest dismay of the satirist. Death Porn was chernukha done for laughs.

As an exaggerated portrait of Russian misery, Death Porn is less than reliable, but as a distillation of the excess of post-Soviet journalism, it is perfectly on the mark. The coverage of violent crime in the Russian media is about far more than simply reporting the news: the grisly details, sexualized photographs (usually staged), and sheer repetitive content suggest the voyeuristic pleasure and the need for endless, minor variations on a limited number of acts that characterize pornography. Throughout the 1990s, central newspapers such as *Moskovskii komsomolets* and *Komsomol'skaia pravda* desperately tried to outdo each other with graphic, sensationalist stories of lurid violence, while specialized publications such as *Vne zakona* (*Outlaw*) were devoted entirely to crime. The prominence of violent crime reporting is abundantly clear if one simply picks up any of these newspapers at random. The headline in the bottom left corner of the June 19, 1997, issue of *Moskovskii komsomolets* informs its readers that a "sadist tried to slice up all the women on one particular street"("Sadist"). The story is presented as good news but only in the context of the overall bad news: "Muscovite women can rest easy—the number of predators [*man'iaki*] in the capital has shrunk by one."[13] The previous day's *Megapolis-Express* (a weekly newspaper whose motto is "The exotica of urban life") portrayed a veritable sea of troubles: the gang of young thugs (*otmorozki*) who had been torturing and killing homeless people in Krasnodar for the past year (Shtamm 9) got only a brief write-up, while a two-page spread entitled "Awful event in Liubery" was filled with disgust at a gathering of bikers in a Moscow suburb, although the only crime to take place was a bar fight leading to a handful of arrests (Perfilev 9–10). Not that the paper was short on reports of "real" crimes: other headlines included "Thugs with suitcases full of bucks" (bus hijackings to extort ransom) (Kribosheev 11); "Grandma hit with hammer six times (T. Borovik 11); "Clever girl attacked her savior" (Logachev 11); and "*Banditskaia Rossiia*" (a two-page excerpt from Andrei Konstantinov's latest guide to organized crime) (Konstantinov and Sidiachko 14–15).

---

[13] I have chosen to render the Russian word "man'iak" as "predator," since it makes more sense in its context of obsessive sexualized violence than "maniac."

The Russian yellow press was remarkably self-conscious in its insistence that ordinary Russian citizens must never be allowed to forget how terribly dangerous their world had become. The June 1, 1997, issue of *Moskovskii komsomolets* attempted to instill two parallel levels of fear: the danger is not only in the prevalence of crime itself but in the possibility that other events might distract attention from the criminal threat. Svetlana Antonova's "Diagnosis: predator" attempts to breathe new life into the already tired genre of the serial killer profile with a prefatory warning: "The wave of terrorism and hired killings that have swept the country has caused society to forget for a while about the crimes of sexual predators, which so recently sparked such horror" (25). In other words, Russians must never forget any of the terrible threats that lurk outside their doors—the truly aware public must somehow manage to keep terrorism, hit men, sexual predators, thugs, random murders, rapists, and kidnappers in mind at the same time.

The daily reports of murders, rapes, and cannibalism constituted bespredel as an endless flow, a process consisting of infinite iterations of the same horrific acts. As a function of the daily crime chronicle, bespredel is "without bounds" precisely because it lacks a beginning, middle, and end: all the stories run together into a single, nightmare narrative of a Russia that is out of control. Russia is hardly unique in its fascination with bloody violence, but, as with so many of the phenomena discussed in this book, the sensationalism of post-Soviet crime reporting was shocking and anomalous because it was so recent. Russia went from virtually no coverage of violent crime to a bloodbath of yellow journalism in under a decade, with the result that the journalistic representation of violence was even more prominent for its relative novelty. The United States and Britain have long-established traditions of "true crime" reporting and fiction, which means that true crime, like pornography, has a comprehensible place within the culture at large, both as a niche for dedicated consumers and as a visible, but not predominant, aspect of the larger culture. In her comprehensive study of late-twentieth-century British true-crime narratives, Anita Biressi makes the Foucauldian argument that true crime shows "the emergence of modern notions of lawlessness, the divisions between the criminal subject and the law-abiding citizen and the creation of the 'dangerous individual,' " interrogating the "rhetorical division between the criminal and the good citizen . . . through an examination of the discursive relationship between British true crime and the social construction of crime and criminality" (6). A similar dynamic is at work in Russian crime reporting, including a broad spectrum of newspaper and TV crime reporting, nonfiction books on the criminal scene and famous lawbreakers, and novelizations of famous cases;

but, as is to be expected, the discourses of crime and citizenship in post-Soviet Russia are not developing along Anglo-American lines. Anglo-American true crime strikes a balance between terrifying consumers and reassuring them of their civic power. As Biressi notes, the "vigilant citizen" is one of the primary categories of moral subjectivity created in Thatcher-era true crime: British television shows such as *Crimestoppers* combined with civic organizations such as Neighborhood Watch to suggest that vigilance and surveillance could empower law-abiding citizens both to prevent crime and to apprehend offenders (73–84). Thus crime becomes manageable thanks to the insistence on the cultural consumer's investment in the discourse of law enforcement and the institutions of crimefighting.

In Russia, true crime could neither inculcate nor rely on such a civic ethos; nor did it strengthen faith in the power of state institutions to fight the growing crime wave. The 1990s were a low point for popular investment in civic institutions or civic-mindedness. Decades of Soviet campaigns exhorting the citizenry to take part in public good works led to a virtual civic exhaustion; the brief period of broad interest in and enthusiasm for civic life in perestroika ended with the Soviet Union itself, leaving a populace far more concerned with bread-and-butter economic issues. Just as the Russian language lacked an accessible, neutral vocabulary for sex, the discredited, slogan-based Soviet discourse of civic involvement left post-Soviet Russia without a credible language for appealing to the initiative of what was more often called the "population" than the "citizenry."[14] TV crime programs, particularly the police-produced *Petrovka 38*, did include a "wanted" segment, but the only sustained appeals to personal initiative in crime prevention were in the advertisements, which focused on self-protection and secure barriers rather than vigilance: in 1999, all the central crime shows featured commercials for the "Mongoose" home security system. Crime reporting and true crime in the 1990s did not help constitute an active, empowered civic subject; on the contrary, it facilitated atomization and abject fear.

Bespredel would not be bespredel if it could be conceived as manageable by and for ordinary people or subject to remediation through collective social action. The protagonists of bespredel narratives who manage to survive in a world of boundless crime do so by leaving their ordinary lives behind, removing themselves from any rational, civic order, and becoming

---

[14] Only by the end of the Yeltsin era did the government develop a publicity campaign for civic-mindedness that neither resembled Soviet propaganda nor invoked nationalism: a 1999 series of television ads and billboards featuring impoverished pensioners and underequipped schools and the simple slogan "Please pay your taxes."

vigilantes or vengeance-driven lone wolves. If they are part of a team or group to fight bespredel, then the team engages in battle with the forces of chaos on their enemy's own terms. In his two-volume true crime novelization of the life and death of Aleksandr Solonik, one of the most notorious hit men of the 1990s, Valerii Karyshev claims that Solonik was actually the product of a top-secret KGB operation dedicated to fighting crime in secret, thereby circumventing the legal niceties that protect criminals.[15] Solonik's KGB handler argues that the only way to fight "criminal bespredel" is through "state bespredel" (Karyshev). The only way the forces of law and order can be victorious over bespredel is by abandoning law and order entirely. This particular scenario was quite popular in the 1990s, though usually accompanied by concerns that the state, having engaged in lawlessness, would not be able to restrain itself once the battle was over. However appealing the fantasy may be (and we will return to it in the next chapter), it threatens to perpetuate bespredel rather than end it. In Karyshev's account, Solonik becomes a liability for his handlers and must be removed using the same lethal force that Solonik wielded so well.[16]

If Russian crime reporting and true crime posited the noncriminal subject as a passive witness or helpless victim, they came closer to their Western counterparts in their treatment of criminals themselves. Anglo-American true crime is distinguished by a fascination with the character and life story of the murderer (Biressi 173–77), with a particular emphasis on the serial killer, who can be easily represented with "a Gothic rhetoric of 'the monster' " (Ingebretsen 27). Russian true crime, which was arguably still in its embryonic stages, attempted to create a criminal taxonomy, employing the monster rhetoric for murderous predators while carefully situating lesser criminals within recognizable, established social categories. Returning to our story of the sadist attacking random women on his street, we see a rare hybrid of these two extremes: before attacking five women on the street, the "29-year-old maniac" had only been arrested for theft before. But today his girlfriend had left him: "This banal scandal was the last straw—the criminal became bitter at the entire fair sex." After drinking vodka and taking "some

---

[15] In Sergei Norka's paranoid thriller, *Zagovor protiv Rossii* (*The Plot against Russia*) (2004), Solonik has fled the country and is living as "Brother Alessandro," a pentitent monk in Milan. The leaders of the "Holy Russian Inquisition," a conspiratorial organization dedicated to Russia's salvation, bring him back home to complete his mission (707–27).

[16] Karyshev, who identifies himself as Solonik's lawyer, claims that the novels are based on voluminous notes his client left with him for safekeeping. Yet the scenario he describes seems awfully familiar from earlier novels and films, include *La femme Nikita*, among others. Elena Borovik blames Karyshev for a number of the "myths" that have sprung up since Solonik's death, in particular the idea that he was actually working for the government. According to her, Karyshev was not actually Solonik's lawyer, a detail that renders his story even less believable (E. Borovik).

sort of pills," he began attacking random women ("Sadist"). The anonymous author wrings as much sensationalism from this wild story as possible, but the result is an imperfect iteration of the Russian true-crime
formula, which usually demands extensive biographical and psychological
detail for its serial killers while leaving ordinary criminals to their banal
sociopathologies.

After the 1990 arrest of the notorious Ukrainian serial killer Andrei
Chikatilo exposed the Soviet public to the details of fifty-three murders accompanied by mutilation, rape, and cannibalism, the Russian mass media
indulged the public's fascination with sexual predators. Such killers were
frequently featured in crime fiction, such as Voronin's *Slepoi protiv man'i-
aka* (*Blind Man versus the Predator*). By the time the Russian media and culture industry turned their attention to serial killers, their story was such an
established part of Western true-crime genres that the Russian versions differed only slightly from their Western counterparts. Where they diverged
was in the body of "scientific" knowledge to which Russian true crime narratives turned in their creation of the "monster." For example, the March
28, 1999, broadcast of *Catastrophes of the Week*, a profile of the serial killer
Anatolii Onoprienko, combined a facile misinterpretation of contemporary genetics (the hunt for a "criminal" gene) and post-Soviet anxieties
about degeneration and the decline of the national "gene pool" (*genofond*)
with digressions about Soviet and Nazi labor camps and a serious treatment of the long-discredited theories of Cesare Lombroso, whose work has
sustained numerous reprintings since perestroika (*Katastrofy*, 1999). The
common thread in all these approaches was an emphasis on the deviant as
a distinct physical or biological type rather than the consequence of social
upheaval. Thus the fears of criminal chaos were intensified even further.
Somehow, the terrible social conditions resulting from the Soviet collapse
had irrevocably changed the Russian body itself, transforming crime into a
dominant biological mutation.

Most of the crime reported in the media was simply not as Gothic as
serial killings, and the approach taken to them was rather different. Attention was paid to the immediate context of a given crime and to the bodies
of the perpetrators and victims. The larger social context was established
more subtly by the manner in which the stories were presented, with the
result that the criminals and victims fell into familiar, prepackaged social
categories whose validity and rigidity were reinforced through sheer repetition. This implicit criminal taxonomy was most efficiently achieved on
television, which made the daily and weekly criminal roundup an important part of regular programming. Each of the major television networks

had its own version of these real-crime shows: *Petrovka 38* (TV6, TV-Tsentr), a ten-minute, police-produced broadcast named after the address of Moscow's central police headquarters (and a popular Soviet crime drama); *Kriminal* (*Crime*) (NTV); and *Dezhurnaia chast'* (*Duty Station*) (RTR, Rossiia); and *Dorozhnyi patrul'* (*Road Patrol*) (TV6, Rossiia). The events featured on these shows fell into four broad categories: organized criminal schemes (both violent and nonviolent), disasters (usually automobile accidents), drug busts, and the domestic disturbances covered by the police term *bytovukha* (everyday violence ranging from drunken fights to sexual assault to murder). The offenders themselves were usually the familiar representatives of late- and post-Soviet deviance: ethnic minorities from the Caucasus (presumed to be bandits as a matter of course), tattooed professional thugs, wayward youth, and hopeless (and often homeless) drunks.[17]

The most striking feature of all these reports was the explicit presumption of guilt: those who were arrested were never described as "suspects," and the only attempts to protect privacy were for the occasional witness or victim who feared reprisal (their faces were digitally blurred). Moreover, in keeping with the Russian and Soviet emphasis on the criminal's admission of guilt, the viewers were often treated to the criminals' video confessions, in which they explain exactly what they had done and why (Olcott 42). *Petrovka 38* attempted to put these crime stories in a legal context, interviewing experts who speculated on the outcomes of the eventual trials and the legal recourse for dealing with particularly recalcitrant or troubled offenders. On the opposite end of the spectrum was *Road Patrol*, the crime broadcast that was most relentless in conveying the message of *bespredel*. In its weekend edition, it showed the highlights from the past week's annals of murder, rape, arson, and car accidents. After each clip, a table of statistics about a given crime's frequency that week appeared on screen. *Road Patrol* was also noteworthy for its aesthetics; where the other real-crime shows stuck to the tried-and-true studio format, with anchors, interviews, and taped special reports, *Road Patrol* framed its stories in scenes of a police car driving across the road, presumably on its way to or from the scene of the latest tragedy. Each episode opened with a montage of the patrol car, an all-seeing eye, and images of crimes and objects associated with criminality (most notably the

---

[17] I watched crime reports frequently throughout my trips to Russia in the 1990s but unfortunately did not realize that I would be doing research on them until 1999, when I began taping the broadcasts. Thus my admittedly impressionistic approach is based on a thorough familiarity with the ephemeral nightly flow of these broadcasts at various points in the 1990s, but the only individual episodes available to me for analysis after the fact are from the period beginning in 1999.

cell phone), and the words: "Road Patrol . . . watches . . . shows . . . accidents . . . crimes."

While the squad car framework might seem lifted from *Cops*, a reality show that has been running on Fox TV in the United States since 1989, there are some important differences. *Cops* is based on a counterpoint between the camera's dehumanization of both perps and victims and an emphasis on the human, personal qualities of the policemen themselves, who usually talk into the camera and convey a world-weary sense of duty (Rapping 257–59). But *Road Patrol* dispensed with this device entirely; there were no admirable, reasonable representatives of law and order for the viewer to identify with; the camera itself stepped in and filled their place. The viewer was left with nothing but the crime and its victims.

In a typical *Road Patrol* segment from the June 13, 1999, weekly summary episode, the voice-over announces that the body of a forty-year-old man named Zelinskii has been found in his apartment, whereupon the camera shows his corpse lying on a mattress, with close-ups of his face and outstretched hand. The police quickly determine that the killer is Vladimir Egorov, a friend of Zelinskii's who has just been released from prison and who has killed him in a drunken brawl (the camera lingers obligingly on a set of empty bottles of beer and vodka). The story behind his crime undermines any relief that we might have at his arrest. If anything, the crime grows even more senseless once it is explained. The audience is horrified and titillated twice: first by the graphic presentation of the crime scene, then by the killer's own explanation of his actions. Egorov admits his guilt during his interrogation, and he repeats his confession for the cameras:

EGOROV: What can I tell you, guys. That . . . I won't swear . . . that scum [*mraz'*]. Can I say that? That scum told me to go [bleep] myself, and I said, "Think it over. Think it over." Who are you saying this to, you animal, and that's when I stabbed him. [The camera closes in on his dirty socks.]

JOURNALIST (OFF CAMERA): So you're a harsh person, would you say?

EGOROV: Yeah, I'm harsh, I'm a harsh person.

JOURNALIST: You stabbed him many times, a lot . . .

EGOROV: Oh, yeah, many times, I stabbed him many times. I wasn't counting . . .

The level of sheer objectification in this clip is both typical and, for the unaccustomed viewer, jarring. Throughout *Road Patrol* (and, to a lesser extent, its competitors on other networks), bloody, lifeless bodies are offered up to the camera (in the case of car accidents, the mangled, blood-stained automobiles serve as stand-ins). But even more noteworthy is the focus on the daily pathology of crime: the filthy apartment, the uneducated drunk, the terrible grooming. Both the criminals and their victims are a perfect fit with their social surroundings, but their presentation hardly inspires reformist zeal for social action.[18] In this, *Road Patrol* does resemble the American show *Cops*, which Elayne Rapping argues is an effective vehicle for transforming the deviants into thoroughly pathologized aliens with no place in an ordered society: "[T]he conditions in which these people live—filth, squalor, chaos—are seen as of their own making, a result of their own degraded natures" (Rapping 267).[19] In their confessions, the criminals show themselves to be dim-witted or inarticulate, or their accents reinforce ethnic stereotypes that pathologize them further.[20] Yet simply showing the criminals' bodies, an expressive counterpoint to the frozen tableaux of their victims, serves to pigeonhole them. The red-eyed faces of the disheveled, unshaven drunks speak volumes, while the tattooed bodies of habitual criminals are displayed in loving close-up, with the offenders obligingly lifting their shirts to provide a better view (*Petrovka 38*). Watching *Road Patrol* was a nightly ritual based on simultaneous fascination and repulsion, enticing the viewer to stare at the unspeakable, confirming that the world was a senseless place fraught with random, inexplicable dangers, and, in the wee hours before both the viewer and the television retired for the night, reassuring the audience that, once again, it had not happened to them.

The True Lies of True Crime

The pervasiveness of *bespredel* as a readily available context for violent crime and state chaos in the 1990s was the result of a synergy that any

---

[18] Drunken murderers and the corpses of their victims were also prominent on *Dezhurnaia chast'*, May 25 and August 20, 1999, and *Kriminal*, May 14, 1999.

[19] Even here, though, the difference between *Cops* and *Road Patrol* is significant: Rapping argues that on *Cops*, the viewers are protected from these "aliens" "only by the thin blue line of the police, who are presented as the true salvation of American civilization" (266). While the Russian police were sometimes cast as heroic in the police-produced *Petrovka 38*, they were virtually absent from *Road Patrol*.

[20] In the July 10, 1999, episode of *Crime* (*Kriminal*), Yemenite graduate students from the Patrice Lumumba International University are arrested for operating an illegal international telephone network; when one of the ringleaders explains how the operation worked, the reporter states that the criminal "spoke with the expressiveness typical of a person from the East."

marketing executive would envy: the concept arose in the zone, spread
through narratives of gangland conflicts, was exemplified and reinforced
in the sensationalist media every day, and, finally, was distilled in new fictional narratives that made bespredel their ostensible theme. In addition
to the detektiv and the boevik, the Russian entertainment industry in general and book publishers in particular recognized a third category: *kriminal* ("crime"), a mixture of both true crime (documentary accounts such
as Konstantinov's original *Bandit Petersburg* and nonfiction novels such as
Karyshev's Solonik series) and pure fiction about organized crime but
without any representatives of an incorruptible legal establishment. *Kriminal* was a triumph of niche marketing in the post-Soviet book world: in
the 1990s, EKSMO Press fielded several different series dedicated to bespredel. Though the individual books published in a given series varied
widely in content and approach, their packaging and marketing promised
readers a guided tour of criminal hell. Readers could pick up these books
in stores or from street vendors, or, if they were particularly dedicated to
the product line, monthly subscriptions were available (along with a free
quarterly full-color catalog). The book referred to in the beginning of this
chapter, *You're Just a Slut, My Dear!* was published in a series called
Russkie razborki (*Russian Gang Wars*), which billed itself in classic bespredel fashion:

> Every criminal knows: prison isn't as frightening as a sentence by your own
> people. As is well known, organized crime's iron fist never misses its target.
> And the most important thing is to strike first. This thrilling new series of
> criminal novels, "Russian Gang Wars" is about the cruel fights between crim-
> inal groups, operations to annihilate their enemies, and the intricate ways of
> escaping justice. (Pugachev, back matter)

The same publisher also had as series called *Vne zakona* (*Outlaws*), whose
emblem was a balding Russian thug with a cigarette dangling from his
mouth (the emblem for *Russian Gang Wars* was a closed fist with brass
knuckles). *Outlaws* promised "crime novels whose plots rule out the customary conflict between the criminal world and law enforcement. Here
everything is unpredictable, for the hero fighting the criminals is, as a rule,
himself the object of persecution and defends the very law that made him
an outlaw" (Pugachev, back matter)And finally, EKSMO Press had a series
of alleged nonfiction called simply *Bespredel*, including the aforementioned
Solonik novels as well as titles such as *Who's Who in Russian Crime*, *Criminal Russia*, and *Bandit Russia*. All of these series were part of EKSMO's

Criminal Club, which insistently created the illusion that the readers had been given exclusive access to the world of crime that they otherwise could only glimpse each day on the nightly news.

The perennial stories of gang wars and zone life under the *Kriminal* rubric are tales of *bespredel* by default: a conflict among prison camp inmates is almost always between the forces of order and chaos. Bespredel is at the heart of the early installments of Evgeny Sukhov's long-running series *I Am a Thief-in-Law (Ia—vor v zakone),*[21] in which the powerful and honest thief Varyag enforces the thieves' code in the face of challengers who do not know the meaning of the word "honor."[22] The reader has little choice but to identify with the "good" thief, since the alternative is clearly reprehensible. But when *bespredel* fiction moves beyond gang wars, the result can be an even greater compression of the distance between the cultural consumer and the world of uncontrolled violence. We have already referred to the revenge plot in our discussion of *Antikiller,* but Fox's story is still about a cop, albeit a disgraced one. The audience is implicated far more directly in *bespredel* revenge stories that purport to be about ordinary people, as is the case in the 1995 film *Vultures on the Road.* The blurb on the videocassette box reads: "The hero independently begins to investigate his friend's murder. Finally he finds the killer, but he himself becomes a criminal. Now they're looking for him. . . ." Most telling, however, is the sentence that introduces the plot: "This is a story that could happen to anyone." Of course, this statement is patently false; not every would-be Miss Marple becomes Dirty Harry, and even fewer would attempt to take justice into their own hands. But the illusion of commonality here is crucial, allowing the viewers to suspend their disbelief and, at least for a time, imagine themselves in the criminal role.

Such stories work along the same lines as Polina Dashkova's *detektivy* but with a crucial difference. Though they display great ingenuity and previously untapped reserves of courage, Dashkova's heroines come out of their adventures morally unscathed. When their underworld safaris are over, their lives have changed (often because they have found the love of a good man), but their characters have not: they remain the same good girls they were when their stories began. Their journeys parallel the experience of the reader, who gets sucked into a whirlwind of adventure but can

---

[21] *Hunting Blind (Okhota v slepuiu),* the fifteenth volume in this series, was published by AST-Press in 2005.

[22] As the series has continued, particularly in recent years, Sukhov has slowly developed Varyag's character and even shown him working with the authorities, something that would have been unthinkable in the first novels.

breathe a sigh of relief upon closing the book, returning to her ordinary world. *In* bespredel revenge stories, the hero can never go back to his or her old life. Only the audience survives.

In fiction, the bespredel narrative is embodied almost to perfection by *You're Just a Slut, My Dear!* which begins with a scene straight out of classic, perestroika-era chernukha: Rita Prozorova has been fighting with her mother, whom she holds in utmost contempt. In the eighties this story would probably have continued in this vein, with mutual recriminations, screams, copious vodka consumption, and perhaps slaps in the face. It surely would have been a tacit condemnation of the soullessness of the children and the moral failures of the parents. But as we recall, *You're Just a Slut* immediately takes a different turn: instead of just yelling at her mother, Rita rubs her out. Moreover, the book is marketed as though it were true to life: the author's rather amusing biographical blurb on the back cover reads: "Sergei Pugachev is a mathematician by education. But he has had to change professions many times in his life, and to travel around the world. So Sergei Pugachev knows the world he writes about not just by hearsay." Thus even though we are reading a work of obvious fiction, part of the work's entertainment value is its connection to a particular, prepackaged view of real life in all its ghastly glory.

While bespredel fiction is packaged as reality, bespredel heroes experience their travails in terms of film and television: like the amateur detectives of mystery novels throughout the world, who know how to solve crimes because they are avid consumers of Agatha Christie and Dorothy Sayers, bespredel heroes know how to act in dangerous situations precisely because they have seen so many action movies and crime dramas. While the connection between violence in the media and violence in real life is a controversial proposition, in bespredel narratives good viewers do make good fighters. Media violence is shown to be mimetic, if only within the closed bubble of the popular entertainment itself. This in turn further strengthens the identification between bespredel reader and bespredel hero, since the hero is often a reader or viewer whom circumstances oblige to use the lessons violent fictions have taught them.

And it could explain at least some of these stories' appeal: not only do the readers and viewers become desensitized to extreme violence by exposing themselves to it again and again, but they also get the chance to see people like themselves navigate through a harsh land devoid of law and decency, armed only with their wits and their familiarity with the genre. So such stories are ultimately reassuring, if only on a subconscious level: tales of bespredel afford readers and viewers a limited sense of mastery and control in a time of chaos, letting them entertain the possibility that they can be more than the victims of violence. It is a winning situation for everyone involved. Audiences vicariously engage in the very acts of torture and bloodshed that they otherwise fear with no threat to their safety or conscience. And the culture industry that offers up regular doses of virtual violence can reap the financial rewards of its success; it is the one who is making a killing.

CONCLUSION

Someone Like Putin

My boyfriend got into trouble again
Got into a fight, took some junk.
I'm so tired of him, I dumped him.
And now I want someone like Putin.
Someone like Putin, full of strength,
Someone like Putin, who doesn't drink.
Someone like Putin, who won't hurt me.
Someone like Putin, who won't run away.
I saw him yesterday on the news.
He said that the world was at a crossroads.
With someone like him, things are easy, at home and at friends'.
And now I want someone like Putin.

—Singing Together, "Someone Like Putin"

"If there's no obvious breaking news, we start with the president."

—Mikhail Antonov, news anchor on *Rossiia*

In the summer of 2002, an unknown female duo called Singing Together (*Poiushchie vmeste*) released a surprise hit, literally singing the praises of Vladimir Vladimirovich Putin, the man who became president of the Russian Federation after Boris Yeltsin's unexpected resignation on the last New Year's Eve of the 1990s. The group's name was modeled on that of a patriotic, pro-Putin youth group calling itself Moving Together (*Idushchie vmeste*), which had recently begun crusading for moral purity and national pride. Even at the height of Yeltsin's popularity, bolstered by the image of Russia's leader standing defiantly on top of a tank during the August 1991 coup attempt, a synthopop encomium to the nation's president would have been unthinkable, and not only because the lumpy and ill-mannered Yeltsin was an unlikely object of desire: one of the most liberating aspects of late- and post-Soviet culture was the freedom not to praise the leader. Readers of the present study will look in vain (and perhaps with disappointment) for extended discussions of the political situation in the 1990s, and the entry for "Yeltsin" in the index will yield limited, and cursory, results. Culturally, the Yeltsin era was a refreshing change for twentieth-century Russia precisely because so little of it was about Yeltsin himself.

Yet thanks to the persistent negativity and hostility with which the Russian 1990s have been characterized in the first five years of the twenty-first century, Yeltsin retroactively becomes a handy symbol for a now-despised decade. Flabby and weak, he was saved from a near-fatal heart condition only with the help of Western experts. His frequent drunkenness and concomitant clownish behavior held up a troubling mirror to a nation long plagued by alcoholism; his famous attempt to dance the twist may or may not have helped him win reelection in 1996, but it also reinforced the image of an aging, awkward man whose attempts to be "with it" were embarrassing. The decline of the president's physical and mental state over the course of the decade threatened to morph Yeltsin into a latter-day Brezhnev, slow of speech and limited in wit, while the corruption of his inner circle (the "Family") was legendary. As centralized authority was dwindling rapidly, Yeltsin incarnated the state perfectly, because by the end of the 1990s he was so often in seclusion: in a country with strong paternalistic traditions, Yeltsin was the absent father.

The political handlers who facilitated the new president's rise to power ("Project Putin") (Baker and Glasser 55–59), created the image of a tough, no-nonsense "man's man" who was sober, athletic, and decisive. Though some aspects of the Putin phenomenon suggest an emerging "cult of Putin" (in particular the fawning, hagiographic depiction of the president in textbooks for Russian schoolchildren) (39–40), the plethora of commodified product tie-ins and the proliferation of his image on items meant for sale point to something closer to a "Putin brand."[1] The fact that he was catapulted from near anonymity to dizzying popularity in the space of a year

---

[1] Putin's own personal role in his increasing commodification is unclear. His contempt for the marketing and glad-handing involved in electoral politics is well known, thanks to his remark that he did not want to be a product sold to the public "like Tampax" (Baker and Glasser 57).

also suggests that there may be unintended wisdom in the title of Singing Together's song: the new president filled a perceived need not necessarily for Putin himself, but for someone like Putin. The song's lyrics superficially displace the discourse of great power politics to personal romance (a boyfriend like Putin), but they also allegorically point back to the drama of national leadership in which Putin participated so well. The old boyfriend is a dead ringer for the latter-day caricature of Boris Yeltsin: weak, intermittently and unpredictably belligerent, and prone to drinking and disappearing. Where the 1990s were marked by a perceived crisis of manhood and the rise of compensatory masculinity, Putin, whose manly and martial virtues have been continually trumpeted in the increasingly submissive media, represents the restoration of long-lost vigor and confidence. The Yeltsin years considerably lowered the bar for the country's next leader: Putin's specific policies and actions arguably matter far less than his reassuring symbolic function as a "real man" who can husband the nation's resources and promise a return to greatness.

This is not the place to chronicle the Kremlin's growing centralization of power, the state's restored control over television news, and the increasing irrelevance of the print media in the court of public opinion. Nor would it be wise to allow the country's new authoritarianism to revive the lazy habits of Western scholarship from the Soviet era. Though the news media have become more tame, films, television shows, and novels still cater to, and shape, perceptions of the public's taste. The Putin administration is not the prime mover of Russian popular culture but rather a part of it (and even, perhaps, a product of it). Moreover, any cultural shifts that can be identified since 1999 did not spring up overnight; the same forces and events that made Putinism palatable could not help but have an effect on the culture and entertainment industry. The proliferation of Chechen terrorism and the revival of Russia's war in Chechnya (under Putin's leadership as Yeltsin's prime minister) played into the hands of nationalists and bolstered the xenophobic tendencies we have seen in the boevik, while the 1999 NATO bombing of Yugoslavia unleashed pent-up resentment of the West.

Meanwhile, the country's 1998 financial crisis made the importation of foreign goods far too expensive, providing the Russian film and television industry the much-needed stimulus to create cheaper domestic alternatives to Western imports. Given the lead time required to make a movie or TV show, it was only after Yeltsin's departure that the effects of this audiovisual renaissance would make themselves known. Six years into the new century (and two years away from a constitutionally mandated change of presidential power that may yet be elided), it would be premature to attempt any definitive characterization of this new stage of post-Soviet Russian culture. Rather, the early years of the post-Yeltsin era are important for our purposes to the extent that Putin-era popular culture is engaged in a demonstrative reassessment of the 1990s. Recent popular culture is attempting to move beyond male insecurity (Yeltsin) to a manly grip on power (Putin) while ostensibly rejecting the violent excess and bleak cynicism of the previous decade in favor of domesticity, comfort, and the continuity of family ties. The major themes of the 1990s have not disappeared but instead have been reconfigured as part of a nascent ideology based on comfort, warmth, and security. The limits of chernukha and bespredel are delineated quite clearly when gangsters become family men, and the police procedural framework provides the backdrop for shopping, lighthearted banter, and, above all, good food. It is as though early-twenty-first-century Russian popular culture were rediscovering all the myriad functions and pleasures of the body that are not limited to sex and violence. The post-Yeltsin body is a different subject from its predecessor, both philosophically and grammatically. This body can also sit, rest, eat, and play.

The cultural climate has begun to change, shifting from the generalized anxieties of the 1990s to a slightly more relaxed mood—despite the increasing death toll from terrorism and the war in Chechnya. Whether or not life in Russia has gotten any better or any less dangerous, the discourse of Russian life has become considerably calmer. No doubt the strict controls on the broadcast news media have played their part (although true crime shows remain as prevalent as ever), but even the fictional storytelling of the Putin era looks almost upbeat in comparison with that of the previous decade. An ethos of sentimentality and "coziness" (*uiut*), already noticeable in certain strands of 1990s entertainment, has come to the fore. Unlike the crass extravagance of the free-spending "New Russians" who were the butt of so many jokes in the 1990s, coziness extols the joys of *inconspicuous* consumption, the pleasures to be had in a good meal, good company, and a pleasant and orderly home. Intimately connected to coziness is the rise of the family chronicle, which becomes prominent in the first decade of the twenty-first century. Even crime stories are not immune to coziness and the inward turn toward home and hearth: the post-Yeltsin boevik and detektiv introduce their audiences to civic-minded gang leaders who exemplify old-fashioned family values.

Indeed, the rise of coziness in the culture at large could not have happened without significant changes to popular narratives about Russian crime; as I have argued throughout this book, crime stories in post-Soviet Russia had become an infinitely elastic genre, encompassing a wide variety of plots, themes, and emotions while colonizing neighboring genres with the thematics and attributes of violent crime. Thus coziness could gain sway over popular culture either by eliminating or marginalizing crime stories (which has yet to happen) or by encouraging the development of crime narratives in a direction that is more congenial to domesticity, family drama, and sentimentality.

The seeds of this new coziness could already be found in the 1990s, in certain noteworthy bright spots of sentimental domesticity that stood out against the general backdrop of chernukha and bespredel. The ten-volume *Chronicles of Ekho* by Maks Frai (Svetlana Martynchik) series, which featured tales of magic and parallel worlds all within the framework of an otherworldly police procedural, indulged in some of the casual violence readers had come to expect.[2] One of her novellas even featured a fight against a latter-day, earthborn Jack the Ripper who disemboweled the hapless inhabitants of this magical land's capital city (*Labrint* 227). Yet this "maniac" was all the more appalling because he inverted the natural, harmonious order of Frai's fictional creation: her protagonists are far more preoccupied with feeding their own guts than with ripping out the entrails of their enemies. Maks and his fellow investigators spend most of their time either eating, ordering, or discussing food. They find any excuse to visit their favorite tavern or occasionally to try out new restaurants, which they inevitably praise at great length. Since the adoption of a set of laws called the "Great Codex" ended the bloody battles among magic users years ago (a Tolkienist wish-fulfillment fantasy about the end of bespredel), Ekho's citizens have agreed to abide by severe strictures on the everyday use of magic. It is the job of Maks and his colleagues to seek out and punish those who violate the codex. Only one exception is made to these stringent rules: powerful magic may still be used by those whose all-important job is the preparation of tasty and satisfying food (111). Nothing happens in Ekho without a good meal: in the absence of technology, the investigators rely on magical, parrotlike birds called "Viribukhi" for data storage and retrieval. They are unfailingly helpful and accurate but only if they are rewarded with a steady supply of treats.

This obsession with food, in Frai and elsewhere, serves as a signal of

---

[2] Maks Frai's literary career began in 1996, with the publication of the first book, whose narrator and protagonist is none other than Maks Frai. When the books first appeared, the author "Maks Frai" was officially two people: Svetlana Martynchik and an artist named Igor Stepin. However, Martynchik asserts that she was always the sole author of the Frai texts, while Stepin contributed to the design of her imaginary worlds, supplying her with useful details while also painting the books' initial covers ("Sobranie sochinenii" 15; Lintsova and Sorokina 30; "Maks Frai—gazeta" 1).

lightheartedness and even optimism. In Frai's work, it is accompanied by a similar preoccupation with home furnishings and comfort (everyone in Ekho lives in spacious houses equipped with multiple baths), pets (Maks's twin cats, Armstrong and Ella, who eventually lend their names to yet another new restaurant), and rather fussy verbal etiquette and clumsy repartee.[3] Frai's characters and narrators also tend to end their sentences in exclamation marks, as if their world were simply too exciting to be contained by more prosaic punctuation.

That Frai's novels are escapist fantasies should come as no surprise; escapism is one of the functions that popular genres fill so well. But *Chronicles of Ekho* and Frai's later books are self-conscious in their escapism, to the point that they are *meta-escapist*. The hero of *Ekho* is an ordinary man who exchanges a dull life in post-Soviet Russia for the excitement and adventures of the magical land of Ekho, extending a fantasy tradition going back at least as far as Edgar Rice Burroughs's John Carter of Mars novels, C. S. Lewis's *Narnia* series, and Frank Baum's *Oz* books. But Frai the hero is a Moscow couch potato who can barely bring himself to turn off the television in order to leave his apartment and search for the gateway to his future home. Upon his arrival in Ekho, Frai immediately acquires crucial importance for this world's welfare, and yet his new life rapidly becomes domestic. Far more attention is paid to his home, his food, and his friends than is devoted to his battles, perhaps because his true triumph over the forces of darkness is his ability to lead a demonstratively (even nauseatingly) happy and satisfied life. Frai's fantasy world is one of belonging, rather than actual adventure, and the novels' escapism resides in the hero's own constant awareness of his good fortune in finding a better world and in the unrelenting sunniness of nearly all the characters' dispositions. The hero initially finds out about Ekho through dreams in which he meets his future boss in a cozy bar, which in Frai's novels is a far more appropriate mechanism for interdimensional travel than a tornado or an enchanted wardrobe. Frai's fantasy world is exactly like an idealized bar, a compromise between the warmth of home and the alienation of the public sphere: in Ekho, the fictional Maks Frai has found a place where everybody knows his name.

---

[3] Everyone in Ekho is addressed as "Sir" or "Lady," often accompanied or replaced by compliments and nicknames. Maks usually addresses his beloved Lady Melamori as "unforgettable" (*nezabvennaia*) and never tires of making the same joke at the expense of his colleague and occasional rival Melifaro: Melifaro's father wrote a famous eight-volume treatise on magic in Ekho, so Maks insists on calling Melifaro "Ninth Volume" (a phrase that is only marginally less awkward in Russian than it is in English). As a counterpoint to Ekho's playful formality, nearly every character insists on calling every adult male a "guy" (*paren'*) rather than "man" (*muzhchina* or *chelovek*), in a fashion that is more consistent with American usage than Russian.

The coziness of the author Maks Frai, who began her literary career in 1996, would eventually be outstripped by the unrelenting cuteness of crime writer Daria Dontsova. Dontsova's entry onto the literary scene has itself become the stuff of myth, since her runaway success following a brush with death is worthy of her own (at times autobiographical) novels. The story of her midlife career change, which is touched upon in nearly every interview and profile published in the press, can be found on her website (http://dontsova.net/). In 1998, at the age of thirty-six, Agrippina Arakadievna Dontsova, a German teacher and former journalist, was diagnosed with breast cancer and given eight months to live. Her husband, who knew that Dontsova had long dreamed of being a writer, insisted that she fight against both her disease and her depression by writing a book while confined to intensive care. After five days, she finished her first novel, *Krutye naslednichki* (*Hard-Boiled Heiresses*), only to be awakened from a drugged sleep by the hysterical laughter of the duty nurse who became her first reader. Since then, Dontsova has continued to write in bed (or, to put it as precisely as she does, on her "wide Italian bed, covered with a soft, straw-colored bedspread, the color of her beloved '*mopsy*' [dogs]." Dontsova is legendary for her miraculous recovery and for her unfailing humor in the face of death (all her novels are intended to be funny), a feat that is outshined only by her astonishing productivity. In her first five years as a writer, she published thirty-four novels and wrote nine more. As of August 2005, sixty-five books were available for download from www.ladoshki.com, the result of a pace that the author herself describes as roughly a book per month. Through sheer volume and popularity, she handily displaced Alexandra Marinina as the queen of Russian crime fiction in the post-Yeltsin era.

Dontsova has four different series, each centered on its own protagonist, and at least two of them have been developed for television so far. Her first novels featured her most recognizably autobiographical heroine, the French teacher Dasha Vasilieva. Like her creator, Dasha has been married numerous times, never quite shedding the family ties she has acquired along the way. Her extended family features children, stepchildren, and former in-laws, as well as a large menagerie of cute and pampered pets. Dasha's adventures begin with a stroke of unbelievable good fortune: through a complicated and unlikely chain of events, she inherits millions of dollars left by a friend who emigrated to France. She moves her entire clan to a French chateau, though she eventually chooses to divide her time between Moscow and Paris. Like the heroine of the American television series *Murder She Wrote*, Dasha has a strange proclivity for wandering onto the scenes of crimes and an even stranger knack for solving them.

Distantly related to the popular novels by Polish detective writer Joanna Chmielewska, Dontsova's books are published under the rubric "ironic detektiv," yet true irony in Dontsova's unfailingly lighthearted and upbeat work is almost impossible to find. Rather, irony here is synonymous with humor: corpses aside, Dontsova's novels are comedies. Dontsova has hit upon a winning formula, reveling in luxury and world travel in a context that emphasizes domesticity, family ties, and simple pleasures. Her heroes, like those of Maks Frai, are obsessed with food and creature comforts: like *Intergirl* of the 1980s, Dontsova's books have somewhat sensationalist plots that are actually excuses for long inventories of exciting commodities available for consumption. Dasha's family spends most of its time in Paris shopping and eating, and its amazement at the wondrous delicacies on the menu in a French hospital indulges in the long-standing humor about unsophisticated Russians faced with European luxuries (*Za vsemi zaitsami* 190–91). Yet the laughter is never at the heroes' expense; nor does their wealth expose them to envy or disdain. Dontsova offers her readers a guilt-free fantasy of conspicuous consumption because her characters, as the recipients of a fantastic stroke of luck, are untouched by the criminality and crude materialism associated with New Russians and mobsters. If anything, the characters' improved circumstances only emphasize their homeyness: wherever they go and whatever they do, they enjoy the comforts of their self-consciously idiosyncratic home.

Indeed, Dontsova's coziness is perfectly timed with a confluence of political and economic features suggesting that the Putin era will be remembered as a time of renewed domesticity, when the culture began to turn away from the horrors of the street in order to look inward at house and hearth. The opening of an Ikea superstore on the outskirts of Moscow inaugurated a boom in home furnishings aimed not at the richest of the rich but at urbanites whose incomes could allow them to rethink their conception of their own domestic space. Such television shows as *The Apartment Question* (*Kvartirnyi vopros*) offer useful decorating tips to an eager audience. If the hectic scramble of the Yeltsin years was detrimental to the kitchen culture that had arisen under Brezhnev (the cult of the "circle of friends" so handily dismantled by Liudmila Petrushevskaia), the early twenty-first century turned the home into a site of both coziness and consumption.

Thus the early twenty-first century has witnessed a revival of an old and popular genre, the family saga. If Russia has yet to produce an ongoing series to rival the ever-popular Latin American soap operas, both the television and the publishing industries have begun to explore the potential of the family saga. Novels and miniseries such as *Two Fates* (*Dve sud'by*) follow in the footsteps of Soviet classics such as *Moscow Does Not Believe in Tears* (*Moskva slezam ne verity*), chronicling the tribulations of migrants from the provinces who want to take the capital by storm. Vasily Aksyonov's trilogy *The Moscow Saga* (*Moskovskaia saga*), a minor publishing phenomenon of the late 1990s, was a great success as a television miniseries, while Booker Prize-winning author Liudmila Ulitskaia has made the highbrow family chronicle her forte (*Kazus Kukotskogo* [*The Kukotsky Case*]). Particularly noteworthy is the new life that has been bestowed upon Anatoly Rybakov's *Deti Arbata* (*Children of the Arbat*). Rybakov's trilogy about life under Stalin was one of the great sensations of perestroika but seemed headed toward literary obscurity once the novelty of such fiction wore off. Now Russian television has repackaged this perestroika hit by emphasizing an aspect that was always central to the trilogy, but that had not seemed so important twenty years ago: the televised *Children of the Arbat* is a multigenerational family saga.

Even Alexandra Marinina has gotten into the act. After exposing the intricacies of family dynamics in novels such as *Illiuza grekha* (*The Illusion of Sin*) and tentatively exploring the intergenerational dynamics of Nastia Kamenskaia's clan, Marinina has begun to turn her attention even further away from the world of work. Since resolving her extended midlife crises in the late 1990s, Nastia herself has become somewhat less focused on her office and more on her home and her body. More than any other popular writer in Russia today, Marinina ties her character's life and adventures closely to real time, and her books always reflect the major events and minor incidents that could presumably have an effect on someone living in Moscow at the time in which the novel takes place. From the beginning, Kamenskaia has been allowed to age; her body is prey to all the misfortunes one begins to dread in one's forties.[4] She has a perennial bad back, was recently confined to bed after breaking a leg, and now is nonplussed to discover she has begun menopause—a frank and human detail that is not only unprecedented for the *detektiv* but also perhaps an indirect signal of its author's dissatisfaction with the genre in which she has been pigeonholed. The only reprieve from the series' perpetual bloodletting is interpreted by the heroine as a distressing sign of impending obsolescence. One senses that her exhaustion mirrors that of her creator, who had been finding the world of serial crime fiction increasingly constricting. Her 2001 novel *Tot, kto znaet* (*The One Who Knows*), the story of an extended family who at one

---

[4] As Marinina explained in an interview, Nastia "changes and ages just as I change and age" (Nikolaeva 8).

point all shared a communal apartment, ventures far from her well-trodden territory, nearly leaving the murder mystery behind.[5] Again the novel has a strong metafictional element, since it is a family saga about a young woman named Natasha whose crowning achievement is to create a televised miniseries about an extended family in a communal apartment. After almost two dozen books about Kamenskaia, *The One Who Knows* seems remarkably fresh, but Marinina immediately retreats from her tentative steps out of her generic cave. Not only does she return to Kamenskaia in her next novel, but she even incorporates the main characters from *The One Who Knows* into a Kamenskaia story. Natasha's husband becomes a suspect in a murder investigated by Kamenskaia, while Natasha's unofficial stepdaughter starts a love affair with one of Kamenskaia's colleagues, thereby subsuming even this apparently independent novel under the all-encompassing series.

Just as crime stories colonized other genres in the 1990s, crime fiction itself has begun to adapt to the themes of home and family. One of the great Russian literary success stories of the late 1990s and early twenty-first-century was the arrival of Boris Akunin in the bookstores and bestseller lists. Akunin (the pseudonym for literary scholar and translator Grigorii Chkhartashvili) has come to be seen as the virtual savior of Russian popular fiction, writing detective novels with a solid literary style and intertextual links to Russian and European classics, essentially creating airplane reading for educated readers.

Akunin's novels, most of which are set in the nineteenth century, appeal to a nostalgia for an imaginary time when chernukha did not exist, as best exemplified by the packaging of his Erast Fandorin series in the hardcover editions brought out by Zakharov, which feature the motto: "In memory of the nineteenth century, when literature was great, belief in progress was limitless, and crimes were committed and solved with elegance and taste." When Akunin introduces his readers to Erast Petrovich Fandorin in *Azazel'* (*The Winter Queen*), the young hero is an orphan, and Fandorin's rootlessness is thematically crucial. The plot opposes him to a worldwide conspiracy made up entirely of orphans, raised by the progressive but ruthless

---

[5] Marinina's fascination with extended and blended families is a recurring feature of her work. Not only is the nature of the family the thematic center of *Illusion of Sin*, but Kamenskaia's own family is a self-conscious mix of blood relatives and "adopted" step relatives (Kamenskaia is much closer to her stepfather than to her biological parents). Another example is the family of Marinina's other fictional doppelgänger, the police detective Tatiana Obrastsova, who writes crime novels under the pen name Tomilina; she lives with the sister of one of her ex-husbands, who serves as the unofficial housekeeper even after she marries a private detective, becomes a stepmother to his daughter, and gives birth to a child of her own.

Lady Esther, a visionary who treats her charges as the raw material from which to create a new world. Even more important is Fandorin's own desperate need for a mentor who can train him in the ways of the world. Yet Fandorin's search for father figures inevitably leads him to men whose callousness toward human life makes them just as unacceptable as Lady Esther (the bad mother). Fandorin becomes a full-fledged adult only with the help of villains whom he must reject: in *The Winter Queen*, he hones his reasoning skills thanks to the example of a free-thinking police investigator who turns out to be part of Lady Esther's conspiracy, even acquiring mannerisms that he will keep for the rest of his life. In *Almaznaia kolesnitsa* (*The Diamond Chariot*), another criminal surrogate father teaches him Eastern wisdom and Japanese fighting techniques, giving him new life as a latterday ninja.[6]

The Erast Fandorin series would appear to follow the classic model of the detective as lone wolf; with the exception of his faithful Japanese servant, Masa, Fandorin has no long-term supporting cast. The women in his life tend to die young (although the lucky ones simply leave him before it is too late). Through a cruel twist of fate, his illegitimate son, the product of a love affair in Japan, becomes his enemy, and Fandorin captures him and indirectly causes his death, without even knowing that he had ever sired a child (*The Diamond Chariot*). In 2000, Akunin began a new series that supplied Fandorin with an unexpectedly large number of relatives, even if they never intersect with Erast Petrovich himself. *Prikliucheniia magistra* (*The Adventures of an MA*) features Erast's descendant, Nicholas (Nika) Fandorin, a British Russophile whose obsession with his family tree has brought his graduate studies in history to a standstill.[7] Relocating to his ancestral homeland after his parents' sudden death, Nika nearly loses his life on several occasions but along the way acquires a wife, two children, and a private investigation business that shows all the signs of being just as successful as his previous academic career.

Just as the Erast Fandorin novels allow Akunin to explore a variety of mystery genres while never entirely losing his ironic distance, the books that comprise *The Adventures of an MA* indulge in all the excesses of the family saga while undercutting the biological determinism and naive faith

[6] Given that the name "Akunin" is Japanese for "evildoer," Fandorin is truly the product of a villain.

[7] The narrator describes Nika as Erast Petrovich's *vnuk*, a word whose primary meaning is "grandson." However, the Russian term is vague enough that it could also mean "grandnephew." For Erast to be the father of a line of British Fandorins would not only require a drastic change in his lifestyle but also mean that he became a parent in his sixties. Nika's father is never identified by a patronymic, so Akunin's options for elaborating the Fandorin family tree remain open.

in genealogical destiny that are so prevalent in the genre. Nika's enthusiasm for his family history is both charming and laughable; his interest in history is confined almost exclusively to people who happen to share some version of his family name. By the second novel, *Vneklassnoe chtenie* (*Recommended Reading*), Nika's genealogical pursuits have descended into onanistic self-parody: rather than drumming up new clientele for his failing business, Nika has wasted an enormous amount of time creating and then playing a video game based on his family's history. Nika's obsessions make him an appropriate stand-in for Akunin's faithful readers: he is less hero than fan.

Nika's story is usually part of a parallel plot involving the Fandorins' distant ancestors; in the first novel, *Altyn'-Tolobas*, Nika's arrival in Moscow is contrasted with that of the first von Dorn to come serve the tsar centuries before. In *Recommended Reading*, the historical plot involves palace intrigues under Catherine the Great. *Recommended Reading* features a twist that undermines both the reader's and Nika's preoccupations with all things Fandorin: the biological line of Fandorin's descent was interrupted in the eighteenth century, and the continuation of the family name resulted from a complicated arrangement in which a young wunderkind was saved from death by changing his name and being adopted by a Fandorin. If the Fandorins can lay any hereditary claim to a great intellect, it is because one of their ancestors happened to adopt a genius. Adoption, which is so fraught with revolutionary implications in the first Erast Fandorin novel, paradoxically turns out to be the key to the Fandorins' hereditary uniqueness. In *Detskaia kniga* (*A Children's Book*), an eccentric relative from the European branch of the family (the Dorns) is desperately searching for a young Fandorin who can go back in time in order to avert global disaster. Nika's young son, Lastik, proves to be the ideal candidate, but had Lastik refused, the European Dorn has a back-up plan: he would have adopted another boy, given him the family name, and sent him on the mission.[8]

Five years into the post-Yeltsin era, it seems that few are immune to the allure of the family theme. Even the least family-friendly of all Russian popular genres has managed to accommodate itself to a renewed fascination with hearth and home. We should recall that Russian tales of organized crime involve heroes who are much more isolated than their American counterparts: the Italian mafia, the archetypal criminal organization, is a

---

[8] Appropriately enough, when Lastik does travel to the past, he ends up involved in Russia's Time of Troubles, an interregnum that resulted from the suspicious death of the tsar's young heir and the appearance of a young man claiming to be the long-dead tsarevich.

Figure 9: DVD cover of Aleksei Sidorov's *The Brigade*, a miniseries about the mob that was a runaway hit in the early Putin years.

family structure, while Russian mobs are not. In 2002, the RTR television network broadcast a miniseries called *Brigada* (*The Brigade*) (directed by Aleksei Sidorov), a twelve-part synthesis of the previous decade's tales of gang wars and bespredel, with heavy echoes of American gangster classics from *The Godfather Trilogy* to *Once Upon a Time in America*.[9] With a story that begins in the 1980s, *The Brigade* also invokes the perestroika-era panic

[9] The series' tagline is "Once upon a time in Russia . . ." (*Odnazhdy v Rossii*), while the *Godfather* borrowings are equally hard to miss. The eighth episode shows the Brigade ruthlessly destroying its enemies while their leader is at a classical concert with his wife, an obvious homage to the christening scene in *Godfather Two* (the concert in *The Brigade* is even followed by a christening).

over wayward youth even as the series manages to suggest that post-Soviet criminals can develop a conscience and evolve beyond bespredel.

The Brigade is the story of·four friends: Cosmos, the privileged son of a well-connected scientist; Fila, a would-be boxer who has taken too many punches to the skull; the happy-go-lucky Pchola; and Sasha Belyi, a clever and charismatic Afghan veteran who emerges as their leader. After a com-plicated set of circumstances forces Sasha (played by Sergei Bezrukov) to run from the law, his friends save his life, and the four of them swear an oath of unbreakable loyalty to one another. Sasha's "brigade" quickly makes its way up the criminal hierarchy, thanks in part to his old army connections and his willingness to work with the authorities. Early on, Sasha falls in love with Olia, an aspiring violinist who eventually marries him, gives up her career, and has a baby. Sasha is clearly not an old-style thief, yet neither is he a coarse and unprincipled bandit (thanks in part to the moderating influence of his cultured wife). Unlike his counterparts in other boeviki, Sasha treats violence as a last resort. As the series moves closer to the present day, Sasha gets baptized, shifts his activity into legiti-mate business, establishes charities, and even runs for political office. Along the way, his marriage nearly collapses, but Sasha and Olia reunite in time to pose as a happy family during the electoral campaign.

The Brigade is still a crime story, so the plot is hardly all sweetness and light. Sasha's die-hard enemy hatches a plot against him that comes to fruition in the last episodes, killing Pchola, Kosmos, and Fila, and obliging Sasha to send his wife and child abroad for safety. Nonetheless, *The Brigade* operates in a different moral universe from that of its immediate Russian predecessors. The criminal heroes are not bloodthirsty degenerates, and the emphasis on the brigade's male solidarity is counterbalanced by a fully de-veloped love story involving a female character who manages to rise above her initial role as a plot device. The emphasis on romance made *The Brigade* a hit with women as well as men (Sergei Bezrukov's dashing good looks didn't hurt either). The end of the series seems to put Sasha on the more familiar path of the lone wolf hero, but the very fact that he has a wife and son to save humanizes him.[10]

Russian popular culture has not changed radically since the end of the Yeltsin era, but the trends observed so far point to a growing emphasis on order, structure, and domestic harmony. Chernukha gives no indication of

---

[10] *The Brigade* has inspired a series of novels retelling and continuing the story under the byline of Aleksandr Belov (Sasha Belyi). Sasha continues to look for a way out of his life of crime and dan-ger, but circumstances (often involving his family's safety) always prevent him from leading a nor-mal life. The fourteenth book was released in August 2005.

vanishing: sex, violence, and crime are still central features in the cultural landscape, and the pockets of lighthearted optimism represented by Frai and Dontsova are still noteworthy in contrast to the bleakness of so many novels and films (and this despite the high body counts on which both authors depend for their plots). But it does appear that Russian cultural consumers who are exhausted after a decade of bespredel and cynicism might be able to look forward to a softer variety of violent entertainment, populated by kinder, gentler killers, civic-minded godfathers, and self-satisfied bystanders who are content to watch the bloody spectacle from the comforts of their well-appointed living rooms.

WORKS CITED

Books and Articles

Adorno, Theodor W. "Culture Industry Reconsidered." *Media Studies: A Reader*. 2nd ed. Ed. Paul Marris and Sue Thornham. New York: New York University Press, 2000. 31–37.

Agamben, Giorgio. *Homo Sacer: Sovereign Power and Bare Life*. Trans. Daniel Heller-Roazen. Stanford: Stanford University Press, 1998.

Aitmatov, Chingiz. *The Place of the Skull*. Trans. Natasha Ward. New York: Grove, 1989.

Aksenov, Vasilii. "Matushka-Rus' i igrivye synochki." *Playboy* July 1995: 50–58.

Akunin, Boris. *Almaznaia kolesnitsa*. Moscow: Zakharov, 2004.

———. *Altyn'-Tolobas*. Moscow: OLMA, 2000.

———. *Azazel'*. Moscow: Zakharov, 2002.

———. *Detskaia kniga*. Moscow: OLMA, 2005.

———. *F.M.* (2 volumes) Moscow: OLMA-Press, 2006.

———. *Vneklassnoe chtenie*. Moscow: OLMA, 2002.

———. *The Winter Queen*. Trans. Andrew Bromfield. New York: Random House, 2003.

Aleksandrov, Valentin. "Vashe Seksual'noe Erotichestvo!" *Nezavisimaia gazeta* 10 June 1993: 8.

Ames, Mark, and Matt Taibbi. *The eXile: Sex, Drugs, and Libel in the New Russia*. New York: Grove, 2000.

Antonova, Svetlana. "Diagnos—Man'iak." *Moskovskie novosti* 1–8 June 1997: 25.

Andrei: Russkii zhurnal dlia muzhchin 1 (1991).

Andrei 5 (1994).

Andrei 8 (1997).

Anin, Aleksandr, "Chechnia: O chem molchat soldaty." *Andrei* 7 (1996): 84–93.

Attwood, Feona. "Reading Porn: The Paradigm Shift in Pornography Research," *Sexualities* 5.1 (2002): 91–105.

Attwood, Lynn. *The New Soviet Man and Woman: Sex-Role Socialization in the USSR*. Bloomington: Indiana University Press, 1990.

——. "Sex and the Cinema." *Sex and Russian Society*. Ed. Igor Kon and James Riordan. Bloomington: Indiana University Press, 1993. 64–85.

Austen, Jane. *Northanger Abbey*. New York: Modern Library, 2002.

Avins, Carol. *Border Crossings: The West and Russian Identity in Soviet Literature, 1917–1934*. Berkeley: University of California Press, 1983.

Babel', Isaak. *Sochineniia*. 2 vols. Moscow: Khudozhestvennaia literatura, 1990.

Baker, Peter, and Susan Glasser. *Kremlin Rising: Vladimir Putin's Russia and the End of Revolution*. New York: Scribner, 2005.

Baldaev, D. S., V. K. Belko, and I. M. Isupov, *Slovar' tiuremno-lagerno-blatnogo zhargona*. Moscow: Krai Moskvy, 1992.

Baraban, Elena V. "Russian in the Prism of Popular Culture: Russian and American Detective Fiction and Thrillers of the 1990s." PhD diss., University of British Columbia, 2003.

Barker, Adele. "The Culture Factory: Theorizing the Popular in the Old and New Russia." *Consuming Russia: Popular Culture, Sex, and Society since Gorbachev*. Ed. Adele Barker. Durham, NC: Duke University Press. 49–75.

Baudrillard, Jean. *The Gulf War Did Not Take Place*. New York: Power Publications, 2004.

Beaudoin, Luc. "Masculine Utopia in Russian Pornography." *Eros and Pornography in Russian Culture*. Ed. M. Levitt and A. Toporkov. Moscow: Ladomir. 622–638.

Beeston, Richard. "Chaste Designs on Power by Virgin Party." (London) *Times* 23 Aug. 1997.

Belova, Valeriia. "Kak Interdovichku obviniali v prostitutsii." *Kino-park* 5.24 (May 1999).

Belyi, Aleksei, Boris Voitsekhovskii, and Viktoriia Kuz'mina. "Aleksandra Marinina: 'Ia ne mogu Nastiu Kamenskuiu zastavit' zaberemenet' . . . '" *Komsomol'skaia pravda* 29 Jan. 1999.

Benjamin, Walter. *Illuminations*. New York: Shocken, 1969.

Bernstein, Frances L. *The Dictatorship of Sex*. De Kalb: Northern Illinois University Press, 2007.

——. "Envisioning Health in Revolutionary Russia: The Politics of Gender in Sexual Enlightenment Posters of the 1920s." *Russian Review* 57.2 (1998): 191–217.

——. "Prostitutes and Proletarians: The Labor Clinic as Revolutionary Laboratory in the 1920." *The Human Tradition in Modern Russia*. Ed. William Husband. Wilmington, DE: Scholarly Resources, 2000. 113–128.

Bernstein, Laurie. *Sonia's Daughters: Prostitutes and Their Regulation in Imperial Russia*. Berkeley: University of California Press, 1995.

Bershidsky, Leonid. "Liberal Media Neglect 'Zippergate's' Legal Side." *Moscow Times* 29 Jan. 1998.

Beumers, Birgit. Introduction. *Russia on Reels: The Russian Idea in Post-Soviet Cinema.* Ed. Birgit Beumers. New York: I.B. Tauris, 1999. 1–11.

Biressi, Anita. *Crime, Fear and the Law in True Crime Stories.* New York: Palgrave, 2001.

Blakely, Allison. *Russia and the Negro: Blacks in Russian History and Thought.* Washington, DC: Howard University Press, 1986.

Bly, Robert. *Iron John.* Reading, MA: Addison-Wesley, 1990.

Boele, Otto. "Melodrama as Counter-literature? Count Amori's Response to Three Scandalous Novels," *Imitations of Life. Two Centuries of Melodrama in Russia.* Ed. Louise McReynolds and Joan Neuberger. Durham, NC: Duke University Press, 2002. 99–126.

Borenstein, Eliot. *Men without Women: Masculinity and Revolution in Russian Fiction, 1917–1929.* Durham, NC: Duke University Press, 2000.

——. "Public Offerings: MMM and the Marketing of Melodrama." *Consuming Russia: Popular Culture, Sex, and Society since Gorbachev.* Ed. Adele Barker. Durham, NC: Duke University Press, 1999. 49–75.

——. "Slavophilia: The Incitement to Russian Sexual Discourse." *Slavic and East European Journal* 40.1 (1996): 142–147.

——. "Tekst kak mashina smerti: Voennye rasskazy A. Platonova." *Voina i literatura, 1941–1945.* Ekaterinburg: Ural States Pedagogical University Press, 2000. 109–117.

Borovik, Elena. "Solonik—.killer mafii." *Monokl'* 2 Feb. 2004. http://www.borovik.com/index.php?zh=15&st=5. Last accessed 29 June 2005.

Borovik, Tat'iana. "Babushku ogreli molotkom shest' raz." *Moskovskii komsomolets* 19 June 1997: 11.

Braterskii, Aleksandr. "Poslednii devstvennik SSSR." *Makhaon* 4 (1995). 24–26.

Brooks, Jeffrey. *When Russia Learned to Read: Literacy and Popular Literature, 1861–1917.* Princeton, NJ: Princeton University Press, 1985.

Bulgakov, Mikhail. *Sobranie sochinenii.* 5 vols. Moscow: Khudozhestvennaia literatura, 1990.

Bushkov, A. *Na to i volki.* 2 vols. Moscow: OLMA, 1999.

Camus, Albert. *The Stranger.* Trans. Matthew Ward. New York: Knopf, 1993.

Carpenter, Dave. "Russians Warm up to Racy Talk Show." Associated Press. 21 Nov. 1997.

Cassiday, Julie A. and Leyla Rouhi. "From Nevskii Prospekt to Zoia's Apartment: Trials of the Russian Procuress." *Russian Review* 58.3 (1999): 413–431.

Cawelti, John G. *Adventure, Mystery, and Romance: Formula Stories as Art and Popular Culture.* Chicago: University of Chicago Press, 1976.

Cherniak, Mariia. "Russian Romantic Fiction." *Reading for Entertainment in Contemporary Russia: Post-Soviet Popular Literature in Historical Perspective.* Ed. Stephen Lovell and Birgit Menzel. Munich: Verlag Otto Sagner, 2005. 151–172.

Chernyshevsky, Nikolai. *What Is To Be Done?* Trans. Michael R. Katz. Ithaca: Cornell University Press, 1989.

"Chto dlia vas bylo samym priiatnym v ukhodiah schem godu?" *Vecherniaia Moskva* 29 Dec. 2003: 1. http://dlib.eastview.com/sources/article.jsp?id=5746505.

Clark, Katerina. "Not for Sale: The Russian/Soviet Intelligentsia, Prostitution, and the Paradox of Internal Colonization." *Russian Culture in Transition.* Ed. Gregory Freiden. Stanford Slavic Studies 7. Stanford: Stanford University Press, 1993. 189–205.

———. *The Soviet Novel: History as Ritual.* Chicago: University of Chicago Press, 1985.

Collins, Max Alan, Sam Mendes, and Richard Piers Reyner. *The Road to Perdition.* New York: Paradox, 1998.

Condee, Nancy. "Body Graphics: Tattooing the Fall of Communism." *Consuming Russia: Popular Culture, Sex, and Society since Gorbachev.* Ed. Adele Barker. Durham, NC: Duke University Press, 1990. 339–361.

Daniel, Yuli. *This Is Moscow Speaking, and Other Stories.* Trans. Stuart Hood, Harold Shukman, and John Richardson. New York: Dutton, 1969.

Dashkova, Polina. *Efirnoe vremia.* Vol. 2. Moscow: EKSMO, 2001.

———. *Krov' nerozhdennykh.* Moscow: EKSMO, 1999.

———. *Legkie shagi bezumiia.* Moscow: EKSMO, 1999.

———. *Prodazhnye tvari* [*Chechenskaia marionetka*] Moscow: EKSMO, 1999.

Dickens, Charles. *The Mystery of Edwin Drood.* New York: Penguin Classics, 2002.

Dobrenko, Evgeny. *The Making of the State Reader: Social and Aesthetic Context of the Reception of Soviet Literature.* Trans. Jesse M. Savage. Stanford: Stanford University Press, 1997.

Dobrolyubov, Nikolai. "When Will the Real Day Come?" *Belinsky, Chernyshevsky, and Dobrolyubov: Selected Criticism.* Ed. Ralph E. Matlaw. Bloomington, Indiana University Press, 1976. 176–226.

Dobrotvorskii, Sergei. "Nasledniki po krivoi." *Iskusstvo kino* 7 (1991): 25–29.

Dondurei, Daniil. "Ne brat ia tebe, gnida. . . ." *Iskusstvo kino* 2 (1998): 64–67.

Dontsova, Dar'ia. *Kontrol'nyi potselui.* Moscow: EKSMO, 2002.

———. *Krutye naslednichki.* Moscow: EKSMO, 2005.

———. *Za vsemi zaitsami.* Moscow: EKSMO, 2002.

Dostoevsky, Fyodr. *Crime and Punishment.* Trans. Richard Pevear and Larissa Volkhonsky. New York: Vintage, 1993.

———. *Demons.* Trans. Richard Pevear and Larissa Volkhonsky. New York: Vintage, 1995.

———. *The Idiot.* Trans. Richard Pevear and Larissa Volkhonsky. New York: Vintage, 2003.

———. *Memoirs from the House of the Dead.* Trans. Jessie Coulson. New York: Oxford University Press, 2001.

Dotsenko, Viktor. *Beshenyi zhiv!* Moscow: Vagrius, 2002.

———. *Komanda Beshenogo.* Moscow: Vagrius, 1998.

———. *Kremlevskoe delo Beshnogo.* Moscow: Vagrius, 2000.

———. *Liubov' Beshenogo.* Moscow, Vagrius, 1999.

———. *Mest' Beshenogo.* Moscow: Vagrius, 1998.

——. *Nagrada Beshenogo*. Moscow: Vagrius, 1999.

——. *Okhota Beshenogo*. Moscow: Vagrius, 1999.

——. *Ostrov Beshenogo*. Moscow: Vagrius, 2000.

——. *Otets Beshenogo*. Moscow: Vagrius, 2000.

——. *Pravosudie Besehnogo*. Moscow: Vagrius, 2000.

——. *Srok dlia Beshenogo*. Moscow: Vagrius, 1998.

——. *Sled Beshenogo*. Moscow: Vagrius 2001.

——. *Tridtsatogo unichtozhit!* Moscow: Vagrius, 1998.

——. *Uchenik Beshenogo*. Moscow: Vagrius, 2003.

——. *Voina Beshenogo*. Moscow: Vagrius, 1999.

——. *Vozvrashchenie Beshenogo*. Moscow: Vagrius, 1998.

——. *Zoloto Beshenogo*. Moscow: Vagrius, 1999.

Draitser, Emil. *Making War, Not Love: Gender and Sexuality in Russian Humor.* New York: St. Martin's, 1999.

Drobyshev, Igor'. "Borets i koliun. S sozdatelem zhurnala 'Andrei' govoit Igor' Drobyshev." *Andrei* 8 (1997): 19–12, 36–39.

Dubin, Boris. "Ispytanie na sostoiatel'nost': K sotsiologicheskoi poetiki russkogo romana-boevika." *Novoe literaturnoe obozrenie* 22 (1996): 252–275.

——. "The Action Thriller (*Boevik*) in Contemporary Russia." *Reading for Entertainment in Contemporary Russia: Post-Soviet Popular Literature in Historical Perspective.* Ed. Stephen Lovell and Birgit Menzel. Munich: Verlag Otto Sagner, 2005. 101–116.

Eco, Umberto. "The Myth of Superman." *Contemporary Literary Criticism: Modernism through Post-Structuralism.* Ed. Robert Con Davis. New York: Longman, 1986. 330–344.

Engel, Barbara Alpern. *Between the Fields and the City: Women, Work, and Family in Russia, 1861–1914.* Cambridge: Cambridge University Press. 1994.

——. "St. Petersburg Prostitutes in the Late Nineteenth Century: A Personal and Social Profile." *Russian Review* 48.1 (1989): 21–44.

Engelstein, Laura. *The Keys to Happiness: Sex and the Search for Modernity in Fin-de-Siècle Russia.* Ithaca: Cornell University Press, 1992.

Epstein, Mikhail. *After the Future: The Paradoxes of Postmodernism and Contemporary Russian Culture.* Amherst: The University of Massachusetts Press, 1995.

Erdrich, Louise. *Last Report on the Miracles at Little No Horse.* New York: HarperCollins, 2002.

Erofeev, Viktor. *Muzhchiny.* Moscow: Podkova, 1997.

——. "Polet 'oblaka v shtanakh.'" *Andrei* 6 (1995): 44–46.

——. *Russkaia krasavitsa.* Moscow: Vsia Moskva, 1990.

Erofeyev, Viktor. *Russian Beauty.* Trans. Andrew Reynolds. London: Penguin, 1992.

"Erotika i vlast': Kto kogo . . ." *Ogonek* 17–18 May 1994: 12–18.

Essig, Laurie. *Queer in Russia: A Story of Sex, Self, and the Other.* Durham, NC: Duke University Press, 1999.

Etkind, Aleksandr. *Eros nevozmozhnogo: istoriia psikhoanalisa v Rossii.* St. Petersburg: Meduza, 1993.

——. *Sodom i psikheia: Ocherki intellektual'noi istorii Serebrianogo veka*. Moscow: ITs-Gigant, 1996.

Fal'kovskii, Il'ia. "Massovaia literatura." *Ex Libris NG* 14 Jan. 1998: 5.

Fedorov, N. F. *Filosofiia obshchego dela*. Ed. V. A. Kozhevnikov and N. P. Peterson, 2 vols. London: Gregg Press, 1970.

Foucault, Michel. *The History of Sexuality: An Introduction*. Trans. Robert Hurley. New York: Vintage Books, 1990.

Frai. Maksim. *Labirint*. St. Petersburg: Terra, 1998.

——. *Volontery vechnosti*. St. Petersburg: Amfora, 2002.

Franchetti, Mark. "Sauna Scandal Opens Russian Eyes." (London) *Sunday Times*, 30 June 1997.

Gambrell, Jamey. "Russia's New Vigilantes." *New York Review of Books* 16 Jan. 2003: 40–43.

Genis, Alexander. "*Perestroika* as a Shift in Literary Paradigm." In *Russian Postmodernism: New Perspectives on Post-Soviet Culture*. Ed. Mikhail Epstein, Alexander Genis, and Slobodanka Vladiv-Glover. New York: Berghan, 1999.

German, Pavel, and Yuly Khait. "Ever Higher." *Mass Culture in Soviet Russia: Tales, Poems, Songs, Plays ad Folklore, 1917–1953*. Ed. James van Geldern and Richard Stites. Bloomington: Indiana University Press, 1995. 257–258.

Gessen, Masha. *Dead Again: The Russian Intelligentsia after Communism*. New York: Verso, 1997.

——. *The Rights of Lesbians and Gay Men in the Russian Federation: An International Gay and Lesbian Human Rights Commission Report*. San Francisco: IGLHRC, 1994.

——. "Sex in the Media and the Birth of the Sex Media in Russia." *Postcommunism and the Body Politic. Genders* 22. Ed. Ellen E. Berry. New York: New York University Press, 1995. 197–228.

——. "We Have No Sex." *Out/Look* (Summer 1990): 43–54.

Goldman, Wendy Z. *Women, the State and Revolution: Soviet Family Policy and Social Life, 1917–1936*. New York: Cambridge University Press, 1993.

Golod, Sergei. "Nesmotria ni na chto, muzhskaia seksual'nost' po-prezhnemu otlichaetsia ot zhenskoi. I eto khorosho." *Chas-pik* 10 (Aug. 1994): 11.

Goldschmidt, Paul W. *Pornography and Democratization: Legislating Obscenity in Post-Communist Russia*. Boulder: Westview, 1999. 90–91.

Gondusov, Vladimir. "Ia ne pishu o tom, chego ne znaiu, govorit avtor populiarnykh detektivov Aleksandra Marinina." *Sankt-Peterburgskie vedomosti* 22 Sept. 1998. http://dlib.eastview.com/sources/article.jsp?id=2168999.

Gorbachev, Mikhail. *Perestroika: New Thinking for Our Country and the World*. New York: Harper & Row, 1987.

Goscilo, Helena. "Big-Buck Books: Pulp Fiction in Post-Soviet Russia." *Harriman Review* 12.2–3 (1999/2000): 6–24.

——. "Body Talk in Current Fiction: Speaking Parts and (W)holes." *Russian Culture in Transition*. Ed. Gregory Freidin. Stanford Slavic Studies 7. Stanford: Stanford University Press, 1993. 145–177.

——. *Dehexing Sex: Russian Womanhood During and After Glasnost*. Ann Arbor: University of Michigan Press, 1996.

——. "Feminist Pulp Fiction: Detecting Murder and Aleksandra Marinina." *Women East-West* 50 (1997): 15–16.

Goscilo, Helena, and Andrea Lanoux. "Introduction—Lost in the Myths." *Gender and National Identity in Twentieth-Century Russian Culture*. Ed. Helena Goscilo and Andrea Lanoux. Dekalb: Northern Illinois University Press, 2006. 3–29.

Gould, Jennifer. *Vodka, Tears, and Lenin's Angel*. New York: St. Martin's, 1997.

Goven, Joanna. "Gender Politics in Hungary: Autonomy and Anti-Feminism." *Gender Politics and Post-Communism: Reflections from Eastern Europe and the Former Soviet Union*. Ed. Nanette Funk and Magda Muelle. New York: Routledge, 1993. 224–40.

Graff, Peter. "Russian Lawmakers Slam "Armageddon" Film." Reuters 9 Oct. 1998.

Graham, Seth. "Chernukha and Russian Film." *Studies in Slavic Cultures* 1 (2000): 9–27.

——. "A Cultural Analysis of the Russo-Soviet Anekdot." PhD diss., University of Pittsburgh, 2003.

Gudkov, L. D. "Massovaia literatura kak problema. Dlia kogo? Radrazhennye zametki cheloveka so storony." Reitblat. A. I. *Drugie literatury*. Special issue of *Novoe literaturnoe obozrenie* 22 (1996): 78–100.

Gudkov, Lev, and Boris Dubin. *Literatura kak sotsial'nyi institut*. Moscow: Novoe literaturnoe obozrenie, 1994.

Gutterman, Steve. "Russian Police Investigate Prominent Writer on Pornography Charge." Associated Press 11 July 2002.

Hashamova, Yana. "Post-Soviet Russian Film and the Trauma of Globalization." *Consumption, Markets, and Culture* 7.1 (2004): 53–68.

Healey, Dan. "Masculine Purity and 'Gentlemen's Mischief': Sexual Exchange and Prostitution between Russian Men, 1861–1941. *Slavic Review* 60.2 (2001): 233–265.

Heller, Dana. 'Russian 'Sitkom' Adaptation." *Journal of Popular Film and Television* 31.2 (2003): 60–72.

Herbert, Frank. *Dune*. New York: Ace, 1990.

Herman, David. "Stricken by Infection: Art and Adultery in *Anna Karenina* and 'Kreutzer Sonata,'" *Slavic Review* 56.1 (1997): 15–36.

Hopkins, William. "The Development of "Pornographic Literature in Eighteenth- and Early Nineteenth-Century Russia." PhD diss., Indiana University, 1977.

Horton, Andrew, and Michael Brashinsky. *The Zero Hour: Glasnost and Soviet Cinema in Transition*. Princeton, NJ: Princeton University Press, 1992.

Howard, Lucy, and Arlyn Tobia Gajilan. "Periscope/Russia: A Real Man." *Newsweek* 9 Mar. 1998.

Humphrey, Caroline. *The Unmaking of Soviet Life: Everyday Economies after Socialism*. Ithaca: Cornell University Press, 2002.

"Intermediia" *Andrei* 5 (1994): 2.

"Intermediia." *Andrei* 7 (1996): 2.

Il'ichev, Valerii. *Psikh protiv mafii*. Moscow: Vagrius, 1998.

Ingebretsen, Edward J. "The Monster in the Home: True Crime and the Traffic in Body Parts." *Journal of American Culture* 21.1 (1998): 27–34.

Irving, John. *The World According to Garp*. New York: Ballantine, 1999.

Kaganovsky, Lilya. "How the Soviet Man Was (Un)Made." *Slavic Review* 63.3 (2004): 577–596.

Karyshev, Valerii. *A. Solonik—Killer mafii*. http://www.ladoshki.com/?books& author=1243&id=16286.

Kelly, Catriona. *Refining Russia: Advice Literature, Polite Culture, and Gender from Catherine to Yeltsin*. Oxford: Oxford University Press, 2001.

Kermode, Frank. *The Sense of an Ending. Studies in the Theory of Fiction*. Oxford: Oxford University Press, 2000.

Khanga, Yelena, with Susan Jacoby. *Soul to Soul: A Black Russian American Family, 1865–1992*. New York: Norton, 1992.

Kipnis, Laura. *Bound and Gagged: Pornography and the Politics of Fantasy in America*. New York: Grove, 1996.

Kivinov, Andrei. *Ulitsa rabitykh fonarei*. Moscow: OLMA-PRESS, 1998.

Kon, Igor. *The Sexual Revolution in Russia: From the Age of the Czars to Today*. Trans. James Riordan. New York: Free Press, 1995.

Kon, Igor, and James Riordan, eds. *Sex and Russian Society*. Bloomington: Indiana University Press, 1993. 1–14.

Kondakov, Evgenii. "Amerikanskie kukly." *Andrei* 6 (1995): 6–11.

Konovalov, L. "Ot redaktsii," *Makhaon* 1 (1997): 1.

Kontsantinov, Andrei. *Advokat*. Moscow: OLMA, 2001.

——. *Arestant*. Moscow: OLMA, 2001.

——. *Banditskii Peterburg*. Moscow: OMLA, 2001.

——. *Ment*. In *Arestant*. Moscow: OLMA, 2003.

——. *Sud'ia*. Moscow: OLMA, 2001.

——. *Vor*. Moscow: OLMA, 2001.

——. *Vydumshchik*. Moscow: OLMA, 2001.

Konstantinov, Andrei, and Aleksandr Sidiachko. "Banditskaia Rossiia." *Moskovskii komsomolets* 19 June 1997: 14–15.

Kornilova, Natal'ia. *Pantera*. Moscow: EKSMO, 1998.

Korestkii. *Antikiller*. Moscow: EKSMO, 2002.

——. *Antikiller-2*. 2 vols. Moscow: EKSMO, 2001.

Kress, Nancy. *Beggars in Spain*. New York: Eos, 2004.

Kribosheev, Pavel. "Otmorozki s chemodanami baksov." *Moskovskii komsomolets* 19 June 19 1997: 11.

Krylova, Anna. "Saying 'Lenin' and Meaning 'Party': Subversion and Laughter in Soviet and Post-Soviet Society." *Consuming Russia: Popular Culture, Sex, and Society since Gorbachev*. Ed. Adele Barker. Durham, NC: Duke University Press, 1999. 243–65.

Kurkov, Andrei. *Piknik na l'du*. Kharkhov: Folio, 2001.

Kurkov, Andrey. *Death and the Penguin*. Trans. George Bird. London: Harvill, 2001.

———. *Penguin Lost.* Trans. George Bird. London: Harvill, 2004.

Lahusen, Thomas. *How Life Writes the Book: Real Socialism and Socialist Realism in Stalin's Russia.* Ithaca: Cornell University Press, 1997.

Larsen, Susan. "National Identity, Cultural Authority, and the Post-Soviet Blockbuster: Nikita Mikhalkov and Aleksei Balabanov." *Slavic Review* 62.3 (2003): 491–511.

———. "Zhenshchina v zerkale sovetskoi pressy: Vzgliad so storony." *Russian Culture in Transition.* Ed. Gregory Freidin. Stanford Slavic Studies 7. Stanford: Stanford University Press, 1993. 178–185.

Lebina, N. B., and M. V. Shkarovskii. *Prostitutisiia v Peterburge.* Moscow: Progress-Akademiia, 1994.

Leiderman, N. L., and M. N. Lipovetskii. *Sovremennaia russkaia literatura. Vol. 3, V kontse veka (1986–1990-e gody).* Moskva: Editorial URSS, 2001.

Levinson, Aleksei. "O plokhom otnoshenii intelligentsii k telereklame. *Neprikossnovennyi zapas* 1 (1998). http://magazines.russ.ru/nz/1998/1/nzlevins.html.

Lévi-Strauss, Claude. "The Structural Study of Myth." *Contemporary Literary Criticism: Modernism through Poststructuralism.* Ed. Robert Con Davis. New York: Longman, 1986. 308–322.

Levitt, M., and A. Toporkov. *Eros and Pornography in Russian Culture.* Moscow: Ladomir, 1999.

Lintsova, Liubov', and Tat'iana Sorokina. "Maks Frai po imeni Svetlana okazalsia strannym, no neprikhotlivym chelovekom." *Rossiiskaia gazeta* 24 Sept. 2004: 30. http://dlib.eastview.com/sources/article.jsp?id=6770890.

Lipnitskii, Aleksandr. "Viktor Sukhodrev: PLAYBOY v moem bagazhe." *Playboy* July 1995: 97–103.

Lipovetskii, Mark. "Rasstratnye strategii, ili metamorfozy chernukhi." *Novyi Mir* 11 (1999): 193–209.

———. "Veskh liubliu na svete ia!" *Iskusstvo kino* 11 (2000): 55–59.

Lipovetsky, Mark. "POST-SOTS: Transformations of Socialist Realism in the Popular Culture of the Recent Period." *Slavic and East European Journal* 48.3 (2004): 356–377.

Lodge, Robin "Crimean Prostitutes to Retreat from NATO." 24 April 1997.

Logachev, Viktor. "Shustraia devitsa naekhala na spasitelia." *Moskovskii komsomolets* 19 June 1997: 11.

Lotman, Iurii M. and Boris A. Uspenskii. "Binary Models in the Dynamics of Russian Culture (to the End of the Eighteenth Century)." *The Semiotics of Russian Cultural History.* Ed. Alexander D. Nakhimovsky and Alice Stone Nakhimovsky. Ithaca: Cornell University Press, 1985. 30–66.

Lovell, Stephen. *The Russian Reading Revolution: Print Culture in the Soviet and Post-Soviet Eras.* New York: St. Martin's, 2000.

Luk'ianenko. *Dozor. Nochnoi dozor. Dnevnoi dozor. Sumerechni dozor.* Moscow: AST, 2004.

L'vova, Valentina. "Briuzga nedeli. V poiskakh neporchennogo zhanra." *Komsomol'skaia Pravda.* 28 May 1999.

MacFadyen, David. "Literature Has Left the Building: Russian Romance and To-day's TV Drama." *Kinokul'tura* 8 (2005). http://www.kinokultura.com/articles/apr05-macfadyen.html.

Maiakovskii, Vladimir. "About That." *Sochineniia v dvukh tomakh.* Vol. 2. Moscow: Pravda, 1988.

"Maks Frai—Gazeta. 'Nas s p'ianitsei rodnit gotovnost' k samoistrebleniiu." *Gazeta* Feb. 3 2005: 1.

Maksimovskii, Edvard. *Imperiia strakha.* Moscow: Market Limited, 1991.

Manstov, Igor'. "Strogii iunosha." *Iskusstvo kino* 2 (1998): 62–63.

Marinina, Aleksandra. *Chernyi spisok.* Moscow: EKSMO, 2002.

——. *Chuzhaia maska.* Moscow: EKSMO, 1998.

——. *Ia umer vchera.* 2 vols. Moscow: EKSMO, 1998.

——. *Igra na chuzhom pole.* Moscow: EKSMO, 1998.

——. *Illiuziia grekha.* Moscow: EKSMO, 1998.

——. *Kogda bogi smeiutsia.* Moscow: EKSMO, 2000.

——. *Muzhskie igry.* 2 vols. Moscow: EKSMO, 1998.

——. *Nezapertaia dver'.* Moscow: EKSMO, 2002.

——. *Prizrak muzyki.* Moscow: EKSMO, 1998.

——. *Sed'maia zhertva.* Moscow: EKSMO, 2000.

——. *Stilist.* Moscow: EKSMO, 1997.

——. *Smert' i nemnogo liubvi.* Moscow: EKSMO, 1998.

——. *Soavtory.* Moscow: EKSMO, 2004.

——. *Stechenie obsotaitel'stv.* Moscow: EKSMO, 1998.

——. *Tot, kto znaet.* 2 vols. Moscow: EKSMO, 2001.

——. *Ukradennyi son.* Moscow: EKSMO, 1998.

——. *Za vse nado platit'.* Moscow: EKSMO, 1998.

Matich, Olga. "Dialectics of Cultural Return: Zinaida Gippius' Personal Myth." *Cultural Mythologies of Russian Modernism: From the Golden Age to the Silver Age.* Ed. Boris Gasparov, Robert P. Hughes, and Irina Paperno. Berkeley: University of California Press, 1992. 19–51.

——."A Typology of Fallen Women in Nineteenth Century Russian Literature." *American Contributions to the Ninth International Congress of Slavists.* Vol. 2, *Literature, Politics, History.* Ed. Paul Debreczeny. Columbus: Slavica, 1983. 325–343.

——."The Symbolist Meaning of Love: Theory and Practice." *Creating Life: The Aesthetic Utopia of Russian Modernism.* Ed. Irina Paerno and Joan Delaney Grossman. Stanford: Stanford University Press, 1994. 24–50.

McLaren, Bronwyn. "Big Brains Bog Down in Hunt for the Russian Idea." *St. Petersburg Times* 18–24 Aug. 1997.

McNair, Brian. *Mediated Sex: Pornography and Postmodern Culture.* London: Arnold, 1996.

Melville, Andrei, and Gail W. Lapidus, eds. *The Glasnost Papers: Voices on Reform from Moscow.* Boulder: Westview, 1990.

Menzel, Birgit. "Writing, Reading, and Selling Literature in Russia, 1986–2004." *Reading for Entertainment in Contemporary Russia: Post-Soviet Popular Litera-*

ture in Historical Perspective. Ed. Stephen Lovell and Birgit Menzel. Munich: Otto Sagner, 2005. 39–56.

Mickiewicz, Ellen. *Changing Channels: Television and the Struggle for Power in Russia.* Rev. ed. Durham, NC: Duke University Press, 1999.

Mil'ianen'kov, Lev. "Damy i gospoda." *Po tu storonu zalona: Entsiklopediia prestupnogo mira.* St. Petersburg: Damy i gospoda, 1992.

Miller, Donald E., and Lorna Touryan Miller. *Armenia: Portraits of Survival and Hope.* Berkeley: University of California Press, 2003.

Modleski, Tania. *Loving with a Vengeance: Mass-Produced Fantasies for Women.* New York: Routledge, 1996.

Moller, Peter Ulf. *Postlude to the Kreutzer Sonata: Tolstoi and the Debate on Sexual Morality in Russian Literature in the 1890s.* Trans. John Kendal. Leiden: E. J. Brill, 1988.

Morson, Gary Saul. *Narrative and Freedom: The Shadows of Time.* New Haven: Yale University Press, 1994.

Myers, Steven Lee. "On Russian TV, Whatever Putin Wants, He Gets." *New York Times* 17 Feb. 2004.

Naiman, Eric. "Historectomies: On the Metaphysics of Reproduction in a Utopian Age." *Sexuality and the Body in Russian Culture.* Ed. Jane T. Costlow, Stephanie Sandler, and Judith Vowles. Stanford: Stanford University Press, 1993. 255–276.

——. *Sex in Public: The Incarnation of Early Soviet Ideology.* Princeton, NJ: Princeton University Press, 1997.

"National'naia gordost'." *Andrei* 6.4 (1995).

Nekrasov, N. A. *Polnoe sobranie stikhotvorenii v trekh tomakh.* Vol. 1. Leningrad: Sovetskii pisatel', 1967.

Nepomniashchy, Catharine Theimer. "Markets, Mirrors, and Mayhem: Aleksandra Marinina and the Rise of the New Russian *Detektiv.*" *Consuming Russia: Popular Culture, Sex, and Society Since Gorbachev.* Ed. Adele Barker. Durham, NC: Duke University Press, 1999. 161–191.

Nikolaev, Konstantin, and Irina Lyshchitskaia. " 'Tridstatyi vozvrashchaetsia, za-khvativ s soboi nashatyr.' " *Moskovskii komsomolets* 11 June 2004: 16.

Nikolaeva, Elina. "Aleksandra Marinina: Mafiia na pal'tsakh." *Moskovskii komsomolets* 9 Nov. 2000: 8. http://dlib.eastview.com/sources/article.jsp?id=76824.

"Nostalgiia po komsomolke." *Andrei* 7 (1996): 113–118.

Novikova, Lizaveta. "Vladimir Sorokin vne podozreniia." *Kommersant-daily* 25 April 2003: 8.

Nuikin, A. *Muzhskoi razgovor.* Moscow: Detskaia literatura, 1990.

Olcott, *Russian Pulp: The Detektiv and the Way of Russian Crime.* Lanham, MD: Rowan & Littlefield, 2001.

Orlova-Novopol'tseva, Anna. "Kak sochinit' krutoi zhenskii detektiv." *Komsomol'skaia Pravda* 21 June 1999. http://dlib.eastview.com/sources/article.jsp?id=6684858.

Oushakine, Sergei. "Crimes of Substitution: Detection in Late Soviet Society." *Public Culture* 15.3 (2003): 427–451.

——. ed. *O muzhe(n)stvennosti.* Moscow: NLO, 2002.

Paperno, Irina. *Chernyshevsky and the Age of Realism: A Study in the Semiotics of Behavior*. Stanford: Stanford University Press, 1988.

Paramonov, Boris. "Chevengur i okrestnosti." *Kontinent* 54 (1987): 333–375.

Pelevin, Viktor. *Homo Zapiens*. Trans. Andrew Bromfield. New York: New Directions, 2002.

———. *Omon-Ra*. Trans. Andrew Bromfield. New York: Farrar, Straus & Giroux, 1994.

———. *Zhizn' nasekomykh*. *Romany*. Moscow: Vagrius, 1997.

Perfilev, Aleksei. "Zhutkoe proisshestvie v Liuberakh." *Megalopolis-Express* 18 June 1997: 9–10.

Pesmen, Dale. *Russia and Soul: An Exploration*. Ithaca: Cornell University Press, 2000.

Petrushevskaia, Ludmila. "Gigiena." *Sobranie sochinenii v piati tomakh*. Vol. 2. 99–106.

Petrushevskaya, Ludmila. *The Time: Night*. Trans. Sally Laird. New York: Vintage, 1994.

———. "Our Crowd." Trans. Helena Goscilo. *Glasnost': An Anthology of Russian Literature under Gorbachev*. Ed. Helena Goscilo and Byron Lindsey. Ann Arbor, MI: Ardis, 1990. 3–22.

Petryna, Adriana. *Life Exposed: Biological Citizenship after Chernobyl*. Princeton, NJ: Princeton University Press, 2002.

———. "Sarcophagus: Chernobyl in Historical Light." *Cultural Anthropolgy* 10.2 (1995): 196–220.

Phillips, Sarah H. "Chernobyl's Sixth Sense: The Symbolism of an Ever-Present Awareness." *Anthropology and Humanism* 29.2 (2004): 159–185.

Pilipov, V. *Tak li plokh byl domostroi?* Moscow: Panorama, 1991.

Plutser-Sarno, Aleksei. "Filosofiia 'pizdy.'" *Materialy k slovariu russkogo mata. Tom vtoroi. Pizda*. St. Petersburg: Limbus, 2005. 18–40.

"Pro-Putin Youth Group Takes Stand against 'Pornographic' Modern Russian Novel." BBC Worldwide Monitoring, Ekho Mosvy Radio, 27 June 2002.

Prokhorova, Elena. "Fragmented Mythologies: Soviet TV Mini-Series of the 1970s." Phd diss. University of Pittsburgh, 2003.

Proshina, Larisa. "Tat'iana Leshenko Sukhomlina: Biurokraty otniali u muzhchin vse." *Rossiiskaia gazeta* 17 July 1993: 8.

Proulx, E. Annie. *Accordion Crimes*. New York: Scribner, 1997.

Pugachev, Sergei. *Ty prosto shliukha, dorogaia!* Moscow: EKSMO, 1999.

Pustz, Matthew J. *Comic Book Culture: Fanboys and True Believers*. Jackson: University Press of Mississippi, 1999.

Pynchon, Thomas. *The Crying of Lot 49*. New York: Harper Perennial, 1999.

Rapping, Elayne. "Aliens, Nomads, Mad Dogs: Tabloid TV and the New Face of Criminal Violence." *Mythologies of Violence in Postmodern Media*. Ed. Christopher Sharrett. Detroit: Wayne State University Press, 1999. 249–274.

Reeves, Phil. "Russia: So What Can You Get Away With?" *Independent* 1 Feb. 1998.

Remnick, David. *Lenin's Tomb*. New York: Vintage, 1994.

Rezin, M. "Po-latyni—*Sex*, a po-russki?" *Professional'no-tekhnicheskoe obrazovanie*

1 (1989): 78–83.

Rice, James. *Freud's Russia*. New Brunswick, NJ: Transaction, 1993.

Ricoeur, Paul. *Time and Narrative*. Trans. Kathleen McLaughlin and David Pellauer. Vol. 2. Chicago: University of Chicago Press, 1985.

Ries, Nancy. "'Honest Bandits' and 'Warped People': Russian Narratives about Money, Corruption, and Moral Decay." *Ethnography in Unstable Places: Everyday Lives in Contexts of Dramatic Political Change*. Ed. Carol J. Greenhouse, Elizabeth Mertz, and Kay B. Warren. Durham, NC: Duke University Press, 2002. 276–315.

——. *Russian Talk: Culture and Conversation during Perestroika*. Ithaca: Cornell University Press, 1997.

Robinson, Kim Stanley. *Red Mars*. New York: Spectra, 1993.

Rostokina, Viktoria. *Bogatyi muzh*. Moscow: AST, 1996.

Roth-Ey, Kristin. "Mass Media and the Remaking of Soviet Culture, 1950s–1960s." Phd. diss. Princeton University, 2003.

Rudnev, V. P. "'I eto vse o nem': 'Khui': Fenomenologiia, antropologiia, metafizika, pramasemantika." *Materialy k slovariu russkogo mata. Tom pervyi. Khui*, Aleksei Plutser-Sarno. St. Petersburg: Limbus, 2001. 16–34.

"Russian Writer Blasts Pro-Kremlin Critics," United Press International 29 June 2002.

"Russia Would Prefer Sex Scandal." Reuters 19 Aug. 1998.

Rybakov, Anatoli. *The Children of the Arbat*. Trans. Harold Shukhman, Boston: Little, Brown, and Co., 1988.

"Sadist pytalsia vyrezat' vsekh zhenshchin na otdel'no vziatoi ulitse." *Moskovskii komsomolets* 19 June 1997: 1.

Sanjian, Andrea Stevenson. "Prostitution, the Press, and Agenda-Building in the Soviet Policy Process." *Soviet Social Problems*. Ed. Anthony Jones, Walter D. Connor, and David E. Powell. Boulder: Westview, 1991. 270–295.

Savkina, Irina. "Gliazhus' v tebia, kak v zerkalo. Tvorchestvo Aleksandry Marininoi v sovremennoi russkoi kritike: Gendernyi aspekt." *Tvorchestvo Aleksandry Marininoi kak otrazhenie sovremennoi rossiiskoi mental'nosti. Mezhdunarodnaia konferentsiia, sostoaiavshchaiasia 19–20 oktiabria 2001. Institut slavianovedeniia, Parizh*. Ed. E. F. Trofimova. Moscow: Rossiiskaia akademiia nauk, Institut nauchnoi informatsii po obshchestvennym naukam, 2002. 5–18.

Selivanova, Natal'ia. "Odin, no beshenyi." *Izvestiia* 26 Sept. 1997. http://dlib.eastview.com/sources/article.jsp?id=3161437.

Shargodska, Julia. "U.S. Interngate Doesn't Faze Russia." *Moscow Times* 26 Feb. 1998.

Shcherbakov, Andrei. "Dopros na zadannuiu temu." *Rossiiskaia gazeta* 5 April 1997. http://dlib.eastview.com/sources/article.jsp?id=1840642.

Shcherbakov, Dmitrii. *Nimfomanka*. Moscow: EKSMO, 1998.

——.*Nimfomanka: Besposhchadnaia strast'*. Moscow: EKSMO-Press, 1999.

Sheets, Lawrence, and John Ydstie, "Dispute in Russia over a Book by Vladimir Sorokin and Whether or Not It Is the Dissemination of Pornography." *All Things Considered* 8 Aug. 2002.

Shevelev, Igor'. "Uspekh po prozvishchu Beshenyi." *Ogonek* 11 Mar. 1996: 68–70.

Shklovskii, Viktor. *Sobranie sochinenii v trekh tomax.* Vol. 1. Moscow: Khudozh-estvennaia literatura, 1973.

Shtamm, Mikhail. "Iunye ubliudki demonstriruiut vlast'." *Megalopolis-Express* 18 June 1997: 9.

Shteyngart, Gary. "Letter from Russia: Teen Spirit: On the Rise of Post-Soviet Youth," *New Yorker* 10 Mar. 2003: 46.

Siegel, George. "The Fallen Woman in Nineteenth Century Literature." *Harvard Slavic Studies* 5 (1970): 81–107.

Sinclair, Upton. *The Jungle.* New York: Penguin, 1985.

Smith, Kathleen E. *Mythmaking in the New Russia: Politics and Memory During the Yeltsin Era.* Ithaca: Cornell University Press, 2002.

"Sobranie sochinenii. Maks Frai, navsegda!" *Slovo* 4 Mar. 2005: 15. http://dlib .eastview.com/sources/article.jsp?id=7430730.

Solovyov, Vladimir. *The Meaning of Love.* Ed. and trans. Thomas R. Beyer, Jr. West Stockbridge, MA: Lindisfarne, 1985.

Solzhenitsyn, Alexander. *Cancer Ward.* Trans. Nicholas Behtell and David Burg. New York: Farrar, Straus & Giroux, 1972.

——. *The Gulag Archipelago.* Vol. 2. Trans. Thomas P. Whitney. New York: Harper & Row, 1975.

Sorokin, Vladimir. *Goluboe salo.* Moscow: Ad Marginem, 1999.

Spark, Muriel. *The Prime of Miss Jean Brodie.* New Yorker: HarperPerennial, 1994.

Sotnikova, Tat'iana. "Funktsiia karaoke." *Znamia* 12 (1998): 168–172.

SPID-Info. February 1994.

Stanley, Alessandra. "On Russian TV, Suddenly the Screen Is Steamy." *New York Times* 13 Nov. 1997: A4.

——. "The Sauna Scandal—Steamy Stuff in High Places." *New York Times* 26 June 1997.

Stites, Richard. "Prostitute and Society in Pre-Revolutionary Russia." *Jahrbücher für Geschichte Osteuropas* 31.3 (1983): 348–364.

——.*Russian Popular Culture: Entertainment and Society since 1900.* Cambridge: Cambridge University Press, 1995.

——. *The Women's Liberation Movement in Russia: Feminism, Nihilism and Bolshevism (1860–1930).* Princeton, NJ: Princeton University Press, 1988.

Strukov, Vladimir. "*Masiania*, or Reimagining the Self in the Cyberspace of Rusnet." *Slavic and East European Journal* 48.3 (2004): 438–461.

Sukhov, Evgenii. *Ia—Vor v zakone. Oboroten'.* http://www.ladoshki.com/?books& author=605&id=6846.

——. *Okhota v slepuiu.* Moscow: AST, 2005.

Tarkhova, Lina. *Vospitat' muzhchinu.* Moscow: Pedagogika, 1992.

Tiger, Lionel. *Men in Groups.* New York: Marion Boyars, 1984.

Tikhomirov, Sergei. "Russkaia kul'tura v predchuvstvii 'Sodomizatsii': Ili Gomoseksualizm kak demokraticheskaia problema." *Nezavisimaia gazeta* 16 June 1993: 5.

Tishler, Jennifer Ryan. "*Menty* and the Petersburg Myth: TV Cops in Russia's 'Crime Capital.'" *Journal of Criminal Justice and Popular Culture* 10.2 (2003):

127–141.

Todd, William Mills III. "The Responsibilities of (Co-) Authorship: Notes on Revising the Serialized Versions of *Anna Karenina*." *Freedom and Responsibility in Russian Literature. Essays in Honor of Robert Louis Jackson.* Ed. Elizabeth Cherish Allen and Gary Saul Morson. Evanston, IL: Northwestern University Press, 1994. 159–169.

Todorov. Vladislav. *Red Square, Black Square: Organon for Revolutionary Imagination.* Albany: SUNY Press, 1995.

Tolstoi, L. N. *Sobranie sochinenii v dvenadtsati tomakh.* Moscow: Pravda, 1987.

Trifonov, "The Exchange." *The Long Goodbye: Three Novellas.* Trans. Ellendea Proffer. Ann Arbor: Ardis, 1986. 17–98.

——. *The House on the Embankment. Another Life. The House on the Embankment.* Trans. Michael Glenny. New York: Simon & Schuster, 1983.

Trofimova, Elena. "Fenomen detektivnykh romanov Aleksandry Marininoi v kul'- ture sovremennoi Rossiii." *Tvorchestvo Aleksandry Marininoi kak otrazhenie sovremennoi rossiiskoi mental'nosti. Mezhdunarodnaia konferentsiia, sotoa- iavshchaiasia 19–20 oktiabria 2001. Institut slavianovedeniia, Parizh.* Ed. E. F. Trofimova. Moscow: Rossiiskaia akademiia nauk, Institut nauchnoi informatsii po obshchestvennym naukam, 2002. 19–35.

Troitskii, A. K. "Rossia v pleiboiskom prishchure." *Playboy* 1 1995: 94–96.

Tsivian. Yuri. "Early Russian Cinema: Some Observations." *Inside the Film Factory.* Ed. Richard Taylor. London: Routledge, 1994. 7–30.

Tukh, Boris. *Pervaia desiatka sovremennoi russkoi literatury.* Moscow: Oniks 21 vek, 2002.

Tuller, David. *Cracks in the Iron Closet: Travels in Gay and Lesbian Russia.* Boston: Faber and Faber, 1996.

Uehling, Greta. *Beyond Memory: The Crimean Tatars' Deportation and Return.* New York: Palgrave, 2004.

Ulitskaia, Ludmila. *Kazus Kukotskogo.* Moscow: EKSMO 2006.

Uspenskii, Mikhail. *Kogo za smert'iu posylat'.* St. Petersburg: Azbuka, 1998.

Ustiuzhanin, Vasilii. "The Lovely Ms. Lewinsky Was Aimed at Clinton But Has Hit Albert Gore." *Komsomol'skaia pravda* 12 Feb. 1998.

"Vas ushchemliali po polovomu priznaku?. Vopros nedeli." *Kommersant"-Vlast'* 7 Mar. 2000. http://dlib.eastview.com/sources/article.jsp?id=3201208.

Veitsler, Aleksei. "Bronenosets Marina." *Andrei* 5 (1994). 6–15.

——. "Konversiia. 'Etu dorogu domoi nuzhno proiti . . ." *Andrei* 3 (1992). 76–89.

——. "Sto verbliudova za russkuiu baryshniu." *Andrei* 7 (1995): 43–50.

Verdery, Katherine. *What Was Socialism and What Comes Next?* Princeton, NJ: Princeton University Press, 1996.

Vladin, V., and D. Kapustin. *Garmoniia semeinykh otnoshenii.* Petrozavodsk: Kareliia, 1991.

Vladislavskii, V. Z. *Esli ty muzhchina.* Minsk: Vysshaia shkola, 1991.

Volkov, Vadim. *Violent Entrepreneurs. The Use of Force in the Making of Russian Capitalism.* Ithaca: Cornell University Press, 2002.

von Geldern, James, and Richard Stites, eds. *Mass Culture in Soviet Russia: Tales, Poems, Songs, Plays and Folklore, 1917–1953.* Bloomington: Indiana University

Press, 1995.

Vonnegut, Kurt. *Galapagos*. New York: Dial Press, 1999.

Voronin, Andrei. *Slepoi protiv man'iaka*. Moscow: AST, 1997.

Waters, Elizabeth. "Prostitution." *Soviet Social Reality in the Mirror of Glasnost*. Ed. Jim Riordan. New York: St. Martin's, 1992. 133–154.

——. "Victim or Villain: Prostitution in Post-Revolutionary Russia." *Women and Society in Russia and the Soviet Union*. Ed. Linda Edmonton. Cambridge: Cambridge University Press, 1992.

Wertham, Frederic. *The Seduction of the Innocent*. New York: Rinehart, 1954.

Wood, Elizabeth. "Prostitution Unbound: Representations of Sexual and Political Anxieties in Post-Revolutionary Russia." *Sexuality and the Body in Russian Culture*. Ed. Jane T. Costlow, Stephanie Sandler, and Judith Vowles. Stanford: Stanford University Press, 1993. 124–135.

Yurchak, Aleksei. *Everything Was Forever, Until It Was No More: The Last Soviet Generation*. Princeton, NJ: Princeton University Press, 2005.

——. "Muzhskaia ekonomika: 'Ne do glupostei, kogda kar'eru kuesh.'" *Neprikosnovennyi zapas* 5 (2001).

Zetkin, Clara. "From My Memorandum Book." *My Recollections of Lenin*. Moscow: Foreign Languages Publishing House, 1956. 53–86.

"Zhirinovsky Courts Gay Voters in St. Petersburg." NTV 26 Mar. 1998.

"Zhirinovsky Throws Wedding Party to Boost Campaign." Reuters 11 Feb. 1996.

"Zhirinovsky 'Like a Virgin' Before Wedding." Reuters 9 Feb. 1996.

"Zhirinovsky to Clinton: Let's Swap Sex Tales." Reuters 23 Jan. 1998.

Zholkovskii, Aleksandr. "Topos prostitutsii." *Babel'/Babel*. Ed. A. K. Zholkovskii and M. B. Iampl'skii. Moscow: Carte Blanche, 1994. 317–368.

Zimovets, Sergei. "Son of the Regiment: Deus ex Machina." *Socialist Realism without Shores*. Ed. Thomas Lahusen and Evgeny Dobrenko. Durham, NC: Duke University Press, 1997. 191–202.

Zolotonosov, Mikhail. "Kul'tura: Drova izdatel'skoi topki." *Moskovskie Novosti* 12 Mar. 2003: 26.

Zolotov, Andrei, Jr. "Santa Barbara: 'Matter of National Security." *Moscow Times* 26 Nov. 1998.

Zorin, Andrei. "Kruche, kruche, kruche . . . Istoriia pobedy: Chernukha v kul'ture poslednikh let." *Znamia* 10 (1992): 198–204.

——. "Legalizatsiia obstsennoi leksiki i ee kul'turnye posledstviia." *Russian Culture in Transition*. Ed. Gregory Freidin. Stanford Slavic Studies 7. Stanford: Stanford University Press, 1993. 123–144. http://www.doktor.ru/onkos/mop/don.htm

Films and Television

Afganets (1991). Dir. Vladimir Mazur.

Agent national'noi bezopasnosti (several episodes).

Ameriken boj (1992). Dir. Boris Kvashnev.

Amerikanskii dedushka. Dir. Ivan Shcheglev. Moscow, Iupiter, 1993.

Antikiller (2002). Dir. Egor Mikhalkov-Konchalovskii.

Assa (1987). Dir. Sergei Solov'ev.

Banditskii Peterburg: Baron (2000). Dir. Vladimir Bortko.

Banditskii Peterburg: Krakh Antibiotika (2001). Dir. Vitor Sergeev.

Brigada (2002). Dir. Aleksei Sidorov.

Dezhurnaia chast'. 25 May 25 and 20 Aug. 1999.

Dorozhnyi patrul. 11 June 1999.

Dorogaia Elena Sergeevna (1988). Dir. El'dar Riazanov.

Escrava Isaura (1976). Dir. Milton Gonzales and Herval Rossano.

Interdevochka (1989). Dir. Petr Todorovskii.

Ironiia sud'by, ili s legkhim parom (1975). Dir. El'dar Riazanov.

Katastrofy nedeli. 28 Mar. 1999.

Krestonosets (1995). Dir. Aleksandr Inshakov and Mikhail Tumanishvili.

Kriminal. 14 May and 10 July 1999.

Liubit' po-russki (1989). Dir. Evgenii Matvev.

Liubit' po-russki-2 (1996). Dir. Evgenii Matvev.

Liubit' po-russki-3 (1999). Dir. Evgenii Matvev.

Los ricos tambien lloran (1979). Dir. Fernando Chacyn.

Malen'kaia Vera (1988). Dir. Vasilii Pichul.

Melochi zhizni (1999). Dir. Viacheslav Brovkin, Gennadi Pavlov, and Aleksandr Pokrovskii.

Menty. (1997–1998). 32 episodes.

Mesto vstrechi izmenit' nel'zia (1979). Dir. Stanislav Govorukhin.

Osobennosti national'noi okhoty (1995). Dir. Aleksandr Rogozhkin.

Petrovka 38. 10 July and 7 Sept. 1999.

Po prozvishchu zver' (1990). Dir. Aleksandr Muratov.

Priiatel' pokoinika (1997). Dir. Leonid Boiko and Viacheslav Khristofovich.

Pro urodov i liudei (1998). Dir. Aleksei Balabanov.

Psy: Posledniaia krov' [Psy 2: ostatnaia krew] (1994). Dir. Wladyslaw Pasikowski.

Rosa Salvaje (1987). Dir. Ernesto Arreola and Beatriz Sheridan.

Russkii tranzit (1994). Dir. Viktor Titov.

Santa Barbara (1984–93).

17 *Mgnoveniia vesny* (1973). Dir. Tat'iana Lioznova.

600 sekund (1987–1993). Dir. Aleksandr Nevzorov.

Sledstvie vedut znatoki (1971–89). Dir. Viacheslav Brovkin, Iurii Krotenko, et al.

Sluzhebnyi roman (1978). Dir. El'dar Riazanov.

Sterviatniki na dorogakh (1990). Dir. Samvel Gasparov.

Superkhirurg (1999). Dir. Andrei Badin.

Tak zhit' nel'zia (1990). Dir. Stanislav Govorukhin.

Tsirk (1936). Dir. Grigorii Aleksandrov.

Tridstatogo unichtozhit! (1992). Dir. Viktor Dotsenko.

Twin Peaks (1990–91). Dir. David Lynch.

Voroshilovskii strelok (1999). Dir. Stanislav Govorukhin.

Vse to, o chem my tak dolgo mechtali (1997). Dir. Rudol'f Fruntov.

INDEX

Page numbers in *italics* indicate illustrations.

detektiv and, 128–34

See also feminist movement

Yeltsin, Boris

in Dotsenko's work, 180

"Russian idea" and, 2, 56 n, 191

as symbol of 1990s Russia, 225–27

You're Just a Slut, My Dear! (Pugachev), 89, 195–96, *197*, 221, 223

youth, narratives of perestroika and, 15–16

Zalkind, Aron, 32

Zhirinovsky, Vladimir, 42–43

Zorin, Andrei, 12 n, 14, 59

Zorin, Valentin, 40